CONSTRUCTING
THE CHILD
VIEWER

Constructing the
Child
Viewer

A HISTORY OF THE
AMERICAN DISCOURSE
ON TELEVISION
AND
CHILDREN,
1950–1980

Carmen Luke

New York
Westport, Connecticut
London

Library of Congress Cataloging-in-Publication Data

Luke, Carmen.
    Constructing the child viewer : a history of the American
discourse on television and children, 1950-1980 / Carmen Luke.
        p.   cm.
    Includes bibliographical references and index.
    ISBN 0-275-93516-7 (alk. paper)
    1. Television and children—United States—History.   2. Mass media
and children—United States—History.   3. Discourse analysis.
    I. Title
HQ784.T4L85   1990
302.23′45′083—dc20   90-7354

British Library Cataloguing in Publication Data is available.

Library of Congress Catalog Card Number: 90-7354
ISBN 0-275-93516-7

First published in 1990

Praeger Publishers, One Madison Avenue, New York, NY 10010
An imprint of Greenwood Publishing Group, Inc.

Printed in the United States of America

(∞)

The paper used in this book complies with the
Permanent Paper Standard issued by the National
Information Standards Organization (Z39.48-1984).

10 9 8 7 6 5 4 3 2 1

Contents

Preface

This project began as an archeology of knowledge. My initial aim was to search out and document the discursive constructions of the child in the U.S. research literature on TV and children. From the onset of this project, it became clear that I had underestimated the enormity of the task. Following Michel Foucault's methodological template, outlined in *The Archaeology of Knowledge* (1972), I recognized early on that a comprehensive archeology was impossible. That is, within the generic conventions and constraints of writing an academic book, it is impossible to account for all the textual sites upon which TV and the child were mapped over a 40-year period. Hence, I decided to exclude a range of texts such as federal reports, school curricular documents, teachers' professional journals, and the wide range of popular cultural texts wherein strictly academic knowledges are transformed into publicly accessible and "commonsense" knowledges. My first move, then, was to concentrate on the purely "scientific" domain of knowledge production about TV and children. But even narrowing my research to scholarly texts turned out to be a much larger task than I had anticipated.

The genealogical aspect of a Foucauldian archeology calls for a historical trace of discursive (re)configurations. I was thus compelled to outline how the child was conceptualized in relation to the cinema, radio, and comics in order to then map possible continuities, discontinuities, or transformations of prior discourses. As I began to investigate those scientific knowledges established about the child and mass media in the pre-TV era, I quickly encountered a relatively large volume of research on the cinema, radio, and comic books. For purposes of textual economy, these three distinct discourses had to be condensed and unified in one chapter. The 1950s discourse on the early years of TV research still seemed manageable. Yet the volume of 1960s research foreshadowed what I was to encounter once I moved into the 1970s: The massive amount of research data became increasingly more difficult to account for within the textual framework and limitations of the book.

The problem, it became apparent, was that the methodology I had chosen appeared unsuitable to the historical time frame I had initially set myself. In a print culture, the sheer proliferation, redundancy, and intertextuality of academic discourse makes it increasingly difficult to catalog, describe, and analyze both marginal and central texts within a discourse. Further, my methodological approach precluded any arbitrary exclusions, for in order to avoid the hermeneutic trap of interpreting a disciplinary field, genre, or research domain according to unproblematicized a priori themes or paradigms, archeology requires that we let the text speak as and where it occurs. Each published study, then, needed to be laid out according to its disciplinary and textual site, methodological rule system, and theoretical orientation; citation networks needed to be traced; and authors' interpretation of the data and the conclusions drawn from such data needed to be outlined. In this way, I was able to extract historically variant concepts of the child, of TV, and of the relation between them.

By the time I was working my way through the 1970s, the sheer volume of research rendered my own text nearly beyond control: The manuscript printout stack was growing exponentially week by week. One obvious solution to this problem was to conclude the textual analyses with research ending in 1979. Suffice it to say that what you have before you is a highly abridged and revised version of a longer, more exhaustive and exhausting history. The 1980s post–"Ferment in the Field" research on TV and children will require a separate study, one which I foreshadow in the last chapter. Notwithstanding these methodological compromises, this volume offers an extensive bibliographical resource, a preliminary introduction to Foucault's discourse theory, and an experimental application of that theory to one major strand of the discourse of mass communications research.

One of the unanticipated outcomes of doing an archeology, particularly one such as the discourse on TV and children, is that although archeology writes a different kind of history, it nonetheless risks reinscription of the very history it aims to critique and subvert. And since this text is bound at every turn to similar academic rules as those that circumscribed the 30-year research enterprise that I focus on here, I have in some ways reproduced the very history which I saw to be in need of a critical rewriting. I have given the scientific "truths" and author-authorities on TV and children a textual space in yet another discursive forum which redeploys and potentially revalorizes them. This is not my aim. But it seems that even a poststructuralist archeology cannot critique or "write difference" from outside the power/knowledge nexus, or without rearticulating, albeit in critical terms, the texts that are its object of study. As Foucault noted, we must learn to read below the manifest text if we are ever to get at the politics of truth by which science produces knowledges about the social and the human subject. I have tried here to write such a reading: a reading which at times cuts across and reframes, but always traverses below, the manifest texts of three decades of empirical social science.

In preparing this text I have received much support and advice from many sources. I wish especially to thank Allan Luke and Richard Baldauf, Jr., for their careful and thoughtful readings of a very lengthy manuscript, and for the many hours of proofreading, discussion, and editorial advice; and Bill Routt and Rowland Lorimer for critical comments on earlier versions. My thanks also go to Richard Smith for administrative and collegial support which enabled me to finish this project.

Introduction

Television historically has been positioned as principal cause of a host of individual problems and social evils: TV has been blamed for everything from falling literacy and numeracy standards, increased juvenile delinquency and promiscuity, and aggressive and violent individual behaviors to a decline in the nation's moral fabric, an increasing desensitization to crime and violence, and an increasing fearfulness of a world perceived as hostile and violent. In response to foregrounded, often media-enhanced social "crises," educators and parents, governments, the public, and advocacy groups look to scientific research to explain and solve social problems. Historically, science tends sooner or later to come up with root causes and definitive cures for social ills. But what we must ask is: What kinds of knowledges does scientific research produce? What about those discourses of the social to which we look for answers? Can any discourse claim ascendancy or claim to provide better truths than another independent of its ideological structure, institutional politics, and historical moment? It is my contention that no discourse, no "science," is outside history or outside what Foucault calls the politics of truth production.

TV emerged in the social domain at a particular historical moment in the development of North American social science. Those discourses that claimed to be able to explain, describe, and define TV's role in and influence upon the social, in effect, laid claim to TV and the child as objects of study. Subsequently, between and within existing discourses a distinct, identifiable field of study—TV and children—emerged in the 1950s. This field of inquiry was founded upon a particular historical configuration of then dominant disciplinary knowledges, and in conjunction with established scientific "truths" about previously conceptualized movie/viewer and radio/listener relationships.

This book traces and analyzes the development of ideas about TV, the child as TV viewer, and the relations between them, as these were constructed in scholarly discourses from 1948 to the mid-1980s. From a poststructuralist position—drawing in particular on the works of Michel Foucault—I delineate how TV and children were constituted in discursive formations. In contrast to narrative or revisionist histories, the history of discourse undertaken here outlines how epistemological, sociocultural, political, and institutional rules converge in historical configurations that enable and constrain the production, authorization, and legitimation of scientific knowledges.

The central aim of this study is to locate disciplinary sites and junctures at which the discourse on TV and children formed (and re-formed), and to trace the discursive trajectories along which the discourse was mapped over a three-decade period. A further concern is to uncover the conceptual conditions under which the construct of "media literacy" became possible. During the 1980s, "the media-literate" became a constitutive definition and descriptor of the contemporary human subject—particularly the subject as constituted in the discourses of schooling. In addition to an analysis of how concepts of the televiewing child emerged and were transformed and reconstituted in discourse, I also describe the epistemological-discursive underpinnings of the recent professed shift in U.S. mass communications discourses from a positivist to a critical orientation.

The vast amount of data produced during nearly four decades of scientific research on TV and children has been central to the discursive production of the passive viewer, the active viewer, the interactive viewer, and the media-literate viewer. These scientific facts are recirculated and stand unchallenged in every new media textbook. However, these viewer constructs remain problematic. The received histories of modern mass media research are narrative histories: accounts of significant media events, dates, names, statistics, and research models. Textbook histories describe a progression of media research "paradigms": the hypodermic model of the 1920s and 1930s; the two-step flow model of the 1940s; the behaviorist model of the 1950s and 1960s, and, in the 1970s, the cognitive-developmental information processing model (e.g., Liebert & Sprafkin, 1988; DeFleur & Ball-Rokeach, 1982; DeVito, 1985; Wimmer & Dominick, 1983; Agee, Ault, & Emery, 1985). Even recent critical reevaluations chronologically reassemble these "paradigms" as *historical fact* (e.g., Gitlin, 1978; Rowland, 1983; Rowland & Watkins, 1984; McQuail, 1987).

How did this linear, progressivist development of a "science" of televiewing develop? During the early period of electronic mass media from the early 1920s to the 1930s, movie and radio media were considered to have direct effects on audiences. That is, no mediating variables were seen to significantly influence the medium's impact on viewers—hence, the concept of hypodermic effect. In the 1960s, the TV violence effects model is said to have prevailed. Research evidence supported the equation that TV violence causes aggression in child viewers (e.g., Bandura et al., 1961, 1963; Berkowitz & Geen, 1966; Hicks, 1965). It was taken for granted that the child viewer was directly affected by television's audio and visual messages. This appeared a natural, not a methodologically manipulated process and consequence. The behaviorist construct of the human subject, in effect, precluded the conceptualization of the (viewer) "respondent" as an active, cognate, and skilled mediator of the omnipotent (TV) "stimulus." Hence, human agency was theoretically precluded. The viewer, conceptualized on the basis of a cause-effect rationality, could only be seen as a passive, cognitively and experientially blank target upon which media messages would inscribe effects.

In contrast to a passive viewer posited by behaviorists, what came to be labelled as the "uses and gratifications" approach constructed an active viewer, one who seeks out media experiences to gratify psychosocial needs. However, the inability of this model to explain effects left a discursive space for the then ascendant behavioral model. While the uses and gratifications model could provide self-reports of perceived needs and viewing choices, it could not provide the clinical evidence in support of effects. By contrast, experimental research generated empirical evidence of direct, socially uncontaminated effects following TV exposure. The experimental construct of the passive viewer held sway during the 1960s and well into the 1970s.

While U.S. mainstream applied research throughout this century has set as its goal the maximization of message impact in commercial advertising, political advertising, and public (government) information campaigns, media research on children has looked at effects primarily in terms of children's learning. That is, whereas media messages for adults were seen to be targeted at consumers and voters whose responses to media exposure could be identified in political (voting) and economic (purchasing) behaviors, media messages aimed at children were seen to influence primarily learners and, only secondarily, future consumers and voters.

Since the onset of modern mass media research, children constituted a distinct group for whom separate research questions were formulated. The history of research on TV and children, like the broader mass media–audience research history, has been written as an instantiation of these models. No history has been undertaken which renders these paradigms and truths themselves problematic. This book turns on the discursive constitution of historical subject constructions. Since a history of discourse on TV and children is radically different from traditional narrative or revisionist histories, I begin in Chapter 1 with a broad introduction to poststructuralist theory and method.

1

Discourse Analysis:
A History of Knowledge Production

Historical and contemporary popular and professional debates about TV and children are based on assumptions about, inter alia, the child, the medium, cognition, behavior, learning, culture, and society. The terms, concepts, arguments, and positions of these debates are lodged in what are taken as authoritative, scientific research and disciplinary knowledges bases. From a poststructuralist perspective we would reread knowledge neither as a transparent reflection of objects and relations in the world nor as a natural process. This is the discursive position taken in this study. Objects about which we speak and write, and of which we have knowledge, are products of discourse.

The guiding principle of a poststructuralist discourse analysis, then, is discourse-in-history. Poststructuralism rejects a sovereign subject and a history that has self-proclaimed itself as "History." Discourses form the epistemological horizons which enable and limit what can be known, how it is known, and what kinds of subjects are implicated in these knowledges. Whether in oral, manuscript, or electronic information cultures, discourses-in-history regulate social practices as well as understandings of self and other, and make possible articulations of the subject and, indeed, of history itself.

At the formative level of scientific knowledge production (i.e., research procedures, epistemological assumptions, and translation of research data into scholarly text), discursive rules and relations are at work which regulate, make possible, and yet delimit who can speak, under what conditions, about what kinds of problems. These rules and relations constitute discursively formalized knowledges which, in turn, construct historical versions of the human subject. An archeology of knowledge thus tracks the rules and relations operant in knowledge production sites. These rules systematize both the practitioners in and the procedures for knowledge production. And since, for

Foucault, knowledges are by definition historical products of socio-cultural, economic, and discursive-political interests and conditions, construction of the human subject within discourses is always a historical contingency.

This chapter provides a broad overview of these and other key aspects of Foucault's discourse theory—posed here as a means for rereading and reframing the historical discourse on children and television. Following a general introduction to Foucault's theoretical position, I turn to a description of how discourses are formed through "rules of formation" and on "fields of emergence." The methodological procedures of discourse analysis thus outlined, I then describe how such analysis is applied to historical investigation.

Since the historical constructs of history and of the subject are central to Foucault's work and to this study, the remainder of this chapter focuses on current debates surrounding the poststructuralist project of historically locating the subject in discourse. But how adequate is poststructuralism for the study of contemporary discourse-subject relationships in postindustrial, information-based society? I here make the case that, given the current transition from industrial to information production, an analysis of discourses that define the relationship between the subject and the new information order is a central task for critical social theory. The discourse on TV and children warrants such scrutiny.

ARCHEOLOGY OF DISCOURSE: QUESTIONS OF METHOD

An archeological analysis of discourse can reveal the strategic formations, locations, and deployment of knowledges (concepts, theories, assumptions) that construct human subjects: their assumed ontology, their social positioning, practices, and relations (e.g., Bowers, 1980; Hacking, 1982; Donald, 1985; Luke, 1989). Foucault (1972:26) argues that in the investigation of discourses, the archeologist's principal methodological task must be to dismantle discursive unities: "*I shall take as my starting-point whatever unities are already given* ... ; but I shall not place myself inside these dubious unities in order to study their internal configurations. . . . I shall make use of them just long enough to ask myself what unities they form. . . . I shall accept the groupings that history suggests only to subject them at once to interrogation" (my emphasis).

The historical text, then, as it is given in discursive unities, must be laid out in a field of statements wherein all continuities and unities are provisionally suspended: "One is [then] led ... to the project of a *pure description of discursive events* as the horizon for the search for the unities that form within it" (p. 27). Mark Cousins and Athar Hussain (1984:84) caution that "what is *not* at stake is the mad project to describe all that has been said and written, an exhaustive history of all utterances." Rather, the aim must be to map "effective state-ments"—those that have been given in discourse as authoritative, that have a regularity in their articulation and reference to an object of study. Thus, by "freeing them of all the groupings that purport to be natural, immediate, universal unities, one is able to describe other unities, but this time by means of a group of controlled decisions" (Foucault, 1972:29). While it is important to map discourse "as and when it occurs" (p. 25)—in order to deconstruct imaginary unities and to lay bare the discursive field according to rules that enable discur-sive formations—it nonetheless remains impossible to physically gather and conceptually (re)combine all statements within various discourses that make claims about an object of study. What this suggests for this present study is that the sources here are selective and not exhaustive. An attempt is made, however, to account for as many discursive groupings of authoritative statements (i.e., published works) as possible within the constraints of the academic genre and discourse delimiting this text.

Authoritative statements are those that "qualified" speakers make from "authorized" institutional positions. In Foucault's (1972:224–225) view, "none may enter into discourse on a specific subject unless he has satisfied certain conditions or if he is not, from the outset, qualified to do so." Conditions for entry and participation are them-selves discursively constructed rules or "constraints of discourse: those limiting its powers, those controlling its chance appearances and those which select from among speaking subjects" (p. 224). Accord-ingly, Foucault (1980b:11) argues that an important task in undertak-ing a history of discourse is to account for "the positions and viewpoints" of speakers and for "the institutions which prompt people to speak . . . and which store and distribute the things that are said." Only by accounting for the various discourses, and the diverse locations of "authorized" speakers of "authoritative" statements, can a history of knowledge and knowledge encoding practices (according to which we "think" and "know") be undertaken. From this follow guidelines for the selection of authoritative statements:

> It is not possible to describe all the relations that may emerge
> . . . without some guide-lines. A provisional division must be
> adopted as an initial approximation: an initial region that analy-
> sis will subsequently demolish and, if necessary, reorganize. . . .
> On one hand, we must choose, empirically, a field in which the
> relations are likely to be numerous, dense, and relatively easy to

describe: ... [and] consider ... all the statements that have chosen the subject of discourse (their own subject) as their 'object' and have undertaken to deploy it as their field of knowledge. (Foucault, 1972:29–30)

In accordance with these guidelines, my selection of sources is based on the following criteria and research procedure. Starting with the discursive "unities" as "given," I began with books and articles that focused specifically on TV and children. My starting point was the research of the 1970s and early 1980s. From these texts I traced references to preceding decades. Moving from 1970s research to the 1950s and 1940s enabled the reverse crossing of the threshold from research on TV and children to research on children and radio, comics, and movies. A computer search of the literature was not conducted. Rather, the discourse has been reconstructed by tracing text back through the citation network, using what Foucault calls the genealogical method. A citation network, in Foucault's scheme, is itself a discourse-specific rule system upon which disciplinary knowledge production is partially based and which, indeed, legitimates such knowledges as authoritative.

Children and media, specifically movies, radio, comic books, and TV, constituted the guiding concepts for the selection of sources. The concept of discourse, which is discussed in detail in the following section, is applied in this study to its textual dimension and confined to academic text. I argue in that section why academic text can be read as constituting a regime of rationality in which (scientific) "truths" and (rational) "justifications" are produced around objects of study and interest such as, for instance, the child, the media, society, or mind. The discourse under analysis here, then, is published academic text, which means that conference presentations, book review articles, consumer advocate and popular press materials, Senate committee hearing transcripts, curriculum and professional magazine materials, and media productions have been excluded. Each of these constitutes a separate aspect of the discourse on media and children, and warrants separate study. Professional teachers' journals are included here only for the early 1950s, when academic research and commentary on TV and children was still commonly published in them. Conference presentations are noted where such "discursive events" are incorporated as part of the text, which signals an earlier circulation of knowledge preceding the discursive formalization of ideas in print in a scholarly journal.

The textual focus throughout this study, then, is on the construction of knowledges about the subject as they are ritualized and manifested in the media of "scientific" knowledge exchange and communication:

the scholarly journal and monograph. Social scientific discourse is scholarly discourse at the level of knowledge production and formalized scholarly discourse is knowledge-in-text.

DISCOURSE: DEFINITIONS AND ASSUMPTIONS

Language, communication, and discourses are social phenomena: "To speak of discourse is to speak of practice and to speak of 'social' as opposed to 'natural'. . . . To identify 'social' and 'discursive' serves to prevent any naturalistic approach to social relations and processes. Given the persistence of naturalism in the social sciences, this is not a small achievement." (Laclau & Mouffe, 1982: 98 – 99). The historically varying concepts of the child that have emanated from the social sciences are the product of discursive practices which are rooted in social and political interests and relations. Academic social science does not function outside such constraints, but rather functions within social and political (and, not least, economic and cultural) relations and interests that are institutionalized and highly ritualized.

Discourse thus does not precede the social organization of its articulation. Rather, it is identical with and formed in concurrence with the formation of social practices and relations. These concurrent processes are made possible by sets of rules which delimit what can be said, by whom, and under what historical, social, or institutional conditions: "These rules are not put there by the subject nor are they even conscious to the subject who uses these discursive systems" (D'Amico, 1982:203). Key here is the imperative to question the "givenness" of discourses as "the true ordering of historical reality . . . as a window through which one looks but does not look at" (p. 203).

Text is one form—since the advent of typography, a dominant form—in which knowledges become reified, objectified, and discursively grouped in the material forms of books, lists, maps, accounts, registers, and transcripts, and in the conceptual forms of authorship and genre. Text thus can be seen both as historical trace and as material ground for discourse. Text also is linked to the institutions within which text is practiced (e.g., examination records of schools, scholarly journals of disciplines, transcripts of court proceedings), and is linked to the position of speakers within those institutions who produce, resist or restructure, sanction, register, and authorize discourse.

Among the discursive rules that procedurally prescribe the parameters for this study—in terms of what can be said and how it can be said—the rule that stipulates authorial identification with statements is paramount. For instance, my text here is bound to that rule and thus qualifies as part of a formal discourse insofar as it situates statements within a reference network of author-authorities. Hence, the "sacred" status of the author is preserved (and reproduced) in the citation network within which discourse authorizes itself. In this sense, this text too becomes but one more discursive unity—a unit of discourse that is the product of academically authorized text production.

Discourse, then, *is* the social. And while such a claim may seem itself self-evident, it is important to emphasize the identity of the social and the discursive at the outset, because the very discourse under investigation here has its discursive basis—its speakers, institutional sites and practices, and epistemology—in this century's preeminent social science discourse: psychology. As the flagship discipline of the human sciences, psychology has developed such a ubiquitous and comprehensive textual corpus about human activity that it is difficult for either layperson or scholar to conceive of the human subject without reference to psychological description. Moreover, it is nearly impossible to think or know about the child outside of psychological referents and classifications. For instance, what appear as commonsense educational practices in schools, such as procedures of motivation, reward, and reinforcement, are based upon seemingly natural assumptions about children's social and cognitive developmental stages, their motor or language development.

Such taken-for-granted knowledges have their theoretical counterparts in scientifically authorized "true" knowledges. Foucault (1977:132) explains:

> In societies like ours, the "political economy" of truth is characterized by five important traits. "Truth" is centred on the form of scientific discourse and the institutions which produce it; it is subject to constant economic and political incitement (the demand for truth, as much for economic production as for political power); it is the object . . . of immense diffusion and consumption (circulating through apparatuses of education and information whose extent is relatively broad in the social body . . .); it is produced and transmitted under the control, dominant if not exclusive, of a few great political and economic apparatuses (university, army, writing, media); lastly, it is the issue of a whole political debate and social confrontation ("ideological" struggles).

Discourse and the social, then, are seen by Foucault as co-constitutive and institutionally embedded within the greater political economy of knowledge and truth production.

Discourse is based on the interplay of two knowledge axes: one specifying "code" and "rule," the other "truth" and "justification"

(Foucault, 1981). Practices "don't exist without a certain regime of rationality" and such regimes should be analyzed along two axes: "On the one hand, that of codification/prescription (how it forms an ensemble of rules, procedures, means to an end, etc.), and on the other, that of true or false formulation (how it determines a domain of objects about which it is possible to articulate true or false propositions)" (p. 8). A history of discourse thus studies "this interplay between a 'code' which rules ways of doing things (how people are to be graded and examined, things and signs classified, individuals trained, etc.) and a production of true discourses which serve to found, justify and provide reasons and principles for these ways of doing things" (p. 8).

By "true discourses" Foucault does not suggest that knowledge statements correspond to the real, or are to be seen as equivalent to universal, ahistorical truths. Rather, he claims that statements are considered true if they pass certain formal epistemic criteria and validity tests that authorized, qualified speakers within a discourse use to judge statements as true or false. When a discursive formation has reached the "threshold of epistemologization" (Foucault, 1972:187), then articulation, codification, and formalization of certain validity tests are formulated. These, in turn, allow for the critical reflection deemed necessary to sift fact (truth) from error. By the time statements are codified and materialized in print according to disciplinary rules and rules of academic publishing, such statements have undergone further validity testing by academic review. "True" statements do not appear in the formalized and public forum of the academic journal without having been certified as "true" by academic peers (authorized speaker-critics) according to epistemic criteria and methodological rules of inquiry that comply with canons of empirical investigation.

Such validation procedures are self-referential and self-justificatory. The certification of statements as true by authorities from within the discourse is further endorsed and rationalized by other collectivities of inquirers (i.e., producers of knowledge in other scholarly discourses) as a professional, objective, and logical process of producing true knowledges. In the social sciences, for instance, scientific procedures for appropriating the social for quantifiable ends are collectively practiced and rationalized across disciplines. Yet at the periphery of all formalized knowledges, marginal "truths" circulate. Under varying historic-discursive conditions, the marginal can displace, be incorporated by, or remain at the margins of prevailing dominant discourses. The material surface of academic text, then, is the arena upon which "truths" are inscribed and upon which contests of appropriation and counter-appropriation are fought. It is the material space upon which the production of true knowledges is discursively mapped.

DISCURSIVE FORMATION: RULES AND RELATIONS

Discourse-specific rules make possible the formation or transformation of an object of study, groupings of concepts, or emergence of concepts. These Foucault (1972:38) calls "rules of formation." Such rules can be identified in a guiding theory, a methodology, or in epistemological "givens" that set the conditions of possibility for the form and appearance of statements in discursive formations. Moreover, the organization of knowledge statements within dominant discourses and on the material textual surface upon which they are inscribed is further governed by rules including, inter alia, "methods of observation, techniques of registration, procedures for investigation and research, apparatuses of control" (Foucault, 1980b:102). Such rules are themselves products of discursive practice. A revised methodology, for instance, suggests new or modified methodological procedures or designs which set rules for organizing knowledge in different ways.

Objects of study are "an effect of certain 'rules' or regularities [of practice] which make knowledge possible" (D'Amico, 1982:209). Thus discursive formations produce "knowledge effects." Take one knowledge effect, one conceptualization of the media-subject relation as an example: In contrast to the passive viewer of the 1960s, the 1970s' cognitively active viewer generated the conceptual possibility for self-directed intervention in TV's putatively harmful effects. Media literacy programs and the teaching and testing of critical viewing skills thus became widely institutionalized school practice, adding yet another pedagogical technique of control. This move was an effect of historic-specific knowledges brought to bear on understandings of a particular mass medium and its relationship to a particular version of the human subject.

Because discourses and discursive practice are historical, each writing (and reading) reinstantiates and thus potentially remakes the rules. Even within a dominant discursive order, rules and knowledges can be subverted, resisted, and contested. Historical change—the disappearance of old or the emergence of new rules, objects of study, or statements within existing discourses—is made possible by certain opportune discursive configurations and juxtapositions within and among adjacent discourses. The emergence of the active viewer, for instance, was made possible in part by a reconfiguration of the child as a cognitive, developmentally segmented entity in adjacent educational discourses. Foucault maintains that the formation and "presence" of a "manifest discourse" is always situated in relation to other systematized sets of ideas or concepts (1972:25). The manner in which a new or transformed discourse (or concept) emerges, then, is in juxtaposition to ideas already "enunciated" elsewhere—that is, ideas organized within other contemporaneous or historical discourses. Hence a given discourse may stand in relations of analogy, opposition, or complementarity with certain other discourses (p. 66).

During its formative years, the discourse on TV and children was derived in large part from psychological principles and assumptions. Such cross-disciplinary and intertextual moves complemented and helped diffuse the then dominant discourse on children in an expanded system of ideas which Foucault calls a "discursive constellation" (p. 66). To explain the "child television viewer," as this object of study appeared in the 1950s, archeology must examine the "constellation" of adjacent "networks of concepts," and attend to how other discourses are ordered and systematized. That is, it must look at how and why ideas are ordered as they are; how institutional systems reflect the ideas and knowledges they in fact produce; in what mode of articulation ideas are encoded (i.e., what system of documentation fixes and disperses ideas); under what conditions epistemological boundaries are weakened at specific historical junctures to enable new ideas and practices to dislodge traditional norms and assumptions; which individual and institutional "authorities of delimitation" have the de facto and de jure right to reject or legitimate new ideas; and, finally, which historical conditions sanction authority in the first place.

In efforts to uncover identifiable knowledge relations and underlying presuppositions which influenced (re)conceptualizations of the child viewer, this present analysis will focus on circumscribing power/knowledge relations ("authorities of delimitation") and on the sociopractical dimension of knowledge relations. In this study, "authorities of delimitation" are, inter alia, institutionally based academics, journal editors, and state officials (i.e., those involved in Senate subcommittee hearings and reports).

The sociopractical level of knowledge relations is, very simply, that level where the ordering of dominant and marginal knowledges occurs. Academic journals disseminate, albeit in a restricted yet public domain, acclaimed "true" knowledges into spheres such as governments (e.g., U.S. Senate Committee and Congressional hearings) and public lobby groups (e.g., Action for Children's Television). In turn, public and government reactions to findings exposed and authorized by academic expertise can also be read as a "knowledge effect" of prevailing theory and research which frames the TV/youth debate.

For example: As Willard Rowland (1983) notes in *The Politics of TV Violence*, the data produced in the early 1970s for a federal inquiry into TV violence and children were modified editorially before publication in order to appease broadcasting and advertising industry pressures. Statements that did become formalized in the resultant 1972 Surgeon General's Report can be seen from an archeological perspective as knowledge effects of a particular discursive formation. In this and similar cases, the extension of scientific knowledges can be traced to and along the level of diffusion of academic text: We can trace the making of the TV effects discourse within and among disciplines, as it transgresses discursive boundaries, as it is deployed into the domain of government, and as it then circulates in the public societal domain via popular press reports.

Despite the difficulty of undertaking a systematic description of discourses, rules of formation, and objects of discourse independent of a priori analytic categories such as ideology, discourse, or history—it nonetheless is possible to deconstruct "manifest" levels of discourse and identify rules of formation, authorities of delimitation, and discursive formations. An archeology of knowledge, however, does not claim historical neutrality. That is, it does not claim a value-free analytic strategy and terminology, since any inquiry is historically and culturally situated, as is the subject-inquirer. As Hubert Dreyfus and Paul Rabinow (1982:166) have noted, "one is always already in a particular historical situation, which means that one's account of the significance of one's cultural practices can never be value-free, but always involves an interpretation. The knower, far from being outside of all context, is produced by the practices [s]he sets out to analyze." The present analysis is situated in and speaks from one locus on the grid of social science discourse, a discourse of which critical social theory is but one discursive "branching" (Foucault, 1972:147), and wherein what has been conceptually grouped and named "poststructuralism" is but another discursive formation.

OBJECTS OF STUDY AND SITES OF EMERGENCE

The field within which objects of study emerge, and are assigned an identity, is ordered according to three levels of discursive formation: (1) the surface of emergence, (2) the authorities of delimitation, and (3) grids of specification (Foucault, 1972:41–42). As distinct from doing a history of scientific paradigms as suggested by Thomas Kuhn (1962), this archeological approach accepts no a priori truths: no essentialist definitions, labels, concepts, theories, or discursive unities. What is presupposed are the historical presence of discourse, and the discursively produced child and mass media. To provide an analytic template for the present study, what follows below is an outline of the three levels of discourse formation.

The *surface of emergence* is the site where an object first appears: the social, historical, political, cultural, or economic domains. Nineteenth-century psychiatric discourse, for instance, initially emerged on the surfaces of "the family, the immediate social group, the work situation, the religious community" (Foucault, 1972:41). These sites eventually came under the gaze of medical discourses which would claim, "if not the responsibility for treatment and cure, at least the burden of explanation" (p. 41). Looking to the 1950s, the TV-child relationship emerged in the family, but the burden of explanation, treatment and cure for TV's (ill) effects on children became the focus of institutional academic scrutiny and analysis.

The child as a TV viewer emerged on several public and disciplinary sites, similar to those where the child as a viewer of movies emerged in the 1920s and 1930s. Movies and television have always been situated in the social domain. The cinema is public entertainment available outside the home and TV is public entertainment but consumed in the privacy of the home. On another level, the child viewer—whether of movies or TV—is an object of family attention and of informal pedagogical procedures and knowledges. As an object of surveillance already institutionalized in the school, the child is also a public object of study and scrutiny in the educational documentary film, the teacher training film, the audio-taped classroom transcript, the filmed recording of ethnographic data. Unlike the movie-viewing child, however, the youngster watching TV is engaged in practices more closely linked to the family. Unlike movies that are viewed outside the home, or educational movies viewed under professional supervision in the classroom, TV watching occurs in the home and most often amidst family members.

As a sociopractical surface of emergence, the discourse on children and TV emerged in the domain of the social. Yet official knowledges about the relation between the medium and youth did not derive from that site. Instead, concepts, theories, and data about TV and children came from those institutional sites and authorities "authorized" to speak about children: from field and laboratory experiments conducted by some educationists, but mostly by psychologists and sociologists. The scientific knowledges imposed on TV-viewer relationships, situated predominantly in the private domain of family and household, came from those disciplinary authorities, sites, and perspectives that claimed privileged knowledges about children. Insofar as access to children was limited to their only public location, in the school (unlike the adult's public profile as worker, consumer, or voter), the production of knowledge about TV and children occurred in school-associated sites, rather than at the site and in the context of the home viewing situation.

Authorities empowered de facto and de jure to code, interpret, and control knowledge are, according to Foucault (1972), individuals of institutionalized professional rank. Foucault considers both the individual(s) of rank within institutions and the institutions themselves as "authorities of delimitation" (p. 41). Within institutions such as the penal system, the school, the church, or government, individuals such as lawyers and judges, teachers and academics, clerics, and administrators produce and reproduce knowledge, and control and oversee the practices derived from and rationalized by the institutional discourse. These professionals—professing knowledge—are the same authorities who have the "right to speak": the authority to construct meaning, to interpret, to judge. Discursive formations authorize "certain kinds of *speaking, writing,* and *analyzing* . . . in a fully formed system, not just anyone can speak or occupy the position of a subject" (my emphasis; D'Amico, 1982:210). As Foucault (1972:224–225) notes, "a discourse impos[es] a certain number of rules upon those who employ it, thus denying access to everyone else. . . . None may enter into discourse on a specific subject unless [s]he has satisfied certain conditions . . . [and] is not, from the outset, qualified."

The authorities who constituted the child in the mass media discourse were predominantly academics employed in universities, from whence their institutional authority and status were derived. "Certain kinds of speaking"—the discourse of university-based research—can be considered as a system of institutional rules that frame a discursive formation, one shaped in the disciplinary and pedagogical "field" of the university. Similarly, "certain kinds of writing" at this same site delimit what can be said and how it can be said: in a conference paper, a journal article, or a monograph.

At these sites, possibilities of analysis are just that, a possible choice among a limited range of analytic procedures (only "certain kinds of analysis") constrained by the reigning "positivity" within a given discipline (p. 178). Not just anyone can "speak." Not anyone can lecture, publish, or present a conference paper, despite ostensibly anonymous and democratic manuscript or proposal review. Furthermore, those who do have the authority to speak must do so within a framework of authorized norms and procedures which govern what will count as methodological accuracy, theoretical validity, and conceptual coherence. As an "object of study" emerges in such a field, the process of discursive formation subtly alters how an object is discussed and positioned and, in turn, alters the object itself. It is this dynamic of formation that enables objects of study to appear, to be transformed, or to be eliminated altogether. This present study is a case in point: My subject position is authorized to speak, the authorized norms and procedures frame the production of this discourse, and constituted within this very text is a sanctioned (traditional) object of study—the individual child. That object of study, in turn, is hereby in the process of discursive transformation: from one historically constructed as objective fact, to one being rearticulated as discursive construct.

Foucault's third field of emergence is the "*grid of specification.*" He writes that this category refers to "the system according to which different 'kinds of madness' [or any object of study] are divided, contrasted, related, regrouped, classified" (1972:42). That is, grids of specification are loci (e.g., the soul, the body, the mind, the case study) upon which an object is mapped by discourse: divided, differentiated, classified, regrouped, contrasted, and so forth. Nineteenth-century psychiatric discourse, Foucault suggests, was mapped on four levels of differentiation: the soul, the body, the case study, and the neuro-psychological system (p. 42). The soul was conceptualized as a hierarchized group of interpenetrable faculties; the body as a three-dimensional configuration of interacting organs; the case study as a linear succession of stages recurring in cyclical repetition; and the neuropsychological system as interplay and reciprocity within a tautology of circular causality.

The grids upon which the televiewing child of the 1950s was mapped occurred on two levels. The medium's "impact" was located in mind (cognition), yet response to the medium was located in body (behavior). Grids of specification impose their own conceptual order on the object of study as it emerges in a particular disciplinary or practical field. These historic-specific grids, in turn, are evident in the ways (medical, psychiatric, or pedagogical) authorities define the object. An authority speaking from within the psychological discourse of the 1960s about the influence of TV on children would locate media influence in the measured behaviors of the experimental sample. By contrast, sociological discourse would analyze TV influence on child viewers according to categories such as attitudes and social expectations, and would consider children's susceptibility to TV effects as a "function" of social class backgrounds, parental reading habits, family use of other media of entertainment and information, and so forth. The point here is that objects of study are variously mapped on "grids" which are, furthermore, conceived of differently within different discourses or domains of practice. Methodological emphases on independent and dependent variables thus construe and construct the subject on distinct grids of specification.

A discursive formation takes shape between levels of relations possible among authorities of delimitation, fields of emergence, and grids of specification. A discourse and its objects emerge in between existing discourses, on uninscribed spaces, and the conditions and characteristics of this appearance are delimited by circumscribing discursive relations. These relations partially contribute to the formation of new discourses/objects, yet also make claims upon them. New representations, ideas, theoretical choices, and practices may emerge with concepts, rules, or practices borrowed from adjacent fields. To return to Foucault's example: The description of psychopathological behaviors embodies classificatory categories that resemble descriptions of deviant (e.g., criminal) behavior. Yet these categories also embody concepts that can explain the same behaviors via psychological concepts of mental derangement. The educational discourse of the 1920s, for instance, applied agricultural terms to describe educational "yield." The 1960s saw the transposition of the medical model to educational discourse in describing diagnosis, treatment, and remedy—remedial intervention. The conceptualization in the 1970s of cognition as critical in the viewing process reframed the child but retained the methodological procedure of isolating and observing behaviors. Cognitive psychology transposed the Piagetian child from educational and developmental discourses, retained behaviorist methodologies, and applied cognition implicated in print learning to audiovisual text comprehension.

Historically emergent discourses embody transposed and/or modified conceptual baggage from existing discourses, and yet, as new discourses become visible on a given field of emergence, surrounding disciplines make claims upon them. Criminality becomes an object for the medical gaze. Knowledge of madness and its treatment is shared by medical and psychological discourses. Experts on penal incarceration also contribute qualified knowledges to the therapeutic/punitive confinement of the criminally insane. Similarly, today's school dropout/juvenile offender becomes a site of knowledge and intervention practices dispersed among: clinical sociologists, psychiatrists and psychologists; educational and perhaps legal authorities; and social welfare and rehabilitation experts. This dispersion of knowledges about the subject, then, constitutes a fragmented subject whose "formation" is mapped across numerous grids in various discourses. Such a "formation is made possible by a group of relations established *between* authorities of emergence, delimitation, and specification" (emphasis added; Foucault, 1972:44). It is within this three-fold analytic grid, then, that this study maps the emergence and transformation of the TV-viewing child as articulated in discourse.

DISCURSIVE HISTORY: AN ARCHEOLOGY OF KNOWLEDGE

A history of discourse does not reject the notion of a history of ideas per se. It does, however, cut adrift knowledges from conventional epistemic anchors such as "stream of consciousness," "progress of ideas" or "rationality," and from the a priori conceptual unities these presuppose. The task of archeological analysis is to reject the anthropological project of searching for genesis, precursors, and antecedents along a fabricated historical continuum of increasingly rational, scientific, and true knowledges. An archeology of ideas is "an abandonment of the [traditional] history of ideas, a systematic rejection of its postulates and procedures, an attempt to practice a quite different history of what men have said" (Sheridan, 1980:104).

Foucault's postulate that discursive relationships construct objects of discourse enables an analysis of the historic specificity of an object of study (i.e., the subject), whereas a traditional history of ideas constructs "coherence" and "unity" around an object (i.e., the idea of the subject). Positivist narrative histories, then, commonly describe statements as derivative of or produced by the founding subject, rather than constitutive of it: Whether overtly or covertly, a kind of genetic fallacy is at work. An archeology of knowledge, by contrast, sets out to render knowledge, the quotidian production of knowledge and the quintessential object of knowledge—the human subject—as problematic. Thus, in order to decenter the subject, "one has to dispense with the constituent subject" (Foucault, 1980b:117).

An archeological approach "digs at the discursive site," so to speak, in search of textual artefacts—statements indicating appearance or contradiction—"to be described for themselves" (Foucault, 1972:105). It is only after statements have been recataloged according to their relations to other statements at the site, or with statements in adjacent fields, that claims can be made about how networks of statements construct a discursive (and, possibly, interdiscursive) configuration which may have at its center a principal idea, object of study, or set of practices. By contrast, a traditional history of ideas pursues statements from the inside out, moving from the object of study outwards to collect, accumulate, and harness statements derived from the object. This "slow accumulation of the past," this "silent sedimentation of things said" (Sheridan, 1980:104) is the work of building disciplinary traditions, of valorizing founding fathers, of proving disciplinary maturation—in short, of writing History.

Epistemic shifts are transformations which do not all occur at the same time or in the same (discursive) place. Moreover, Foucault's notion of historic rupture and discontinuities does not imply a neat structuralist parceling of knowledges at various historical junctures.

Unlike structuralist anthropology or literary criticism, archeology does not "try to freeze the continuous flow of history in synchronic systems that remain motionless between one transformation and the next" (Foucault, 1972:109). What archeology does attempt is "to determine the extent and form of the gap that separates them [knowledge transformations]" (p. 152). Conversely, an archeology—by looking beneath the manifest discourse—can trace continuities where transformations are no more than imaginary appearances: superficial discursive constructs that claim change but only obscure the continuation of established regimes and practices. Cases in point are current claims within U.S. mass communications discourses of a shift from positivist to critical research. The epistemological and methodological residue of the established (liberal positivist) regime of truth production, meanwhile, remains firmly entrenched. Hence, archeological analysis does not confine itself to the synchronic site, identifying and describing statements only in the immediacy of their appearance. Such description would deny the historicity of discourse.

Central to this present archeological enterprise is the historicity both of Foucault's archeological method and of discourse per se. An archeological expedition into the domain of discursive practices and formations enables historical reconstruction that traces the emergence, transformation, marginalization, or elimination of ideas, concepts, and objects independent of fixed a priori historical unities, an expedition independent of such unities as would constitute fixed "ends," toward which analysis is compelled to proceed. To "do" archeology and to bracket history does not mean that inquiry is dehistoricized or that inquiry cannot proceed historically. Rather, it suggests that discourse can and must be situated historically but not rewritten from within and according to the historical logic of enlightenment epistemologies.

HISTORICAL CONSTRUCTS OF THE SUBJECT

Foucault not only brackets universal, rationalist History but dismisses the human subject as an a priori category as well. This study is concerned with outlining changes in the concept of the child concomitant with changes in the discourses established to scrutinize and define the child. Hence, I review here how poststructuralist theory has been applied in analyses of historical constitution of subjects by and in discourses.

The phenomenological subject, for Foucault, is a historical object of study much like history itself. Both are historical creations of discourse. There is no subject for Foucault, as Ian Hacking (1986:36) comments, "no 'I' or 'me' prior to the forms of description and action appropriate to a person." Hacking (p. 36) further explains that "it is a Foucauldian thesis that every way in which I can think of myself as a person and an agent is something that has been constituted within a web of historical events."

Not until the nineteenth century did "man" focus on himself as an object of study. The gendered collectivity here, admittedly, signifies correspondence with the real conditions of historical knowledge production. "The nineteenth century saw the birth of biology, the study of man as an organism, political economy, the study of man as an economic producer and philology, the study of man as a language maker" (Weeks, 1982:116). Foucault suggests that the nineteenth century constitution of "man" as a biological or economic entity was not a reconceptualization or refinement of concepts from preexisting disciplines, but that these concepts were, in fact, new objects of study that occupied previously uninscribed knowledge spaces. Discourses create the subject and discourses delimit the subject, "in the sense of being imprisoned, 'subjected' within a discourse" (p. 117).

To dispense with the subject enables a trace of constitutive discursive elements that define a particular human subject as, for instance, the laboring and alienated (Marxist) subject, the (Kantian) transcendental subject, the (sociological) subject caught between a top-down ideological apparatus and bottom-up material relations, the psychoanalytic ego, or the sociolinguistic language user and psycholinguistic ideal speaker. Paradigmatically, modern social scientists and humanists alike take what appear as commonsense notions such as human nature, or the individual as "natural," and thereby as a logical unit of analysis, as ahistorical and universal givens. Yet, in fact, "the very notion of a human essence, the truth of specific individuals, is itself a product of discourse. . . . Our idea of individuality is itself a historical creation" (p. 117). The ahistoricity and universality of the subject's androcentric essentialism points to the importance of preserving a nonidealist concept of history, and of historical analyses. Furthermore, the individual subject not only is the product of singular discourse/disciplines but is constituted interdiscursively by and through a range of discursive practices and disciplinary constructions. In this way, in any given era the subject can be co-constituted, fragmented, or unified by a range of disciplinary texts and attendant disciplinary, normalizing practices.

In what follows, examples of the historical constitution of the individual subject will clarify the poststructuralist position on the epistemological problem and historical contingency of privileged subjectivity. The psychological subject, for example, is but a recent invention. Prior to Freud, the individual was not seen to harbor repressed fantasies in the unconscious, women were not equated with lack or seen to suffer from penis envy, and men were not positioned in struggle with oedipal fixations. Piaget constructed a subject with distinct cognitive developmental stages. Kohlberg gave us a subject with distinct moral developmental stages. Closer examination reveals that both the Piagetian and Kohlbergian subjects are constructs derivative and constitutive of a Western masculinist ideal(ized) subject (cf. Gilligan, 1982; Lever, 1976). The individual appears, disappears, and reappears at different historical junctures in different knowledge domains, described, defined, compared, and reclassified differently with each (re)surfacing. Particularly since Kant and Hegel, notions of the universal subject have evolved within a false teleology of idealized reason.

Similarly, the individual as a sexual being has undergone numerous historical (re)conceptualizations in Western discourse. The seventeenth and eighteenth centuries, Foucault (1980a:42–43) tells us, generated "a secular campaign . . . around the sex of children" and constituted the homosexual as a "species." "This new persecution of the peripheral sexualities" led to a "*new specification of individuals . . .* a steady proliferation of discourses concerned with sex-specific subjectivities, different from one another both by their form and by their object, [which] generated a discursive ferment that gathered momentum from the eighteenth century onward" (p. 18). The child and adolescent as sexual beings emerged on the surfaces of "a whole literature of precepts, opinions, observations, medical advice, clinical cases, outlines for reform, and plans for ideal institutions" (p. 28).

By contrast, in the centuries prior to the end of the sixteenth century, sexuality circulated in "open spaces" and in "free expressions" (Aries, 1962). Children, sexuality, and children's sexuality were not institutionally, socially, or discursively differentiated from the realm of adults. At least, this is how discourse has reconstructed children's sexuality in the classical era. Children in medieval society are said to have mingled freely in an adult world which did not conceal sexuality from the young (cf. Aries, 1962). Instead of the traditional image of medieval times as an era of moral piety, strict religious morality, and sexual prudery, Aries (1962:315, 328) characterizes medieval society as "a wild population . . . given to riotous amusements." In this raucous atmosphere children participated freely: "Transmission from one generation to the next was ensured by the everyday participation of children in adult life . . . wherever people worked and also wherever they amused themselves, even in taverns of ill-repute, children mingled with adults" (Aries, 1962:368).

Yet by the eighteenth century, pedagogues, physicians, parents, administrators, and clerics had isolated children from the general population. Children were relocated from the street, fields and taverns and embedded (and enclosed) in discourses concerning their sexuality, their learning, their moral and psychosocial development. The young had been moved out of the parental bedroom as part of the century-long physical relocation and architectural restructuring of family members into separate, individual spaces (pp. 378–383). Childhood and adolescence were institutionalized in schools. Here the young were collectivized yet individuated through the "dividing practices" of the examination, and by the spatial distribution and ranking of bodies in classrooms to facilitate newly institutionalized regimes of surveillance of large groups of newly classified individuals (Luke, 1989). The European child—that is, male child—during the seventeenth and eighteenth centuries emerged as a learner and a sexual being within pedagogical discourses, social practices, and educative techniques. By the eighteenth century, concern over children and adolescents had generated "innumerable institutional devices and discursive strategies" (Foucault, 1980a:30) with which to observe and control the young.

Another more recent discourse constituting the human subject concerns the quantification of the individual as part of a populace. In his analysis of the statistical study of populations, Hacking (1981, 1982) suggests that the early nineteenth century numerical counting and accounting of the social body generated a discourse ostensibly concerned with a study of the whole, but which covertly classified individuals and groups according to categories not intrinsic to "society" or to the "individual." The science of mathematics was considered an objective means by which information about the populace could be accumulated. The aim of statistics was to organize "information about and control of the moral tenor of the population" (Hacking, 1982:281). Classifications of individuals according to occupation, a historically new category according to which individuals thought of themselves, laid the early foundations of "the class structure in terms of which we view society" (p. 280).

Individuals during the eighteenth century were redefined and classified in terms of new economic categories "into which people had to fall, and . . . [which helped] to create and to render rigid new conceptualizations of the human being" (p. 281). Today, we continue to be counted and classified, in census and social science research texts, according to categories of age, gender, marital status, occupation, income, commodity consumption, place of birth and residence, type of residence and economic relation to the residence, number of offspring residing in the household or elsewhere, and so forth. As part of the quantification of the social body we are assigned an individual location—a unique profile—on the census table of grouped differences. On one level discourse produced social and economic groupings conceptually organized according to individual attributes. On another, individuals were defined in relation to other individuals, all subsumed under categories of division (e.g., socioeconomic status) not inherent in the phenomena in question. The census enumerations introduced a new "individualization technique" within a "totalization procedure" (Foucault, 1982:213). The quantification of the social body produced knowledges about the individual in the context of newly conceptualized collectivities.

Hacking, like Foucault, is not concerned primarily with actual categories and definitions, but with the very idea of categorizing and defining human subjects. Foucault's works on madness (1973), on criminality, prisons, and surveillance (1979), and on sexuality (1980a) show how discourses, social practices, and institutionalized techniques expose the individual as an object of study. As a preliminary to study of the subject in more recent contexts, I have tried in this section to argue that only by avoiding the a priori positioning of the individual as given, fixed, and immutable can analysis uncover how the individual has been historically constituted in knowledges and social practices. The individual subject has a historical specificity and is situated within a historical framework—s/he is not the same entity across time. Importantly, then,

> One has to dispense with the constituent subject, to get rid of the subject itself, that's to say, to arrive at an analysis which can account for *the constitution of the subject within a historical framework*. . . . [Archeology/genealogy] is a form of history which can account for the constitution of knowledges, discourses, domains of objects etc., without having to make reference to a subject which is either transcendental in relation to the field of events or runs in its empty sameness throughout the course of history. (my emphasis; Foucault, 1980b:117)

Foucault's insistence that the archeologist-historian bracket the subject, historical unities and progressions, enables the mapping of discourse and discursive practices which "make" the subject.

If we move from studies of the construction of individuals in eighteenth-century census enumerations, of the criminal in eighteenth-century penal reform discourse, or of the child/adolescent learner in sixteenth-century pedagogic discourse, to a study of the child in twentieth-century mass communications discourse, then the historical framework within which that discourse is situated requires some elaboration. The following and final sections of this chapter discuss the utility of poststructuralist theory applied to a contemporary discourse on the subject.

MODE OF PRODUCTION: MODE OF INFORMATION

Raymond Williams (1980:50) rightly observed: "As a matter of general theory it is useful to recognize that means of communication are themselves means of production." Means of communication produce meaning, subjects, and subject identities in discourses. In the 1980s a theoretical shift of focus occurred in critical social theory from analyses of material commoditization to significatory commoditization, from subject positioning seen within material relations to subjects positioned in symbolic relations. Any study of the child within "postmodern" conditions must take into consideration changing information and cultural environments, as well as discourses that theorize the child in relation to such changes. In agreement with Philip Wexler (1987:133) I would argue that "if discourse is a dominant condition of production, then its de-reification becomes *the* historically appropriate critical practice." Poststructuralist analysis is a move towards such de-reification.

Unlike structuralist theories of information (e.g., structural linguistics, cybernetic systems theory), a poststructuralist conception of information does not separate syntax from semantics, discourse from language (cf. Wilden, 1980:23). By contrast, "classificational information, the notion of 'information' current in the U.S.A.," tends to see information as objective, as carrying universal meaning, and as independent of the contexts within which information is produced and exchanged (Maruyama, 1980:28–29). Poststructuralist and postmodernist theorists of and commentators on the postindustrial information age insist that information is context dependent, whether that context is the billboard, the disciplinary corpus, or the TV ad. Importantly, context in the information age is said to be both medium and the media texts of information technologies themselves. Thus, for example, computer language codes have meaning only in relation to the soft- and hardware which make the production and exchange of information in that medium possible. Commodities tend increasingly to have meaning for consumers primarily in relation to what they symbolize: Meaning, or what a product symbolizes, is defined in the 30-second TV ad. In the West today, the lived experiences that comprise knowledge of and about the world are increasingly experienced in information technology relations, whether at work, at school, or at leisure. Power over knowledge is having knowledge of and thus power over the production and distribution of information. By extension, access to

information production and distribution enables control of information networks and technologies and the attendant social apparatus
that services and consumes them. Such control is not confined only to
the production of TV or computer texts but includes the academic and
corporate production of knowledges about the social body as it is
variously configured in information networks.

Clearly we are no longer in the age of industrial capitalism. Umberto
Eco (1987) concurs with Marshall McLuhan (1964) that information is
no longer an instrument for producing economic merchandise, but has
itself become the chief merchandise. Communication has been transformed into heavy industry. Western information society may very
well be but a phase in the historical permutation of capitalism, but the
new mode of production *is* the mode of information (cf. Harvey, 1989;
Poster, 1984, 1989). Further, "the mass media do not transmit
ideologies, they are themselves an ideology" (Eco, 1987:136). The new
information politics are the new commodity relationships within
which "the struggle over the means of producing discourse, over
language and the practices of forming discourse, becomes the major
locus of social life" (Wexler, 1987:124). And, as Mark Poster (1984:53)
puts it, "labor now takes the form of men and women acting on other
men and women, people acting on information and information acting
on people. Especially in the advanced sectors of the economy, the
manipulation of information tends to characterize human activity."

The point that Poster makes from his reading of "Foucault's premise
of historical materialism" is that the contemporary social field involves "information (electronically processed), not men or commodities"
(p. 53). Hence, "in addition to the older configuration of a labor
society, the labor premise can no longer be the first principle of critical
theory" (p. 53). In other words, in a society in which the dominant
mode of production involves subjects acting upon and being acted
upon by information—that is, by the (soft)wares of signs and not the
(hard)wares of material-industrial objects—the classical Marxist concept of domination/power is inadequate, delineated as it is in
master/slave, subject/object, and base/superstructure dualisms.
Substituting discourse for the subject as the focus for the analytic
enterprise suggests a new appraisal of the relationships between
power and subjects. On this thesis, technologies and discourses of
power such as science are considered constitutive of subjects, as
distinct from the traditional premise of capitalist subjects holding
power over laboring subjects within industrial commodity relationships. A poststructuralist analysis, then, reads all subjects as discursively located in power/knowledge networks. This includes those
subjects who, in neo-Marxist models, appear to be at the center of the

power/knowledge nexus, whether in science, technology, corp
or academic knowledge production.

THE SUBJECT IN TWENTIETH-CENTURY MEDIA
DISCOURSES

The cinema, radio, and TV changed in irreversible ways the social
location and practice of leisure and public entertainment. These media
produced a historically different kind of subjectivity, one organized
in mass-produced and -consumed collective symbolic structures. Perhaps more significantly than in movies and radio, today "the mass
discursive definition of the subject occurs quintessentially in
television-watching" (Wexler, 1987:159). Moreover, each medium
generates and delimits a series of medium-specific discourses: at the
level of content and audience analyses, and at the level of metadiscourse commenting on itself (e.g., Horkheimer & Adorno, 1944/1972;
Lasswell, 1948; Lazarsfeld & Stanton, 1944; McQuail, 1987; Gerbner,
1983a). Emergent information technologies in this century have added
new dimensions to the book and newspaper reader; they have
redefined the print-literate subject. This century witnessed the emergence of the movie goer, radio listener, TV viewer, and, more recently,
the computer user. A substantial theoretical and practical discourse
already has been established and institutionalized for the making of
the computer- and media-literate child.

Foucault considered the "apparatus of writing," the media and
modes of information encoding, as central discursive elements in the
production and deployment of power and knowledge (p. 190). In his
analysis of the emergence of notions of criminality and the correlative
institutional and conceptual construction of the criminal subject, "the
whole apparatus of writing," "the examination," "modes of transcription," and "techniques of notation," played a central role (Foucault,
1979). Particular modes of transcription, such as "arranging facts in
columns and tables that are so familiar now, were of decisive importance in the epistemological 'thaw' of the sciences of the individual"
(pp. 190–191). Not only does Foucault point here to an epistemological
shift consequential of specific information recording techniques, but
he further highlights the importance of linking analysis of discourse
to historical modes of information. Hence, analysis that takes discourse, discursive practice, and modes of information into account can
enable access to one constitutive aspect of power-knowledge relations. And such relations are always encoded in media of communication—whether in speech, the document, the memo, the artifact, or the
electronic image.

The "'power of writing'" that situated the conscript, the child-learner, or the criminal "in a network of writing" (p. 189) has contemporary electronic counterparts that "write over" subjects. TV text partially and in different ways constitutes subject identities, but the network of theoretical writing that describes and defines the TV-viewer relationship writes over that relation. At a metatheoretical level, a network of writing constitutes that knowledge axis which Foucault (1981:8) distinguishes as the discourse of (scientific) truth from the discourse of practice ("codification/prescription"). Foucault's notion of a "network of writing" underscores and supports Poster's (1984:168) premise that "Foucault's discourse analysis takes on its full significance for critical theory when the mode of information is taken into account." If, as Foucault (1982:213) suggests, the twentieth-century sciences of individuation and "political structures of individualization-techniques" are historically unprecedented, and if we accept that information capital has replaced industrial capital as the dominant order of power-knowledge relations, then any discourse analysis must take modes of information into account, and must focus on those discourses which constitute the subject in the new information order. Television and the child is one such discourse.

This present archeology of discourse will map transformations in the ways "authorities of delimitation" have constructed the child in relation to TV. By locating "fields of emergence"—investigating how and where ideas about this relationship developed—I will identify those discursive (trans)formations that gave rise to knowledges about the televiewing child in general, and the media-literate in particular. How different concepts of the televiewing child mapped the subject on "grids of specification" will be outlined. Rules of discursive formation will be identified from analysis of the epistemological ground upon which theories (and attendant methodologies) of the child, of TV, and of the relationship between both were configured as central objects of academic scrutiny and inquiry. Rules that regulate the textual production and organization of discourse in the forum within which knowledge statements are contested and appropriated—that is, the scholarly text—will be identified.

Chapter 2 outlines the discourse on children and movies, radio, and comic books. The aim of this chapter is to establish the parameters of the academic debate on children and the newly emergent popular cultural forms of public entertainment. Film, radio, comic books, and TV each engendered public and professional debate—alternately resistant and hostile to each new medium, and yet also heralding each as potentially emancipatory, democratizing, and educative. With the advent of each new technology, social scientists and critics drew on formal discourses and conventional wisdom established about previous "new" media. The discourse emergent with the large-scale introduction of TV in the late 1940s drew on and was located within already existent discourses on mass media and children. "Theories" had been established, research agendas set, problems defined, and founding figures named. Hence, Chapter 2 begins at the very beginning: with a survey of the discourse on cinema and youth in the early decades of this century. The aim in that chapter is not to map precursors or locate points of origin from which to trace historical progression. Rather, the aim is to identify what conceptual residue was transposed to the TV-child discourse, and to establish a discursive field against which subsequent transformations in the mass media-child relationship can be identified.

Chapter 3 outlines the TV-child discourse of the 1950s, Chapter 4 of the 1960s, and Chapter 5 of the 1970s. These chapters focus exclusively on the textual trace. Statements extracted from books and journal articles that define the child, articulate rules, and identify and position authorities of delimitation are analyzed. For purposes of methodological economy and order, and yet mindful of the poststructuralist imperative that historical analyses not reproduce or reinstate alleged historical unities or continuities, I have ordered all studies surveyed chronologically. The published output of research on TV and children during the 1950s is small in contrast to the volume of studies produced during the 1970s. Therefore, the studies reported in Chapter 3 (1948–1959) are organized chronologically but not alphabetically for each year. The increasing volume of research analyzed in Chapter 4 (1960–1969) and in Chapter 5 (1970–1979) necessitated alphabetic ordering within chronological segmentation.

Periodization, problematic in all historical research, remains an issue in this text. Although the progression of this text through the movie, radio, and TV eras is not a methodological construct but in fact follows the chronological introduction of these media into the public sphere, the discursive rule specifying the need for chapters forced the imposition of textual units and divisions. Rather than thematize the discourse according to research models, I arbitrarily decided to organize the text chronologically. This, of course, unavoidably constituted another set of discursive groupings.

Chapter 6 summarizes and concludes this study. Discursive re-formations during the early 1980s within the U.S. mass communications discourse are outlined. The implications of an alleged epistemological shift, or discursive "ferment," are examined. The chapter concludes with a discussion of the historical and epistemological implications, and indeed methodological problems, of poststructuralist discourse analysis.

2

1917–1953:
Children and Cinema, Radio, and Comics

This chapter surveys studies concerned with the influence of film, radio, and comic books on children. The aim is to identify how the movie-viewing, radio-listening, and comic-book–reading child was conceptualized in relation to these media. By the end of the 1940s a formalized discourse had been established which focused specifically on mass media and children. My focus here is on how those disciplines concerned with childhood and youth—principally sociology, psychology, and education—had conceptualized the media as a social information source for children, and the child as learning from and socialized by the media of film, radio, and comic books.

FILM

In 1933 children were estimated to spend nearly 167 hours per year in movie theaters, or about 1.6 movies per week per child. In relation to time spent at school, Paul Cressey (1934:505) noted that "since most children are known to remain frequently for a second showing of the photoplay it is a conservative estimate that they spend annually at least a fifth as much time at the cinema as in attending school." In 1941 cinema attendance and radio listening were ranked at the top of favorite activities for high school students from among the "big four (activities) in the passive-spectator category: . . . listening to the radio, going to the movies, riding in an automobile, and watching athletic sports" (Witty, Garfield & Brink, 1941:176). Figures on movie attendance had remained essentially the same since Cressey's 1934 estimate: In 1941 high school students were attending movie theaters about "once or twice a week" (p. 176). W.W. Charters (1933:44) noted that "the average boy of age 5 to 8 attends 24 picture programs a year and the average girl 19. In the age range 8 to 19 . . . the average boy in this range attends 57 picture programs a year and the average girl 46 in the same period." According to Edgar Dale (1933c), youngsters of early elementary school age attended the cinema roughly twice a month, whereas high school and mid- and upper-elementary students attended the movies, on average, once a week.

In response to the significant amount of time children purportedly spent at the movies, serious academic debate about potential effects on children began early in the 1920s. An early paper by Jane Stannard Johnson (1917), published in *Social Service Review*, proposed a solution to the perceived social "problem" of movies and children. Johnson was concerned over children's attendance at Saturday-morning movies, which may be one of the early forerunners of the Saturday children's matinee and, decades later, the Saturday-morning "kid-vid ghetto." For Johnson, children were exposed to too many objectionable movies, and "psychologically, the impression of such acts [crime, theft, dishonesty, lying, cheating] picturized in the screen's vivid manner, is more harmful to children than the vampire films" (p. 11). Her solution: Saturday-morning movie performances which are "clean, wholesome, entertaining and instructive," organized by the women of the Woman's Press Club of New York with the assistance of Boy Scouts. According to Johnson, and the mothers she claimed to represent, children should not be exposed to "films showing prisons and convicts, strikes, riots, fighting, shooting, saloons, gambling . . . [or] discordant relations between parents in the home . . . questions of divorce and the 'eternal triangle'" (p. 11).

Teachers also saw unsupervised and unregulated access to movies as problematic. One principal explained to Johnson: "The children come to school in the morning so sleepy they cannot study their lesson. . . . They see pictures they ought not to see and their minds are so filled with excitement and sensation of it all that they are unable to apply their minds properly to the study of their textbooks" (p. 12). For Johnson, the movie "problem" could be circumvented by active participation in, selection of, and organization of children's movie exposure and attendance. Moreover, the solution to the movie problem was the responsibility of women, not of industry or theater managers: "Women must take the initiative in starting the performances, and women must take the responsibility of arranging the details. . . . The permanence and success of the performances depend, not upon film men, but upon the women" (p. 11). The message here is that this new medium constitutes a problem for children both in terms of the "psychological" effects of content and the substantial amount of time that children reportedly spent at the movies. Although not stating this in so many words, Johnson calls for adult, particularly women's, mediation: censorship, participation, supervision, and regulation to counteract the problem.

Emanating from a socially privileged site—a bourgeois philanthropic site as distinct from an academic site of authority—Johnson's statements in *Social Service Review* must be seen as a contribution to the public, popular discourse on mass media and children. Although public concerns over the effects of movies on children may have been a widespread adult concern, those in positions to voice such concerns in print had both the social status and prestige to enable authorship, and the leisure time for reformist pursuits. Conceptualization of the mass media/children problem by authors such as Johnson thus cannot be taken uncautiously as indicative of de facto public sensibility.

Writing in a more specialized, less public forum for debate, the *International Journal of Ethics*, Joseph Geiger (1923:73) noted of the child viewer of movies: "His attitude is, relatively speaking, passive and receptive. His experiences are imposed on him from without. No opportunity is afforded him for spontaneous and creative activity." He further deplores the commercialization of "literary masterpieces" by the movie industry, specifically the translation of literary characters into suggestive and sensational portrayals, and the creation of undue violent action requisite to adapt literary text to the "necessities of the screen." Geiger sees the effects on "juvenile minds and morals" (p. 70) of most movies popular in the early 1920s with alarm. He suggests that "sympathetic participation," coupled with "instinctive tendencies," can incline cognitively and experientially immature viewers to "certain antisocial types of behavior" (p. 73). Movies, according to Geiger, are partially "responsible for the eye strain which is so prevalent among children today" (p. 73). The poor ventilation and lack of fresh air in the theater is unhealthy for children, and the "morbid and unwholesome" content of many motion pictures "can easily become the germs of nervous and mental disorders" (p. 73). In short, although Geiger does not condemn all motion pictures, he considers most morally and socially unsuitable for and physiologically harmful to children and youth.

Geiger's is one of the earliest commentaries constituting part of the early formalized discourse on children and the mass media. His concern lies with the impact of the movie message—"impressions"—on the immature mind, which lacks "apperceptive mass" (p. 70). He concludes that children's immaturity, the movies' prescriptive "pictorial representations" which preclude imaginative expression or spontaneous creativity, and the morally dubious content of many movies combine to leave the child vulnerable to emotional manipulation and the learning of antisocial and immoral messages. In addition to children's learning about violence from the screen, their innocence is jeopardized by the movies: "Evidence of the demoralizing and degrading effects of the sex-inspired picture on the youth of the land is to be seen on every hand. Immodest clothes, indecent dancing, promiscuous drinking parties, midnight joy rides . . . are an expression of the spirit of the times, a spirit of immodesty and irreverence and lawlessness generated in part . . . by the unparalleled assault which, for a decade or more, has been made, through the motion picture, on society's most valuable assets, namely, its innocency and its youth." (p. 79). Although Geiger does not fault only the movies for influencing the moral degeneracy of youth, he attributes a fair amount of blame to the "moving pictures." As a psychologist—alluding to precursors Hall and Wundt to establish the authority and disciplinary affiliation of his statements—his concern is not with effects in relation to other background variables in children's environment. This, in turn, leads him to make rather overgeneralized claims about the influence of the movies on (all) children and youth.

The first monograph concerned exclusively with movies and children was published in 1929. Alice Miller Mitchell's *Children and Movies* is a study of 10,052 children who were interviewed and given questionnaires or, in Mitchell's words, "written quizzes." Her sample, a "small army," was divided into three groups, or viewer types: public school children, juvenile delinquents, and boy and girl scouts (1929:xiv). Mitchell's objective was to find out what children liked about what kinds of movies, how preferences and habits related to certain kinds of children at different ages, children's attendance patterns, and how children's movie experience related to other interests. According to Mitchell's interpretation of the children's reports, movies do not negatively affect children, including those labelled delinquents (p. 141), who reportedly spent a greater amount of time at the movie theater than did the public school or scout groups in her sample. The delinquent is likely to be most at risk from any negative effects if the assumption is that movies influence viewers in a unidirectional, unmediated way. But as Mitchell observes, for delinquent children, movies provide an escape "through the magic door into movieland" (p. 91) from the "drab realities and cruel certainties of their surroundings and [give] them for a brief time another life" (p. 134). According to Mitchell and the juvenile offenders, movies did not provide a blueprint for unlawful acts. Rather, they were seen to provide an escape from the "poor, overcrowded, and drab . . . homes in which these delinquents live" (p. 134). She comments: "Not many of the delinquent boys felt that movies . . . were to blame for their delinquency. . . . Quite a few of them said that if they had been 'in a movie at the time it [the offense] happened, it would not have happened'" (p. 141).

Delinquency, according to Mitchell, does not lead to more frequent movie attendance and, conversely, excessive movie exposure does not appear to lead to delinquent behaviors. For Mitchell, then, film is a relatively benign influence on children, including reform school children. She discounts the public "charges hurled against the movies and their makers" and, unlike Geiger (1923), sees the potential of the moving picture with optimism: "the immense educational and artistic value of many films, the stimulation of ambition and widening of horizons by the revelation of other and better modes of life, the richer compensations of vicarious experiences" (p. xii). Like the 1933 Payne Fund studies, published only a few years after the publication of *Movies and Children*, Mitchell does not view the advent of film with alarm, and she conceptualizes children's movie viewing preferences and habits as a function of differential home backgrounds.

In contrast to Geiger's (1923) orientation, commentary on movies and youth emanating from quarters in sociology such as Mitchell's study took a different tack: an emphasis on sociodemographic influences which were seen differentially to circumscribe children's uses of and experiences with mass media. Cressey, writing about movies and children in the *Journal of Educational Sociology* in 1934, comments on the 1933 Payne Fund studies. He notes that the effects of movies on children are not uniform but, rather, depend upon "a variety of conditioning factors, important among which are the character, temperament, and personality . . . the nature of his varied social backgrounds represented in racial and nationality heritages, economic and occupational levels, religious experiences, and community traditions" (p. 506). For Cressey, and most of the authors of the Payne Fund studies, effects of movies on young viewers "cannot be seen except by reference to the specific social backgrounds of each individual" (p. 511). Moreover, all seemed to agree that film could be used by the school to educational advantage. Instead of advocating censorship and bemoaning the loss of culture, the Payne Fund authors seemed to have accepted, as Cressey put it, that "the cinema is here to stay" (1934:514).

The Payne Fund studies formed the first comprehensive textual unity in the mass media–children discourse, a formalized body of research not reproduced in scope until many decades later. For example, Ellen Wartella and Byron Reeves's (1985:120–121) reconstruction suggests: "The 1933 Payne Fund studies—twelve volumes of research conducted by the most prominent psychologists, sociologists, and educators of the time—represent a detailed look at the effects of film on such diverse topics as sleep patterns, knowledge about foreign cultures, attitudes about violence, and delinquent behavior." In their estimation, these studies "represent a research enterprise comparable to the 1972 Surgeon General's Committee on

Television and Violence." The depth and scope of the Payne Fund project "generated significant press attention, academic review, and critical comment, and were the basis of recommendations for government action on what the authors believed were significant social problems" (p. 121).

As a significant and authoritative set of constitutive texts of the early development of the discourse on children and mass media, the Payne Fund studies warrant closer scrutiny in order to outline how the relationship between cinema and the child viewer was conceptualized. The research took four years to complete (1929 to 1932 inclusive), and all 12 volumes were published in 1933. The 12-volume work was prefaced by a separate volume written by W. W. Charters, *Motion Pictures and Youth* (1933), which summarized the aims, methodologies, and findings of the entire project. Discussion of the findings from each of the 12 volumes, as reported in this section, is derived from Charters's summary volume. While the 12 research studies historically have been grouped into the discursive unity of "the Payne Fund studies"—paying homage to the funding source, not the object of study—the Charters text as well constitutes a discursive and textual unity, or metacommentary on a diverse range of statements. The Payne Fund studies have been discursively constituted as synonymous with the first definitive and comprehensive research on mass media and children (cf. Wartella & Reeves, 1985), and as representative of early research that conceptualized mass media as having a powerful influence on audiences *in relation* to intervening variables (cf. McQuail, 1987). From an archeological perspective, the Payne Fund studies can be seen to have formed the "root" at the "tree of derivation of a discourse." Foucault (1972:147) explains:

> Archeology—and this is one of its principal themes—may thus constitute the tree of derivation of a discourse. . . . It will place at the root, as *governing statements*, those that concern the definition of observable structures and the field of possible objects . . . prescribe the forms of description and the perceptual codes that it can use . . . reveal the most general possibilities of characterization, and thus open up a whole domain of concepts to be constructed, and . . . while constituting a strategic choice, leave room for the greatest number of subsequent options.

The Payne Fund studies articulated particular concerns, conceptualized effects, and produced a construct of the child which partially set future research agendas. The questions asked and not asked—the initial "strategic choice"—opened up a field of possibilities upon which the discourse would subsequently generate "branchings" (p.

147) of diverse formulations of the child, particular media, and the relationship between them.

The titles of the Payne Fund volumes indicate the kinds of questions academics and researchers considered important. Charters (1933:vi), chairman of the project, enumerated these key topics in the preface to his volume:

> Specifically, the studies were designed to form a series to answer the following questions: What sorts of scenes do the children of America see when they attend the theatres? How do the mores depicted in these scenes compare with those of the community? How often do children attend? How much of what they see do they remember? What effect does what they witness have upon their ideals and attitudes? Upon their sleep and health? Upon their emotions? Do motion pictures directly or indirectly affect the conduct of children? Are they related to delinquency and crime, and, finally, how can we teach children to discriminate between movies that are artistically and morally good and bad?

The contributing authors—the Committee on Educational Research— framed the potential effects of motion pictures on children as a "social problem" (vii), not a behavioral problem. Furthermore, potential effects were not taken for granted as unmediated and direct.

Getting Ideas from the Movies (1933) by P.W. Holaday and George D. Stoddard set out to examine "what . . . amount of knowledge [is] gained and retained from motion pictures by children of various ages and the types of knowledge most likely to be thus gained and retained" (Charters, 1933:2). "What effect motion pictures have on the attitudes of children toward significant social concepts, standards, and ideals of children" (p. 2) was the focus in *The Social Conduct and Attitudes of Movie Fans* (1933) by Frank K. Shuttleworth and Mark A. May, and by Ruth C. Peterson and L.L. Thurstone in *Motion Pictures and the Social Attitudes of Children* (1933). "The extent to which motion pictures influence the conduct of children and youth in desirable or undesirable directions and particularly in regard to patterns of sex behavior" (Charters, 1933:2) was analyzed by Herbert Blumer in *Movies and Conduct* (1933); by Herbert Blumer and Philip M. Hauser in *Movies, Delinquency, and Crime* (1933); and in *Boys, Movies, and City Streets* (1933) by Cressey and Frederick M. Thrasher. Another focus of study concerned the possible effects of motion pictures on children's health: "While no direct attack was made on the problem an interesting indirect attack was developed by Samuel Renshaw, Vernon L. Miller, and Dorothy Marquis [in *Children's Sleep*], in the study of the influence of motion-picture attendance upon restlessness in sleep which is in turn related to the health of children" (Charters, 1933:2–3).

The extent to which "motion pictures influenced the emotions of children and whether this influence . . . was exerted in wholesome or in harmful ways" (Charters, 1933:3) was examined in *The Emotional Responses of Children to the Motion Picture Situation* (1933) by W.S. Dysinger and Christian A. Ruckmick, by Blumer and Hauser in *Movies, Delinquency, and Crime* (1933), and by Cressey and Thrasher in *Boys, Movies, and City Streets* (1933). Finally, Dale in *The Content of Motion Pictures* (1933a) analyzed the content of several hundred films and collected data on *Children's Attendance at Motion Pictures* (1933c) in order to establish "that if it were proved that children acquired information, changed attitudes, and modified conduct as a result of movie attendance the directions in which these changes occurred would be determined by what they saw in the movies" (Charters, 1933:3). As a result of his research for the Payne Fund Studies, Dale (1933b) produced the first formal textbook on media literacy, "a textbook on motion-picture appreciation for high-school children" (p. 4). This text, *How to Appreciate Motion Pictures*, constituted the first formal trace in the adjacent educational discourse on applied mass media literacy.

In all, the Payne Fund studies took what could be read as a sociological view of the medium-viewer relationship. Repeatedly the authors emphasized the importance of linking effects to a network of contributing social variables. Cressey and Thrasher, for instance, found no direct effects between movies and delinquency, noting that "a simple cause and effect relationship does not prevail. To say that the movies are solely responsible for anti-social conduct, delinquency, or crime is not valid" (Charters, 1933:13).

Shuttleworth and May (1933) examined the attitudinal effects of movie stereotyping on children and found that movies did exert an influence on children's attitude formation, but "this influence is specific for a given child in a given movie" (Charters, 1933:16). Charters comments, however, that "the May-Shuttleworth study is of chief value as a caution. It indicates clearly that the influence of a motion picture is only one of several influences and the attitudes of children are a product of many influences. Native temperament, past experience, family ideals, school instruction, community mores, all theoretically have an effect" (p. 17).

While "the attitude of children toward a social value can be measurably changed by one exposure to a picture" (Charters, 1933:20) as Peterson and Thurstone found, movie messages can also counteract each other in their influence on children: "The movies themselves conflict with one another in the direction of their influence—a good picture may be followed by a bad one, an anti-Chinese film may be neutralized by a pro-Chinese movie.... Home influence may be stronger than the movie in specific cases. School instruction may neutralize the influence of a picture. Sometimes the movie may crash through and overpower the influence of the home, the school, or the community" (Charters, 1933:17–18).

Blumer (1933) gathered data in the form of "movie auto-biographies" from 1,800 subjects—college and high school students, office and factory workers—and conducted personal interviews with 81 university students, 54 high school students, and "a number of grade-school children" (p. 9). He found that movies apparently did influence the emotions and attitudes of youth, but that levels of influence varied with subjects' educational levels. Moreover, from a developmental perspective, movies were found to be more influential on adolescents than on young children because, as Blumer (p. 195) put it, "the influence of motion pictures upon the mind and conduct of the adolescent is more understandable if we appreciate this condition—to wit, that he is confronted with a new life to whose demands he is not prepared to respond in a ready and self-satisfying way; and that he is experiencing a new range of desires and interests which are pressing for some form of satisfaction." But even for adolescents, the reor-ganization of conduct as a consequence of portrayals or "schemes of life" in the movies, "may be quite temporary, as it frequently is. However . . . it may be quite abiding" (p. 198). Experiences of fright, sorrow, love, and excitement generated by the motion picture were found to influence youth in the long term differentially.

Concluding the introductory section of his summary, Charters (1933:61) comments on the overall implications of the Payne Fund studies: "The motion-picture . . . is one among many influences which mold the experience of children. How powerful this is in relation to the influence of the ideals taught in the home, in the school, and in the church by street life and companions or by community customs, these studies have not canvassed." Noting that some of the studies found no attitudinal differences among frequent moviegoers and non–movie-attending children, and yet other studies found "specific and significant differences," Charters surmises that these discrepancies "complicate the question of total influence" (p. 61).

An anomaly was emerging in the discourse: While the findings suggested an absence of clear-cut patterns of effects between the medium and children's attitudes, world views, and affective states, the findings also suggested that movies did generate some identifiable effects in many of the subjects studied. Hence, the Payne Fund re-searchers agreed on the necessity for an "experiment with one con-structive safeguard against bad movies and one aid to good movies"

(Charters, 1933:59); namely, preparing a textbook for high school use on "motion-picture appreciation and criticism" (p. 59). Such a move suggests that young viewers were considered as active, educable interpreters of audiovisual content and not as mere passive recipients.

The perceived need for teaching viewing skills to children and adolescents stems from Dale's (1933a) content analysis of 500 movies which indicated to Charters (1933:52) that most movies "produce an unbalanced diet . . . too narrow for the [moral] welfare of children." Dale's analysis of 500 movies shown in 1920, 1925, and 1930 found ten dominant movie themes, of which "the Big Three"—love, crime, and sex—were identified in seven out of ten movies in 1930. Some of the romantic love themes were perceived to be "beautiful and in good taste" (Charters, 1933:51), whereas "others are sensual and in conflict with the mores of every group studied by Peters" (p. 51). The "matter of aggressive love-making by girls" (p. 59) seems to have been of particular concern.

Crime themes were considered to depict simplistic solutions to complex social problems: "The fundamental philosophy of movie criminology is that the crimes are committed by bad people. Therefore, jail or deport the criminals and the crime problem is solved" (p. 50). Of 115 movies analyzed, 59 showed a variety of "killing techniques"; "in 45 [movies], killings occurred, and in 21, killings were attempted"; "the revolver was used in 22 pictures, knifing in 9 . . . " (p. 50). Hanging, stabbing, lynching, machine-gunning, and so forth, all contributed to the movie portrayal of crime equated with carnage. As Charters (p. 50) noted: "This is a rather sorry layout for . . . children to see when they go to the movies. One out of four of all the films are crime pictures and crimes are committed in many more than those in which they are the central theme."

Finally, sex themes constituted 15 percent of the movie sample for 1930. In light of Blumer and Hauser's findings that "sex pictures have an extremely powerful influence upon many delinquents" (Charters, 1933:54), the influence on (nondelinquent) children of movies with an overt sexual theme was of grave concern. Charters (p. 51) outlines the major sex themes identified by Dale: "living together without marriage being apparent; loose living, impropriety known or implied; plot revolving around seduction, adultery, kept women, illegitimate children . . . sex situations; 'women for sale' stuff; bedroom farce with incidents on the fringes of impropriety." On behalf of the Payne Fund authors, Charters (p. 60) expresses his concern about 1930s motion picture content: "for children the content of current pictures is not good. There is too much sex and crime and love for a balanced diet for children" (p. 60).

Clearly, crime, sex, and love themes in the movies were perceived as a moral problem with social and educational implications. Yet by implementing motion picture appreciation and criticism into the school curriculum, it was believed that "a discriminating audience would be a constructive power for control of what would be produced" (Charters, 1933:59). Capitalizing on the "unusual interest of high-school students in motion pictures," this appreciation course "promises to be a constructive measure in teaching adolescents how to discriminate among motion pictures—to help them to enjoy good art and drama more deeply and criticize bad pictures more intelligently" (p. 60). The program was piloted in several high schools in 1931 and was revised in 1932 and 1933. At the time of the Payne Fund publications, efforts were being made to link the movie appreciation course with radio broadcasts for transmission to students and adult discussion groups.

Calls for teaching critical viewing skills to the young, then, were not uncommon during the movie era or during the early years of TV. Most often, those who urged the school to play a role in educating children about movies also called for teachers of English to teach skills of aesthetic appreciation. More than 15 years after the publication of the Payne Fund monographs, Barbara Gray (1950)—in efforts to dispell the public concern "about the effects of cinema-going upon young people" (p. 135)—based much of her argument on Dale (1933a), and Dysinger and Ruckmick (1933). She suggested that "every effort should be made to strengthen children's resistance to the insidious attack of frivolous film by suitable training and discussions. This training could take the form of lessons in film appreciation as a normal part of the school curriculum . . . with the purpose of helping adolescents 'to consider before going to a film . . . to be selective in their cinema-going'" (Gray, 1950:143).

The "movie criticism and appreciation" course generated by the Payne Fund studies was the only curricular material derived directly from the "formalized" discourse on mass media and youth in the 1930s. Other, local initiatives were taken by some teachers to incorporate movie-related studies into the classroom. Cressey (1934:514–515) reports on one such teacher who had "recently reversed her official attitude and allowed her girl students to introduce pertinent comments regarding movie actresses, and even permitted a judicious use of the fan magazines, [from which] a marked improvement in classroom morale and . . . interest of the students resulted." Cressey was optimistic for the potential of the movies. He recognized that, "for the most part, the incipient attitude of school and teacher has probably been one of antagonism" (p. 514), and he maintains that the school should "adopt a more enlightened attitude towards it," since "the cinema is here to stay" (p. 514). Unlike Blumer (1933:200), who saw few redeeming features in movies and charged the "directing personnel" with improving the movie diet for children, Cressey (1934:515) advocated school-based media studies courses, and envisioned significant educational potential for the motion picture: "It is also possible for the school, through motion-picture appreciation courses and other ways, to exert a positive influence in the child's selection and response to photoplays. . . . The wider use of motion pictures in school programs and as aids in visual instruction represents a tremendous field for educational advance and coordination."

Contributing to the burgeoning discourse, Mary Preston (1941) in "Children's Reactions to Movie Horrors and Radio Crime," published in the *Journal of Pediatrics*, claimed that in comparison with "nonaddicts," "movie addicts" suffered from increased fears, nervousness, sleep disturbances, eating disorders, and nail biting. Here, the entry of the medical discourse into the mass media and youth debate introduced a medical metaphor for viewers—"addicts"—which conceptualizes viewing as a pathology. Severe addiction was classified as movie attendance between two and five times per week; moderate addiction, one to two movies per month; mild addiction, attending several movies a year; children who attended no movies at all were classified as non-addicts.

Preston bemoans the loss of an earlier time when families engaged in entertainments such as "games, handiwork, reading aloud, and so on" (p. 148); "poor families, on or off relief . . . drag . . . the whole family along to the movies, since there is no money left to pay for someone to stay with the children at home" (p. 148). With the advent of movies and radio, she "wonders how the old Sunday school attendance has fared" (p. 148). "Movie horrors" and "radio crime" affect the child, who through "sympathetic participation . . . takes on the action he is seeing or hearing as his own" (p. 149). Preston does concede differential effects among children, but suggests that the only mediating variables are emotional security in the home, secure peer relationships, school success and, lastly, "a good physique": "Naturally, the effects of [movie/radio] addiction were found to vary in different children, whether expressed by the general health, nervousness, sleeping, eating, thinking, fears, and so forth. . . . Naturalizing agents were found to be a good physique, a comforting security at home, a satisfying relationship with one's own fellows, and a desirable success in the school world" (pp. 148–149). A decade later, Edward Riccuiti (1951:75) commented on Preston's claims: "A study by Preston in 1941 claimed spectacular evidence for the harmful effects of both movies and radio. Her results are highly questionable. One gleans from her writing the preconceived notions of the writer. Also, her subjects (or "addicts") were children who had come into the clinic or private practice for care."

In contrast to Preston's evident personal and professional bias and her "direct effects" premise and findings, another study published in 1948 in the *Journal of Educational Research* found no differences between "Movie and the Non-Movie Goers in achievement, mental age, chronological age, personality or parental socio-economic level" (Heisler, 1948b:545). According to Florence Heisler, "one would think that moving picture attendance would help increase the child's vocabulary; give an added number of concepts and as a result improve the reading; help with language development; and increase the child's information in literature, social studies, and science" (p. 546).

Clearly, Heisler assumes beneficial influences of movies on children. Since her findings did not confirm her hypotheses, she speculates that perhaps the achievement battery may not have been able to identify facts learned from movies; subjects may have "missed or forgotten historical or geographical facts because the plot of the picture over-shadowed this information"; the sample "may not have been 'set' or ready to absorb the information presented"; or, the movies "these children saw may have been barren of any historical, geographic, or literary material" (p. 546). Heisler offers a tentative explanation for the lack of effects not in relation to mediating variables, but in terms of medium and viewer characteristics.

In another study published in the same journal in the same year, Heisler sought to identify differences according to the same factors of age, educational achievement, parental socioeconomic status, and so forth, among elementary age school children "who attended the moving pictures, read comic books and listened to serial programs to an excess [and] . . . those who indulged in these activities seldom or not at all" (Heisler, 1948a:183). She reportedly found no differences among heavy and light mass media consumers. Heisler admits that the *Stanford Achievement Tests* do "not have a test on current events and on social behavior and it may be that the vocabulary learned through these activities [radio listening, movie viewing, comic book reading] was not measured by the achievement test" (p. 190). Reflecting what perhaps may have been a commonly held view among teachers, she notes: "Many teachers . . . believed that these activities helped to increase the child's vocabulary, reading ability, and information. The results of this study do not substantiate this belief" (p. 189). In other words, heavy mass media consumption did not appear to decrease educational achievement, and light or no mass media consumption apparently did not improve educational achievement. She did note, however, that those children "who did not read comics, listen to serial radio programs or attend the moving pictures owned more books" (p. 189), which may be a function of parental socioeconomic status, although she does not make this link.

These findings contributed to the discourse a radically different view of the relationship between medium and viewer from Preston's claims some seven years earlier. Heisler's position is more akin to the orientation of the Payne Fund studies and, as such, can be seen as indicative of an extension of or continuity with the general perspective espoused by the Payne Fund studies. Preston's study, on the other hand—judging by its noncirculation as a citation in subsequent studies—is of more marginal status. Preston's article, appearing in the *Journal of Pediatrics*, was undoubtedly more likely to circulate among the medical establishment, whereas Heisler's studies in the *Journal of Educational Research* and the Payne Fund study monographs were more likely to circulate in professional and academic educational quarters. Given the relative paucity of research on movies and children in the 1930s and 1940s—that is, in comparison to research on TV and children published in the early years of TV—those studies that were published in the formal domain of academic journals undoubtedly received considerable notice by practitioners dealing with children. It seems, then, that the discourse on movies and children, by and large, conceptualized the relation between medium and viewer as highly dependent upon individual differences among viewers. Although all researchers agreed that movies had powerful effects on the young, most recognized that factors such as developmental level and social class mediated media uses and influences.

Studies of the influence of movies on children overlapped with studies on the effects of radio on children. The effects of radio on the public, particularly the political effects of government campaigns (e.g., Lazarsfeld & Stanton, 1941, 1944) and the effects of consumer advertising, were an important research focus before and during World War II. The influence of radio on children as well came under research scrutiny and is an intrinsic part of the development of the discourse on mass media and children.

RADIO

Writing seven years after the introduction of radio, the author of a 1927 paper in the *American Journal of Sociology* predicted that the radio would have no significant social effects because "there are fundamental things in human nature that will prevent broadcasting from wielding any greater influence on us than the phonograph has" (Beuick, 1927:615). As a focus for social congregation and interaction, broadcasting "does not encourage association or herding," and will, "therefore, never compete injuriously with the theater, the concert, the church, or the motion picture" (p. 615). Radio, like print, privatized individuals in the process of information acquisition from a mass medium and did not, in Beuick's terms, "herd" individuals together like the cinema or theater. Beuick did not specifically consider the influence of radio content on individual listeners but considered its medium-specific form in terms of broader social effects, a concern that also would accompany the introduction of TV. In that sense, he saw the possibilities of radio as most beneficial for the disadvantaged and the isolated: "Today radio broadcasting is cheering thousands of people in hospitals: it brings instruction and entertainment to isolated groups; in the prison it plays its part in social welfare; to the sightless it is of inestimable value" (p. 617).

Like McLuhan (1962) some 30 years later, Beuick compared radio with the printing press insofar as it enabled the conquest of time and space. The radio, he noted, could overcome geographic isolation and transmit information faster and to more diverse and inaccessible regions than print. Communities would be united in an "international brotherhood and a world of intelligent and rational communities all metamorphosed under the potency of democracy" (Beuick, 1927:618). Radio, in fact, as seen by Beuick, not only positively influenced politics, education, and religious and international consciousness, but had the potential to bring about world peace: "These programs have stimulated the conclusions that we shall have a greater religious consciousness, that we shall take a greater interest in politics than we are wont to, that we shall find less apathy for education, and that we shall wake up one bright morning with an international conscious-ness, the result of world-wide broadcast programs, and the dawn of mutual understanding and world peace will have come" (p. 617).

So while radio was seen to have the potential for uniting com-munities, if not nations, it nonetheless was seen to lack the socializing qualities that the "theater, the cinema, the church, the concert, the political meeting, and the lodge" (p. 622) embody. For Beuick, "men must go among men," and it is the "social" and "psychological" appeal of group association "of which broadcasting is almost entirely devoid" (p. 622). Several decades later, researchers would assess the social impact of both radio and TV quite differently—by relocating the importance of socialization through group association in the more private nucleus of the family. Radio and TV were both seen as reunit-ing the family, relatives, friends, and neighbors in front of the tech-nological hearth.

One of the earliest studies on the effects of radio on children was published in 1936 in the *Journal of Educational Psychology*. Some 93.4 percent of households in cities over 250,000 reportedly owned a radio in the mid-1930s (H.P. Longstaff, 1936:210). Children voluntarily listened to radio approximately two to three hours daily, and their favorite program type was the radio drama (DeBoer, 1937:456). Longstaff sought to find out what cognitive and value links children make between radio program and product advertisements, and whether and to what extent children's knowledge of advertised products influences parental purchasing behavior. Based on his interview data of 1,020 children, Longstaff claimed that children associate programs they like with the advertised products that sponsor the program; that children who make such associations tend also to have access to and use the product; and that girls make less program/product associations than boys because, according to Longstaff, there are fewer programs targeted at girls than at a general (male) audience. Finally, IQ was found not to make a difference "in determining who listens and what programs will be remembered" (p. 220). That "retarded, average, and accelerated children" (p. 217) are attracted to the same kinds of programs suggests, for Longstaff, that program content has been "geared down intellectually" (p. 218) to a common denominator formula to appeal to all groups.

According to Longstaff, radio affects children because they seem to learn commodity names and associate these with the sponsored programs. The secondary effects of learning product names from radio, according to Longstaff, are channelled toward mothers of whom children make product purchase requests. Although Longstaff does not draw any implications from his findings for children's value formation or social behaviors, the implicit construction of the child (radio) listener is that s/he learns messages from the medium which, in turn, are translated into social behaviors (purchase requests). Children's purchase requests, furthermore, indirectly influence the social behaviors of the family group through product acquisition and use.

In 1937 John DeBoer published the findings of a study conducted to test the validity of empirical observation of children's behaviors ("outward reactions") in response to radio programs. Although John DeBoer stated that "more reliable evidence may be derived from a direct observation of children in the listening situation" (1937:457), his subjects were observed in classroom settings where the children "were encouraged to play games and in general to assume an attitude of relaxation" (p. 457). The objective of the experiment was to determine "children's interest in radio programs [and] . . . to discover which programs are most popular with children" (p. 456). Measurements of subjects' emotional expressions to the experimental radio programs were used to identify rising and falling interest in various programs and program segments. For DeBoer, a method that can accurately discriminate among the radio preferences of children "will have a distinct advantage over the techniques which require elaborate psychological apparatus" (p. 459). So while his aim was to provide evidence of children's responses to radio program content derived from a "naturalistic" setting—whereby he hoped to show that observation is a more accurate indicator than psychological measurement instruments—a classroom setting does not remotely approximate the everyday situation of family and household life within which radio listening occurs. Yet DeBoer remained cautious with his conclusions, noting that "the results thus far do not justify the conclusion that children's emotional responses to a radio program can be reliably measured through the observation and recording of their physical reactions" (p. 463).

In an era when the child's cognition, social behaviors, attitudes, and skills were seen as measurable entities, when the child was individuated and specified as a discrete identity according to numerical quantification, DeBoer's effort marks a deviation from the methodological norm of the day by rejecting psychological measurement instruments in favor of observational technique. Yet he conforms to the norm of the controlled experimental situation by his use of the controlled environment of the classroom. DeBoer's conceptualization of the medium-child relationship suggests that children's responses to radio programs cannot be adequately described numerically, and that even observational techniques may bias the findings since, as he found in one early experiment, "the presence of 28 observers in the room seemed to put the pupils on their 'good behavior' and to cause them to inhibit their normal responses to the program" (p. 458). In the 1930s, few studies advocated alternative approaches to psychological testing and, as such, DeBoer's contribution can be considered as the incorporation of marginal statements within the dominant discourse.

Two years later DeBoer reported on his 1937 findings in *School and Society* (1939a). Here he cited no statistics but discussed the potential merits of radio in terms of children's emotional reactions to the medium and the formation of their attitudes and values. In agreement with "the current belief of psychologists that the formation of attitudes is essentially emotional rather than intellectual in character," (DeBoer, 1939a:371), he argues for the positive potential of radio. Referring to Peterson and Thurstone's (1933) study that suggested that movies can significantly modify children's attitudes towards more positive, socially egalitarian and democratic ends, DeBoer proposes that with concerted efforts of producers, script writers, and educators, "radio drama can help children solve problems in their personal relations with other members of the family, their schoolmates, the adult world and members of other community institutions" (p. 372). For DeBoer, "it is in the constructive use of radio drama in the field of children's emotions that the chief educational challenge to radio lies" (p. 371). Effects of radio on children are seen by DeBoer as principally affective ones which, in turn, are influential in children's political value and attitude formation: towards "questions like war and peace, labor and capital, socialism and capitalism, fascism and communism, other races and other nationalities" (p. 371). For the most part, radio programs are "perhaps relatively harmless—but they are also relatively useless" (p. 371).

The notion of the child as passive radio listener was supported by Paul Witty, Sol Garfield, and William Brink (1941), who considered radio listening as one of "the big four (activities) in the passive spectator category" (p. 176). Comparing speech in interpersonal communication with radio listening, DeBoer (1939b) also claimed that children were more "passively receptive," less critical, and less analytical when listening to the radio in contrast to engagement in interpersonal speech. Witty et al. (1941) found in their study of 1,687 high school students—of whom 701 were "white" and 986 were "black"—that radio program preferences fell along gender and racial lines. Girls were found to prefer romantic programs whereas boys preferred mystery, adventure, and gangster programs. White males and females were said to prefer comedy programs, whereas "gangster films were far more popular with Negroes [who] . . . showed unusual interest in gangsters films and pictures dealing with criminals" (pp. 181, 182). Gender and racially delineated preferences can be read both to suggest and reinforce stereotypical orientations. Quoting DeBoer's 1939 article, "Radio—The Pied Piper of Education," Witty et al. (1941) suggest that because, unlike speech, radio renders the listener "passively receptive," it is imperative that schools intervene "to help pupils . . . select broadcasts and photoplays intelligently and to evaluate them critically" (p. 183). Because children and youth spend such significant amounts of leisure time with radio and movies, and because these media are such powerful influences on attitude formation (p. 182) and on public opinion (p. 183), it appears vital to the authors that the critical study of radio and the cinema be integrated "in every area of the secondary school" and taught as "a continuous process to be pursued on all levels" (p. 183).

Existing media studies programs, according to the authors, are limited in scope. They propose, instead, that "the classroom . . . should be a place where information secured over the radio or from a film is introduced freely by students and analyzed as to its accuracy and implications. . . . The psychological time to guide students' interests in these media of learning and recreation is when opportunities naturally present themselves, rather than at related intervals or by means of set units or courses of instruction" (pp. 182, 183).

The proposal to teach adolescents critical listening and viewing skills which would mediate media-specific content is based on assumptions that radio listeners and movie viewers are not affected unilaterally by either medium. Such assumptions imply less of an effects, or hypodermic, model of media effects and suggest, instead, an interactive relationship. Of particular interest is this article's lengthy discussion of and insistence on the need for the secondary school to teach critical viewing/listening skills: to enable students to discriminate among programs; to identify media content "tinged with propaganda" (p. 183); to distinguish between valid and biased interpretations in efforts to preserve democracy (p. 182); to use media as sources for discussing personal and community problems; to aid in the development of human relations; and, finally, to lead students "to understand how their own attitudes on social, economic, and political issues are colored or determined by radio programs and movies" (p. 183). Such a comprehensive agenda for school-based media studies, focused on critical evaluations of the media as well as on the individual, was not proposed again until calls for media literacy instruction became a significant part of the formal discourse on TV and children in the late 1970s and 1980s. As Witty et al. saw it, "the possibilities of the radio and the movie for the enhancement and improvement of life are indeed great" (p. 183).

Adelle H. Mitchell (1949), in her "scientific investigation" into the effects of radio on reading achievement, saw no such potential for radio. Published in the *Journal of Educational Research*, Mitchell's study is prototypical of later experimental studies in which concern with method overrides theoretical considerations, and where discussion of methodological design and procedure takes precedence over discussion of the object of inquiry. Ninety-one public school students randomly selected from fourth to ninth grade were administered an IQ test (Otis Test of Mental Maturity) and the Iowa Silent Reading Test. Students were given the reading test under three radio-listening conditions: no radio, musical programs, and variety radio. Mitchell's five-point conclusion noted that radio adversely affected all children's reading achievement, that musical programs affected children less than did variety programs, that boys were slightly more affected by either type of program than were girls, and that the reading achievement of children with a high IQ score was less affected by radio than that of low-scoring children—although children scoring below 90 IQ points were found not to be adversely affected by musical programs. Mitchell draws no inferences from her findings, provides no agenda for further research, and makes no recommendations as to how schools or the family might help mediate radio's allegedly negative influences on reading achievement. Mitchell conceptualizes the young radio listener as a measurable entity and as one whose reading ability is negatively influenced by radio listening. Moreover, effects of commercial radio are assumed to be legitimately deducible from the interference of listening to radio programs with achievement test scores.

Studies of children's radio program preferences and listening habits (Lyness, 1951), radio and reading achievement (Mitchell, 1949), radio and children's emotions (DeBoer, 1937, 1939a), and radio and product requests (Longstaff, 1936; Grumbine, 1938) appeared in monographs and journals until the early 1950s, when the first studies were published that combined radio with TV research (e.g., Lyness, 1952). The most prevalent research interest focused on identifying "patterns of interest" (Lyness, 1951:449) in specific media among children and adolescents (cf. Ricciuti, 1951). A decade earlier, Herta Herzog (1941:2) also noted that the main topic of published studies on radio and children centered on "what children listen to or what they prefer." W.R. Clark (1939), DeBoer (1937), A. Eisenberg (1936), Herzog (1941), Paul Lazarsfeld and Frank Stanton (1941), H.P. Longstaff (1936), Paul Lyness (1951, 1952), J.G. Peatman and T. Hallonquist (1945), Wilbur Schramm (1948), Witty and Ann Coomer (1943), and Witty et al. (1941) were all concerned in one way or another with youth's preferences for particular media and specific media content. Preferences were commonly delineated according to subjects' age, sex, IQ, and parental socioeconomic status. Given the disciplinary orientation of the researcher, these standard variables were further delineated according to other background data such as health records (e.g., Preston, 1941), social-emotional adjustment (e.g., Ricciuti, 1951), book ownership (e.g., Heisler, 1948a), possession of library cards, preferred presidential candidate, ownership of automobiles, telephone, radio and TV sets (e.g., Lyness, 1951), and personal adjustment (e.g., Heisler, 1947).

Ricciuti (1951), summarzing pre- and postwar studies on radio and children in preface to his own comparative study of listeners and nonlisteners in terms of ability, attitude, and behavior, noted that "the study of the effects of what they [children] listen to or of the relationship existing between listening habits and the everyday behavior of children has been neglected" (p. 75). According to Ricciuti, the limitations of "research studies which have been concerned with the influence of radio on learning and behavior . . . were for the most part conducted under controlled laboratory conditions" (p. 75). Studies such as DeBoer's (1937) and Preston's (1941), which Ricciuti severely criticizes, and studies which sought direct effects in "controlled laboratory conditions" provide an incomplete and distorted picture of the influence of radio on children since "the applicability of laboratory results to the everyday situation" (p. 77) is highly questionable. By contrast, Ricciuti's study "was conducted with children in their natural life setting" (p. 77). Published as a 74-page ethnographic study in *Genetic Psychology Monographs* in 1951, it constituted a marginal yet important departure from the epistemological and methodological norms of this particular strand of psychology. It stands, nonetheless, as part of the formalized discourse and, as such, mitigates the unilinear effects data produced by the pre- and posttest methodology of most experimental studies.

Highlights of Ricciuti's findings were that certain radio content differentially influences some children in some areas of behavior and performance: "Radio programs have different meanings to children depending upon their age and sex . . . [and] while age, grade, sex, intelligence, social-emotional adjustment, and other factors may account for a child's interest in certain types of radio programs, the habitual listening to specific types of programs influences to different degrees, directly or indirectly, the child's behavior and performance in some areas" (p. 140). Best reflective of Ricciuti's findings of potential direct and indirect influences, and of the general scope of findings of the social and psychological research on radio and children during the first 30 years of radio—divided among beneficial, harmful, and no effects—is Berelson's classic observation that "some kinds of *communication* on some kinds of *issues*, brought to the attention of some kinds of *people* under some *conditions* have some kinds of *effects*" (cited in Schramm, 1960a:527). As with research on the impact of movies on children, research on radio and children cannot be categorized within a consensual "effects" model.

COMICS

Like the introduction of movies and radio, the advent of comic books generated much public and academic debate. The research on comic books as a mass medium of popular culture in which children took a particular interest warrants attention as an important part of the discourse on mass media and youth.

A quotation from Fredric Wertham's 1953 text, *The Seduction of the Innocent*, exemplifies the popular anticomics campaign in Britain during the late 1940s and early 1950s:

Superman (with the big S on his uniform—we should be glad, I suppose, that it is not an SS) needs an endless stream of ever new submen, criminals, and 'foreign looking' people not only to justify his existence, but even to make it possible. It is this feature that engenders in children either one or the other of two possible attitudes: either they fantasy themselves as supermen, with the attendant prejudices against the submen, or it makes them submissive and receptive to the blandishment of strong men who will solve all their social problems for them. (cited in Barrett, 1986:9)

According to Wertham, comics—particularly *Superman*—affect children in one of two ways: Children adopt attitudes either of dominance or of submissiveness, and "no credit is given to a child's ability to perceive comic characters as unreal or fantasy figures" (Barrett, 1986:9). Wertham's position on comic books was apparently well publicized in the United States during the late 1940s, judging from Thrasher's (1949:195) critique:

Wertham, who is a prominent New York psychiatrist, has stated his position on the comics in the following articles: "The Comics—Very Funny!" *Saturday Review of Literature*, May 29, 1948; "What Your Children Think of You," *This Week*, October 10, 1948; "Are Comic Books Harmful to Children?" *Friends Intelligencer*, July 10, 1948; "The Betrayal of Childhood: Comic Books," *Proceeding of the Annual Conference of Correction*, American Prison Association, 1948; "The Psychopathology of Comic Books" (a symposium), *American Journal of Psychotherapy*, July 1948; and "What Are Comic Books?" (a study course for parents), *National Parent Teacher Magazine*, March, 1949.

Wertham took his message to the public through publications in the popular press, conference addresses, and workshops for parents, thereby extending the professional/academic discourse into a broader domain of public debate which seems to have been of national proportions. *Time* magazine, for instance, published "Are Comics Fascist?" in October 1945. The association between comic book reading and juvenile delinquency, a dominant theme in the emergent discourse on comics and children, was strongly supported by Wertham, and strongly rejected by sociologists (Hoult, 1949; Thrasher, 1949; Frank, 1944).

Arguing against Wertham's single factor theory of "delinquency causation," Thrasher dismisses his nonscientific research and "illogical" findings. He agrees with Katherine Clifford (1948) that the anti-comic book hysteria may have reflected the sociopolitical frustrations of postwar times: "Wertham's dark picture of the influence of comics is more forensic than it is scientific and illustrates a dangerous habit of projecting our social frustrations upon some specific trait of our culture, which becomes a sort of 'whipping boy' for our failure to control the whole gamut of social breakdown" (Thrasher, 1949:195).

Drawing on Cressey's (1938) findings which "showed that the movies did not have any significant effect in producing delinquency in the crime breeding area in which the study was made" (Thrasher, 1949:199), Thrasher notes that there exists no research evidence to support the popular claims that comic book reading leads to juvenile delinquency (p. 200). Popular claims he refers to the "psychiatrists, lawyers, and judges" who support "the position of the leading crusader against the comics, New York's psychiatrist Fredric Wertham" (p. 201). For Thrasher, "the current alarm over the evil effects of comics" is spearheaded by those professionals and parents "who were once offended by the dime novel, and later by the movies and the radio" (p. 200).

The debate over comic books is indicative of historical controversies that commonly follow the introduction of a new medium of mass communication, to which public and academic debate tends to respond with suspicion and alarm, and to attribute to it a host of negative social causes. As Thrasher implied in the title of his article "The Comics and Delinquency: Cause or Scapegoat," the highly emotionally charged and "scientifically" unsubstantiated debate over the alleged effects of comics on youth may have reflected nothing more than the use of comics as a scapegoat for sociopolitical problems, the source of which lay elsewhere. In Thrasher's estimation, "each of these scapegoats [movies, radio] for parental and community failures to educate and socialize children has in turn given way to another as reformers have had their interest diverted to new fields in the face of facts that could not be gainsaid" (p. 200). And "facts that could not be gainsaid," such as the purported links between comics and delinquency, decreased reading achievement, language development, or social adjustment, had sufficient counter-evidence in the research literature to disprove many of the sensational claims made by Wertham and his supporters, and to suggest that comic book reading had few, if any, significant measurable effects on children's language and vocabulary development, reading achievement (Heisler, 1947), or delinquent behavior (Hoult, 1949).

Indeed, comics were seen to have possible beneficial effects, such as providing for readers "a release for their feelings of aggression" (Frank, 1944:220), or showing the comic book hero in a positive role as one who "must always be brave, utterly honest, altogether scrupulous" (Emery, 1944:90). And Heisler (1947), who found no differences in reading or vocabulary scores among proficient and poor readers, or among "bright, average, and dull children" (p. 464), speculates that children may very well learn from comics, but that the test instruments administered in her study were incapable of measuring such achievement. Abandoning the standard research question of the day, "What effects do the media have on children?" Heisler calls on future research to determine "whether maladjusted children preferred to read comic books, or, whether the comic books caused the maladjustment" (p. 464). A decade earlier, Cressey (1933) also had observed that individual predispositions (i.e., aggression) may lead to preference for certain kinds of (gangster) movies which may, in turn, reinforce those susceptibilities in certain individuals. Cressey restated this formulation in 1938, and Thrasher used it a decade later to buttress his argument against Wertham's claims of a monocausal relationship between comics and juvenile delinquency. The acknowledgment of individual psychosocial variables as possible determinants of media choice and preference mitigated what appears to have been the popularly held view of comics as a powerful source of universal and unmediated effects on influential young minds.

The most comprehensive study in its day of children and comic books, "The Children Talk About Comics" (Wolf & Fiske, 1949), also argued for children's individual and developmental differences in assessing comics' effects: "Comics satisfy a real developmental need in normal children and are harmful only for children who are already maladjusted and susceptible to harm" (p. 50). Katherine Wolf and Marjorie Fiske observed that children themselves take a similar perspective. As one 12-year-old girl put it: "I don't think they [comics] are bad. They have different reactions on different children. You have to know the emotional set-up of a child before you can tell" (p. 49). The authors noted the "tensions" generated among adults over comics, which have been "blam[ed] . . . for everything from children's bad language to international crises" (p. 37). Parents, they found, level the most vehement and "irrational" criticisms against comics. Conversely, the children reported that parents condone comic book reading. And, as Wolf and Fiske argue, adult complaints are by and large unfounded: "Their voiced objections to comics are for the most part vague . . . blind, irrational blows at an inflated straw man . . . and their accusations, of doubtful validity" (p. 37).

Wolf and Fiske conducted semistructured one-hour interviews with 104 children, of whom half were 11 or 12 years old, and the remainder ranged from 7 to 17 years of age. Data on parental attitudes toward and interventions on children's time spent reading comic books were derived from the children's reports. The study recounts hundreds of children's responses and provides only a few tables of percentage response distributions. As Lazarsfeld and Stanton note in the introduction, the "study dealing with children's comics is . . . of a descriptive psychological nature" (p. xvi). Comic book preferences, according to Wolf and Fiske, follow a distinct developmental pattern. Children under age 10, in the "egocentric or animistic stage" (p. 11), prefer "funny animal" comics which center on action and animal characters with which young children readily identify. At approximately age 11 or 12, children's preferences switch to "Fantastic Adventure Comics" of the *Superman* and *Batman and Robin* kind. At this age, "the satisfaction derived from reading comics . . . seems to be one primarily of escape from the real world into a world where the child becomes powerful" (p. 13). From roughly age 12 onward, children are said to prefer the "True and Classic" comic books. At this age children seek "comics which are based on actual events" (p. 17), and "also demand psychological reality" (p. 18). In short, "ego-identification with an invincible hero is no longer necessary, and the child seeks instead for facts and advice which will help him in direct participation in the real world" (p. 19).

For most children at this age, "the comic habit is thus broken" (p. 19), but children do not reject comics entirely and prefer to continue reading more realistic comics. As well, they "turn back to the funny animals for fun" (p. 19). As Wolf and Fiske conceptualize the children/comics relationship, "the normal child needs different kinds of comics at different stages of his development" (p. 20); and, as each developmental stage is outgrown, the "normal" child returns to the favorites of the past. By contrast, the "maladjusted" child is one who fixates on comics at any one of these stages. The source of maladjustment, according to Wolf and Fiske, is the family: Such children "seem not yet to have emancipated themselves from their parents . . . [and] they have apparently witnessed instances in which their parents manifested injustice, ignorance, or weakness" (p. 34). Such experiences, in turn, lead children to "search for a more perfect father-figure" which they find in, for instance, Superman (p. 34).

In Wolf and Fiske's estimation, comics are not the source of moral degeneracy, delinquency, or maladjustment. Rather, they propose that psychosocial maladjustment is present in the child before s/he turns to comics: "The possible dangerous effects of comics on fans must not be overestimated. The child's problems existed before he became a fan, and the comics came along to relieve him" (p. 35). Home environment and age are the two main factors which contribute to differential interests in and potential effects of comic books. Not only do problematic family relationships influence children to become comic book "fans," but social class background is also seen as a contributing factor. For instance, children of "professional" families ("those which provide other interests") were "moderate comic readers" (p. 45). Wolf and Fiske set off their principal conclusion in italics: "*Home atmos-*

phere . . . seems to be a basic factor in determining whether a child will be a moderate reader or fan" (p. 45).

In all, the discourse on comic books and youth does not represent a unified view either on the effects of comics or on the viewer. The public debate, as interpreted by the studies examined here, was marked by assumptions that posited the medium as powerful and highly influential on children, and characterized its content as "vicious," "dangerous," and "evil." The child, in this context, was considered a tabula rasa, open to and defenseless against the ideological messages of the comics. The academic debate, by contrast, seems to have been equally divided between opponents and defenders of the anti-TV crusade.

Unlike the movie and early radio era, the advent and early years of the comic book coincided with the major social, cultural, economic, and political upheavals of World War II. Given the apparent heightened awareness among academics and the public alike during the postwar years, of the meaning and implications of "propaganda," "public opinion," and the social consequences of propaganda (cf., Horkheimer & Adorno, 1944/1972; Smith, Laswell & Casey, 1946; Lazarsfeld & Stanton, 1941, 1944), the negative public response to comics, perhaps, is not surprising. For in an era wracked by political strife and uncertainty, and at a time when media heroes defending freedom and democracy were seen as necessary to buoy the public spirit, comic book heroes whose "virtues and methods are purely fascist in nature" (Frakes, 1942:1350) were perceived by many as a threat to malleable and morally defenseless young minds. The discursive construction via mass media of "public opinion" or external "threats" to national security in times of mass social insecurity may partially explain the vehemence with which the public denounced comic books. Moreover, the mass media–produced and disseminated constitution of the "individual voice," collectivized in "public opinion," exemplifies the discursive, symbolic, and representational construction of illusory subjectivity. The child or adolescent reader of comic books also is positioned in a particular ideological construct of the (real or fantasy) world: the discursive construction of the state, enemies of the state, the democratic public, the individual hero. The academic discourse about comics and readers similarly reflects that kind of liberal individualism: Effects on the individual child were in question even though the child was methodologically grouped in demographic or psychosocial collectivities.

The consensus that did emerge from the academic discourse on comics and their effects on youth was a general agreement over the two-step effects model and the perniciousness of Wertham's work. Importantly, by the late 1940s, the child and adolescent were (re)constituted as consumers of a new medium of mass communication, namely comics. Henceforth, comic book reading often would be used by researchers as one of three indices of mass media activities that children engaged in: radio listening, TV watching, and comic book reading. Movie attendance and preference were superseded in the early 1950s by TV viewing and program preference as an index of children's interest in, preference for, and use of an entertainment mass medium. Radio program, TV program, and comic book preferences for the same text regardless of media, such as for *The Lone Ranger*, was common among children (Gesselman, 1951).

EARLY MASS MEDIA AND CHILDREN: AN OVERVIEW

On the eve of the TV era, the educational discourse had attributed to children a new dimension. By the late 1940s children and adolescents had been transformed into consumers of mass culture and mass media. For social critics, academics, and the public, the problem with children's access to and relationship with popular culture and mass media was their susceptibility to the messages of a cultural text directed at mass society, not necessarily or solely directed at children. The potential harm that messages associated with sex, love, and crime in movies, radio, and comics might have on the young seemed to pose serious concerns for parents, educators, and academics. Prevailing standards of aesthetic taste and morality informed the kinds of questions asked about media content, and prevailing knowledges about children's social and cognitive development informed conceptualizations of media influences on children. Reflecting public concerns over the media's impact on children, and reflecting the theoretical and research concerns among those disciplines concerned with the study of children, researchers set out to find answers to questions previously not asked in relation to children's learning and socialization.

The data accumulated in research reports, monographs, and academic and teacher's journals dispersed into the public domain via the popular press. Contending assumptions about children's affective, behavioral, cognitive, and social development merged with assumptions about the relative powers of influence of each new medium and constituted a newly formed discourse on childhood and youth. This discourse emerged on disciplinary fields that had already well-established claims to knowledge about children—predominantly the applied fields of educational psychology and educational sociology. Researchers from both disciplinary fields brought contemporary theoretical truths and methodologies to their research tasks. In the absence of an established discourse on the child and mass media, research initially proceeded on the basis of a comprehensive body of scholarship on the child as educational object. Given this disequilibrium in disciplinary background knowledge applied to a historically emergent phenomenon—one which consisted at its most elementary of two primary components: mass media and child—it is not surprising that mass media would be a conceptualized correlative to the manner in which educational psychology or sociology had conceptualized other agents or agencies of learning and socialization (the school text, the school, family, peers, etc.). Educational sociologists considered radio, film, or comics to be but a singular contributing influence among many in children's social learning and development. By contrast, educational psychologists in the early decades of the cinema tended to view the medium as having powerful effects, but only in relation to cognitive, affective, and behavioral differences among children. Experimental studies and a focus on children's cognitive reactions to the movies (i.e., long- and short-term information retention) characterized many of the early psychological studies on movies and children reflecting Wundtian mentalist concerns with cognition, not with behaviors.

A corpus of disciplinary propositions already established as scientific truths served as a contextual backdrop, a "verbal network" which both informed the formation of new statements and accommodated them within already existing formulations. As Foucault notes, "the psychological halo of a formulation is controlled from afar by the arrangement of the enunciative field" (1972:98). That is, an enunciative field serves as host to emergent statements which are controlled "from afar" by the arrangement of existing formulations within that field. Existing formulations, in turn, are "reactualize[d]" or mediated by emergent formulations. Against this background of enunciative co-constitution, formulation, and modification, an object of study— such as the radio-listening or movie-viewing child—emerges, becomes appropriated by discourse(s) which rule(s) its position, status, role, and definition from afar, and becomes itself a part of the propositional (disciplinary) context which will delimit subsequent possibilities for as yet unarticulated statements.

Insofar as statements, in order to belong to a particular discipline, "must refer to a specific range of objects, which . . . changes from one period to another" (Sheridan, 1980:126), the statements produced in print concerning mass media and children changed in tandem with consecutive introductions of new media technologies, and changed according to the dominant epistemological assumptions governing the discourse on pedagogy. For it was in the discourse on pedagogy and not, for instance, pediatric discourse that knowledges about children's social and cognitive development resided.

The Payne Fund studies can be considered the first discursive unity on mass media and children formulated and bordered by educational, sociological, and psychological discourses. As a formally grouped system of statements—in individual monograph form and those monographs further grouped as "The Payne Fund Study"—they emerged as "a unity of another type" (Foucault, 1972:46): a unity not reducible to any one of the contributing discourses, but a unit of discourse comprised of a blend of disciplinary statements and situated at a particular interdisciplinary juncture. For several decades following the publication of the Payne Fund studies, statements derived from and referring to the Payne Fund monographs circulated in the medium of knowledge production and exchange: in academic journals wherein "authorities of delimitation" constructed and interpreted the medium-child relationship (cf. Gray, 1950).

Juxtaposed to the restricted, publicly invisible academic discourse, a public discourse on mass media and children developed in the popular press (e.g., *Time, Parents Magazine, Newsweek, Collier's*). Many of the statements circulating in this public domain were derived from the scholarly discourse and, as such, reflected its theoretical divisions. Statements about children and the mass media, then, were articulated primarily on two enunciative fields: the popular press and the scholarly journal. On both fields of emergence, the objects of study (media and child) were identical; yet the construction of the medium-child relationship differed within each field and between fields. Within academic and popular discourses, scientific judgment and public opinion was divided into two opposing views of the medium's beneficial and/or detrimental effects on children.

Statements in the popular press function ostensibly to educate and inform a lay public, whereas statements in the academic journal serve to educate and inform the already educated and informed authorities of delimitation. This latter group is comprised of literally certified members of an interpretive community who often author statements that consequently surface in the popular press. In the popular press, particularly women's magazines, the child is an object of public (family and community) concern; in scholarly discourses, the child is an object of science. Of course, not all statements in the popular media are editorial opinions. Most information concerning media and children is interpretation and paraphrase of statements made on a given topic by professional authorities and experts. The published texts on media and children that are produced for public consumption are "outposts," popularized versions of "true" statements produced by the formal, institutionalized discourse of scientific scholarship.

In sum, at the advent of TV a scholarly and popular discourse on mass media and children had been established. Sociology and psychology, in the context of educational study and research, had laid claim to mass media and children as objects of academic study. The early pre–Payne Fund research on children and movies had focused on children's movie preferences and attendance patterns, on the moral consequences of movie messages on children, and had stressed the need for educational, wholesome movie content. The Payne Fund studies, a seminal and landmark group of studies on movies and children, considered mass media effects on young viewers primarily in terms of intervening variables that were seen to mediate between exposure and effects. Children's movie attendance and preferences received substantial attention, and from this data, in conjunction with the first comprehensive movie content analysis, children's viewing patterns of morally questionable content were forwarded. This led to the first calls for school-based media literacy programs. The research questions posed by the Payne Fund committee laid the research agenda for subsequent research on radio and TV. The concept of the viewer as derived from the Payne Fund studies was that of a physically passive but cognitively active viewer who interpreted content on the basis of individual socioeconomic, age, gender, cultural, IQ, and affective variables.

3

1948–1959:
The Televiewing Child

This chapter surveys and discusses the academic discourse on TV and children as it emerged during the 1950s. As in Chapter 2, studies will be examined chronologically rather than according to research topics. Since the overall volume of published research on TV and children during the 1950s is substantially less than for the 1960s and 1970s, the data in this chapter is divided into three sections: 1948 to 1951, 1952 to 1955, and 1956 to 1959. These divisions are entirely arbitrary. The texts under investigation in this chapter are those that were published in monograph form, in scholarly journals, and include some publications in professional teachers' journals. As in Chapter 2, text published in popular magazines is excluded.

1948–1951

Although the first commercial station began broadcasting telecasts in 1930 and the first regular program schedule was in effect by 1939, a wartime freeze on commercial broadcasting, followed by postwar equipment shortages, suspended the large-scale introduction of commercial TV until 1948. Studies on TV's effects did not appear in significant numbers until the early 1950s. One of the first research projects undertaken to determine the social consequences of the new medium was conducted by the Columbia Broadcasting System in conjunction with the Department of Sociology at Rutgers University. A report of initial findings appeared in 1949 in *Public Opinion Quarterly*. Noting that "children and teen-agers in television homes form a unique group in that they will be the first to grow up with television" (Riley, Cantwell & Ruttiger, 1949:230), the CBS-Rutgers project sought to determine "how the medium is going to chang[e] the habits, attitudes, and values of individuals and family groups" (pp. 231–232). As with the introduction of film, children were seen as a special group in relation to the new medium, since it was assumed that TV would profoundly influence their socialization, value, and attitude formation. Questions regarding whether TV would "enhance family solidarity," forge "a bridge between adults and children," and create "new ties between family members" (p. 232) by uniting family members in front of the set, were seen as central.

Citing interview data from adults in 278 TV homes, John W. Riley, John W. Cartwell, and Katherine F. Ruttiger argued that the introduction of TV into households did not displace other valued activities such as social interaction and sports. Riley et al.'s argument was against the notion that TV generates viewer passivity. Instead, they expounded TV's positive social effects: Families reported that TV brought the family together, that new friendships had been formed since the acquisition of a set, and that families were experiencing a renewed sense of family unity. "Regardless of length of ownership, the changes reported by TV families are entirely in the direction of increased sociability. . . . it is currently stimulating new interests within the family, a new awareness of family unity, and enlarging the immediate circle of social relationships" (p. 233).

According to parental reports, this new family cohesion included the bridging of an alleged intergenerational communication gap between children and parents. A year earlier, Thomas E. Coffin (1948) also found that families reported spending more time together as a consequence of new TV set ownership. In one of the first qualitative studies on family viewing habits and attitudes toward TV, Coffin found that non-TV-owning families spent more time engaged in out-of-home social activities than TV families (pp. 552–553), and that time spent reading was reportedly less in TV homes than in non-TV homes (p. 555). In the 137 TV families interviewed, the average viewing time reported was 24.4 hours weekly in an area where the overall broadcasting time was 25 to 30 hours weekly (p. 555). For Coffin (and Hofstra College), the potential impact of this new medium was significant. In response to the medium's potential "social and psychological effects," "the psychology department of Hofstra College has set up a Television Research Program to conduct periodic studies" of these effects (p. 550). The aim of this program was to "orient ourselves to the [TV] problem." The first "qualitative probings," reported in Coffin's 1948 study, claimed that "television tends to pull the family together as a unit once more, preempts time and attention formerly given to hobbies, radio, movies, and other leisure-time activities, and engenders an intensity of feeling which leads some to refer to their sets as 'practically a member of the family'" (p. 550).

A study conducted in early 1950 of matched TV and no-TV families reported similar findings: less reading, less visiting with friends, less "driving for pleasure," less participation in sport activities, less radio listening and movie attendance, and less conversational interaction among TV families in contrast to no-TV families (McDonagh, 1950:116–121). Edward C. McDonagh found that "it is the family with more children that is likely to have television" and that in these families, "parents disclose that they think television programs are 'educational'" (p. 121). McDonagh sees a change in family interaction patterns as a result of TV, which clearly disturbs him: "The television family during the evening hours is changing from a social group characterized by conversation to an audience sitting in the semidarkness and silently gazing at their commercially sponsored entertainment via television" (p. 122).

In contrast to Riley et al.'s (1949) optimism about the social cohesion function of TV, Coffin's concern over TV's preemption of traditional social activities, and McDonagh's dismay at the silent family in semidarkness, Eleanor Maccoby (1951) questioned the quality of shared family time in front of the set: "The social context of television viewing . . . is not one of a group of friends but primarily one in which several members of a family are looking at a program together. . . . In general, the amount of inter-personal communication which occurs when people are together watching TV is very small" (p. 426). Watching TV together is considered by Maccoby to be a social activity uniting family members only in the sense "of being in the same room with other people" (p. 427). What may foster a sense of family cohesion, according to Maccoby, is "the shared experience of TV programs [which] gives family members a similar perceptual framework with which to view the world, so that there are fewer differences in point of view among family members and fewer grounds for conflict" (p. 427).

According to Riley et al. (1949), TV did not displace other childhood activities; rather, TV reportedly was incorporated "over and above the regular activity patterns" (p. 223). Maccoby (1951) too found that time spent with other children was the same for children in TV households as for those in non-TV households. In contrast to Coffin's and McDonagh's anticipation of TV as a problem, Riley et al. did not herald TV with alarm, nor support a negative effects model situating children as passive targets of an omnipotent medium.

"TV and Teen-Agers" (Lewis, 1949), published in *Educational Screen*—a professional journal for educators—reports on a questionnaire and interview survey of 1,700 high school students. The fact that "screen" information was considered educational, as the journal's title indicates, signals that film had already been incorporated into the

educational discourse and had already achieved a level of formalization significant enough to warrant a separate, specialized forum for
debate: the professional journal. Philip Lewis heralds the advent of
TV with cautious alarm and finds the rapid spread of the new technology "electrifying": "The [questionnaire] returns were electrifying—almost 100 students lived in homes already equipped with video
receivers!!" (p. 159). And, since the students in his survey reported an
average viewing of 23.5 hours weekly, the serious implications for
students of the displacement of other activities by this new technology
seemed obvious: "It must be remembered that, when watching a
television program, it is impossible to do anything else where concentration and attention is required . . . Students of today . . . can listen to the radio and still go through the motions of doing homework
at the same time. This is absolutely impossible with TV. Expressed in
different terms, *the effect is as though the student attended a three-hour
movie every night of the week (Saturday and Sunday included)!*" (p. 160).

Lewis suggests that TV is a medium for uniting the family in a
shared activity but notes that, even though the family is brought
together physically by TV, "televiewing is . . . a deterrent to normal
conversation" (p. 160). Turning to the question of TV's effects on
homework, Lewis reports numerous students' comments, which are
equally divided among those who judge TV to benefit, to deter, or to
have no influence on their homework. As Lewis sees it, "regardless of
the replies, it is easy to conclude that *TV certainly influences the lives of
the children exposed to its magic screen* . . . It should be realized that
*television has usurped the 23.5 hours per week (average) that were devoted,
previously, to other activities*—many of which were necessary and even
vital to the normal growth of the youngster" (p. 161).

Given the rapid proliferation of sets and the significant amount of
time teenagers devote to TV, Lewis implores parents to "regulate the
time their children spend at the TV receiver," and calls for teachers to
"recognize this rapidly-maturing colossus and make it serve their
purposes" (p. 161). For Lewis, then, TV has educational potential, but
if left unchecked by parental and educational neglect, TV can have
potentially serious effects since it displaces those activities "vital to
the normal growth of the youngster." Finally, Lewis conceptualizes
the viewer as passive and wholly enslaved to the medium to the
exclusion of other activities.

In October 1950, *Elementary English* published "Children's, Parents'
and Teachers' Reactions to Television" (Witty, 1950). This article summarizes then prevailing public attitudes toward TV. Witty acknowledges parental and teacher concerns over TV's alleged effects, citing
parents' complaints that TV induces "over-stimulating experiences
which lead to sleepless nights and fatigued eyes" (p. 349). He notes

that one teacher had left the teaching profession "since she finds that she cannot compete with the fascinating antics of the favored comedians," and notes that many teachers feel that school subjects are no "match for the adventure and excitement of the cowboy programs" (p. 349). He argues, however, that the problems allegedly associated with TV are not intrinsic to the medium but, rather, are problems of parental control over children's viewing time and program selection. To this Witty adds that, by and large, parental responses on his questionnaire survey indicate "a curious mistrust of their own ability to deal with the problems created by television" (p. 355). He suggests that "the criticisms of parents and teachers are similar to criticisms leveled at the comics, the radio, and the movies" (p. 355). Witty seems to consider parents more of a catalyst of the "TV problem" than TV itself. The inclusion in his article of numerous parental comments may not be uncommon in a teachers' journal—as distinct from a publication in an academic journal—but they seem to serve more as an indictment of parental inability to cope with TV *and* their children in the context of family life than as ammunition for a denunciation of TV. The following comments are illustrative of the kind of parental reactions to TV that Witty documents:

—We have friends . . . whose children are no longer on the honor roll since TV came into the home. . . . We wouldn't have a set in our house because of its bad and wholly disruptive influence.
—It [TV] converts our children into a race of spectators. . . . Life should be lived, not watched.
—Our daughter holds us in contempt for not buying a set. (p. 353)

For Witty, "the inescapable conclusion seems to be that television is a real problem or liability largely in homes where it is permitted by the parents to become one" (p. 355). Predicting that TV "may be a liability or an asset" for children, and that TV may "cause children and young people either to read less or to choose materials of inferior quality and doubtful value" (p.355), Witty calls for a two-pronged "antidote" to TV. First, "parents, teachers, and commercial agencies should cooperate to develop a series of more worthwhile programs" (p. 355) and, second, teachers should incorporate TV studies in the classroom, as well as generate interest in other "worthwhile" activities such as "reading good books" (p. 396). Providing "other desirable experiences" besides TV for children, according to Witty, is the responsibility of both home and school.

Most of the early studies on movies, radio, and TV and children sought to identify children's media interests, preferences, and viewing/listening patterns. The emergent discourse on TV was no exception. Witty found that the average time spent viewing by pupils in his sample (kindergarten to eighth grade) was 2.5 hours daily. The top five favorite programs listed by children were, in order of preference: "Hopalong Cassidy," "Howdy Doody," "Lone Ranger," "Milton Berle," and "Arthur Godfrey." Only one program, "Howdy Doody," was specifically a children's program, the remaining four falling under the variety program and cowboy Western categories. The "Lone Ranger" was first among the top five favorite programs of 30 third graders surveyed by Daisy B. Gesselman (1951) that same year. Similarly to Witty, she found from her questionnaire data that children spent, on average, three hours daily watching TV. During TV's early years, children already were tuned into adult programs (cf. Maccoby, 1951) and were apparently watching then nearly as many hours as they reportedly watch today.

Gesselman's (1951) study focused on TV influence on reading achievement and comprehension. In addition to administering the Stanford Achievement Test, which indicated "no appreciable difference in reading comprehension" (p. 386) between the TV and the non-TV group, she compared magazine, book, and comic book reading habits between the two groups. Gesselman chides "critics [who] have even gone so far as to predict that TV will eventually kill reading, and that we can look forward to a future generation of human potted plants, content to only sit and watch [TV]" (p. 388). In fact, almost 40 percent of her sample reported that TV had encouraged them to read a book (p. 388). Gesselman does not see TV as a threat to children and suggests that once TV loses its novelty effect, parents and teachers will be less alarmed and concerned over potential negative effects. The parents interviewed in her study all agreed "that young children ought to be kept strictly on a very bland diet of TV: puppet shows, gay films, circuses, with all horror pictures eliminated" (p. 391). She advocates incorporating discussions about TV in the classroom and, like Witty (1950), strongly encourages parents and teachers "to help children to become interested in and to read good books" (p. 391). Ensuring a "proper balance" between TV time and reading time is seen as a task for parents, and exerting pressure on networks and sponsors to schedule programs suitable for children as a task for the viewing audience. In sum, Gesselman's message to teachers is that "actually there is nothing to fear about what TV is doing to our children" (p. 391).

Several studies showed that children's viewing hours decreased with the length of time households owned a set (e.g., Coffin, 1948; Lewis, 1951; Witty, 1951). The reported decline in children's viewing hours relative to increased length of TV ownership may have contributed to fairly widespread assumptions that TV was nothing to be fearful of. In Coffin's (1948) sample, families who had owned a TV for six months or longer reportedly watched 2.5 hours less per week than those who had owned a set for six months or less. Lewis (1951) found that the "levelling- off point, where television viewing normalizes and fits in with a balanced program of living" (p. 118), occurred after four years of set ownership, at which time the high school students in his sample averaged 13.5 hours weekly compared to 17.5 hours weekly during the first 12 months of TV ownership. In relation to academic achievement, Lewis found that students viewing 11 to 15 hours weekly "were also identified with the peak profile in the [achievement] rating profile" (p. 119). In other words, once TV's novelty effect had worn off and adolescents' viewing had leveled off to approximately 11 to 15 hours a week, TV was seen not to affect school achievement adversely.

Lewis, like Gesselman, extolled the positive effects of TV, noting that TV can stimulate students' interest in new topics, can help with homework, and can generate career interests. Out of 959 students, Lewis reported, 438 claimed to have "definite career interests in the video field" and, surprisingly, "99 of these students have already appeared on television in some capacity" (p. 121). Most researchers at the time seemed compelled to respond to parental and educational concerns over TV's effects, frequently citing parental and teacher complaints. Lewis's study is one of the first to take a different tack, citing students' comments of their experience with TV in relation to doing homework:

— Most programs on television are not worthy of close attention. While doing my homework my attention is on the work, but should anything sound worth seeing, I shift my eyes to the screen.
— I can rewrite papers for various subjects, do simple geometry problems, go over spelling or language vocabulary while watching television. However, television programs have to be musicals, etc.
— Most of my homework is typed and music provides a rhythm for me to type by.
— I find the many commercials helpful, for the minute they appear, I study. (p. 120)

Lewis obviously considered his subjects' view of their own experiences with TV significant enough to record. In Lewis's estimation, TV has no adverse effects on adolescents, who claim to have incorporated the new medium into their everyday lives: "Yes, the students have learned to live with television, it is now up to the teachers to learn to work with it" (p. 121). Lewis implies here that teachers (and, by implication, adults in general) have not made peace with TV.

Another study on TV and adolescents by Witty (1951), published in *Education*, concurred with Lewis on the potentially positive effects of TV, as well as on decreases in viewing amount in relation to length of TV ownership, and on the link between excessive viewing and decreases in scholastic achievement. Witty concludes his discussion with a near-verbatim reiteration of his conclusion for his 1950 article published in *Elementary English*. Witty altered his prose only slightly in the conclusion written for the 1951 study: Statements are couched in more complex terminology and grammatical structure in the article discussing high school students, compared with the same concluding statements written about elementary school–age children. The discursive context of these statements differ: The 1950 study focuses on grade school children, and the discursive statements aimed at elementary school teachers are simplified in contrast to those about high school students and written for high school teachers. However, the need for an antidote to TV remains an important point for Witty. His invocation of a medical metaphor equates TV watching without adult intervention with a medical disorder.

Witty (1951) claimed that most studies on TV and children tended towards the polemical rather than providing empirical evidence. To counter the lack of empirical research, Witty set out to determine "the relationships between amount of televiewing and factors such as intelligence, personality, and educational attainment" (p. 242). The discursive linking of these categories with TV suggests that the influences of "televiewing" can be read from correlations between hours watched and IQ scores, personality test measures, and scholastic achievement scores independent of mediating social factors such as, for example, parental supervision or social class background.

Witty prefaces his study with a summary of some of the major surveys published in teachers' journals, magazines, and the *New York Times*. The titles of these publications indicate the kind of negative attitude toward TV and youth the discourse was promoting on the public front: (1) "TV Viewing Hurts Grades of Sophs and Juniors, but Helps Seniors" in *Advertising Age* (1950); (2) "TV—Enemy of Education?" in *Senior Scholastic* (1950); (3) "Pupils' Time Spent at TV Rivals Hours in Classes" in the *New York Times* (1950). Citing the results from "TV Lifts Students' Grades in Texas but Lowers them in N.J.," published in *Advertising Age* (1950), Witty sides with the inconclusive findings, noting that "studies of grades in relation to amount of time devoted to TV reveal conflicting results" (p. 245). For Witty, studies of students' school achievement are not the key to assessing TV's effects; rather, he sees IQ and personality as more accurate indicators, even though he does not report on his subjects' IQ or personality scores. In fact, subsequent to his review of the surveys noted above, he reports his own data. These amount to no more than a compilation of his sample's viewing hours, reading amount, and book preferences, radio listening patterns, and movie attendance frequencies. Witty never returns to his research topic on the relationship between IQ and televiewing, personality, and educational achievement.

So, despite a promising introductory premise, Witty's article concentrates on what Wartella and Reeves (1985) later argue are characteristic early topics of study on TV and youth: TV use and program preference. However, as in his 1950 paper, Witty chides teachers for their failure to deal with TV in a positive way: "Efforts to relate TV programs to school work and to offer systematic guidance in televiewing are barely started by these teachers" (p. 250).

Maccoby (1951)—like Riley, Cantwell, and Ruttiger (1949), Lewis (1951) and Gesselman (1951)—does not "view the advent of television with alarm" (p. 443). Her study does not focus on program preferences, but rather is concerned with a range of social effects of TV on 4- to 17-year-old children. This study was the first to collect data from "open-ended interviews" with 322 mothers who were also asked to record their children's activities for each hour during one week preceding the interviews; the activity records produced data for 622 children. No mention is made of the potential problems of interpretation associated with self-reports, but her methodology does give those closely involved with children's televiewing—that is, mothers—a voice.

Maccoby found that set ownership was concentrated in the "middle socio-economic group ... while the high-income group is conspicuously low in set ownership" (p. 424). Among those in the higher SES (socioeconomic) bracket, "there is a tendency for the children ... to spend less time viewing TV" (p. 423). In terms of program preferences, Maccoby notes "that at all age levels children seemed to do a majority of their TV-watching during hours which are not exclusively devoted to children's programs, so that their exposure to a variety of adult programs must be considerable" (p. 426). Both Lewis (1951) and Maccoby considered set location an important part of TV's social influence. Unlike Lewis, however, Maccoby found that in the majority of homes TV had retained its prominent position in living rooms, whereas Lewis found that after two years of ownership, "TV sets were on the move" (1951:120). Maccoby considered set location important, for it indicated what other family activities might be inhibited by its presence. Maccoby questioned mothers about other activities family members engage in while viewing, and found that "the nature of the family social life during a program could be described as "parallel" rather than "interactive" (p. 429). She also questioned mothers about the extent to which conflict arises over TV and mealtimes, and reported that "a third of the families report a certain amount of tension over getting children to come to meals" (p. 429). With regard to conflict over TV and bedtimes: "All the [mothers'] concessions mean later average bedtimes for children in television households" (p. 431). Children in non-TV households apparently went to bed during week-days a half-hour earlier than children from TV households.

Moving from the social effects of TV on family life, Maccoby ex-amined TV's influence on children's homework patterns. The "majority of parents (86%) are convinced that television has not inter-fered with their children's homework" (p. 432). Most reported to have set fairly non-negotiable rules for homework, and that their children tended to complete homework before televiewing without parent-child conflicts. Moreover, children from non-TV and TV households reportedly spent similar amounts of time on homework. For the most part, the families in Maccoby's sample did not consider TV to have serious negative consequences: "From the mothers' standpoint, TV is often a solver rather than a creator of problems. In fact, many mothers are enthusiastic about television as an aid in taking care of the children" (p. 434). Maccoby explains: "For busy mothers the modera-tion in their children's behavior while they are watching TV comes as a welcome relief. One mother commented 'it's much easier—it's just like putting them to sleep.' A frequent comment, too, is that television keeps the children in 'off the street'" (p. 434). But Maccoby is critical of mothers' praise of TV, noting that "mothers commonly regard quiet children as virtuous children, so to them, the change is all to the good" (p. 435). And, commenting that many mothers noted increased cooperation among their children to parental requests, Maccoby at-tributes this to parental use of TV "as a form of reward, or its denial as a form of punishment" (p. 435). The parental use of TV privileges as either reward or punishment had apparently earned it the title of "pacifier" (pp. 435, 439), of which Maccoby is suspicious.

Interpreting her data in light of unspecified "relevant psychological theory" (p. 439), Maccoby attempts to outline "whether any judg-ments can be made about the probable long-range effects of continued exposure to television on developing personalities" (p. 439). Maccoby makes no judgments but speculates that TV, through the process of vicarious experience, may reduce a child's momentary need for ag-gressive outlets but may, in the long term, increase the probability of aggressive behaviors. She proposes that TV can function as a safety valve in the control of certain (psychological) needs, and yet can also provide too much "needs satisfaction," in which case the provision of "too many avenues of [TV] 'escape' from social pressures . . . may retard the development of social responsibility" (p. 443). Habitual identification with TV characters (e.g., Hopalong Cassidy) can lead

some children to become "identifier[s]" in general—[which] may increase . . . [the] tendency to get power satisfactions through particular
kinds of power figures in later life" (p. 443). Finally, she comments
that while TV does appear to decrease "the amount of interactive
social contact a child has, which may produce social deficits" (p. 443),
TV compensates for this potential loss by providing experience with
other, program-specific skills. For example, in Maccoby's view: "TV
might increase a child's recognition vocabulary and interfere with the
development of recall vocabulary and the ability to combine words
spontaneously into spoken sentences" (p. 443).

Maccoby's detailed attention to the social context of viewing is
unique in the early 1950s discourse on TV and children. Like Witty
(1950), she remains tentative with conclusions, and posits possibilities
rather than arguing for unequivocal effects. Her intepretation of
mothers' reports of their children's televiewing habits in relation to
family life suggests that children, in their mothers' estimation, had not
been negatively affected by TV. Although families reported that they
spent more time together since a TV set had been acquired, Maccoby
is suspicious of the quality of shared family time in front of the set.
Speculating that the role of TV in children's lives is probably not much
different from the role of other media, she concludes: "The part
television plays in a child's life is probably not qualitatively different
from that of the movies and other mass media, and in many ways TV
probably plays a role similar to that of the fairy stories and fantasy
play" (p. 443).

"Patterns of interest" were a central problem in the academic discourse during the first few years of the 1950s (Lyness, 1951, 1952;
Maccoby, 1951; Seagoe, 1951; Witty, 1950, 1951, 1953). The kinds of
programs children and adolescents liked and amounts viewed commonly were delineated according to age and gender. In larger urban
centers, where most of the early studies were conducted, length of
TV ownership ceased to be used as an indicator of how much TV and
what kinds of programs children watched. Hence, by approximately
1952 to 1954, TV was considered established in the American
household, and the novelty effect ceased to be a relevant research
question. Consequently, researchers began looking for background
factors in children's psychosocial identities and home environments
to account for TV's effects. Age, SES, and sex were obvious targets,
and individual differences were explained accordingly. Chronological
and mental age and sex were also the easiest categories to isolate in a
research design, the data easily gleaned from school records (cf. Riley
& Riley, 1951).

May V. Seagoe (1951) was one of the few researchers to posit
children's social class background as a mediating variable between TV

and child viewers. She published "Children's Television Habits and Preferences" in *Quarterly of Film, Radio, and Television,* a journal probably not widely circulated among teacher-educators or teachers. She comments on the difficulty of isolating three SES levels and admits to the subsequent imprecision of her findings (p. 145). Nonetheless, from such approximations discursive truths were derived about the influence of SES on children's viewing habits and preferences. The two links Seagoe makes between children's SES and televiewing are that (1) in terms of media use, upper-SES children spend less time with radio and TV, attend movies more frequently, and have more "theater experience" than lower-SES children, and (2) low SES is no deterrent to TV ownership (pp. 146–147). Moving outside the "subject"—the subject's personal psychosocial "qualities," such as measured IQ and personality—Seagoe introduces an economic category to explain the TV-child relationship. Better-educated, more affluent families, according to Seagoe's data, tend to watch less TV than those with lower income and education. This link between low SES and above-average viewing time, previously noted by Maccoby (1951), would become a dominant and central discursive feature of audience profile construction. SES would come to be included as a classification intrinsic to the individual child viewer, along with defining characteristics such as personality, IQ, and educational achievement.

Lyness (1951) similarly tried to incorporate SES as part of his sample's background data along with "ownership of automobiles, telephones, radios and TV sets; church affiliation and attendance; years of residence . . . ; preferred presidential candidate in 1948; possession of a library card; and recreational activities at home and away from home" (p. 451). Although Lyness's aim in this study also was to survey, as the title of the article indicates, "Patterns in the Mass Communications Tastes of the Young Audience," he saw a broader scope of background variables contributing to media "tastes." But since "figures on parental education and occupation for all public school children [in the sample] were not available" (p. 451), Lyness estimated representativeness by statistical comparison of his sample with SES data "on city adults with children in school" gathered by the "Iowa Poll," "a weekly, state-wide survey of what Iowans think on leading topics of the day . . . sponsored by *The Des Moines Register* and *Tribune*" (p. 451). One can only speculate how representative such "an estimate of 'representativeness'" is (p. 451). However, in the explication of his data and findings, Lyness makes no mention of the background data he considered so important (e.g., possession of a library card; car, radio, TV ownership; church affiliation; or parental political persuasion). He focuses, instead, exclusively on children's sex and grade level in relation to media preferences. The age-sex doublet, then, becomes the base formula in the classificatory grid which specifies the child from a TV household.

The emergent discourse of the early 1950s on TV and children, much like the early discourse on children and movies and radio, began with the rudimentary definition of the child classified according to sex and age. Upon these primary defining characteristics additional dimensions of the child would be constructed, in tandem with refinements in statistical method which would provide more complex possibilities for quantifying the human subject.

Lyness's second publication the following year in *Journalism Quarterly* was of the same study published the previous year (1950) in the *Journal of Educational Psychology*. As with Witty's duplication (1950, 1951, 1953) of the same statements on separate discursive planes, Lyness's statements materialize on two distinct discursive fields: one in the domain of education, the other in the domain of mass communications and journalism. Lyness's two versions of the same study published in two distinct journals are of interest here because they illustrate the deployment of one set of statements—his interpretation of one set of research data—on two separate knowledge fields. Assuming that *Journalism Quarterly* circulated predominantly among authorities on broadcast journalism and associated knowledges, and that *Educational Psychology* circulated among teacher-educators and psychologists, Lyness's study formed a micronetwork of statements in separate yet adjacent disciplinary knowledge fields. Throughout the 1950s, the study of children in relation to popular culture was to be mapped on two fields: mass media (TV) became a concern for scholars in education, and children became a concern for mass media scholars.

Matilda White Riley and John W. Riley (1951) focused their study on children in efforts to identify how sociological theory might inform communications research. Drawing on the work of Mannheim, Merton, and Parsons, Riley and Riley cast the (child) viewer and TV in a utilitarian relationship: Media serve to fulfill different needs for different children. According to Riley and Riley (p. 454), exclusion or inclusion in peer groups, aspirations to belong to peer groups and to meet the group's expectations, and failure or success at meeting parental expectations can all contribute to what Parsons termed "strain": "When the social structure imposes undue strain upon the individual . . . we should expect him to be highly productive of fantasies, and therefore to select a kind of media material, such as little animals or violent action, which would foster such fantasies."

The "frustrated" child, the one who wants to belong to a peer group, who may not receive sufficient recognition from family or peer groups, is a child under considerable "strain." This same child tends to choose TV content to fulfill certain needs. The implication here is that children are active selectors of media content in response to needs. The "uses and gratifications" model would employ the same logic to explain selective viewing. Riley and Riley (p. 456) also suggest that older children, particularly those who are peer group members, select media for specific purposes: "Peer group members, oriented as they are to the need for getting along in the group, appear to judge media in terms of a criterion which we might call 'social utility,' to select media materials which will in some way be immediately useful for group living."

In Riley and Riley's estimation, children's complex and often fluctuating social relations may have more to do with children's TV program preferences than age, sex, or social and educational background (p. 456). Children and TV were seen to intersect in this article at a unique discursive juncture: where "such sociological concepts as 'group membership,' 'reference group,' and 'strain'" coincide with communications research. "The concept of the 'social utility' of mass media, depending as it does on the individual's group relationships may, we believe, be used to go far beyond the traditional approach in explaining communications behavior" (p. 460).

Aside from positing the viewer as an active selector of media content, and attributing to the media a "social utility," the Riley and Riley article can be seen as representative of an early application of functionalist sociology to the study of TV and the child. "Social needs" of individuals for group (and role) participation here are seen as a motive force in child media use. Moreover, the utilitarian argument foreshadows the media "uses and gratifications" model which would emerge more visibly a decade later (cf. Katz & Foulkes, 1962).

1952–1955

In 1952, TV and children came under the scrutiny of a federal authority (Dunham, 1952) in the U.S. Office of Education. Franklin Dunham reported on a study conducted by Xavier University and published in *School Life*, a teacher's journal. Children's viewing habits were conceptualized as a function of chronological and mental age, school achievement, and parental control over televiewing (p. 88). For teachers, the message from the Xavier study was this: Preference for mystery-crime programs and wrestling shows, coupled with minimal parental intervention, was found predominantly in low-IQ children. Dunham views with alarm the fact that children were found to spend more time in front of the set than with print in the classroom. Of course, Gesselman (1951), Lewis (1951), Sarah I. Roody (1952), Seagoe

(1951), and Witty (1950, 1951, 1953) had all argued for the need to preserve print traditions and practices, but they also tried to counteract the kind of alarmist messages espoused by Dunham. Dunham concludes by quoting from the Xavier study, which posits TV as a "problem" in need of "constructive action" (pp. 89, 91). The problem was clearly located in low-IQ children who, because of minimal parental mediation of their viewing, reportedly favored the most violent kinds of programs (mystery-crime, wrestling), to watch these in greater amounts, and to watch these later in the evenings than children in "the higher IQ brackets" (p. 89).

Roody (1952), by contrast, considers the mass media to have positive psychological effects on students, "particularly in helping our pupils to develop emotional maturity" (p. 245). Published in *English Education*, a journal of the National Council of Teachers of English, "Effects of Radio, TV and Motion Pictures on the Development of Maturity" was read in 1951 at the Council's annual meeting. Again, one set of statements was enunciated on different discursive sites (the professional conference and professional journal), which can be read to signal the increasing conflation of academic, professional, theoretical, and applied "truths" about TV and children.

Referring to Allport's premise that "humor helps one attain insight into one's own nature and is therefore a sign of maturity" (p. 247), Roody encourages English teachers to make use of popular TV comedies—such as "Jack Benny," "Ozzie and Harriet," "Milton Berle," "Red Skelton," "and other top bananas" (p. 247)—to help students develop a sense of humor, learn to laugh at themselves, and learn to look at the self objectively (p. 247). TV and film can serve as an introduction to classroom literature study, and can encourage out-of-class reading interests. Importantly, Roody sees the fostering of a "love for reading" and a "fondness for the subject of English in general" among students as an "index to emotional health" and "success in college" (p. 248). Citing an "investigation scientifically conducted at Yale" which showed a "very high correlation . . . between maturity of personality and love of reading" (p. 247), Roody buttresses her argument with an invocation of scientific evidence. Scientific truths established elsewhere are here reincorporated as unassailable, objective evidence of a particular social equation: Love of reading equals maturity of personality equals success at college.

Roody posits the mass media as potentially beneficial in triggering this peculiar developmental equation. Yet unlike many anti-TV traditionalists—those whom Witty, Gesselman, and Lewis address—Roody articulates a positive role for TV in the discursive field of English education, a field which has clung tenaciously to an anti-TV stance in favor of the sanctity of print. She concludes: "In our efforts to help our pupils benefit psychologically, there is no need for us to relegate a piece of literature to the status of a lesson on mental hygiene. We can prepare our students for the performance" (p. 250).

Witty's 1952 follow-up report to his 1950 and 1951 studies indicated that average viewing time among elementary and high school students had increased, that TV ownership had increased, and that twice as many teachers owned TV sets as in 1951. Program preferences among children, adolescents, parents, and teachers had changed as well, and Witty attributes this to a greater variety of program offerings. The disparity between children's and teachers' program preferences remained: Children claimed to dislike anything educational, and teachers listed educational and public affairs programs as favorites. Witty's conclusion is a much-abbreviated version of his eight-point ("antidote") "suggestions for parents and teachers" listed in the 1950 and 1951 studies.

In his earlier studies Witty located the source of the TV problem with parental lack of intervention. In the 1952 study Witty links the TV problem to other sources of entertainment in the child's environment: "It should be recognized that the problem of TV is related intimately to that found in dealing with other favored activities of children today—reading comic books, going to the movies, and listening to the radio" (p. 473). And, while comic-book reading, movie attendance, and radio listening are out-of-school activities, Witty suggests that teachers attack this combined media use problem: "In dealing with the combined problem, teachers should study each child's leisure pattern and help him cultivate a balanced program of recreation" (p. 473). One way to achieve this is for teachers (and parents) to provide children with books, to facilitate reading and encourage children "to use the library to advantage" (p. 473). In the educational discourse on TV and children, then, the central antidote to the electronic media problem remains focused on print.

Witty's longitudinal study is the only one of its kind undertaken and published—all of them in *Elementary English*—in the early 1950s. As such, the combined text constitutes a substantial portion of the formalized expression of the early discourse on TV and children and, moreover, positions Witty as "authority of delimitation." I do not mark Witty here as hallowed author—the "actual individual" (Foucault, 1977:131). Instead, I suggest that Witty (or any author) can be read as a discursive marker denoting author-authority, a ritualized part of all published academic work. In this early case, Witty—having published several works in both refereed and non-refereed journals over a relatively short period of time—can be seen to have held substantial influence in the early formation of the discourse on TV and children. He would continue to do so for more than a decade.

Throughout the remainder of the 1950s, Witty's name circulated consistently in the citation network of the developing discourse on TV and children.

In 1954 two short articles on TV and children (Brumbaugh, 1954; Scott, 1954) were published in teachers' journals; both referred to statements made by Witty as their only reference. An article published the previous year in the *Catholic Educational Review* (Mahoney, 1953) also cited Witty as the only reference to empirical work amidst references to newpaper and news magazine articles. Articles in teachers' journals did not commonly cite academic references. The appearance of Witty's statements as the sole reference to substantiate claims made in all three articles signals how "Witty"—the text—was being established as an authoritative discourse on TV and children.

For Katherine Mahoney (1953), TV is the "most wonderful medium of communication yet invented, [which] seems to have taken its place as a permanent fixture in the home and school" (p. 234). Mahoney aimed to identify the "television viewing preferences and viewing habits of elementary school children . . . [of] which no survey has been made" (p. 235). A questionnaire was administered to 808 third and fifth grade children; the data suggested that children from TV households read less, that TV has "drastically curtailed . . . most recreational activities" including "out-of-door play," radio listening and movie-going (pp. 241–242). Children in both third and fifth grade reported that church attendance had increased since the introduction of TV into their homes; whether this survey was conducted in a denominational or public elementary school was not noted. The significant impact that TV appears to have made on the American family leads Mahoney to conclude that "parents and teachers must be progressive and modern enough to accept and turn it to advantage in the training and instruction of children" (p. 234). She encourages teachers to take advantage of children's home viewing and encourages parents "who watch television with their children, [to] discuss the programs, criticize the vulgar, criminal, or any display of bad taste, and [to be] just as free in their praise and enjoyment of the wholesome, clean entertainment that will develop in their children the power of discernment and the ability to create for themselves standards of behavior and entertainment that will remain with them through life" (p. 241). Effects of TV on children are harmful insofar as both teachers and parents fail to take control of children's viewing: TV's "undesirable effect on the health or scholastic achievement of pupils" can be mitigated "if the programs viewed were properly supervised and controlled by parents" (p. 245). Like Witty, Mahoney sees the TV problem as residing with inadequate parental involvement in and supervision of children's viewing.

"What Effect Does TV Advertising Have on Children?" (Brumbaugh, 1954) is a two-page discussion of a report on the effects of TV advertising on children, previously published in a news bulletin of the Association for Childhood Education (*Bulletin* 93, 1953–1954). Six- to 12-year-old children were found to remember advertisements targeted at adults better than those targeted at children; beer, detergents, cigarettes, pharmaceuticals, cosmetics, and automobiles were listed more frequently than cereals, candy, and milk (p. 32). Also, children's "spelling of trade names was correct in almost every case," even though these were "far more difficult than words in spelling lists" (pp. 32–33). Today, the salience of product brand names and commercial jingles for children's verbal learning remains a focal concern of educators and media researchers. Florence Brumbaugh supports Witty's (1952) claim that TV is not children's only source of entertainment and learning: "The degree to which televised advertising is conditioning children is difficult to determine, since the same articles are usually advertised on radio and in newspapers and magazines. It is unlikely that they will remember or know which of the media influenced them, or whether their attitudes were changed because of television" (p. 33). Hinting at the possibility that the same media message may influence different children in a variety of ways, Brumbaugh forwards a solution for teachers: "The same stimulus is accepted by one and rejected by another, so that the best solution at the present time appears to be to help children develop a sense of discrimination in regard to the exaggerated claims that may be made by some advertisers" (p. 33).

The use of terms such as "conditioning" and "stimulus" in Brumbaugh's text is one of the first instances of what would be labeled behaviorist terminology to surface in the TV-child discourse. Concluding her discussion with a quote from Witty which states that "the most avid watchers of TV . . . are children between the ages of four and six" (p. 33), Brumbaugh implies that children are heavily influenced by TV in their preschool years and that, hence, a substantial part of the knowledge they bring with them when starting school is TV knowledge—that is, commercial product information. Cleansing children of such knowledge can be accomplished by teachers, who, in Brumbaugh's view, should teach children to view TV commercials discriminately.

In "Social Attitudes of Children Revealed by Responses to Television Programs," published in the *California Journal of Elementary Education* (1954), Lloyd Scott reviews a questionnaire survey he conducted in 1951 of 478 elementary school–age children "from two significantly different socioeconomic groups in the East San Francisco Bay Area" (p. 176). How children's SES was identified remains unspecified, and Scott does not delineate his sample according to age or sex. Scott is concerned that "the advent of television has made available a powerful medium for forming concepts and attitudes in children" which are suspect: Are they "true" and do they promote "healthy" attitudes? Citing Witty (1951), Scott notes that what the research has not considered, and what his study examines, is TV's "influence on [the] formation of attitudes and concepts" (p. 176). While acknowledging that "analysis of the influence of any single source can give at best only a partial picture," Scott makes no reference to any background influences among his subjects, other than SES, that may contribute to their attitude and concept formation. Hence, despite the rhetoric of multiple causation, the text supports the unqualified equation of TV as the single factor cause of attitude and value formation.

A listing of Scott's survey questions, for which he supplies the response percentages, is instructive because it indicates the kinds of concerns about TV violence voiced during the early years of TV. The influence of TV crime programs on audience attitudes toward law enforcement and perceptions of crime in the real world was still being systematically investigated over two decades later (cf. Gerbner et al., 1976, 1977, 1978, 1979, 1980).

1. Do cowboys on ranches out in the country still have big fights and catch outlaws?
2. Are the sheriffs on TV programs usually dishonest men?
3. Are our sheriffs today usually dishonest?
4. Are outlaws on these programs usually treated mean?
5. Are criminals in big cities usually treated mean today?
6. Do all cowboys on the program carry guns?
7. Do cowboys on real ranches today carry guns?
8. Is it okay for the Lone Ranger or Hopalong Cassidy to beat up outlaws to make them confess?
9. Do we beat up criminals today to make them confess?
10. Is it okay for the Lone Ranger or Hopalong Cassidy to be dishonest to help him trick an outlaw?
11. Is it okay for police today in big cities to be dishonest to help them trick a criminal?
12. Do you think most of the outlaws on the TV programs were smart?
13. Do you think today's criminals are smart?
14. Do you think you would rather have lived on a ranch in stagecoach days than on one of today's ranches? (Scott, 1954:177–178)

Scott's data suggested that his low-SES group more readily supported TV-portrayed law enforcement tactics than did the upper-SES group. The former also tended to believe that TV criminals and outlaws are authentically portrayed. Gerbner and his associates would ask subjects the same questions some 25 years later about the legitimacy of police brutality or the use of "dirty tricks" by police in the "real world" to capture and bring to justice the criminally deviant. In Scott's view, his findings "indicate that television programs are having some effect upon children's attitudes towards law enforcement" (p. 179). Importantly, "this effect appears to be more apparent in children in a low socioeconomic group than in children in a high group" (p. 179). Scott here establishes support for a unilinear, single-factor effects argument, and he targets negative effects in low-SES children. Published in a teachers' journal, the message for teachers is that in addition to a host of sociocultural and cognitive "deficiencies" among lower-SES pupils, TV is now seen to contribute to the formation of "unhealthy" attitudes and values in these same children.

In the academic discourse of 1954 four articles were identified as dealing with TV and children, two of which focused on the effects of TV on children's schooling (Wells & Lynch, 1954; Greenstein, 1954). One questioned children's motivations for watching TV (Maccoby, 1954), the other resurrected Preston's (1941) TV addiction and pathological behaviors argument (Meerloo, 1954). Dallas Smythe (1954) published the first comprehensive content analysis and Theodore Adorno (1954) discussed TV and "cultural 'consumers'" (p. 217) in the context of the "present setup of cultural industry" (p. 229)—the "curse of modern mass culture" (p. 219). The following year, Lazarsfeld (1955)—by then an already established authority on mass communications and public opinion—published a paper on TV and children.

In many ways 1954 can be considered an early stage—a watershed year—of a shift in orientation among researchers toward TV and its effects on children. An almost imperceptible seriousness began to characterize the discourse, signposted in the terms by which researchers approached their tasks. This reorientation was reflected in the tone of textual statements, which appeared to take on a new scientific register, rigor, and authority. That is, a subtle shift took place from the more conversational prose style characteristic of earlier, more polemical works (often reliant on popular opinion articles published in newspapers and women's and news magazines) to a more restrained, scientific objectivism that would become more pronounced during the next several years.

TV had become a permanent sociocultural artifact entrenched in nearly all American homes by the mid-1950s, and could no longer be ignored by social scientists. TV could no longer be construed as a cultural fad. Furthermore, by the mid-1950s the discourse on TV and children had established a small body of research on which to base further research projects. The discourse could claim a (minor) history, a domain of study, and authorities in the field (e.g., Witty, Maccoby). Apparent was a subtle relocation of serious research on TV and children from the less formal and less prestigious domain of teachers' journals to the more formal domain of the scholarly journal. The discourse was moving toward an early stage of "epistemologization." The formalization of a discourse-specific technical vocabulary emerged alongside discourse-specific rule systems to which participants in the discourse increasingly seemed bound to adhere. The eminent authority on children and TV was Witty, whose name and text recirculated in various interpretations and juxtapositions within an expanding discourse. Authors contributing to the TV-child discourse referred and deferred to Witty until well into the 1960s.

Jack Greenstein's (1954) study, "Effect of Television Upon Elementary School Grades," published in the *Journal of Educational Research*, is a response to Witty's (1950) paper on children's, teachers', and parents' reactions to TV. Noting the TV-children debate as marked by "rampant" and "divergent" opinions and "emotional bias," Greenstein aims to provide some "objective evidence upon one aspect of the problem" (p. 161). His evidence was derived from three teachers (interviews) and 67 students (questionnaires) drawn from "what the investigator judged to be a typical lower-middle income community of mixed ethnic groups" (p. 162). Only students whose families had owned a TV set for six months or more were included in the study. From his data, Greenstein found no evidence to support the "novelty effect": Increased length of TV ownership among his sample did not parallel less viewing time (p. 175). Importantly, he found that "the grades of the TV group are consistently higher than those of the non-TV group" (p.175). This is the first study that claimed to find a positive correlation between televiewing and school achievement. How much TV was viewed by his subjects, the kinds of programs they watched, relative levels of parental mediation, and previous school grades were not considered. Greenstein concludes by proposing that the TV "problem" must be considered in broader social and health terms other than school grades: "Certainly the influence of television upon children should be considered in wider terms than its effect upon school grades. Its influence upon their social life, their eyesight, their general health, their interest in other activities, their adjustments to the world in which they live—these are all important aspects of the problem" (p. 176). So while on one hand his evidence bears out positive effects of TV (even though he does not specify how these effects occur), Greenstein posits these as almost trivial in relation to the greater social problem.

Maccoby (1954), in "Why Do Children Watch Television?" published in *Public Opinion Quarterly*, again took up the question of home background as a possible influence on children's televiewing habits and preferences. Working from an acknowledged Freudian perspective (p. 240), she hypothesizes that children are likely "to spend more time watching television if they are highly frustrated in real life than if they are not" (p. 240). And, according to Maccoby, "the number of hours of TV-watching and the frustrations experienced by the child are functions of social class, as are the attitudes of mothers towards television itself" (p. 241). On the basis of 52 two-hour interviews with 379 mothers of kindergarten children, Maccoby found that among lower-class, "permissive, warm and non-punitive" (p. 243) families, children tend not to be overtly frustrated, and will imitate parents and spend time with them "which makes [the child] a TV fan, since that is what his parents are" (p. 243). Frustrated children of low-SES parents, by contrast, "may seek television as an escape and a source of vicarious satisfaction" (p. 243). Thus, according to Maccoby's conceptualization of a social class–based family profile: "In the lower-class groups, the amount of frustration does not differentiate the children who are greatly interested in television from those who are not" (p. 243).

Regardless of levels of permissiveness among lower-class parents and relative levels of frustration among their children, these children will tend to be avid TV watchers. By contrast, middle-class families "are busy doing other things"—that is, besides watching TV—and since middle-class families apparently tend to be more permissive and less restrictive (p. 241), their children tend to experience lower levels of frustration. This then tends to motivate the child "to be like them [parents] and to be near them" which means that "he will not spend as much time at television" (p. 243). Yet, as in lower-class families, if children of middle-class families are frustrated, they too will seek "television as an escape and a source of vicarious satisfaction" (p. 243). Clearly there are problems with the kinds of questions asked of mothers about home discipline: "permissiveness of sex behaviour in the child," "level of obedience demands," "extent of use of physical punishment," "punishment for aggression towards parents" (p. 242), etc., which Maccoby does not acknowledge. Nonetheless, she claims that lower-SES families are "less permissive and more restrictive in general" (p. 241), and that lower-SES families and their children watch TV as a main leisure activity. In contrast to her earlier (1951) paper, Maccoby here shows a marked lack of concern for social context within which families, childrearing, and TV are embedded.

The construct of social class—the "classification of people in minute divisions according to their 'work'" (Hacking, 1982:292–293)—was itself a recent, ninteenth-century discursive reinvention of the individual. The concept of social class mapped subjects on grids of difference, upon which the social body was quantified according to class definitions and identities (cf. Hacking, 1981, 1982; Foucault, 1982:215). Maccoby here adds a caveat to the social definition of class-based family dynamics: Working-class parents tend to be restrictive, offer children few alternatives to TV watching, and spend a disproportionate amount of time with TV. Even in permissive working-class families, viewing amount reportedly is high. The frustrated child of the restrictive (low-SES) family watches excessive TV to escape, and the well-adjusted child of the permissive (low-SES) family watches excessive TV by imitating parental "TV fans." In either case, the working-class child and family watch TV excessively compared with middle-class families. The discursive profile of the low-SES family combines a punitive family with heavy viewing and locates TV as the focal family leisure activity.

That same year the notion of TV as an avenue of escape from sociopsychological frustration was also taken up, albeit from the perspective of psychiatry. Television had become an acceptable object of discourse in the fields of education, sociology, and psychology by the mid-1950s. As an object of inquiry, TV had only occasionally emerged in fields of academic inquiry outside these traditional social sciences. Joost Meerloo's (1954) "Television Addiction and Reactive Apathy," published in the *Journal of Nervous and Mental Disease*, was one such exception. Meerloo defined TV as a "dream factory" which, "as a well known fact," has a "hypnotic and seductive action on its audience" (p. 290). Citing three cases of "mental apathy," Meerloo claims that in each case, the subjects were TV addicts who were rehabilitated by "therapeutic intervention." All three, Meerloo comments, were adolescents who neglected their homework, were negativistic and generally apathetic, and "increasingly showed the picture of a schizophrenic episode" (p. 290). TV can hypnotize "special children" (i.e., children at risk) into a dream state, a fantasy world in which committing a crime becomes much easier. For Meerloo, "preoccupation with TV prevents active inner creativity" and tends to isolate family members rather than promote interaction: "It intrudes into family life and cuts off the more subtle interfamilial communication" (p. 291). Psychiatrist Wertham (see Chapter 2) also had denounced comics as catalysts of social deviance and juvenile delinquency; here Meerloo framed TV as a potential breeding ground for mental illness.

Although not explicitly dealing with children's TV program interests or viewing preferences, Smythe's (1954) "Reality as Presented by Television" warrants brief mention here because it is one of the first studies that takes as axiomatic that TV content equals effects: "Content analysis may . . . be thought of as the study of the stimulus field for 'effects' studies (of the audience), or as the study of the effects field for intention studies (of the production process). This frame of reference for content analysis has the implication that *all* of the categories relevant to studies of perception, motivation and learning are equally applicable in the measurement of content" (p. 143). What Smythe suggests is that effects can be analytically read off content, a premise which increasingly characterized research on TV and children in the later 1950s and throughout the 1960s. The viewer here is conceptualized as a psychological subject whose responses to the TV "stimulus" are wholly determined by program content. And program content in 1954, according to Smythe's analysis, was not that dissimilar from the analytic conceptualization of content in subsequent decades: frequency counts, distorted characterizations, and stereotyping.

Concerns over possible deleterious effects of TV—particularly TV violence—on children's moral and social attitudes were the same as those expressed by educators, academics, and the public over the effects of motion pictures on youth (cf. Payne Fund studies, 1933), radio (cf. DeBoer, 1937), or comic books (cf. Thrasher, 1949; Hoult, 1949). Suggesting that the mass media were being used as a scapegoat on which to blame contemporary social ills (e.g., juvenile delinquency), Smythe's (1955) "Dimension of Violence" attacks anticomics campaign leader Wertham with an argument similar to that made by Thrasher in 1949. By the mid-1950s, the public debate over TV and juvenile delinquency had reached a momentum that culminated in a Senate inquiry and, in turn, generated a series of federal reports on the mass media problem. Subsequently, these reports appeared in abbreviated form in a variety of academic and teachers' journals. Under the chairmanship of Sen. Estes Kefauver, the Senate Subcommittee to Investigate Juvenile Delinquency was the first federal inquiry into TV and youth—an extension of the discourse from the domain of academics and teachers into the realm of the state and federal politics. Accordingly, the discourse reached a new level of "epistemologization," formalization, and authority.

"Juvenile Delinquency and Television" (Haines, 1955) appeared in the first volume of *Corrective Psychiatry and the Journal of Social Therapy*. On request by Kefauver, author William H. Haines, M.D. and Director of the Behavior Clinic of the Criminal Court of Cook County (Chicago), was asked to investigate "the degree of influence that crime, violence, sadism and illicit sex . . . in these mass media (violence programs on television) have on the behavior patterns of American youth" (p. 192). But instead of investigating a cross-section of "American youth," Haines picks a particular group: one already incarcerated. Haines interviewed 100 inmates ("64 white and 36 colored") ranging from 16 to 21 years. The initial aim was to report on 200 interviews but, according to Haines, many had to be excluded because of their atypical characteristics, such as one who "was a low-grade mental defective, Mexican by birth. Two of those interviewed were of borderline intelligence and one was a schizoid" (p. 192). The interviews apparently consisted of researchers soliciting inmates' own "reactions as to the role these media played in [their] committing an offense, or offenses, which resulted in [their] incarceration" (p. 192).

Admitting the difficulty of ascertaining what "percentage" of which media influence "certain susceptible youths to crimes of violence, passion, sadism, etc." (p. 192), Haines nonetheless presupposed that his inmates would know whether and to what extent the various media influenced their deviant behavior. And in instances where subjects were not responding as anticipated by Haines, he renders their responses suspect. Whereas some of the white inmates "admitted" buying pornographic booklets, "none of the colored admitted buying them" (p.196). On the topic of TV, Haines found that all inmates interviewed liked to watch sports: "baseball, football, boxing, wrestling, etc." (p. 196). According to Witty (1951, 1952, 1953), Lewis (1951), and Lyness (1951), adolescent boys universally listed sports as a favorite program category. That adolescent boys who also happened to be in detention should also list sports as favorite TV viewing should not be surprising. But Haines, incredibly, interprets inmates' viewing of TV sports to be indicative of their involvement in crime: "It might be inferred from this statement [noted above] that the watchers were able also to improve their technique in hold-ups, robberies and other anti-social acts by watching such television programs" (p. 196). Haines's data predictably suggest "that television, pornography and movies play a distinct role in the creation of anti-social behavior in susceptible teen-agers" (p. 198). This corresponds to his initial premise: "It it our opinion that television will influence certain susceptible youths to crimes of violence, passion, sadism, etc." (p. 192). And "coloreds" fared much worse than white inmates in the profile that emerged from Haines's "susceptible teenagers."

A short notice entitled "Television" follows Haines's article. It reports that an interim report issued by the Kefauver inquiry recommended to the FCC (Federal Communications Commission) that it be "empowered to levy fines and to enforce 'certain minimal standards' of [TV] programming" (p. 198). Although this notice is not part of Haines's text, it serves as a convenient and very powerful summary remark. A textual report on proposals for state intervention to regulate the industry and to regulate, as it were, public morality by means of preventive (punitive) tactics—as part of a grander strategy to regulate the social body—may here be part of a distinct discursive strategy deployed by anonymous editorial authority to lend legitimacy and "truth" validity to Haines's report. That a federal inquiry into TV violence and juvenile delinquency should make a recommendation to another federal agency to monitor the TV industry, based on authoritative data gathered by authorities such as Haines, quite clearly bestows legitimacy on all reports—and in this case, Haines's—commissioned by the Kefauver hearings. It is both reciprocal and self-reflexive authorization, a form of discursive practice.

In its third year of publication, *Audio-Visual Communication Review* published its first paper on TV and children in 1955. In "Dimensions of Violence," Smythe (1955) argues, much like Thrasher did in 1949, against Wertham's (1953) anticomics crusade. Echoing Seagoe's (1951) comments on the public response to the introduction of new media technologies, Smythe observes "that where the technological innovation bears directly on the public, it tends to become the focus of blame for the current social ills" (p. 59). He rejects outright, on the basis of lack of objective evidence, the belief that the provision of the "requisite technical information for committing a crime, by the program or comic book . . . [leads to] commit[ting] the crime" (p. 59). This position contradicts Smythe's aforementioned (1954) direct and unilinear effects premise, which claimed that TV content determines what is learned.

Although Smythe argues forcefully against Wertham and claims that no definitive, "precise" answers are available to most of the questions asked about the effects of TV or comic book violence on children, he does, nonetheless, align himself with viewpoints which suggest that the viewer is indeed "a passive, receiving automaton" at the end of "a one-way conveyor belt" (p. 60). For Smythe, popular fears over TV's effects on children are probably not too far "off the mark": "The intuition of sensitive laymen (such as it is to be found among PTA groups) may not be too far wide of the mark" (p. 61). Smythe felt that "the danger in our mass media lay in the fact that they lead to 'premature graduation of our children into the immaturity of adulthood'" (p. 62). This argument Neil Postman (1982) would resurrect some three decades later. Concluding with a plea for "rational communication between all parties concerned" in efforts to determine and solve the "problem," Smythe opts out of the effects dilemma altogether: "Any thoughtful survey of public information and concerns over the effects of mass media content on children would have to conclude that not much is known about these effects today. As our exploration . . . suggests, it is not at all clear just what we consider the real problem to be" (p. 62).

In addition to Smythe's (1954) study, published in the then newly established journal specifically concerned with the study of mass communication, *Public Opinion Quarterly* published two more articles on TV and children in 1955, while *American Psychologist* and *Review of Educational Research* published one article each. The establishment in the mid-1950s of *AV Communication Review* suggests that communications studies had evolved to a level of disciplinary formalization and academic legitimacy to enable the introduction of a new journal.

By 1955 a significant body of published research had already accumulated on the topic of TV and children. "Social Influences on Children and Youth" (Banning, 1955), published in *Review of Educational Research*, was the first comprehensive literature review on TV and children. Evelyn Banning reviews recent research on the influences on children of nonschool socialization agencies such as television, radio, comic books, newspapers, youth organizations, community organized camping programs, work experience programs, and the family. These areas of research, according to Banning, require "more quantitative than descriptive" as well as more objective, longitudinal studies "of carefully selected groups of children of many different cultures" in order "to identify factors contributing to socialization and to explain the effects of parent-child relationships within the larger complex of society" (p. 44). Citing research by Gesselman, Lewis, Maccoby, Scott, Charles Wells and Timothy Lynch, Witty, and others, Banning recirculates their discourses into the unity of her text. She notes that "no large-scale study of the effect of mass mediums [*sic*] upon children has been attempted since the Payne Fund Studies" (p. 36). The implication here is that contemporary research on the influence of mass media on children is fragmented and, for the most part, inconclusive. Reflecting on the research to date, she notes that "the evidence indicate[s] the value of further study of the influence of television programs on the formation of attitudes and concepts" (p. 38).

Middecade seems to have been marked as a "watershed" year, a time to take stock. Another review of research, a metadiscourse, was published the same year in *American Psychologist* (Coffin, 1955). A subsection entitled "'Effects' of Television" comments that "most of the 'effects' studies to date (especially in the area of TV's effects on children) suffer distinct methodological limitations" (p. 633). Coffin enumerates these limitations and proposes as a remedy "the preferable 'panel' technique" (p. 633). Hence, a mere seven years after the introduction of TV into the American home, the research is already proclaiming itself as "effects research." Although Coffin may seem critical of effects, he nonetheless subscribes to the effects logic. For instance, he groups all previous research into "effects" subheadings: "Effects of Television," "Effects on Other Communications Media," "Effects on Other Entertainment Industries," "Effects on Family and

Social Activities," and so forth. One section, "Effects on Children," surveys the research on TV and children included in this present chapter, as well as industry and university-based research reports and unpublished manuscripts.

Coffin notes that the prevalent public attitude toward TV and children "has been one of sharp concern and controversy" (p. 634), and that the state of research has not progressed beyond counting hours watched and listing program preferences: "The abundance of controversy is accompanied by a corresponding abundance of investigation. Much of it, however, especially in the educational literature, offers chiefly accounts of time spent viewing and catalogues of favorite programs. . . . Most studies 'are inconclusive except at one point: they show that a lot of children are watching a lot of television'" (pp. 634–635). He organizes the existing research according to social, educational, and demographic "effects": "Viewing and school achievement," "Leisure activities," "Behavior at home," "Variations by age and length of ownership," and "Parents' attitudes towards TV." Counter to much of the research of the early 1950s, Coffin's interpretation of the research on TV and school achievement suggests that no significant relationship exists between the two.

According to Coffin, the research suggests that initial displacement effects are not permanent and that children tend to resume non-TV activities once TV's novelty effect has worn off. Moreover, "TV brings the family back together and provides new sources of common interest, but the increased family unity is more 'passive' than 'active'" (p. 639). Children in low-SES households are said to watch more TV than children in middle- or upper-SES households and also have less TV restrictions imposed on them. Parental attitudes toward TV reportedly are generally favorable, although children's passivity in front of the set, coupled with a TV diet of crime and violence, apparently is an ongoing concern: "The 'passive' nature of TV viewing and the content of crime and violence in TV programs have been of concern to observers. However, attitudes of both parents and children toward TV are definitely favorable, and parents see many more advantages than disadvantages in it for their children" (p. 639).

Coffin concludes by noting that since most of the studies he reviewed were conducted while TV was still at a relatively low saturation level, what is needed is ongoing research, particularly in relation to children, to gauge effects on the first generation to grow up with TV: "Among our younger children . . . a generation is growing up which has known television all its life; the adaptation of this group to television might be a sphere of especial interest" (p. 640).

"Home Television and Behavior: Some Tentative Conclusions," by Frank L. Sweetser (1955) is a short report appearing in *Public Opinion*

Quarterly's Living Research section: a forum "devoted to the short and meaty item" (p. 79). Sweetser's research item reports on interviews he conducted with 254 TV families with grade school children to investigate the effects of TV on the behaviors of family members during the first two years of TV ownership. He hypothesized that children, "blue collar families," and "residents of outer metropolitan suburbs" would be more significantly affected by TV than adults, "white collar family members," and inner suburbs residents. Sweetser's interpretation of the data suggests that adults were more likely to change their behaviors than children. Moreover, TV displaced other activities more among white-collar families than among blue-collar families, and this same displacement effect was more pronounced among outer suburb than inner suburb residents; the latter are seen to have more limited access to alternative social activities. Sweetser's study supports the displacement theory of TV effects, which he sees as manifest in altered social behaviors, particularly among those who have recently acquired a TV. This study is somewhat of an anomaly in the research of the mid-1950s, which tended to veer toward specific effects on viewers in relation to a slowly increasing variety of variables. By middecade, research on displacement effects in relation to length of TV ownership was on the wane.

"Psychological Research Using Television" (Carpenter, 1955) outlines the merits of applying contemporary psychological theory and method to the study of TV. The article maintains that, because the FCC allocated 242 TV stations "for use by educational and cultural interest" in 1953, the time has come for psychologists to consider more closely what audiences learn from TV, and to move beyond a focus on compilations of audience's program preferences, time spent viewing, and so forth. For C.R. Carpenter, the audience subjects are "reactors" responding to media "stimulus materials." He rejects research that has examined "intervening variables" as "determinants" of "effects of the communications stimuli," on the grounds that this kind of research leads to "hypotheses which conceptualize communication stimuli as acting like releasor-organizer mechanism (or processes), and points to hypotheses which reveal the fallacies of considering communication processes as being analogous to electrical transmissions" (p. 608). For Carpenter, as for Smythe (1954), "determinants" of effects lie with the medium, not with the viewing subject.

Seymour Feshbach's (1955) "The Drive-Reducing Function of Fantasy Behavior," published in the *Journal of Abnormal and Social Psychology,* and his 1956 publication of "The Catharsis Hypothesis and Some Consequences of Interaction with Aggressive and Neutral Play Objects" in the *Journal of Personality* laid the foundation for what would be labeled the "catharsis" model of televiewing. In 1956 Alberta Siegel would replicate Feshbach's 1955 study of undergraduate psychology students with a study of children exposed to filmed aggression. Briefly, Feshbach's "drive-reducing hypothesis" held that "fantasy expression of hostility will partially reduce situationally induced aggression" (1955:3). In other words, subjects exposed to an induced hostile situation were believed to have measurably lower aggression following "an interpolated fantasy activity" (p. 3). Exposure to aggression was assumed to function as a cathartic release for innate aggressive drives. Borrowing from the discourse of psychoanalysis, Feshbach circulates statements from an adjacent field into social psychology. His text constitutes a discursive formation at the level of initiating a subdiscourse (i.e., catharsis theory of TV effects) which would derive its epistemological regularity from the "thematic choice" articulated by Feshbach.

A central figure in an emergent field, Lazarsfeld was called before the Kefauver Committee in 1955 to provide testimony on the "state of knowledge in the field, the kind of research needed, and some of the limitations of research in "solving" the problem" (1955:243). His report to the committee was published in *Public Opinion Quarterly* that same year. Already a key authority of delimitation in audience and opinion research (e.g., Lazarsfeld, 1940; Lazarsfeld & Stanton, 1944; Lazarsfeld, Berelson & Gaudet, 1944), Lazarsfeld was introduced in this article as witness at the Kefauver Senate Committee Hearings, as "former president of the American Association for Public Opinion Research, as the recipient of a prestigious award, and as chairman of the sociology department at Columbia University" (p. 243). This is the kind of information that is focal to a social history; here, however, it is part of the text which circumscribes the status of authority of both the author and his text.

Deploring the lack of support from foundations for research on TV and children comparable to that provided by the Rockefeller Foundation for radio research, Lazarsfeld comments that "no [philanthropic] foundation has dared to sponsor the necessary research" (p. 245). Lazarsfeld further speculates that the "controversial" nature of this fledgling field of research—the controversy apparently aided by "the harm which resulted from another [committee] investigation last year" (p. 250)—undermines foundation support. Lazarsfeld responds to the "aridity and the negativism of much of the discussion which takes place today" (p. 246) by suggesting that systematic and longitudinal research can dispel this negativism. The "real problem," in Lazarsfeld's view, "is the cumulative effect of television, what it does to children six years, not six minutes, later" (p. 246). He comments: "I submit that only such long-term studies would give us a realistic picture of the role of television in child's personality development.

... Only detailed and large-scale studies of what actually goes on in the home will lead to advice which is concrete enough so that the average mother can make use of it" (pp. 246–247).

Yet short-term research had characterized most university-funded studies on media and children. And herein lies the problem that leads Lazarsfeld back to his plea for large-scale funding from either federal or philanthropic sources. On the question of theory, Lazarsfeld notes that "what might be called a psychological theory of television is still missing, and will continue to be so unless we make collective efforts to help it along" (p. 247). He lauds content analyses, which can be useful to industry decisions about program content and can have potential tie-ins to the toy industry: Instead of toy guns and cowboy suits the toy industry could market scientific or educational toys which would tie in with programs promoting those concepts and toys (p. 248). For over three decades now, the toy and media industries have capitalized on this link between promoting educational (prosocial) concepts with consumer products. As Tom Engelhardt (1987) outlines, media and product networking has reached its most sophisticated levels in the last decade, reaching unprecedented profit and exposure levels with the cross-promotion of prosocial messages and characters via toy, fast-food, movie, cartoon, cereal, apparel, camping, and sports gear tie-ins.

Finally, Lazarsfeld calls for more positive family programs "which dramatize family situations; these could give parents more ideas as to what to do with their children, and, at the same time provide the children with chances to find their own daily lives more interesting and satisfying" (p. 249). Programs with which the entire family can identify would minimize children "using TV as substitutes for what their parents cannot give them for lack of time, energy and insight" (p. 249). Lazarsfeld recommends that if the effects of TV on children are an "urgent social problem" (p. 244)—as the very existence and activity of the Kefauver hearings seems to indicate—then the committee should "raise an emergency flag" (p. 250). That is, the committee "should be able to do something ... to concentrate interest and to speed up research on the effects of television on young people" (p. 250). He concludes by clarifying the alleged controversial nature of the debate over the effects of TV on children: "The effect of television on children is controversial not because some people are against crime and others for it; it is controversial because so little is known that anyone can inject his [sic] prejudices or his views into the debate without being proven wrong" (p. 251).

The message from Lazarsfeld to state "authorities"—which coincided, inter alia, with testimony from Maccoby, Hovland, and Riley and Riley—is that not very much is known about the effects of TV on children. The research results tended toward either inconclusive or contradictory findings. At middecade, then, the discourse on TV and children remained, by its own expert admission, as it were, fraught with inconclusive evidence, an unfocused research direction, and no theoretically based explanation (or even adequate description) of the TV-child relationship.

Research continued in the second half of the 1950s, much as it had prior to Lazarsfeld's appeal at the Kefauver hearings for more systematic and better-focused research. That is, research topics continued along divergent lines, and "microstudies" continued to produce evidence which linked specific viewer variables with specific TV effects. Even though Lazarsfeld emphasized the importance of the role the Kefauver committee could play in systematizing research, he nonetheless recognized that the academic community was unaccustomed to taking directives from the government on research priorities. Judging from the studies published after the Kefauver hearings, government intervention into research on TV and children did not occur.

1956–1959

The study of previously established topics and hypotheses continued. An experimental study to "test the 'release' theory as it applies to the effects of violence in the mass media" (Siegel, 1956:365) was published in 1956 in *Child Development*. Siegel hypothesized that fantasy aggression "reduces the instigation to all other acts of aggression" (p. 267). Thus, exposure to filmed violence, or "any of a diverse variety of aggressive acts" (p. 366), enables viewers to experience that aggression vicariously. Vicarious experience was assumed to decrease the need to act aggressively at some later instigation.

Twelve nursery school boys and 12 girls participated in this study. The experimental group was shown an aggressive film (*Woody Woodpecker* cartoon), the control group was shown a nonaggressive film (*Little Red Hen*). Children were observed during viewing and during play after viewing. Siegel carefully and in great detail describes scoring procedures, experimental controls, operational definitions, hypothesis testing, and so forth. Most of the paper, in fact, is concerned with discussion of the experimental design and procedure. Contrary to her hypothesis, Siegel found that children were more, not less, aggressive after exposure to aggressive film content. Boys reacted more aggressively than girls, and boys rated as aggressive by teachers prior to exposure showed increased, not less, aggression after viewing the film.

In her proposal for future research, which would be taken up by Albert Bandura in the early 1960s, Siegel surmised that incorporation of frustration instigation into the experimental design would provide a more adequate framework within which to test the release theory. Illustrative of the technicist neutrality of the discourse of science, she writes: "These findings suggest that the acceptance of the null hypothesis with respect to the hypothesis of equivalence of forms may be due to the inappropriateness of the scores as indices of drive strength, and that the hypothesis of equivalence of forms should be tested with films of greater immediacy and in a situation in which frustration-produced aggression is aroused" (p. 376). The preoccupation with refinement of method, experimental validity, and precision obscures consideration of the topic of study altogether: Consideration of the child, the medium, and sources of learning and information disappears. The child here is conceptualized as a reactive response mechanism, a passive agent and victim of innate drives. Relatedly, effects of the medium on viewers are seen as unidirectional and immediate.

Two years later, Siegel (1958) conducted another experimental study to examine the "possible influence of violence in the mass media upon what may be called children's *cognitive* development, which includes their conceptual learning of the realities of social life" (p. 35). Specifically, the aim was to study the effects of media violence on children's occupational role expectations. As Siegel saw it, "to date, our information on the learning of role expectations comes from observation, recall, and other informal and uncontrolled sources" (p. 37). The formation of role expectations among children, then, although these are derived from a number of "sources of incidental learning" (p. 37), can be isolated and scrutinized under the controlled conditions of the laboratory experiment.

In this, as in Siegel's 1956 publication, most of the text is devoted to laborious description of design, procedure, and data analysis. Her data revealed that children exposed to dramatized (radio) news stories about taxi drivers held role expectations (of taxi drivers) which included more aggression and violence than did the expectations of children exposed to nondramatized newspaper stories about taxi drivers. Again, children are construed as manipulable by the medium, and, other than age, sex, and IQ, no other background variables are considered as important influences in children's social learning of occupational role expectations. The limitations of a laboratory-based experiment—a highly artificial, decontextualized situation within which to encounter the mass media—here is rendered irrelevant. The only limitation noted is the paucity of experimental data on children's learning of role expectations. This, within the discourse of experimental psychological research, can only be remedied by more experimentation (p. 55).

In 1956 Scott published "Television and School Achievement" in *Phi Delta Kappan*. Scott comments that "little attention has been given to the specific relationships between children and television" (p. 25). Contrary to the research evidence, he claims that "for the most part, interest in television's effect upon children has evidenced itself in more generalized studies" (p. 25). His study, conducted with 456 sixth and seventh graders in the school where he was a principal, sought to identify relationships between amount of televiewing and children's achievement (in reading, arithmetic, language, and spelling), IQ, personal and social adjustment, educational and leisure-time interests, and parental SES (p. 25). Students were provided with checklists on which they were asked to record all programs watched for two school weeks.

Briefly, Scott found that increases in total viewing time correlated positively with decreases in arithmetic and reading scores, with lower IQ scores, and with lower SES levels. Scott found no differences in personality and social adjustment, leisure, or in-school interests between light and heavy viewers. He attempts to avoid positing TV as cause for lowered achievement among heavy viewers by suggesting that low-IQ children may seek cognitively less demanding programs, and that this precludes the possibility that TV can promote learning of language and concepts. Explaining the low SES and heavy viewing relationship, he comments that "an increase in the standard of living makes possible a greater variety of recreational and entertainment experiences and, therefore, less dependence upon television as a means of entertainment" (p. 27). Scott concludes with calls for "further analysis of commercial TV's educational hazard" and further experimentation "to determine cause and effect," for a "strict[er] . . . TV diet," for "planned television viewing," and for planning that must "limit quantity . . . [and] assure some quality" (p. 28). Pleas to parents and teachers for more involvement in children's viewing had almost disappeared in the discourse, despite its direct ties with schooling. Scott, however, saw adult mediation of children's viewing as important in light of "the TV hazard": "Educational achievement must triumph over the television hazard" (p. 25).

Maccoby, meanwhile, was continuing research on learning theory applied to the mass media—specifically film. In 1957 she published with William C. Wilson "Identification and Observational Learning from Films" in the *Journal of Abnormal and Social Psychology*. Here she draws on research such as "Imitation in a home-raised chimpanzee" (1952), "Observational learning by cats" (1944), and "Imitative behavior in the Rhesus monkey" (1935), and invokes Thorndike's and

Dewey's axiom: "We learn by doing rather than by having actions demonstrated to us" (Maccoby & Wilson, 1957:76).

Maccoby and Wilson theorize that viewers identify with on-screen characters of the same sex, age, and status. Identification with media-portrayed characters and vicarious involvement in portrayed action is close to "learning by doing" through observation and vicarious participation in media content. Maccoby's sample (279 seventh grade students) was shown a movie—*Junior G-Men*—during class and was given a multiple-choice questionnaire on the movie a week later. Maccoby and Wilson found that their subjects tended to identify with same-sex characters and with "aspired social class, rather than current objective status" (p. 86). In terms of information recall, viewers tended to "remember somewhat better the actions and words of the characters with whom they identify" (p. 87). For Maccoby and Wilson, character identification is one determinant among others of what viewers learn from media content. However, they admit that viewers can misperceive, and thus will not learn what a (movie) producer intended: "There may be misperceptions . . . in which the viewer misjudges the nature of the cues to which the actor is responding, or misinterprets the actor's responses, in which case the viewer learns something that is not an accurate representation of what the movie producer intended to portray" (p. 76).

Maccoby and Wilson conceptualize the medium as a system of fixed meanings to and from which viewing subjects respond and learn. Meaning, in this view, is not negotiated between viewer and film content, and the viewer who identifies with an opposite-sex character is misreading cues, misperceiving, and misinterpreting the "real" meaning. Maccoby and Wilson's contribution to the discourse, then, forwarded the notion that meaning is intrinsic to the medium's text, and that the producers' and writers' intents were recoverable and "true."

Robert S. Albert published "The Role of Mass Media and the Effect of Aggressive Film Content upon Children's Aggressive Responses and Identification Choices" in *Genetic Psychology Monographs* (1957). This article was a partial reproduction of Albert's doctoral dissertation supervised by "Dr. N. Maccoby and E. Maccoby." Noting that Peterson and Thurstone's (1933) "study of the effect of film material on children's attitudes failed to produce the desired effect" (p. 229), Albert set out to produce effects. That is, he aimed to show the effects of the interaction between aggressive film content and children's personality and behavior. Contrary to Albert's prediction, "subjects shown a conventional cowboy film show a decrease in their aggression" (p. 279). Low-IQ-scoring subjects were found to be more likely to respond to aggressive film content with aggressive behaviors (p.

280). In terms of character identification, Albert claimed that, as Maccoby had found (1957), girls and boys identify with same-sex characters, and increasing age is seen to correspond to a measurable decrease in aggression. Although this study was not concerned with TV, and Albert did not extrapolate his findings to provide explanations for children's (aggressive) behaviors in relation to aggressive TV content, it is illustrative of the kind of quantitative experimental studies on the topic of TV violence and children's aggressive behaviors that would characterize research in the following decade.

In May 1957 the opening address to the National Education Association's Centennial Seminar on Communication was delivered by Joseph Klapper, then research associate at the Bureau of Applied Social Research at Columbia University (1957:453). The address was published as "What We Know About the Effects of Mass Communication: The Brink of Hope" in *Public Opinion Quarterly* the same year. It is, in many ways, an early reading of the discourse as it would reappraise itself in the later "Ferment in the Field" (1983) issue of the *Journal of Communication*. Klapper foresaw a discursive shift underway in communications research: "The new orientation . . . can perhaps be described. . . . as a shift away from the concept of 'hypodermic effect' toward an approach which might be called 'situation,' 'phenomenistic,' or 'functional.' It is a shift away from the tendency to regard mass communication as a necessary and sufficient cause of audience effects, toward a view of the media as influences, working amid other influences, in a total situation" (p. 456).

Klapper, of course, was speaking primarily of mass communication as it pertained to public opinion and attitude research. Discussing the role of the media in changing audience "taste," Klapper turns to research on mass media and children, and observes that "little attention has been paid to the one change which occurs continually—the changing tastes of growing children" (p. 467). In other words, Klapper points out that patterns of children's media interests (comics or TV) parallel development of personality and of regular reading preferences (p. 467). He notes that with the exception of Wolf and Fiske's (1949) research on children's comic book preferences, "no one . . . has ever pointed out the pattern of development [of media interests]" (p. 467).

Calling for research on media and children informed by a developmental perspective, and invoking "the more recent and differently focused work of the Rileys and of Maccoby," Klapper suggests that the new orientation considers the "'functions' served by media, and . . . the role of the media in effects of which they are not the sole cause" (p. 469). For Klapper, this implies a conceptualization of the viewer as active selector or user of media and of media content. The medium-viewer relationship is seen as potentially interactive and functionalist:

Viewers select and use media for specific individual purposes. Meaning, presumably, is constructed on the basis of the interaction between media messages and the viewer. Finally, in Klapper's estimation, communications research had reached "the brink of hope" with the possibilities offered by a more context-sensitive, phenomenological research model. He explains: "The path of the phenomenistic approach . . . seeks to account for the known occurrence and to assess the roles of the several influences which produced it, and . . . attempts to see the respondents not as randomly selected individuals each exchangeable for the other, but rather as persons functioning within particular social contexts" (p. 471).

What would, in the 1960s, be labelled the "uses and gratifications" model of mass communication began to gain ground in the late 1950s. In 1958 Albert and Harry G. Meline published the first article which discursively rephrased the traditional medium-viewer relationship by situating the viewer—in this case, a viewer attribute—as active agent in the title of their paper: "The Influence of Social Status on the Uses of TV." What is implied here, of course, is that viewers use TV for individual purposes and needs, and that SES plays a significant role in delimiting viewers' use of TV.

Albert and Meline sought to identify "the reactions to, and the uses of, television by parents and children in two different socio-economic statuses" (1958:145). Their research aim was "in the possible differences that such a status difference might make in the role of television, and whether or not parents made an effort to utilize its positive potential and to counteract its poorer features" (p. 145). In other words, the aim here was to examine how parental use of TV in children's socialization (i.e., using TV as reward and punishment) differed between upper- and lower-middle-class households. The extent to which parents curtail and direct their children's viewing, the authors hypothesize, would suggest comparable (TV) preferences and uses among children (p. 146). Two classes of fifth graders (one lower-middle-class; one upper-middle-class) were surveyed by class-administered questionnaires. Parents received questionnaires "a few days" later; the kinds of questions used were not reported. The data suggested that "television is reported used as a punishment more often among Lower than Upper status children, but the children's reports of it being used as a reward are about equal" (p. 151). Parents of either SES bracket consistently reported applying more viewing restrictions than what children reported. Estimated amount of viewing was inconsistently reported by parents and children of both SES groups. The authors qualify their findings by hinting at the inherent problem of self-reports: "It is difficult to judge how many of these discrepancies come at the children forgetting the punishments and over emphasizing the rewards or result from the parents reporting what they believe to be more 'socially' acceptable responses" (p. 151).

The validity of this study, or its usefulness for the new functional approach to communications studies, can be summed up by the authors' comment on their findings, which indicates more the inherent methodological flaw of parent and child self-reports than anything substantial about the influence of social class on the uses of TV: "Systematic parent-child disagreements appear consistently throughout the study" (p. 151). The implicit message is that self-reports cannot be relied upon to provide evidence on which to base unequivocal claims of effects, but must be considered as no more than individual constructions in response to a highly artificial form of questioning.

Scott republished his 1956 article, "Television and School Achievement," retitled "Relationships Between Elementary School Children and Television" in the *Journal of Educational Research* in 1958. The data and findings are the same as in the 1957 paper; Scott's prose in the 1958 paper, however, is a much abbreviated version. As in Witty's case, Scott's recirculation of the same statements in different textual sites of academic debate suggests an expansion of the range of knowledge distribution. It is indicative of an expansion of the spatio-temporal parameters of the discourse on TV and children.

The *Journal of Broadcasting* was inaugurated in 1957. This added another discursive forum for mass media studies, thereby expanding and increasing the visibility, recognition, and formalization of mass communications studies as a legitimate field of academic inquiry. The first article on TV and children, "The Effect on Parental Buying Habits of Children Exposed to Children's Television Programs" (Munn, 1958), was published the following year. Mark Munn, "research director of WGN Chicago" (p. 252), writes from a market research perspective. The article itself "constitutes the highlights of a survey conducted by the Research Division of the WGN-TV Sales Promotion Department" (p. 253). Children allegedly had become, by the late 1950s, "indifferent" to children's programs, and therefore, indifferent to the commercials broadcast during children's shows. In response to advertisers' complaints that children "no longer respond actively to commercial announcements" (p. 253), Munn set out to investigate "(1) the effect of commercial announcements on children, and (2) children's effect on their parents" (p. 253). Munn mailed questionnaires to "sample units"—500 "households presumed to have children" (p. 254)—who were asked to respond by describing children's behavior (p. 253). The returned questionnaires represented 221 households with a total of 370 children, of which 80 percent were categorized as preschoolers. Munn interpreted his data to suggest that "almost all children studied are influenced by advertising in children's television programs" and "parents in turn are influenced by their children, though many parents insist upon approving the product" (p. 257). Munn provides no references to similar studies on TV or radio advertisements and children's purchase requests, and he provides no theoretical base from which to speculate, for instance, about children's learning from or socialization by TV commercials, and links to subsequent influences on parental purchase behaviors. This article exemplifies an early version of the kind of research reports on TV and children that typically appeared, albeit in more statistically sophisticated form, in communications journals—as distinct from educational journals—throughout the late 1950s, the 1960s, and a good part of the 1970s.

Maccoby continued to work on social learning theory as applied to movie viewing, first outlined with Wilson in 1957. In a subsequent study written with Wilson and Roger V. Burton (1958) and published the following year in *Public Opinion Quarterly*, she applied a different methodological procedure—"a methodological improvement" (p. 260)—for studying viewer identification (24 college-age men and 24 women) with screen characters. In this study, the methodological refinement over Maccoby and Wilson's previous procedure consisted of recording "eye movements of subjects and measur[ing] the amount of time they spent watching each of the main characters during selected scenes" (p. 260). Maccoby et al. go to substantial lengths to report in great detail the methodological apparatus and procedure which, in retrospect, appears to have been a crude version of later laboratory-based experimental studies such as those conducted by Bandura and colleagues. The lengthy description of "apparatus" and "procedure" itself exemplifies U.S. social science's preoccupation with methodological exactitude at the expense of engagement with theory.

Nonetheless, from observations of subjects' eye movements "through the holes in the screen" (p. 263)—subjects by now having been discursively transformed into "Ss"—which were recorded by "pressing . . . switches," Maccoby reported that "male viewers spend more time, relative to female viewers, watching the male lead in a movie" (p. 267). Maccoby et al. explain this same-sex identification by reference to the 1957 study in which she and Wilson found that girls "remembered better the heroine's actions in scenes of romantic inter-action" (p. 266), even though boys and girls remembered equally well the male protagonist's actions. She explains this difference in sex-based character identification in "light of clinical writings about temperamental differences between the sexes, [which] suggest the possibility that women viewers, being more narcissistic, concentrate upon the character they see as themselves, while men viewers concentrate more upon the cathected object" (p. 266).

Imputing culturally based and derived gender attributes to differentiate male and female viewers inserts into the mass media discourse a Freudian conception of female viewers as inward and self-focused (passive-compliant, domestic) and male viewers as outward and other-focused (active-aggressive, public). These constructs of innate viewer characteristics would, in later studies, be reformulated and reinterpreted to account for the "natural" tendency of female viewers to identify with TV roles which would prepare them for future domestic roles. In 1961, for instance, Schramm, Jack Lyle, and Edwin B. Parker observed that "girls early turn toward programs which relate to the responsibilities they will assume in adolescence and adult life. Boys, on the other hand, maintain 'boy tastes' for adventure, excitement, and physical combat well into adolescence" (p. 46). A decade later, Ann Beuf (1974) noted that boys' and girls' differential preferences for TV content had to do with sex-based differences in career aspirations: Boys aspired to "adventurous" careers such as cowboys, policemen, firefighters, or sports heroes, whereas girls aspired toward less action-oriented careers such as nursing or secretarial workers. These gendered constructs not only are derivative of Freudian conceptions of masculinity and femininity, but must be read as both derivative and constitutive of the epistemological and normative foundations of Western, particularly liberal, conceptions of reason and rationality, rooted as they are in binarist public/private and self/other dualisms.

The "clinical writings about temperamental differences between the sexes" which Maccoby et al. (1958) incorporate into their discourse, suggest that innate biological differences are responsible for differences in media preferences and use between girls and boys, rather than socioculturally based socializing influences such as the school, family, peers, church, and, importantly, the mass media themselves. Maccoby's studies with Wilson and Burton (1958) and with Wilson (1957) are "significant" contributions to the distorted perspective generated by sex-role research on mass media which, inter alia, confuses gender with sex. Nevertheless, the Maccoby studies still counted as "foundational" in the sex-role research branch of the mass media discourse in the 1970s (e.g., Busby, 1975).

In 1958 the first major academic study, *Television and the Child* (Himmelweit, Oppenheim & Vince, 1958), was published in monograph form in England. In contrast to Robert Lewis Shayon's (1951) decidedly less scholarly U.S. publication of *Television and Our Children*, Hilde Himmelweit, A.N. Oppenheim, and Pamela Vince's book was heralded as a landmark study and continues today to be referenced as foundational to the discourse on TV and children. The monograph described a correlational two-year study (1955, 1956) of 908 ten- and eleven-year-olds and 946 thirteen- and fourteen-year-olds, equally divided between viewers and nonviewers and matched for IQ, socioeconomic status, age, and sex. The data consisted primarily of children's viewing diaries and questionnaires, interviews with parents, teacher opinion surveys, several in-depth interviews with children, program content analyses, and observational studies of children's viewing.

Himmelweit et al. (1958:41) suggested that when it comes to TV and children, "whether TV is good or bad for children depends on the programmes, the amount the child views, the type of child, the type of effects to be examined, and the context in which viewing takes place. In the last resort, it is an individual matter with the effects varying from child to child." Himmelweit et al. absolve TV as sole cause of negative effects on children, and locate TV influence in an environmental context of which TV is a part: "Very heavy viewing, very late bedtimes, loss of concentration or interest at school have to do with the child and his [sic] environment rather than with the lure of television—[which] may be mistakenly passed off as the inevitable by-product of having television in the home" (pp. 40–41). TV is conceptualized in neither white nor black metaphors; it is not as "black" a phenomenon as commonly claimed, yet nor is it "the great harbinger of culture and enlightenment" (p. 40). It is a window to the world, but to no lesser or greater extent than any other mass communications media. And, depending on content, TV "can frighten and disturb, particularly those who are emotionally insecure," can make children "less prejudiced and more tolerant," and can encourage tolerance yet "implant or accentuate one-sided, stereotyped value judgements" (p. 41).

Effects were categorized in terms of content and displacement. The study of content was seen as one way to identify how TV influenced "children's knowledge and school performance, and . . . their outlook and values" (p. 2). Displacement effects were to reveal which activities were dropped by children in favor of TV viewing which, in turn, might suggest in which areas of children's leisure time TV was potentially a problem (e.g., free play, organized club activities). Effects, then, are conceptualized as a function of the interaction between TV (content, viewing amount and times) and viewers' individual circumstances. For most children, the authors noted, TV was not found to be the serious problem the public and some researchers had claimed: "the majority of children are not drastically affected [by TV]" (p. 41) and they assimilate TV "smoothly in the majority of cases" (p. 42). However, in a situation characterized by psychological and/or social problems, "television may just tip the scale" (p. 6) toward negative effects.

The widespread lack of adult guidance in children's viewing is of serious concern to Himmelweit et al. In contrast to popular opinion, this lack of interest in children's viewing, they note, is not "a matter of the social level of the home; it is no greater in middle-class than in working-class homes" (p. 44). To this end, a separate chapter is devoted to proposing solutions addressed to parents, teachers, and the public. Proposals include parental involvement in and judicious monitoring of children's viewing choices; demystifying the production process; and teacher familiarization with and incorporation into the classroom of TV material that children are fond of. Importantly, the preoccupation with time spent viewing has been a "misplaced" concern. TV content—too much viewing of "bad" programs to the exclusion of more desirable programs—is seen as more significant in contributing to negative effects; parents must encourage a "programme balance" (p. 44) for their children.

Negative effects repeatedly were found not to be directly related with TV but, rather, were judged by Himmelweit et al. as a function of background factors in children's home environment, personality, and psychological profile. TV did not seem to cause aggression in children, "although it could precipitate it in those few children who are emotionally disturbed" (p. 20). Children's attitude toward school, their school grades, or "general knowledge" did not seem adversely affected by TV (pp. 21–22). In terms of reading, it was found that although TV initially displaced reading time, "in the long run" reading amount and choice of reading material were not adversely affected by TV (p. 24).

The Himmelweit et al. text constructs an interactive viewer whose response to TV is not a direct consequence of viewing content or amount but, rather, a consequence of individual and home background variables (p. 41). Negative effects are seen as associated with excessive and unsupervised viewing which, in turn, is found in children "who have problems," or "in families which have conflicts" (p. 41). Although the entire book is sectioned into various "effects," the authors argue strongly on the basis of their data against direct social, cognitive, or behavioral effects.

In the U.S. that same year, *The Age of Television* (Bogart, 1958/1972) brought together in one volume a broad range of research findings from a variety of disciplinary perspectives on TV in American society. One of the chapters focused on TV and youth. Although Leo Bogart claimed that "there is more opinion than evidence on this point" (p. xi), his volume aimed "to create order out of the evidence, without any pretension to render judgements on the medium" (1972, p. xxxix). In all, his commentary on the evidence indicated an orientation that considered televiewing primarily as a social, not psychological, process.

Discussing the research on TV advertising and children, Bogart notes that TV cannot be blamed for an apparent increase in smoking and drinking among youth. He admits that TV influences children's and adolescents' product identification, yet "the juvenile consumer, like his parents, will decide among the various conflicting advertising appeals and claims on the basis of his own predispositions and tastes" (p. 259). In other words, Bogart situates TV as one among many influences that socialize young consumers. He sees TV as a problem, as a "danger," only in terms of its (mis)use by parents. That is, when TV is used to substitute for parental care and attention, "damage . . . to the child's emotional well-being" is likely, "for if TV is interposed between children and parents this usually reflects attitudes and behavior expressed by the parents in other ways as well" (p. 260).

The largest subsection in the chapter on TV and youth is devoted to the research on TV, violence, and delinquency, which includes a substantial amount of data derived from memos, reports, and testimony submitted by psychiatrists to the Kefauver inquiry. The extent of the textual space devoted to this topic both reflects and contributes to the perceived importance of the question concerning TV violence and aggression (and, by extension, delinquency) among young viewers. Summing up this section, Bogart (p. 284) provides this overview: "Virtually all of the expert testimony submitted to the sub-committee, on both sides of this controversial subject, was based on professional judgment rather than on actual research evidence." Maccoby's (1951, 1954) studies are cited as an exception. Her testimonial statements to Kefauver were based on experimental research rather than mere "professional judgment." In Bogart's estimation: "While a great deal of informed and intelligent judgment has been expressed on the effects of television on children, there is actually very little real research to support either one viewpoint or another" (p. 288).

Thus, for Bogart, effects research on TV and children by the late 1950s remained inconclusive. Bogart himself aligned with that group which conceptualized TV as one of several influences on the child and which had the potential to affect children positively or negatively, depending upon their psychological, social, economic, and cultural background. Criminal behavior, for instance, cannot be "directly linked to a specific television performance [and] is certainly no basis from which to generalize" (p. 288). Neither can TV be said to "create psychological problems, though it may influence the way in which they find expression" (p. 288). The principal problem with TV, as Bogart sees it, is indirectly related to the apparent widespread lack of parental supervision of children's viewing, and directly related to some of TV's content, the "worst" of which "helps to perpetuate moral, cultural and social values which are not in accord with the highest ideals of an enlightened democracy" (p. 289). Yet, in this regard, "television is no different from any other popular art. It has become the focus of recent discussion because it is both the newest mass medium and the one with which children spend the greatest amount of time" (p. 289). In agreement with many, although by no means all, studies of TV and children conducted in the late 1940s and early 1950s, *The Age of Television* reiterates Himmelweit et al.'s (1958) statements that some kinds of (TV) content will affect some kinds of children under certain circumstances—the relationship between TV and children is not one-dimensional or unilinear.

Leonard Pearlin (1959) in "Social and Personal Stress and Escape Television Viewing," published in *Public Opinion Quarterly*, reincorporates Maccoby's (1954) and Riley and Riley's (1951) statements on viewers' use of mass media in response to "stress" and personal needs. Parson's and Merton's premise that social structures and relations can impose undue strain on individuals is taken up by Pearlin, who suggests that "stress is a determinant of escape viewing" (p. 256). Situating theory and TV in a historical context, Pearlin observes that "people's reactions to the strains and stresses induced by their environments take many forms. Watching television, or at least certain types of television programs, appears to be the latest mode of response to stress" (p. 255).

Although Pearlin's study did not focus on children, his references to Riley and Riley's (1951) and Maccoby's (1954) studies examined earlier in this chapter support their premise that child viewers will select TV content as a function of stresses particular to childhood and adolescence. Moreover, this recirculation of discourse relocates previous texts within a new discursive combination. Pearlin puts forth a functionalist model of TV and viewers, proposing that TV can serve an escape function for viewers. He conceptualizes "escape viewing" as one mode of televiewing as distinct from others (presumably watching for information or for entertainment). Furthermore, contrary to the top-down formulation of an effects model, he proposes that individual characteristics (e.g., social and/or psychological stress) "determine" viewing choice. This conceptualization of the viewer, then, would imply that effects are relative to individual needs and motivations for viewing.

"Television Viewing Among High School Boys" by Joseph Balogh (1959) is one of the few studies in the late 1950s that took up the kind of research so prevalent in the early part of the decade, as introduced by Witty (1950, 1951, 1953), Lyness (1951, 1952), and Lewis (1949,

1951). In contrast to Riley and Riley (1951), Gesselman (1951), Witty (1950, 1951, 1953), and Maccoby (1951), Balogh (1959) supports the displacement theory of TV's effects, suggesting that "among various activities (housechores, school-homework, sports, movie-going, etc.) which televiewing has been displacing, nothing has on any level been displaced so much and so consistently as hobbies and creative pursuits. . . . By [which] is meant playing musical instruments, singing, acting or working in theatre arts, painting, photographing, writing, working on periodicals, debating and engaging in forensics and other speech arts" (p. 68).

Balogh's message is clear: TV is a negative influence on children (and, by implication, on society), which inhibits and precludes engagement in the cultured activities of an affluent class. In agreement with Witty, Balogh lays much of the blame of TV's allegedly negative effects on parents, noting that very few parents in his sample exercised any kind of intervention in their children's viewing: "It seems that many of the objections raised by parents relate more closely to themselves than to their children" (p. 71). So while Balogh makes a rather limited case against TV, one guided by his narrow and elitist perception of children's leisure-time activities, he attributes negative effects not solely to the medium but, rather, to parental inability or unwillingness to mediate children's viewing. Such a view implicitly contributes to the discourse the notion that TV effects are consequential of the interaction between medium and viewer—that relative parental input in children's viewing modifies what and how much they view and, by implication, children's learning of and socialization by TV's messages.

The final study published in an academic journal to be considered in this chapter is a revised version of a doctoral dissertation published in *Genetic Psychology Monographs*, entitled "Mass Media and Children: A Study of Exposure Habits and Cognitive Effects" (Baylin, 1959). Lotte Baylin acknowledges her supervisor, Allport, and the assistance of Maccoby, whose theoretical perspective guides the study. "Effects" Baylin conceptualizes as "a causal link starting with [media] exposure and ending with a particular way of thinking" (p. 2). And "cognitive" effects—or "ways of thinking"—do not refer to cognitive processes but are, for Baylin, more akin to values, attitudes, and perceptions: stereotyping, perceptions of (individual, global) threat, and perceptions of self-image (p. 2). Effects as a result of exposure are considered by Baylin as mediated by social and psychological characteristics. Indices of social characteristics are the "occupation of father, education of parents, and religion" (p. 3). Mediating psychological characteristics are identified as the "problems" a child perceives and reports to have with "self, peers, and family" (p. 3). Of interest here is the mutually exclusive positioning of the subject's social and demographic background and psychological profile: Baylin does not acknowledge that parental SES may itself mediate children's perceptions of and levels of articulation of their social "problems" with peers or family.

Baylin's findings suggest that children, primarily boys, who are perceived by adults to have problems in everyday social life tend to use excessive viewing as an escape activity. They also tend to use the pictorial media (TV, movies, comics) more frequently than the print media (newspapers, books). Those children, in turn, tend to hold more stereotyped views and tend to be more passive—that is, to hold "an attitude of acceptance of the socioeconomic situation of the father and a lack of interest in changing it" (p. 32). Among boys, heavy viewing, low IQ, difficulties with peers, school and/or family, a Catholic upbringing, low SES and minimal, if any, parental mediation of televiewing tend to be found within the same individual: "Factors associated with high exposure to the pictorial media are lack of parental restriction, low IQ, fathers with worker or service occupations, and being a Catholic" (p. 32). Most of Baylin's findings recirculate statements (about IQ, SES, viewing amounts, etc.) produced by the discourse throughout the decade and, thereby, added to and diffused what had become, by the late 1950s, a dominant set of truths within the discourse. However, her introduction of religion as a variable adds a new dimension to the viewer profile. Catholics, according to Baylin's data, "turn out to be more stereotyped than Protestants" (p. 6). Catholic boys report a greater perception of threat to nation and world (p. 6), and Catholic children in her sample also appeared to watch more TV than Protestant children (p. 10). Baylin draws no implications from these historically unusual findings, but her very research design and sample selection implies that being Catholic interacts with other background factors which, combined, render the individual more predisposed toward TV's negative effects.

Girls, Baylin explains, are only minimally affected by the mass media. Baylin infers from this that girls, unlike boys, are socialized into and rewarded for conformity. Girls with "problems" have a strong need to conform, to be accepted, to fit in, and they will not tend to use the media as escape from or substitute for unrewarding social relationships. Girls without problems are already conformists with less need to conform and even less need to turn to the media as escape: "One gets a picture, then, of girls trying to fit into an established pattern. They expose themselves to the mass media when it is accepted" (p. 37). Moreover, girls generally seem to have fewer social difficulties than boys and are also seen to be less "rebelliously independent" (p. 5) than boys. Baylin considers levels of rebellious independence as psychological factors, and religion as a mediating factor in children's relative "problem" levels: "Among girls whose fathers are workers, Catholics have more problems than Protestants. . . . Catholic girls, no matter what the occupational level of their fathers, have more self-problems than do Protestants" (p. 4). Protestant girls are said to be least affected by the mass media, in contrast to Catholic boys, who are most susceptible to media effects.

The introduction into the discourse of religious persuasion as a contributing variable in the TV-viewer relationship was, at the least, unusual. Viewer characteristics such as SES, IQ, age, sex, and school achievement were well-entrenched viewer attributes at the advent of TV research. The mass media child consumer profile, in terms of these categories, had been inherited from research on the movies, radio, and comic books. Denominational affiliation, however, had not been considered by researchers as a sufficiently significant variable to warrant inclusion in research design; it would continue to be omitted from the viewer background profile.

Witty's final study in his ten-year longitudinal project was published in 1959 in *Elementary English*, entitled "A Tenth Yearly Study and Comments on a Decade of Televiewing" (Witty, Sizemore, Kinsella & Coomer, 1959). As in Witty's early reports (1950, 1951, 1952, 1953), and the eighth (Witty & Gustafson, 1957) and ninth yearly reports (Witty & Kinsella, 1958), children's program preferences and viewing amounts are outlined, followed by sections on the effects of TV on children's behavior, school achievement, and reading. All studies concluded with what by middecade was no longer called the "antidote" to TV but mere "suggestions" to teachers and parents for constructive intervention into children's viewing. In the 1957 study, as in the 1959 final study, elementary and high school children's preferences and viewing amounts reportedly remained the same as in the early 1950s. By 1958, apparently 79 percent of teachers in the Evanston sample were reported by the children to offer "them guidance and valuable suggestions for televiewing" (1958:455). The perceived threat to reading and school achievement, according to Witty and Kinsella, had not been borne out; in fact, "it appears that children are reading somewhat more at the present time [1958] than before TV came into their homes" (p. 455). A decade of field data, as well, evidenced no decrease in school grades as a consequence of time spent viewing: "Good students tend to remain good; poor students stay poor" (Witty & Gustafson, 1957, p. 540). Witty concludes his final study with an appeal to parents and teachers to encourage reading and outdoor activities, and to guide children to select quality educational and entertainment programs. Finally, at the end of the first decade of TV, Witty et al. found that "the complaints about TV, although expressed each year, have decreased" (1959:581). The focus of teacher and parent complaints apparently had shifted from TV in general to specific programs, such as the "excessive number of Westerns that are being shown for children and adults" (pp. 581–582).

Witty's studies were widely recirculated in the citation networks of 1950s' nonexperimental research. By the 1960s, however, the field survey seems to have fallen into methodological disrepute and, coupled with the academically nonauthoritative discursive site of the professional journal, where all of Witty's studies were published, his work was effectively marginalized and finally exscribed from the "founding" research on TV and children.

THE 1950s: AN OVERVIEW

The academic discourse on TV and children that emerged during the first decade following the introduction of TV surfaced predominantly in the fields of sociology, psychology, and education. Teachers' journals, an academically less scholarly and authoritative forum for academic debate and knowledge production, formed a discursive substratum upon which the TV-child discourse also was mapped. Inscribed on the professional journal, the discourse on TV and children can be assumed to have circulated more widely among those in institutional charge of children.

Studies published in the early 1950s exuded a sense of optimism about the new medium, claiming that TV was reuniting families, increasing social interaction among family members, and increasing children's store of information about the world. The child viewer, by and large, was seen to benefit from TV and to incorporate the new medium into daily life, while maintaining previously established social relationships and activities. Although the child was rendered a physically and cognitively passive participant in the televiewing process, s/he was nonetheless constituted as actively learning content—from commercial slogans and product information to tips on how to commit a crime or how to behave in social circumstances. What was learned from TV was seen, for the most part, as a consequence of TV content in interaction with viewers' psychosocial backgrounds. Age, sex, SES, IQ and achievement scores and, to a lesser extent, indices of social adjustment, personality, and self-image comprised the discursive definition of the viewing child.

These background factors were fundamental variables or, in Foucault's terms, a grid of specification which, by the 1950s, already had a well-entrenched history in the educational discourse. The child, as constructed by educational discourse prior to the advent of TV, became a template upon which further out-of-school (viewing) variables would be mapped. TV did not initially generate a reinvention of the child as much as it generated a discursive interpolation of an already existing, previously defined child.

Although the child initially was constituted by discourse as a passive spectator and learner of TV content, by the end of the 1950s this construct had been modified by an increasing functionalist emphasis on viewers' media uses. The escape function argument proposed that viewers seek out certain kinds of media and particular media content as a function of individual predispositions and social circumstances. Because the "escapist" model was not counter-balanced by a positive thesis such as viewing for pleasure (entertainment) or for self-education, it developed a model of televiewing based on negative, existential, and psychoanalytic assumptions: TV as a means of escape from individually varying levels of alienation, frustration, stresses, or strains. Viewers were conceptualized as selective viewers, choosing media and media content as a function of the need to escape from negative psychosocial conditions.

Excessive viewers were said to have the greatest need to use TV to escape social and psychological difficulties. By implication, then, moderate and light viewers would have fewer needs for escape from presumably less stress and strain. This line of research was not pursued, which limited the definition of the child viewer to one who seeks out TV content in relation to personal and social problems. These problems, in turn, were seen as linked to a host of social-psychological-demographic variables. As the discourse proclaimed, the low-achieving, low-IQ-scoring and low-SES child, is the same child who is least well adjusted socially, has low self-esteem, and whose parents take minimal or no interest in the child's televiewing. These same children were also seen to have the greatest need to seek escape from unsatisfactory school and home life.

At the opposite end of the viewing spectrum, the light or nonviewer was said to pose no problem. This child continued to be classified in mid- to high IQ, SES, and school achievement categories which, taken together, constituted a norm (i.e., the ideal student) against which the heavy-viewing, low-achieving, potentially delinquent student was measured. For the most part, then, the 1950s research conceptualized the child viewer as a passive viewer, one who was subject to TV's negative influences with increased viewing. Heavy viewing and negative effects, in turn, were seen as linked to lack of success at school and unsatisfactory social relations. Most commonly, such a profile was said to be found among lower-SES children, thereby superimposing the definition of the problem viewer on the problem student: They were classified as one and the same.

Commercial TV in the early 1950s was heralded optimistically. TV was said to bring the family together and to increase social contact among friends and within communities, to help students with their homework and to generate interest in topics which would promote reading, and to help the general public become more widely informed. TV as a medium of information and entertainment, insofar as it was discussed in relation to children, was defined in terms of programs. Illustrated by the early program preferences and viewing habits studies, the preoccupation with programs at the exclusion of considerations of TV's symbolic and ideological form and content led to a superficial and one-dimensional conceptualization of TV. This conceptualization underpinned claims made by many that effects are a function of content.

In the early years of the 1950s, TV-as-problem was a common descriptor of TV in the academic discourse. Initially researchers set out to debunk what appears to have been public opinion. The source of the problem with TV was most often traced to program producers as well as to parents, much as the problem with movies had been traced to socially irresponsible producers and to parental indifference and/or inability to effectively mediate children's viewing. Calls for school-based media studies were inconsistent. For the most part, TV emerged in the discourse of the 1950s in rather neutral terms, neither particularly harmful nor beneficial to the average child. Based on what was considered inconclusive evidence in some studies and as definitive truths in others, TV was defined by the late 1950s as a problem mostly for children with problems.

How effects are conceptualized reveals significant insights into the manner in which the TV-child relationship is defined. With few exceptions (e.g., Smythe, 1954; Haines, 1955), effects were not seen as direct and unilinear. Almost all of the published studies, save the more vociferous polemical tracts, conceptualized effects as mediated by social, demographic, psychological, and situational variables. Most were cautious with their research findings, suggesting tentative, indirect links between TV and effects upon children, rather than positing causal, unidirectional effects. Moreover, the methodological orientation prevailing in the social sciences at the time—a still-tenuous emphasis on nonexperimental research—had been transposed to the study of TV and children. This precluded the positing of unequivocal causal effects characteristic of later experimental studies. Reliance on data derived from survey questionnaires and oral self-reports precluded the kind of proclamations made by the discourse the following decade when "overt responses" to TV were rendered empirically observable—hence, seemingly indisputable—through the isolation of televiewing in the laboratory, dislocated from its social context in the home. Toward the end of the 1950s, more complex statistical classification and subclassifications of viewer variables and of the viewing process became evident (e.g., Albert & Meline, 1958; Scott, 1958). This discursive move can be read as indicative of an increasing preoccupation, perhaps more of a fascination, with methodological exactitude in design and procedure.

Research topics followed the agenda initially set down by movie and radio research: media preferences, amount of use, effects on school achievement, particularly on reading, and the relation between TV violence and children's aggression. No specific topic or set of topics seems to have dominated inquiry, as Klapper lamented at mid-decade. Nevertheless, effects of TV violence on children appear to have been a contentious social issue, one seen as pressing enough to become a focus for federal investigation which relied, in turn, on professional expertise. By and large, however, research on the various effects of TV on children was judged to be unsystematic and inconclusive (cf. Bogart, 1958/1972). With the exception of Witty's series of reports (1950, 1951, 1952, 1953, 1957, 1958, 1959) on children's viewing preferences and habits, longitudinal research on the effects of TV on children was absent.

In sum, the methodological limitations of the nonexperimental design which characterized most of the 1950s research on TV and children was unable to account for immediate effects that lay beyond the methodological boundaries of self-reports. Observing what viewers did during and after "exposure" and how such overt behaviors differed from "non-exposed" subjects was increasingly seen as more scientifically accurate and defensible. The forerunner of such "methodological improvements" was Maccoby, Wilson and Burton's 1958 study.

Although the attempt here has not been to marshal evidence in support of a research theme or methodological paradigm with which to characterize a research era, method as well as theory framed the possibilities for questions asked, data gathered, and conclusions drawn. Method is as manifest in discourse as are statements bearing concepts, data, author name, status, and institutional affiliation. The obligatory references to scholarly works on related topics have been an essential and primary rule of institutionalized scholarship. In this manner, scholarly discourse both regenerates and constrains itself by placing a particular text within a discursive framework: restating names, studies, claims, etc. At the same time, it delimits its disciplinary boundaries and intellectual affiliations. The borrowing of concepts and the bibliographic references that trace concepts to textual authoritative sites effectively place statements (i.e., publication data and the disciplinary perspective that names, titles, and journals imply) from adjacent discourses into a new combination or "constellation." Maccoby and Wilson's (1957) references to studies on animal psychology are a case in point.

References to previous works on the same topic, then, serve to establish scholarly credibility and authority for one's own text, as well as to locate text within a historical, discursive continuum. The rule of referencing compels the discourse to reproduce itself intertextually in relation to a discursive past. A return to an earlier textual site is a principal discursive rule of formation upon which the production of modern academic discourse is based. In this sense, and bearing in mind the exclusionary character of referencing, it becomes evident that the early establishment of the TV-child discourse can be traced in the citation patterns that initially emerged, by reference to authorities who produced the discourse, and by tracing the disciplinary fields of emergence wherein the discourse surfaced.

Some texts, and their authors, were marginalized at the outset of their participation in the discourse—their text appeared once and then vanished into obscurity. Others, by contrast, such as Witty, Maccoby, or Lewis, continued to recirculate on a number of textual sites, variously in the form of footnotes, bibliographic references or, most often, as part of the text proper. These authors, then, can be seen to have laid the discursive groundwork, so to speak, on which the subsequent discourse was scaffolded intertextually. In contrast to, say, the novelist, to use Foucault's (1977:131) example, these authors ("initiators of discursive practices") "produced not only their own work, but the possibility and the rules of formation of other texts." Thus, reference to work previously published and thereby rendered authoritative situates a current writing within a discursively constructed tradition. The very act of referring back casts previous statements into what is commonly termed a founding tradition that is, by definition, a retrospective discursive construction.

There is no "tradition" except in discourse. Referencing in conjunction with the temporal dimension of academic debate—the historical process of theory building and deconstruction, and the attendant cumulative amassing of data in support of either—situates any given scholarly text in a pivotal position, one where past statements are rearticulated and realigned within the context of a current discursive construction. Such constructions, in turn, lay the possibilities and delimiting conditions for a future rearticulation. Referencing is always a "return" to a text and a setting of conditions for return by future texts: "The work of these initiators is not situated in relation to a science or in the space it defines; rather, it is science or discursive practice that relate their works as the primary points of reference. In keeping with this distinction, we can understand why it is inevitable that practitioners of such discourses must 'return to the origin'" (pp. 134–135).

The early groundwork set out by the "initiators" of discursive practices compelled future participants in the discourse to abide by certain rules, one of which demanded reference to those initiating works. Authors such as Lazarsfeld, Witty, and Maccoby, who already were labelled as established authorities in fields of mass communication/public opinion, education, and social psychology, respectively, brought to the fledgling discourse on TV and children the academic status signaled by their names and institutional affiliations. In this respect, their presence in the discourse can be seen to have helped formalize and render authoritative the disciplinary study of a topic, TV and children, which lay outside the focus of study of the disciplinary bases from which these authors spoke. Popular culture and mass media became an object of study for educators; children became an object of study for mass media scholars and social psychologists who traditionally had studied adults.

Academic discourse is tied to and is a product of an institutional system of knowledge production: Its rules, procedures, and relations circumscribe its articulation. Institutionalized scholarship articulates its mental production, the labor of discursive practice, in print. The intellectual sparring of contestation, refutation, appropriation, formalization, and marginalization is conducted in the absence of authorial participants on the material, highly ritualized and formalized forums of the monograph and the scholarly journal. The system of rules that underpins the discourse of the university governs, inter alia, who can say what and how. Such discursive rules extend to and are reflected in the criteria and procedures for academic publishing.

Public Opinion Quarterly laid claim early to the discourse on TV and children, as did the *Journal of Education, Review of Educational Research,* and *Genetic Psychology Monographs.* And while these journals shared the cardinal procedural rule of anonymous review—that ostensibly faceless authority of academic censorship empowered to include, invalidate, or exclude discourse—each was and is guided by discourse- and discipline-specific rules that delimit what theoretical choices can be made, what can be enumerated and how, and how an object of study can be conceptualized (cf. Foucault, 1972:181). These discursive choices are signposted via textual markers: titles and headings, discipline-specific lexicon and semantics, and, of course, reference to an acknowledged network of authoritative authors and works. To use momentarily the "positivity" of disciplinary unities, *Genetic Psychology Monographs,* for example, would exclude the formation of a discourse on TV and children that was not principally based on a psychological explanation of the subject in relation to phenomena in the world. Hence, it authorized a psychologizing of the medium-viewer relationship. Similarly, *Review of Educational Research*, for example, would exclude discourse that did not objectify children as pedagogical subjects. In the absence of an established disciplinary niche within which the emergent TV-child discourse could neatly fit, it was mapped, as had been the discourses on children and movies, radio, and comics, across several disciplinary surfaces, each charting a new discursive space alongside and in between traditionally established domains of inquiry. As such, TV and children as objects of study were adrift throughout the 1950s, open to appropriation by adjacent disciplines.

4

1960–1969:
Constructing the Behavioral Subject

This chapter examines how TV and children were constituted in the published academic discourse of the 1960s. Like the previous chapter, this one proceeds chronologically in order that conceptual, theoretical, and methodological transformations can be identified. The 1960s research is divided into three sections: 1960–1963, 1964–1966, and 1967–1969. With the exception of monographs, journal articles are ordered alphabetically for each year.

1960–1963

In 1960, Schramm published the second edition of *Mass Communications*, originally published a decade earlier. The original edition, Schramm notes, "hardly mentioned television; in this volume it has its proper place" (p. xii). Conspicuous by its absence is any reference to mass media and youth: while TV had found its place in mass communications discourse, the TV-child relationship had not. However, Schramm published two more books during the next two years, in which the matter of children and TV was given, in his words, a "proper place."

In 1961 Schramm, Lyle, and Parker published *Television in the Lives of Our Children*, the American counterpart of Himmelweit et al.'s 1958 study of TV and children in Britain. The opening introductory statements specify the authors' position on the relative effects of mass media given audience members' individual backgrounds: "For *some* children, under *some* conditions, *some* television is harmful. For *other* children under the same conditions, or for the same children under *other* conditions, it may be beneficial. For *most* children, under *most* conditions, *most* television is probably neither particularly harmful nor particularly beneficial" (Schramm, Lyle & Parker, 1961:1).

Schramm et al.'s comment still circulates in the discourse today (e.g., Comstock, 1980; Dorr, 1986; Hodge & Tripp, 1986; Luke, 1987), labeled as a "classic" observation, alongside classification of Schramm, Lyle and Parker as "founding fathers of communications" (cf. Dorr, 1986). At the time, Schramm et al. were commenting on the state of the research on TV and children in general as much as on the findings of their own research. In their view, the TV-children debate had been marked by "an impressive lack of agreement" and by the existence of "comparatively few facts to prove any of the points" (1961:2–3).

Based on data derived from questionnaires, TV diaries, and interviews with more than a thousand parents and children, Schramm et al. agreed that TV is not particularly harmful, nor particularly beneficial to children. Children, they claimed, use TV for entertainment, escape, information, and as a social tool: young children use TV primarily to satisfy fantasy needs (p. 170). Children's age, sex, mental ability, social norms, and relationships were considered the most influential indicators of their TV uses (p. 171). Unsatisfactory relationships tend to lead to differential viewing: high ability children reportedly watch more TV whereas low ability children watch comparatively less TV when peer or family relationships are under stress.

Schramm et al. found no evidence of physical effects and emotional effects were found only insofar as very young children tend to get frightened by "violent and stressful programs . . . particularly if they view such programs in dark rooms or alone" (p. 173). Cognitive effects are considered generally insignificant: "in school work" TV is seen as "neither a distinct advantage nor a severe handicap" (p. 173). Schramm et al. note, however, that TV has the potential to become an educational advantage for children if program quality is improved for "informing and teaching the people of a democracy" (p. 173). Behavioral effects are seen in terms of TV violence and aggressive behaviors, and findings indicated that "very little delinquency can be traced directly to television. . . . [it] is at best a contributory cause" (p. 174). Effects are not immediate or even negative, but "cumulative over a long series of exposures to television. This is what we are talking about when we speak of the effect of television on children" (p. 145). Noting that "the term 'effect' is misleading because it suggests that television 'does something' to children," the authors insist on an interactive explanation of the TV-child viewer relationship: "Children are thus made to seem relatively inert; television relatively active. . . .

Nothing can be further from the fact. It is the children who are most active in this relationship" (p. 1).

Schramm edited another anthology on mass communications published two years later in 1963. There he included a chapter on TV and children by Maccoby. That collation of texts was part of a series commissioned and funded by Voice of America, "intended to sum up authoritatively for foreign listeners some of the latest scholarly insights and research findings on a topic of wide interest" (1963:v). Hence, a part of the discourse on TV and children, as selected by Schramm, can be presumed to have circulated—in its material, textual form at least—beyond the physical boundaries of its base of production: the continental U.S. Moreover, without detouring into social history, the sponsorship of the Voice of America could be read as an official "free world," government sanction: The discourse of TV had become, to some extent, recirculated as cold war propaganda. Schramm points out that the essays in this volume represent the heritage of the "founding fathers" of U.S. communications research: the legacy of Lazarsfeld, for instance, inherited by "outstanding young scholars" such as Elihu Katz and Klapper (pp. 2–3). Carl Hovland's legacy, whose "Yale research program between 1950 and 1961 represents the largest single contribution to communication theory any man has made" (p. 5), Schramm bequeathed to Maccoby.

Her chapter "The Effects of Television on Children" reviews some of the then recent research (e.g., Bandura, Ross & Ross, 1961; Himmelweit, 1962; Lövaas, 1961; Mussen & Rutherford, 1961) and briefly discusses some Payne Fund Studies' findings in an attempt to show that a single program (or movie exposure) has been proven to produce effects, but that the "cumulative effects . . . [are] difficult to evaluate" (p. 124). In agreement with Schramm, Maccoby maintains that "the child is not a passive entity . . . but . . . is an active agent, selecting from TV material that which fits his interest and needs best" (pp. 125–126). And TV effects, in this view, can only be seen in terms of a "total environment" (p. 127) within which TV "is not the only, and not even the major, influence upon children's attitudes and values . . . " (p. 125). Maccoby as well as Schramm, Lyle, and Parker clearly reject the notion of TV effects as direct, unmediated, and consistent: "the influence of television is unique with each child" (Maccoby, 1963:126). They also agreed on one social fact: since nearly every household owned at least one set, the post-war generation of children is the first generation in history that rightfully can be labeled a TV generation (p. 117).

Yet the production of "facts" and "truths" about TV and children continued. A minor resurgence of interest in children's mass media preferences and habits appeared in the early years of the decade

(Baxter, 1960–1961; Witty, 1961; Merrill, 1961). Lyness's (1951, 1952) data on Des Moines school children's mass media habits and interests (see Chapter 3) was recirculated in William S. Baxter's (1960–1961) study of a similar sample in the same town. Over a ten-year period, Baxter claims, the place of TV and other mass media in children's lives remained similar to what Lyness had found shortly after the introduction of TV. That is, media interests differed with age and differed between parents and children; content preferences differed among boys and girls; students' description of their and their families' TV behaviors differed from parental descriptions; children overall spent more time with mass media than time spent at school. In all, TV dominated mass media interests among children of all ages, and children apparently spent more time with all mass media than before the advent of TV (pp. 57–58). In other words, not much had changed in the viewing patterns of Des Moines school children over a decade.

Noteworthy in this article, however, is the introduction of a new format. Published in the *Journal of Broadcasting*, which in 1960 was in its fifth year of publication, Baxter's "The Mass Media and Young People" has a subsection on "Method." By contrast, Munn's (1958) publication in that journal (see Chapter 3) included a methods section entitled "Background" followed by "Findings." One of the first articles on TV audiences (Meyerson, 1957) published in the journal's first year of publication had no subheadings whatsoever. This change suggests a shift toward a more structured, scientifically rigorous format for the framing of the textual discourse. Within a five-year period, gone is the essayist style of humanist scholarship, of continuous prose, in favor of a discursive format that valorizes procedure: "method" signifies a far more scientific orientation than does "background." This emergence of a new set of discourse markers signals the movement of the discourse from the disciplinary parameters (and rules of formation) of literary and film criticism, and English education, toward a more formal codification as a social science.

In "Broadcast Viewing and Listening by Children," published in *Public Opinion Quarterly*, Irving R. Merrill (1961) examines how much and when children watch TV. Drawing on combined survey and interview data, Merrill concluded that after 30 months of set ownership, the novelty effect wears off and children's total viewing time decreases; bedtimes for children in radio-only and TV-only households did not differ; parental SES and educational level influenced viewing amount; boys and girls matched for age did not differ in viewing amount; and, finally, radio listening in non-TV households was greater than in homes with TV. While few previous studies had dealt with TV viewing habits of preschoolers, Merrill's study included this age group: "Perhaps the strangest indication of the unusual appeal of television as a medium was the viewing pattern of four- and five-year-olds, who viewed just as much each day as their older brothers and sisters and who chose more frequently to view adult programs after 7 P.M. than the programs intended for children and presented between 4 and 6 P.M. on weekdays" (p. 276). Here, then, the preschooler is constructed not only as a regular TV viewer, but as a consumer of adult TV fare.

A 1958 *Time* magazine article entitled "Opiate of the Pupil" noted that children spent more total time watching TV than in any other activity except sleeping, and that TV had transformed children into "immovable objects" (Witty, 1961:103). In "Televiewing by Children and Youth," Witty (1961) responded to this and other alarmist proclamations by noting that parents and teachers were voicing less concern over TV's effects on children than a decade earlier. Drawing on data from other surveys conducted during the 1950s (e.g., Balogh, 1959; Scott, 1954) as well as from his own questionnaire and interview data, Witty concludes that average viewing amounts do not seem to interfere with reading habits, school achievement, or homework. According to teachers' reports in Witty's study, "In every case of serious maladjustment, the teachers found other contributing factors such as an unfavorable home environment" (p. 110). Witty concludes with the same statements to parents and teachers articulated in his earlier studies: the need for school and parental guidance in children's viewing. The problem with TV, according to Witty, "is a problem mainly in homes where parents allow it to become and remain a problem" (p. 113). Witty situates TV and its possible effects within the context of the family. He remains steadfast in his conviction that parents, not TV, are the problem and that parents, with the aid of the school, can provide the antidote.

Journalism Quarterly published "Who in the Family Selects the TV Program?" (Niven, 1960), which addressed a question previously not considered. Based on interviews with 1,428 housewives from households with at least one TV set and at least one child, Harold Niven concluded that "children of the family are responsible for the highest number of specifically selected programs" (p. 111). According to reports by mothers, children choose programs during the children's hours, whereas the family as a whole tends to select programs after 7 P.M. Yet, who in the family makes the final selection is moot, because fathers apparently select specific programs during the evening more often than mothers or children. Arguably, fathers select prime-time programs for family viewing. Research focus began to move into the family domain and different kinds of viewers—preschoolers, mothers, fathers—were being inscribed in the discourse.

The following year a similar study, "The Selectors of Television Programs" (Smith, 1961–1962) was published in the *Journal of Broadcasting*. In contrast to Niven (1960), however, Don M. Smith found that housewives, not children, select programs in the daytime (85% of the sample), and that housewives (45%) select programs in the evenings more often than fathers (14%) or children (10%), or family (23%). This suggests, then, that mothers decide what (preschool) children watch during the daytime and that mothers predominantly decide what the family watches in the evenings. It follows that whatever effects accrue to children are attributable to parental, particularly mothers', program selection. Programs selected by mothers are not noted, nor does Smith discuss any implications of his findings for children. His argument, instead, focuses on housewives: "unsophisticated housewives" ("low standard of living" and educational level) tend to select programs at a proportionately higher rate than "sophisticated housewives" (high income, college-educated). This difference he attributes to varying interests in TV between the two groups: "in contrast to housewives with a relatively high level of sophistication, housewives who are relatively unsophisticated are more often the selectors of television programs because television is more important to them" (p. 43). Children's viewing, then, is at the whim of mothers who, depending on their level of "sophistication," have differential TV interests. Niven's and Smith's studies exemplify the kind of inconclusive, contradictory evidence which Klapper (1963) and Himmelweit (1962) claimed was endemic to the research on TV and children.

The topic of TV and family life was also taken up by Clara T. Appell (1960) in "Television's Impact Upon Middle Class Family Life" published in *Teachers College Record*. Appell speaks from a sociological perspective, commenting that not much had been published on the impact of TV on family life and American culture. She acknowledges the potential of TV to enrich family life "because it can provide relaxation and education for the family" (p. 274), but also cautions, citing Erich Fromm, of the dangers of marketplace deception and the mass manipulation of individuals' unconscious motives (p. 272).

Appell's middle-class respondents indicated in questionnaires that TV brings the family together and often provides impetus for family discussion, that TV dramas help parents and children discuss family and other interpersonal relationships, and that TV helps stimulate family interests in the cultural arts. Among middle-class families, according to Appell, TV is a problem in households where one or more sets are available: "Disagreements arise over who shall use the receiver with the largest screen" (p. 270). Regarding children's homework and house chores, she notes that "parents feel that children neglect their homework, instrument practice, and chores. This might be related to expectations of middle-class parents regarding their children's achievements" (p. 270). Middle-class families as a special audience—with particular class-based values and (educational) expectations—had not been a special research topic, although family SES had long been incorporated as a rudimentary demographic variable in the construction of a viewer profile.

How family members value TV in relation to other media was examined in "Television's Value to the American Family Member" (Mehling, 1960). From questionnaire and interview data, Reuben Mehling claimed that "with one exception, television was mentioned more than any other medium by all family members" (p. 308) as the one medium they would prefer to keep if asked to give up all except one. Fathers were the one exception, whose preference fell equally between newspapers and TV. High school students and "younger children voted almost exclusively for television" (p. 308). This study indicates very little about the child viewer or about effects; it does not align with any theoretical framework, nor are any references provided. Hence, it is marginal to the mainstream discourse and does not reappear as a citation in subsequent studies.

Parker, coauthor of *Television in the Lives of Our Children* (Schramm, Lyle & Parker, 1961), published several articles in the early 1960s, two of which were based on his 1959 research of two Canadian towns (Teletown, and Radiotown). In "Changes in the Function of Radio with the Adoption of Television" (1961a) he draws on Maccoby (1954) and Baylin (1959) to support his premise that TV has supplanted radio's "fantasy fulfilling function." After a decade of TV, radio has moved into the background—as background sound. TV is said to require more focused viewer attention, and therefore is seen to function as a near total avenue for escape into fantasy. Radio, however, allows "half-listening . . . while engaged in other activities [which] may permit moments of escape from the conflicts of real life into the fantasy world of popular song" (p. 47). Radio provides a "ready escape hatch" while "attention is concentrated on homework lessons or other activities" (p. 47). Comparing such escape-motivated behavior to animal behavior, Parker concludes by noting that "such behavior might be analogous to the behavior sometimes observed in young children or monkeys as they explore a new environment. Temporary returns to the mother or mother-surrogate seem to reassure the young animal and permit renewed explorations of unfamiliar surroundings" (pp. 47–48). Drawing behavioral similarities between children and monkeys was a link not previously suggested quite so explicitly. In "Television and the Process of Cultural Change" (1961b), Parker again tried to show that TV serves a fantasy fulfilling function. According to his findings, children in Teletown did not read fewer newspapers or books, or spend less time on homework than children in Radiotown. He reported that Radiotown children spent more time listening to radio (three hours daily) than children from Teletown (two hours daily). On the other hand, "comic book reading, movie attendance, reading of pulp magazine and radio listening are all displaced by television [which] provides evidence that television is a provider of fantasy materials" (p. 540). Since TV does not displace those activities highly valued by adults, Parker concludes that his evidence "can be viewed as a contradiction of pessimistic claims that television has a negative effect—decreasing learning by taking time away from more serious pursuits" (p. 540).

Parker considers TV as part of a process of cultural change rather than as a cause of change. That is, a new behavioral mode may be "adopted by an individual if and only if such behavior serves his needs more effectively than his present behavior and at least as effectively as each of the available alternatives" (p. 540). In this theorization, the viewer chooses media and media content according to individual needs and perceived utility of media to fulfill those needs. And, in Parker's view, TV serves a fantasy function for children as well or better than traditional sources like the comic book or pulp magazine.

O. Ivar Lövaas claimed in "Effect of Exposure to Symbolic Aggression on Aggressive Behavior" (1961) that exposure to filmed aggression increases aggressive behavior in preschool children. Following B.F. Skinner (1938), Lövaas introduces the notion that "the sight of aggression, like the sight of food, constitutes a discriminative stimulus" (p. 43) to which a response among exposed subjects ("Ss") is conditioned by the absence or presence of a reinforcing stimulus. The films used in this study, as Lövaas notes, "were not unlike those present for children's entertainment, e.g., on TV" (p. 43). Extrapolating from the alleged similarity between the experimental film and commercial TV, coupled with "a growing body of empirical evidence to support generalizations from play behavior to social behavior," Lövaas notes that "the educational implication from this study is that aggressive films are likely to make children more aggressive rather than less aggressive" (p. 43).

He explains in summary of his study: "A bar-pressing response which produced aggressive doll action was observed immediately after the children had been exposed to either an aggressive or nonaggressive film. The study gave evidence for an increase in responding for the aggressive doll action after exposure to the aggressive film when such responding is properly observed" (p. 43). Lövaas's study is a forerunner of what would be considered classic behaviorist laboratory-based research. This mode of research, by the end of the decade, would form a dominant strand in the discourse on TV and children, effectively marginalizing research that did not fit the methodological imperative of experimental treatment and postexposure observation.

Looking to the family as influential in children's televiewing, Robert D. Hess and Harriet Goldman (1962), in "Parents' Views of the Effect of Television on Their Children," consider "a relatively unexamined topic . . . the image that parents hold of television's influence upon their children and the effect that this image has upon the tendency to supervise or regulate their child's viewing" (p. 411). Lövaas's and Hess and Goldman's studies were published in the same year in *Child Development* which, in 1961, apparently was not yet committed to a behaviorist orientation, judging by the inclusion of Hess and Goldman's decidedly nonscientific, nonexperimental study. The data consisted of "face-to-face [semi-structured] interviews with 99 mothers . . . in the home by nonrandom, door-to-door approach" (p. 412). The criteria for selection were age, SES (measured by "occupational level of husband"), and the presence of TV and children between ages 5 and 10 in the household (p. 412). In contrast to Smith's (1961–1962) findings, Hess and Goldman found that according to mothers' reports, "in most homes the young child exercises effective control over the television set during his waking hours" (p. 418). In the majority of families in this study, children are allowed to watch as much as they want and to view programs of their choice. Mothers are said to "make little effort to supervise either program selection by the child or the total amount he watches" (p. 424), and fathers to exercise minimal or no control over children's viewing. Social class, apparently, did not influence children's viewing patterns or mothers' evaluation of the programs children watch (p. 423).

In terms of the image of TV that parents (mothers) in this sample have cultivated, Hess and Goldman found that mothers view TV as alternatively good and bad. Mothers consider it more important to "supervise program content than to regulate the total amount of time a child watches" (p. 424). They considered TV effects as temporary and saw TV "basically as a harmless instrument" (p. 424). Hess and Goldman conflate parents with mothers and make claims for "parental views and images" of TV when, indeed, they gave voice to mothers. In terms of the relation between (mothers') attitudes toward TV and control, no difference was found "in attitudes toward television between mothers who 'say' they prohibit or select shows for children and those who do not" (p. 425).

Noting that research has tended to focus on the measurable effects of particular program types on children's school achievement, reading, and so forth—the authors suggest that long-term "cumulative effect . . . is most difficult, perhaps impossible, to measure in any accurate fashion" (p. 425). In other words, parental attitudes that circumscribe children's viewing contribute to long-term effects, which are unaccountable by (then) contemporary measures in mainstream research. And since parents seem relatively indifferent to children's viewing, what is needed, according to Hess and Goldman, is "a change in the concept of the impact of television" (p. 425). Such a revised concept, if translated into a "concept of norms" and promoted by the public school and church, could provide parents with a set of norms "against which the parent would be inclined to evaluate program content" (p. 425). Hess and Goldman cast the child viewer as an active selector of programs, and conceive of effects as cumulative, long-term, and circumscribed by varying parental involvement in children's viewing. The problem with TV is seen to be in how the medium is used: It is seen as a problem of inadequate criteria by which viewers (parents and children) select programs for rather than against mediocrity. At another, more fundamental level, "This is a problem in socialization of cognitive modes to which the religious, educational, intellectual, and other resources of the society must be brought to bear if we take seriously the goal of adequately developing our greatest natural resource" (p. 425).

Himmelweit's (1962) "A Theoretical Framework for the Consideration of the Effects of Television: A British Report," published in the *Journal of Social Issues*, recasts the data presented in *Television and the Child* (Himmelweit, Oppenheim & Vince, 1958) in relation to a set of principles. These principles, she proposes, will provide "a useful starting point for a systematic program of research . . . and of ordering many of the results of the widely scattered ad hoc studies that characterize so much research in this field" (p. 16). Authorities continued to judge the research as ad hoc, inconclusive, and disjointed. Klapper (1963), too, would revisit the mass communications research the following year and again note the ad hoc nature of mass media studies.

As in the 1958 monograph, Himmelweit (1962) maintains that children's different responses to TV are due to preexisting differences in outlook, values, attitudes, and behaviors rather than due to TV viewing. Young children, she argues, are more susceptible to TV's messages because their worldviews have not been shaped by experience. Furthermore, low-IQ-scoring children watch more TV than high-scoring children; among adults, educational and IQ level, not social class, influence program preferences. After an initial period of heavy viewing and the displacement of traditional leisure activities, Himmelweit finds that the novelty effect wears off and "children read about the same amount as before" (p. 21), attend the cinema as often as before, and maintain involvement in "active sport, outdoor play, companionship with other children . . . [and] club attendances" (p. 21). For Himmelweit, TV functions to fulfill viewer needs, and viewers have to decide among activities that will fulfill those needs: "The individual will sacrifice for viewing most readily those activities which satisfy the same needs as television, but do so less effectively. With the advent of television, the individual is faced with a conflict situation. He has to decide how much to view and how to make room for viewing. Activities which are functionally equivalent, but less effective, will be sacrificed" (p. 20).

Here the viewer is conceptualized as an active selector who chooses from a range of possibilities according to perceived needs. Himmelweit's functionalist orientation fits with Schramm, Lyle, and Parker's (1961) utilitarian conceptualization of media as providing an avenue of escape from social pressures and conflict. Whereas Schramm and his colleagues, and Katz and David Foulkes (1962) the following year, argue that individual viewers' escape into a fantasy world is a positive (nonproblematic) retreat from an alienating or stressful situation, Himmelweit (1962) is reluctant to pinpoint specific social functions and purposes that TV serves for the individual.

Katz and Foulkes (1962) in "On the Use of the Mass Media as 'Escape': Clarification of a Concept," published in *Public Opinion Quarterly*, formally set out a "uses and gratification" model of televiewing. Katz and Foulkes cleave the discourse on mass communications studies into two orientations: one deals with the study of public opinion and the diffusion of new ideas in relation to mass media campaigns intended to persuade rather than entertain; the other approach studies what Katz and Foulkes coin "the 'uses and gratifications' of mass communications" (p. 378). What distinguishes the uses and gratifications approach from "the behavioristically oriented, stimulus-response type of theory which has been prevalent heretofore" (p. 379) is that the approach advocated by Katz and Foulkes "proceeds from the assumption that the social and psychological attributes of individuals and groups shape their use of the mass media rather than vice versa. This is the approach that asks the question, *not* 'What do the media do to people?' but, rather, 'What do people do with the media?'" (p. 378).

Importantly, the research tradition that Katz and Foulkes establish here is not so much a concern with what "people" do with media, but rather with what children do with media. In other words, the series of studies that Katz and Foulkes claim to have been foundational to this approach dealt principally with mass media and children (Riley & Riley, 1951; Maccoby, 1951; Albert, 1957; Baylin, 1959; Pearlin, 1959). These 1950s studies further are aligned historically with 1940s studies appearing in the Lazarsfeld and Stanton radio research series (1941,

1944, 1949). The then most recent research Katz and Foulkes associate with the uses and gratifications approach is Schramm et al.'s *Television in the Lives of Our Children* (1961), which made several important claims about effects at the very beginning of the book (pp. 1–2): "In a sense the term 'effect' is misleading because it suggests television 'does something' to children. . . . Nothing can be further from the fact. It is children who are most active in this relationship. It is they who use television rather than television that uses them. . . . So when we talk about the effects of television, we are really talking about how children use television. A child comes to television seeking to satisfy some need. He finds something there and uses it."

Katz and Foulkes (1962) agreed with Schramm et al. (1961) that the viewer is active, that effects are a function of use, and that use is a function of need. Needs are different for different children, depending upon their mental ability, level of internalization of social norms, social relationships, age, and sex (p. 144). Accordingly, different children use TV to escape boredom or frustration, for entertainment, or for information. However, the "chief needs for which children go to television . . . [are] the needs for fantasy and reality experiences" (p. 170). Unsatisfactory social relationships in the child's environment (school, peers, family) are seen as central in generating the need to escape (p. 172). What Katz and Foulkes (1962) and Schramm et al. (1961) did agree upon was that the media's escapist function was not synonymous with social dysfunction, but that viewers, indeed, select and use media to escape temporarily from an essentially negative social reality.

The discourse on TV and children took a turn with the publication of Schramm, Lyle and Parker's book in 1961, followed the next year by Katz and Foulke's formalization of the uses and gratification "research program." Casting this approach within a tradition by harnessing previous studies and labeling these as foundational to this approach, the Katz and Foulkes text constructs a historical, continuous series within the discourse, while at the same time dissociating this series from the public opinion/mass media campaign strand and the stimulus/response behaviorist orientation. Schramm et al.'s (1961) study, in turn, is heralded by Katz and Foulkes as "one which clearly parallels the emphasis of the present paper" (p. 378). Thus, the Schramm et al. text is incorporated within the newly labeled discourse. That same year, the uses and gratification model (circulating in *Sociological Inquiry*) was associated by Otto N. Larsen (1962:17) with Katz, and Schramm et al.'s study was identified as illustrative of this approach (p. 16).

Klapper resurveyed the then "old communication research road" in 1963 against this backdrop of discursive self-definition. "Mass Communication Research: An Old Road Resurveyed," however, is less of a reappraisal and more of an enthusiastic promotion of the uses and gratification approach: "'Viva los uses and gratifications studies, and may their tribe increase.' We need them badly" (p. 517). Noting those same researchers Katz and Foulkes listed as comprising the "early" uses and gratifications school, Klapper recirculates their studies as early forerunners, but not as "full *functional analyses* in the classic [Mertonian] sense of the term" (p. 516). For Klapper, uses and gratifications research is on the right track, but "if uses-and-gratifications studies are to achieve their potentialities they must . . . proceed further along the road on which many of them have stopped. They must consider not only the observed use, but the *consequences* of that use for the individual user, for social groups, and for society at large" (p. 520). Important for Klapper, then, is that researchers examine the outcomes of specific media-related uses and gratifications in order to identify whether consequences "enhance or maintain the health and integral organization of . . . an individual, a group, or an entire society" (p. 520), or whether certain consequences are dysfunctional: detrimental to or subversive of social cohesion. In order to observe such consequences, Klapper proposes that "We might undertake experiments, within otherwise natural conditions, which collapse the decades of the long-range study to some more easily observable period" (pp. 524–525).

Clearly, Klapper faces a dilemma: how to collapse time to protract long-term effects, yet render them natural and observable. His solution: "Children, whose media tastes are still in process of formation, would seem to be the most logical subjects of such an attempt" (p. 525). The goal-directed nature of school teaching would lend itself as a prototype upon which to build a research model of "induced functional development": "guiding . . . development, overtly or covertly . . . is daily attempted by some teachers, who are primarily interested in the goal rather than . . . the process and modes of achieving that goal. . . . Such a study might serve as a prototype for the kind of induced functional development and accelerated functional analysis that is here being proposed" (p. 525). Klapper, widely considered at the time as an authority, "an old hand at critical surveys of mass communications research . . . a discerning researcher . . . a veteran of seventeen years of active service in the field of communication research" (p. 517), sanctions the uses and gratifications discourse and locates children at the center of the research agenda. Klapper's as well as Katz and Foulkes' texts can be seen as discursive markers, as metacommentaries that attempted to unify a set of texts under one conceptual umbrella. They were deliberate attempts to order one part of what Klapper observed in 1957 (p. 454) to be "a research tradition which supplies . . . a plethora of . . . inconclusive . . . at times seemingly contradictory findings."

Baylin (1962), by contrast, took a different approach in an attempt to unify the discourse. She was editor of a special edition of the *Journal of Social Issues* on "The Uses of Television." This discursive unity itself is indicative of a level of formalization bestowed on the discourse, even though TV as a social issue was readily conflated with social problem. Baylin (1962:1) maintains that only a representative sampling of the diversity of approaches to the same problem can do "justice to the complexity of the problem." In this special issue, alongside Himmelweit's (1962) proposal for a theoretical framework, Baylin includes a discussion of TV in the United States by Bogart (1962) and a discussion of British TV by Raymond Williams. Williams' (1962) entry into the American mass media discourse in the mid-1960s was but a token or guest appearance. Statements such as "capitalist economy," "false consciousness," or "cultural colonization" found no resonance in the discourse. Williams's seminal Marxist/cultural studies orientation was and remained marginal to the U.S. mass media discourse during the 1960s. Until the mid-1980s, there is no evidence of cross-references or citations to his or any other neo-Marxist research in the U.S. mass communications discourse.

In 1963 a large-scale field study "initiated and supported by a grant from the Columbia Broadcasting System to the Bureau of Applied Social Research" was published in monograph form, entitled *The People Look at Television* (Steiner, 1963). As the title indicates, this study was a compilation of public views on TV. A chapter on TV and children reports on parental attitudes toward TV in relation to children and family life. Interviews with 2,498 adults, ages 18 to 70 years, were conducted on weekends and in the evenings over a two-month period in 1960. According to Steiner, parents judge TV for the most part to be more beneficial than harmful for children. One central objection voiced by parents is against violent programs. Gary A. Steiner, however, suggests that such programs are for adults and that parental controls over objectionable programs for children are needed more than a change in program content (p. 106).

In Steiner's view—an authorized set of statements representing (CBS) industry interests as well as his own professional background as a TV writer and producer—the problem with TV's popularized "bad influence" lies not in the programs per se. Instead, he locates direct and sole responsibility for harmful effects with parents (p. 107). And among parents, as the data suggests, "There seems to be a general discrepancy between what parents say worries them most and what they say they do about it. The general impression . . . is that few parents even claim stringent controls over content; the rule in a good many homes, including those that 'oppose' TV for children, is *laissez-faire*" (p. 98).

That this study was commissioned and financed by network funding is evident in Steiner's findings: he suggests that the child suffers no adverse effects from TV and posits TV as a constructive focal point for family life, a veritable hearth which "keep[s] family members at home around a common center of attention" (p. 103). Steiner considers TV a problem for children only insofar as parents neglect to mediate children's viewing by allowing them to watch programs aimed at adult audiences. Although Steiner did not report on "the actual effects as determined by scientific investigation" (Liebert & Sprafkin, 1988:62)—i.e., methodological rules of experimental investigation were not followed—his study did follow the rules of social scientific inquiry, through the large-scale field study of what he considered a representative sample of the average U.S. viewing audience. The study could claim authoritative status by reference to its institutional base at the Columbia University Bureau of Applied Social Research. This organization was headed at the time by Berelson, who was widely considered among social psychologists and academic communications researchers as a distinguished pioneer-scholar of communications research. Stanton, coauthor with Lazarsfeld of several monographs on mass media and public opinion research in the 1940s (1941, 1944, 1949), also was widely considered a preeminent authority on communications research and, as president of CBS at the time of Steiner's study, lent academic credibility and prestige to Steiner's largely corporate-funded study.

At first gaze, the study appears objective enough—the text is liberally augmented by two-tone color charts representing questionnaire responses—and ostensibly detached from the political interests of the funding agency. Yet closer examination reveals a not so subtle orientation toward promotion of a pro-TV discourse. The book was aimed at "the research community, the broadcasting industry, the government officers . . . critics and commentators" (p. x) and was widely cited in the academic discourse following its publication. As such, it counts as part of the authoritative discourse on TV and children, and its stated orientation situates it alongside what Katz and Foulkes (1962) coined the uses and gratifications research, in contrast to the emergent effects research generated by experimental psychology.

A 1963 study published in the *Journal of Abnormal and Social Psychology* noted: "A recent incident . . . in which a boy was seriously knifed during a re-enactment of a switchblade knife fight the boys had seen the previous evening on a televised rerun of the James Dean movie, *Rebel Without a Cause*, is a dramatic illustration of the possible imitative influence of film stimulation" (Bandura, Ross & Ross, 1963:3).

Bandura et al. aligned with previous works on the influence of filmed aggression on children's behavior (Siegel, 1956; Albert, 1957; Lövaas, 1961), with the then recent and definitive study on TV and children by Schramm, Lyle and Parker (1961), and with research on reinforcement in imitative learning conducted with animals (Darby & Riopelle, 1959; Warden, Fjeld & Koch, 1940). Bandura and his colleagues attempted to extend social learning theory along more scientifically rigorous lines (cf. Maccoby & Wilson, 1957) and away from catharsis theory (cf. Siegel, 1956).

Subjects in this experimental study were 48 girls and 48 boys enrolled in the Stanford University Nursery School; the mean age of the children was 2 years and 4 months. Children were divided into three experimental groups: one group was exposed to "real-life aggression" (one male, one female model); the second was exposed to "human film-aggression" (a film of the same "real-life aggression" action); and the third group was exposed to a film of *Herman the Cat* ("a female model costumed as a black cat similar to the many cartoon cats") who was portraying the same aggression patterns as in the two other conditions (p. 4). The aggressive action consisted of a "mallet, and a 5-foot inflated Bobo doll" with which the model interacted in all three "conditions." The discursive construction of those conditions, of behavior, and the human subject speaks for itself:

> In addition to punching the Bobo doll, the model exhibited the following distinctive aggressive acts . . . : The model sat on the Bobo doll and punched it repeatedly in the nose. The model then raised the Bobo doll and pommeled it on the head with a mallet. Following the mallet aggression, the model tossed the doll up in the air aggressively and kicked it about the room. This sequence . . . was repeated approximately three times interspersed with verbally aggressive responses such as, 'Sock him in the nose . . . ' 'Hit him down . . . ' 'Throw him in the air . . . ' 'Kick him . . . ' and 'Pow'" (pp. 4–5).

Children in the experimental groups were moved to another experimental room after exposure to filmed aggression, and their play was observed through a one-way mirror adjoining an observation room. A female experimenter remained in the room, remaining "inconspicuous . . . by busying herself with paper work . . . in the far corner of the room and avoiding any interaction . . . " (p. 5). Children had the choice of aggressive toys (the Bobo doll, mallet, peg board and dart guns, and a tether ball) and nonaggressive toys (tea set, crayons and paper, two dolls, three bears, plastic farm animals, toy cars and trucks) (p. 5). The 20-minute play period was "divided in 5-second intervals by means of an electric interval timer, thus yielding a total number of 240 response units for each subject" (pp. 5-6). A "male model" scored the responses, which were independently checked by another observer. The methodological construct of "televiewing" and the positioning of the child within that context obviously bears little resemblance to any situation a child might encounter outside the laboratory.

The experimental groups were said to exhibit twice the aggression of the control group, which had not been shown the aggressive film. Boys apparently exhibited more "total aggression than girls." Girls were "more inclined to sit on the Bobo doll but refrained from punching it," yet boys who observed the female model were also more likely to sit on rather than punch the doll (p. 8). Sex-appropriateness of the model's behavior, according to Bandura et al., influences children's imitative learning. Filmed aggression "not only facilitated the expression of aggression, but also effectively shaped the form of the subjects' aggressive behavior" (p. 9). Moreover, children's observations of filmed aggression "substantially increases rather than decreases the probability of aggressive reactions to subsequent frustrations" (p. 9). In other words, exposure to filmed or televised violence does not release or "drain" aggressive drives in children, but rather predisposes them to resort more readily to aggressive behavior "on later occasions in the presence of appropriate eliciting stimuli" (p. 9). Since no vicarious reinforcements were given to either the children or the models, Bandura et al. suggest that "a good deal of human imitative learning can occur without any reinforcers delivered either to the model or to the observer" (p. 11).

Bandura, Ross and Ross's study in 1963 followed their 1961 publication on imitative learning, in which the filmed-aggression condition was not included. Their 1963 study marked a step toward methodological refinement. Also in 1963, Bandura and R.H. Walters published *Social Learning and Personality Development*, which argued against the application of psychoanalytic theory to explanations of personality development. In its place, Bandura and Walters proposed that children acquire personalities through vicarious learning: through social experiences with their environment (family, school, peers), a significant part of which is based on learning by imitation and variously sanctioned by positive and negative reinforcements.

These three publications by Bandura and his colleagues set the agenda for a significant part of the research on TV and children for the next decade. Here was an experimental design, unlike Lövaas's (1961) lever-pressing procedure, which could claim unambiguously to describe and explain children's reactions to media content immediately after exposure. Violent film content triggered aggressive behaviors: the photographically recorded evidence was indisputable and the methodology clinically exact. Bandura et al.'s discourse, based on statistical quantifications of behavior, conceptualized the child viewer as one whose behavioral patterns were a function of modeled behaviors; what was experienced was acted upon and acted out. And acting out "responses" was best analyzed by segmenting the analogic continuity of "play" into 5-second units. Effects of a film (the transfer to TV implied) were seen as immediate and not necessarily dependent upon mediating reinforcements. Modeled aggression, in fact, was claimed to be so readily and well learned by children, that future "environmental cues" (e.g., a frustrating experience) might easily elicit hostile behaviors in children. That a laboratory "condition" might not provide accurate data of children's reactions to media content in a naturalistic setting was not an issue for Bandura and colleagues. The peculiarity of the interaction between the "models" and the Bobo doll (classified as "toy"), and the very selection of toys—heavily in favor of male-gendered objects—were also not seen as limitations in methodological design. In all, the principal truth claim made was that modeled aggressive actions, whether filmed or real, cause aggressive behaviors in "exposed" children.

The methodological design and procedure of this study set a new standard, a new rule system, which future psychologically oriented research would follow. The importance of methodological technique over scholarly exegesis and theoretical abstraction, already evident in Siegel's (1956, 1958) and Paul Mussen and Eldred Rutherford's (1961) follow-up study of Siegel's (1956, 1958) and Feshbach's (1955, 1956) catharsis research, gained further momentum with the advent of what became known as the "Bobo doll studies." With Bandura's experiments, behavioral psychology had developed a research strategy that could present objective data derived from tightly controlled laboratory experiments, where hidden observers could score unadulterated behavior. Furthermore, the technique of videotaping behaviors had the potential to render experimenter bias a moot question. Other approaches, questionnaire and interview data, correlational analysis of hours watched, program preferences, and IQ scores, grades, or SES, etc., seemed nowhere near as accurate an indication of TV's effects as direct observation of stimuli inputs and socially uncontaminated behavioral responses.

As researchers began to reconstruct the history of their field during the late 1970s and 1980s, Bandura's (and his graduate students') studies in the early 1960s repeatedly were crowned with emeritus, "founding fathers" status (although several of those founders were women). Such laurels included: "the pioneering investigations of Bandura in the early 1960s" (Siegel, 1975); Bandura as "eminent in academic psychology...for his development of social learning theory...[which] is intertwined with the history of exploring the effects of television on children" (Liebert & Sprafkin, 1988); Bandura's "classic laboratory studies" (Hodge & Tripp, 1986); "granddaddy studies of televised aggression" by Bandura and his students (Dorr, 1986). Behaviorist psychology was making significant inroads into research on TV and children, and its dominance in the discourse had become evident by middecade. However, nonexperimental research continued to probe TV content, viewer uses and preferences, and TV effects on children's learning and socialization.

Illustrative of what Katz and Foulkes (1962:379) called "the behavioristically oriented stimulus-response type of theory" is Leonard D. Eron's (1963) "Relationship of TV Viewing Habits and Aggressive Behavior in Children," published in the *Journal of Abnormal Social Psychology*. This study tried to show that aggressive TV content is related to aggressive behavior in children. Referring to Bandura, Ross and Ross's (1963) work, which showed that "in the laboratory it has been possible to demonstrate that exposure of children to aggressive behavior portrayed in a film increases the probability of aggressive responses to an immediately subsequent frustration" (p. 194), Eron argued that "there is a strong positive relationship between the violence rating of favorite programs, whether reported by mothers or fathers, and aggression of boys as rated by peers in the classroom" (p. 194). Based on interviews with subjects' peers, fathers and mothers, Eron found that amount of violence watched, not total viewing time, was related to viewer aggression. With increased viewing time, aggression apparently drops. This leads Eron to speculate that heavy viewing amount may enable viewers to "discharge their aggressive impulses in this fantasylike way and thus do not have to act them out in real life" (p. 195). Alternately, Eron speculates that heavy viewing may take up so much time that viewers do not have the opportunity to behave aggressively. Eron claims to have no definitive answer for why heavy viewing of violent content is related to aggressive behavior: do viewers with aggressive tendencies chose violent content, does violent content increase aggressive drives, or do viewers imitate (TV) modeled behavior? He maintains, however, that his findings show a relationship between exposure to violent content and aggressive behavior.

In terms of the social relations of viewing, he noted that fathers and mothers differ over their children's viewing habits because fathers "do not know about the child's daytime TV behavior" (p. 196). He furthermore comments that "No consistent relationships were noted between girls' TV habits as reported by either mother or father and aggression as rated in school by the peers" (p. 193). It is quite possible that parents pay less attention to girls' viewing, and therefore parental reports may be less accurate for girls than for boys. Nonetheless, Eron states that one cannot "generalize from boys to girls in research on socialization" (p. 193). Boys here are constituted as a different audience from girls, and TV violence is construed as problematic for boys, not for girls. The concept of the viewer is here loosely constructed according to gender and effects are seen as a function of TV content, not viewing amount.

In response to apparent educational concerns over TV's effects, Joyce M. Ridder (1963) tried to respond to parents' and educators' concerns over "what cumulative effects this passive activity will have upon their children" (p. 204). "Public Opinions and the Relationship of TV Viewing to Academic Achievement," published in the *Journal of Educational Research*, reports on a study that sampled children's opinions about TV, their use of TV, and linked these with academic achievement. Of the 2,428 seventh and eighth grade random sample participants, 84 percent returned the questionnaires and viewing diaries. Ridder concludes: "After . . . comparison of the grades received in English, social studies, and mathematics, and the total amount of time spent viewing . . . it was discovered that there was no significant relationship between academic achievement and the total number of hours spent viewing television" (p. 206).

The viewer is classified by Ridder according to standard educational categories of age, sex, IQ, and scholastic scores; the relationship between IQ and TV viewing is not noted. Instead, Ridder reports on the students' versions of how TV fits into their lives (bedtimes, mealtimes, parental regulation, homework, interest in reading, outdoor activites). Failing to cite a single reference to previous research on TV and school achievement, Ridder does not locate her study in relation to a "traditional" research concern—the relationship between TV and school achievement having long been established as a focal educational issue (cf. Gesselman, 1951; Witty, 1951; Witty & Gustafson, 1957; Scott, 1956; Balogh, 1959). Moreover, Ridder claims no links to a discipline-based theoretical or methodological orientation. If anything, Ridder marginalizes her own text by stating, quite naively for 1963, that "there have been few studies concerning television and the child" (p. 204).

Parker (1963) examined "The Effects of TV on Public Library Circulation," published in *Public Opinion Quarterly*. This study's central, albeit implicit, agenda is to work out a methodological design problem: "The development of the ex post facto before-after design with switching replication to test the hypotheses of this study provides one method for rigorous analysis of nonexperimental data" (p. 589). The vexing problem for Parker is that in mass communications research, "many of the interesting problems cannot be examined by direct experimentation" (p. 589). What appear as by-products of Parker's data, since his aim seems more focused on the validity of his design for hypotheses testing than on the extent of TV's influence on library circulation, are his findings that "library circulations are less after the adoption of television" (p. 585). Yet during that same period, Parker found that juvenile library circulation was greater than that of adults, although this difference was not "significantly influenced by television" (p. 588). Parker claims that although library circulation decreases following the introduction of TV, juveniles nonetheless borrow library books (i.e., fiction) at a greater rate than adults. The implication here is that voluntary reading among adolescents is not negatively influenced by TV although, as Parker notes, rate of book borrowing indicates very little about reading. That "the increase in juvenile fiction circulation is much greater than adult fiction circulation . . . in the television condition" (p. 588) might also imply that TV promotes interest among youth in reading fiction. This contrasts with the "drainage hypothesis" (cf. Eron, 1963:196), which contends that TV watching "funnels off" viewer needs and drives.

Sharpening its focus on audience and network research after a half decade of publication, the *Journal of Broadcasting* came to be less a forum for research on TV and children by the mid-1960s, centering instead more on quantitative research on audience composition, industry economics, policy debates, and network program trends. In "Children's Programming Trends on Network Television," Maurice E. Shelby (1964) traces the "early period" (1948–1952) in children's programming, which he characterizes as a time of experimentation and the introduction of many "quality" programs. Casting a tradition of "founding fathers" by discursive reconstruction—the rearticulation and realignment of authors and texts—is accomplished by the deployment of explicit and implicit rules that also enable the retrospective periodization of "eras." Shelby here reconstructs such historical eras (i.e., children's programming trends) of a discourse not more than a decade in circulation. The "period of adjustment" (1958–1963), in Shelby's view, is one of decreasing program quality for children, and is marked by "speculation that children's programming would decrease in the future, because sponsors would lose interest" (p. 254). Quality programs, because they "could not command audiences large enough to attract sponsors" (p. 254), were judged to be on the wane.

According to Shelby, public response to the drop in quality children's programs was vociferous. As *Newsweek* saw it in 1959, for children who are "too old for Captain Kangaroo and too young for Dick Clark, quality programming . . . is in a virtual vacuum" (p. 256). Unless children were rescued from TV's "wasteland," the "national life" was effectively at stake (p. 257). In 1961, *Newsweek* was still very much outraged: "The junk that floods the air waves during the children's hour comes perilously close to verifying the old suspicion that the average network vice president was without a mother" (p. 254).

The lack of variety of quality children's programs was a concern then as it is today. TV's effects were seen as much the fault of parents who failed to regulate children's viewing (cf. Himmelweit et al., 1958) as of "the industry," which failed to produce quality programs on the premise that such fare would not attract sponsors. As John R. Thayer (1963) had commented the previous year in his "audience composition" study, also published in the *Journal of Broadcasting*, "an automobile dealer . . . would gain little from sponsoring a children's program" (p. 218). In support of the need for "social pressures" on the networks, Shelby enlists the public discourse—statements from *Newsweek*, *The New Republic*, *Time*—to underline the urgency of the need for better children's programs.

1964–1966

In 1964 two content analyses on TV role portrayal were published; one dealt with the portrayal of TV father images, the other with occupational images. "Father Images: Television and Ideal" (Foster, 1964), published in the *Journal of Marriage and the Family*, forwarded the following hypothesis: If TV's father image differed significantly from an 'ideal' father image, or the image a 'real' father was trying to depict, conflict would arise in the child's socialization process (pp. 353–354). June E. Foster (1964) framed potential problems of TV socialization in terms of its long-term cumulative effects on children, and noted the importance of incidental learning in the learning of social roles. In order to conceptualize an "ideal" father image, 24 fathers (15 university faculty members, 7 professionals, and 6 business managers) responded to a semantic differential scale twice over a two-week period, the first time describing themselves, the second describing then current "TV fathers."

Foster interpreted the results to suggest that, for the most part, TV fathers (in "Dennis the Menace," "Father of the Bride," "Danny Thomas") were "less adequate, competent, effective, wise, strong, decisive, consistent, and predictable" (p. 354). The father image in "Lassie" was judged as most similar to the ideal father image. Foster makes no mention of the obvious limitations of her study: the narrow focus of her "ideal" concept derived from upper-middle-class, presumably white males to the exclusion of mothers' and children's conception of an ideal father. Since TV fathers, according to her sample's evaluation, are seen as less desirable than ideal fathers, Foster calls for value clarification: "Teachers . . . can devise television viewing assignments which develop critical observation and evaluation of social roles. . . . Discussion . . . [of] various socioeconomic levels and rural-urban settings. . . . Differences between the television portrayal of father roles . . . can also make for valuable, stimulating discussions" (p. 355). In contrast to Shelby (1964), for instance, who saw the solution to the TV problem in industry responsibility to produce, broadcast, and sponsor more and better quality children's fare, Foster sees a solution to TV's missocialization in teachers and schooling.

Melvin L. DeFleur (1964) in "Occupational Roles as Portrayed on Television," published in *Public Opinion Quarterly*, sets out to analyze the world of work as portrayed on TV and to compare this with children's conceptions of occupational roles and attributes. The content analysis was conducted for 250 half-hour programs broadcast over a six-month period (p. 60). Six- to 13-year-olds were randomly selected from urban and rural areas and were subsequently interviewed about occupational characteristics they considered important. DeFleur cites Schramm et al. (1961) and Himmelweit et al. (1958) in support of his premise that children learn incidentally from TV. Since children spend an inordinate amount of time with TV, "television content undoubtedly plays an important part in the formation of the modern child's conceptions of the world around him" (p. 58). De Fleur speculates that children are socialized by TV into a particular version of the occupational role structure, which may or may not correspond to the world of work that awaits children upon leaving school.

From his data De Fleur concluded that "television tends to make use of stereotyped beliefs and conceptions about a variety of occupations, and to focus upon atypical, dramatic, or deviant aspects of others. . . . As a learning source . . . television content that deals with occupational roles can be characterized as selective, unreal, stereotyped, and misleading" (p. 74). The televised, dramatized labor force, according to DeFleur, overrepresented law enforcement, managerial, and professional roles to the exclusion of less prestigious occupations. Children's most highly valued occupational characteristic is "power," which also characterizes those occupations most overrepresented on TV. DeFleur does not suggest prescriptions for school intervention, but concludes by proposing a "'differential association' hypothesis . . . whereby beliefs and attitudes obtained from television may not be counterbalanced by more realistic information from other sources" (p. 74).

Both DeFleur and Foster view TV effects as indirect and cumulative. For DeFleur, TV is one among many sources of social information to which children are "accidental[ly]" and "haphazard[ly]" exposed (1964:57). Foster, working for the State of Illinois Children and Family Services (1964:353) and, hence, speaking from a site of bureaucratic authority, does not align herself with any disciplinary standpoint and cites no references other than her own master's thesis. De Fleur, Professor of Sociology at the University of Kentucky (1964:57), incorporates children and TV into an established sociological research concern: occupational structures and roles. Speaking from an institutional site of discursive authority, DeFleur's text reflects his membership in the discourse: This is marked by references to a disciplinary corpus and a historical series dating back to Lazarsfeld and Stanton (1944), and the organization of tables and text according to conventional classifications of method, analysis, (viewer) characteristics, summary, and conclusions.

A more technical discourse in "The Effects of Communicator Incompatibility on Children's Judgments of Television Programs" (Greenberg, 1964), published in the *Journal of Broadcasting*, defined child viewers as decoders, or "receivers" whose responses to the TV message were said to be more homogeneous, given a greater degree of compatibility among TV "encoders" (i.e., producers, scriptwriters, directors, etc.). Conversely, "encoder incompatibility leads to grossly heterogeneous viewer judgements" (168). Older children (12-year-olds) demonstrated more "response consistency" than younger children (8-year-olds), which may have to do with "less instrument reliability for the third graders," who may have been "less able to cope with the rating situation in terms of the instrument used" (p. 169). This, in turn, may be a function of their less developed "standards for evaluating what appears on the set" (p. 170). In other words, older children already have been socialized into TV's conventions and will have internalized "the norms of his peers and/or his parents for evaluating television content" (p. 170), which accounts for greater "response consistency" among 12-year-olds. Communication "effectiveness" is thus said to be best achieved when encoders' opinions and judgments are compatible and when such compatibility, transferred to a program, is matched with the appropriate viewer age level. The textual organization of Bradley S. Greenberg's study, like the *Journal of Broadcasting* publications noted earlier, follows the same format: Over half the text is devoted to elaboration of methodological design and procedure, and analysis of results in which the viewer per se virtually disappears.

Reminiscent of Maccoby, Wilson and Burton's (1958) study of differential movie-viewing behaviors (where viewers' eye movements were observed through holes in a screen), eye movements and TV viewing were the focus of what is the classic tachistoscopic study of the decade, published in *Audio-Visual Communications Review*. The title, "Eye Movements and TV Viewing in Children" (Guba, Wolf, DeGroot, Knemeyer, Van Atta & Light, 1964) is misleading: very little is said about TV or children. Children and TV were used in this study not to explore what eye movement responses to moving imagery can indicate about, for instance, attention or learning, but "to develop an appropriate experimental system for the recording of eye-movement data" (p. 387).

Intricate description of the experimental apparatus, the stimulus materials, and data analysis precede "selected findings." Throughout, discourse is couched in acronyms and technical jargon. Despite the obvious problems of generalizing from data of eye movements under the constraint of the "helmet apparatus," to actual eye movements during TV watching in a naturalistic setting, Egon Guba et al. see limitations only with their (small) sample size and the stimulus material. Nonetheless, they conclude that young viewers (21 male and 22 female fifth graders) tend "to focus on a narrator's face when the narrator is present" (p. 401), and that "the majority of low intelligence subjects displayed large amounts of . . . blooming" (p. 394). "Blooming" is when "the eye marker is not on a center of attention" (p. 394): that is, when the gaze begins to wander in an unattentive and unfocused manner. In other words, low IQ scoring subjects apparently are less focused visually when viewing TV—the "dull" viewer of cinema research reappears here. Viewers' IQ was also related to MINs ("minimovements") and NOMs ("no observable movement"): "The curves for intelligence groups differ sharply for NOM's and MIN's. High intelligence subjects display more NOM's than MIN's, while low intelligence subjects display more MIN's than NOM's" (p. 398).

What eye movements can reveal about TV, viewing, or the viewer is not discussed, although it is noted that further experimental research might reveal that certain eye movement patterns "may be related to scene exposure time for maximum learning" (p. 401). Guba et al. conceptualize TV viewing as a physiological response to a visual stimulus, following and reinstating the longstanding reading research tradition initiated by Dearborn, Huey and others in the early twentieth century (cf. Huey, 1906).

Unlike the *Journal of Educational Research*, the *Journal of Experimental Education* had not been a forum for the publication of research on TV and children during the first decade of TV. With "Some Factors Influencing Children's Use of the Mass Media of Communication" (Rush, 1965), "experimental education" entered the discourse or, rather, appropriated children and TV as "factors" for experimental scrutiny. This four-page paper devotes one page to a short introduction, definition of terms, a brief description of the computation for the trend analysis and a short conclusion, followed by four pages of statistical tables. The object of study—children and TV—seems incidental to the study: The greater portion of text deals with description of experimental design, procedure and statistical analyses. In the concluding comments, the child viewer is exscribed altogether: "Though the trend for the latter [parental influence] is not so significant as is the former [peer influence], the trend is evident. The fact that the deviations from linearity are not significant supports the significance of both trends" (p. 302).

Wilmer S. Rush hypothesized that certain factors such as "mode of communication media," "the individual subject," and "grade level" determine children's use of mass media (p. 301). From the "subject responses" (how these were obtained is not stated), Rush found that ninth graders' mass media use (which media also is not stated) is less influenced by parents and peers than that of fifth graders: "As one might expect, there appears to be a significant linear trend with advancing grade level in regard to the factors of friend and parent encouragement" (p. 301). Influences here are conceptualized as "linear trends" and family and peers as "determining factors." The relationships among the child, mass media, and social background are seen in terms of linear coefficients, variance, linearity, and trends. In pursuit of methodological purity, objectivity, and precision, the discourse of science generated statements (cf. Bandura et al., 1963; Greenberg, 1964; Rush, 1965) which removed the object of study—the human subject—from a social context, controlled against extrinsic contextual variables, and recast it into an algebraic network.

David J. Hicks's (1965) replication of Bandura, Ross and Ross's (1963) Bobo doll experiment was reported in "Imitation and Retention of Film-Mediated Aggressive Peer and Adult Models," published in the *Journal of Personality and Social Psychology*. The procedure followed that of Bandura et al. (1963): physical abuse of the inflated doll interspersed with four "verbal stimuli" of "smacko," "take that," "batter up," and "bingo" (Hicks, 1965:98). Six months following the experiment, the children were re-observed (i.e., exposed to a nonfilm frustration condition) to test for content retention. Children who could not readily recall the (aggressive) film shown six months earlier were bribed with a candy reward: "When the children indicated memory of the exposure the experimenter produced a large candy sucker and informed the children that she would give them the sucker if they could tell her all the things they had seen on the film. The sucker was withheld until a child was consistently incorrect or obviously had terminated effort to recall" (p. 99). Prodding children for a response with promise of a reward may very well increase the mental effort to recall events or images which, in the context of children's everyday affairs, might be otherwise forgotten. Yet Hicks takes the information derived from his subjects under manipulated conditions to indicate that "exposure of children to aggressive films appears to remain a relevant antecedent in shaping the form of their aggressive responses for a considerable length of time" (p. 100).

Girls, according to Hicks, and to Bandura and Walters (1963), exhibit lower "imitation scores" than boys. This Hicks attributes to the influence of differential gender socialization, albeit a "psychologized" socialization: "The relatively low imitation scores obtained by girls could be attributed to either response inhibition or inhibition of observational tendencies" (Hicks, 1965:100). Hicks concludes that his study confirms Bandura et al.'s (1963) findings "that exposure to filmed aggression effectively shapes the form of children's aggressive responses" (Hicks, 1965:100). Many more experimental studies (e.g., Geen & Berkowitz, 1966, 1967; Berkowitz & Geen, 1966, 1967; Walters & Willows, 1968; Hartman, 1969) would confirm Bandura's findings, and all would conceptualize the viewer as a defenseless response mechanism in relation to the potent filmed or videotaped (behavioral) stimulus.

Based on a less scientific and, certainly from the point of view of behavioral psychology, on a more traditional sociological approach, "Newspapers or Television: Which Do You Believe?" (Carter & Greenberg, 1965) reports on a telephone survey of 500 adults. The study aimed to establish which of the two media has more credibility with adults. This study does not deal with children, but is included here because Richard F. Carter and Bradley S. Greenberg recirculate Schramm, Lyle and Parker's (1961) findings concerning the credibility that children assign to either medium. In subsequent media related research, even that which did not focus on children, statements referring to Schramm et al.'s (1961) and Himmelweit et al.'s (1958) studies would continue to circulate.

Noting that there "has been relatively little systematic research of the common assumption that the mass media constitute a significant agency of socialization" (Gerson, 1966:40), "Mass Media Socialization Behavior: Negro-White Differences" reports on the differences in media use and socialization between black and white adolescents. For the most part, race as a viewer classification had not been included in previous TV viewer definitions. By the mid-1960s, however, questions of race could no longer be ignored by any discourse in the human sciences. Race had been included by Haines (1955) as one characteristic of the juvenile delinquent profile, since among "coloreds," low educational levels, low SES, drug use, alcoholism, crime, and heavy TV viewing (specifically of violent programs) seemed to coincide. But race as a viewer classification had been largely ignored by the dis-

course until the mid-1960s, when black viewers, juxtaposed to constructs of white viewers, became an identifiable viewer construct
within mass media discourses.

Pointing out that "direct effects are not emphasized" in his study,
Walter M. Gerson situates himself within the "functional," "situational," "phenomenistic," and "uses and gratifications" orientations exemplified in the works of Klapper, Katz and Lazarsfeld, Himmelweit
et al. and Schramm et al. (p. 40). His research questioned: "How do
persons with different statuses and in different social structures use
the media and what are the resulting gratifications and consequences?" (p. 41). Gerson's comparative analysis was based on questionnaire data of "272 white persons" and "351 Negroes" (p. 42); 49 percent
of the total sample consisted of boys and the median age of the total
sample was 15.2 years. Gerson finds that "under almost every condition . . . more Negro than white adolescents used the media as an
agency of socialization" (p. 48), and that "many Negro adolescents are
using the mass media to learn how to behave like whites (i.e., behave
in a socially acceptable way)" (p. 49). Gerson cautions against using
race to explain differential media use among black and white adolescents: "race is merely a socially visible variable about which data have
been gathered . . . racial status is often an indicator of a great many
other factors. . . . These *other* factors are important to a discussion of
"causal" factors" (p. 48).

Gerson observes that "Negroes and other minority groups generally
receive unfavorable symbolic treatment in the presentation by the
media to the broader society" (p. 48). Coupled with black adolescents'
increasing "interaction (through high school) . . . [with] the white-
dominated broader community" (p. 49), this may explain why the
"mass media may represent an agency of the broader community from
which the Negro adolescents can learn to behave in ways acceptable
in the white community. The media constitute an alternative structure
through which symbolic anticipatory socialization can occur" (p. 49).
Gerson speculates that "geographic mobility . . . increases media
socializing for Negro adolescents, but not for whites" (p. 50) and that
for black children in an era of community and educational desegrega-
tion, "relatively large adjustments" (p. 50) need to be made for which
the "Negro subcommunities may not be equipped to advise and direct
youngsters" (p. 49). Hence, black adolescents are "forced into using
the media for socialization purposes" (p. 50).

Gerson introduces the black (adolescent) viewer into the discourse
and conceptualizes the black viewer as one who uses the media for
functional social purposes in efforts to "fit in" with a white society to
which limited entrance has only recently been granted. Media effects
are implicitly seen as positive: the media provide a "convenient nor-

mative source to help him [the Negro] make new adjustments in a dominantly white world" (p. 45).

James W. Carey (1966), by contrast, proposed that blacks select those programs which most closely relate to "Negro culture and social structure" (p. 207). In other words, according to Carey's interpretation of his data, black viewers don't prefer certain programs because they can learn from them the ways of the "white world," but rather they prefer those with which they most closely identify. Carey's study reports on black adult program preferences, but he draws some implications for children that are worth noting.

"The larger size of Negro families" suggests that "such families are more strongly influenced by the taste of teen-agers and children" (p. 210). Children's influence on program selection reflects in the high rankings given by black adults to programs aimed primarily at teenagers and children: "What is striking about many programs rated highly among Negroes, is the degree to which they are programs beamed at youth. . . . For example, in the 1964 rankings "Hullabaloo" was first and "Shindig" third among Negro audiences, whereas they ranked 39th and 35th among white audiences" (p. 209). Carey interprets this preference pattern, noting that "this [music/dance program preference] leads to the suggestion that part of the difference in Negro/white preferences stems from the relatively greater importance of children and teenagers in the selection patterns of Negro households" (p. 209). He makes no claims about effects but emphasizes the importance of taking into consideration "ethnic, religious, regional, and generational group" (p. 199) differences among audience segments, which can indicate "how the structure of group life has some influence over the character of television preferences" (p. 211). Carey's expanded definition of the TV viewer, then, includes race and ethnicity as influential on program selection. Blacks, heretofore absent from the discourse on TV and children, are constituted by Carey and Gerson (1966) as part of the viewing audience.

Witty (1966) summarizes 15 years of research findings in "Studies of Mass Media: 1949–1965" published in *Science Education*; a near verbatim reproduction of this study was published the following year in *Elementary English*. Arguably, the rules governing the production of discourse in professional teachers' journals were not as stringent as those regulating academic discourse, wherein publication of the same text in different journals is indeed prohibited by one of scholarship's most coveted and stringent rules. Sixteen years had elapsed since the publication of his first survey of children's TV preferences and uses, and seven years had elapsed since the publication of the final study in his ten-year longitudinal research (1957), but his message remained basically the same.

Witty observes that over the years, research reports on parental mediation of children's viewing had remained the same: few parents regulate children's viewing. To this end, he again notes that "TV is a problem chiefly in those homes in which parents permit it to become and remain a problem" (p. 126). As in his previous studies, he offers an "antidote" by proposing "a constructive program of guidance at home and in school" (p. 126). Violence, according to Witty, is now a primary concern for parents and teachers who, in previous years, "have complained less frequently about the character of TV programs for children. The criticisms now center mainly in questioning the excessive amount of violence depicted in programs children see" (p. 121).

Witty sees children's program choices in the 1960s as limited by program offerings. Whereas in 1951 children listed "Crusader Rabbit" as their favorite program, a decade later this had been replaced by "Twilight Zone"; by 1965 this was replaced by "Man from U.N.C.L.E." (p. 120). Witty rejects the televiewing–juvenile delinquency equation and agrees with Klapper's (1960) suggestion that TV violence may influence those children already predisposed to aggression. Noting "the scarcity of dependable research on these topics [of violence]" (p. 124), Witty outlines and tersely comments on Bandura's Bobo doll study. While the results show direct behavioral effects, Witty adds that "the children were 'mildly annoyed' before the observations took place" (p. 125).

Reading apparently had not decreased among the TV generation: children reported reading as much, and in many cases more, in 1965 as during the early 1950s. "Reading of books," Witty finds, "generally was just a little greater after TV, but still meager in comparison with televiewing" (p. 122). Watching TV reportedly had not decreased reading amount, but the overall time devoted to reading in contrast to televiewing remained low: "about three hours daily to TV and only one hour to reading" (p. 122). No relationship between TV and school achievement was found, and the initial gains in vocabulary of young children from TV homes were found to level off once schooling begins. Witty concludes, as he had for over a decade, by calling for parental and teacher guidance in helping children "choose programs with greater discrimination" (p. 126).

In contrast, Warren S. Blumenfeld and H.H. Remmers (1966) did find a relationship between program preferences and grades among 2,000 high school students. "Television Program Preferences and Their Relationship to Self-Reported High School Grades" was published in the *Journal of Educational Research*. No references are made to previous research on viewing patterns among high school students. Instead, the two-page text cites four references, of which three refer to studies of statistical evaluation methods; most of the paper is devoted to discussion of evaluation procedure and data analysis. High school students who watch more than one hour of news and documentaries weekly, according to Blumenfeld and Remmers, received higher grades. Conversely, "preference for movies, westerns, cartoons, mysteries, detective stories, variety, and music and dance was associated with reported lower grades" (p. 359). The authors, however, beg the question of effects by concluding that "no cause and/or effect is to be inferred; but these data are meaningful as ends in themselves" (p. 359).

1967–1969

Leonard Berkowitz and Russell G. Geen and, alternately, Geen and Berkowitz, published several studies in 1966 and 1967, all based in part on Bandura's social learning theory and on Berkowitz's (1964, 1965) earlier studies of disinhibiting aggressive cues. These authors set out to disprove catharsis theory and to further refine Bandura's social learning theory. For Berkowitz and Geen, witnessing aggression—whether filmed or real, with or without reinforcements—was seen to trigger aggression in individuals and not, like catharsis theory postulated, to serve as vicarious release for sublimated aggressive drives. Their studies used white male college students, not children, as experimental subjects. All were given course credits for participating in the experiments. Although the object of inquiry was not children per se, the findings produced by Berkowitz and his coauthors contributed significantly to the debate over TV violence and children (cf. Liebert & Sprafkin, 1988).

Using an "aggression machine," subjects administered electric shocks after a variety of combined exposures to and reinforcements of aggressive and anger-arousing stimuli. The Bobo doll experiments were widely considered at the time to have reached new heights of methodological ingenuity in scientific investigation. If, in retrospect, the Bobo doll experiments seem patently nonsensical, then these electroshock experiments surely illustrate the pinnacle of empirical absurdity.

In brief, the Berkowitz and Geen studies (1966, 1967; Geen & Berkowitz, 1966, 1967) claimed that exposure to aggressive modelling does not have a cathartic function in exposed subjects but, rather, elicits aggressive responses. The link to TV violence was obvious: watching violent content would generate aggressive behaviors in viewers. That TV viewing for most children occurs in the context of family life, which includes coviewing with family members, implicit and explicit parental (and school reinforced) sanctions against aggressive and violent behaviors, seemingly was not relevant to the discourse of behavioral psychology. For example, that individuals in everyday contexts do not have access to levers with which to administer electric shocks to "confederates" was never considered a possible conceptual limitation with which to qualify laboratory findings. The viewing subject was conceptualized as a mindless and morally bankrupt victim of stimuli who could be manipulated in various experimental conditions to elicit almost any combination of responses. The discursive rules of experimental psychology had dissected the human subject into the smallest, methodologically possible behavioral "bits": each bit seen as equivalent to behavioral information which, in its minutest detail, explained increasingly less about the complexity of human behavior in everyday contexts.

Given the general research orientation on TV and children—at the time, increasingly a search for effects and for an accurate model with which to measure effects—"Television for Children" (Garry, 1967), published in the *Journal of Education* (1967), is a somewhat anomalous contribution to the discourse. This paper was derived from two seminars, one held in the U.S. and the other in Europe, at which TV producers in both countries discussed children's TV programming. The lengthy 46-page text is a detailed description and discussion of the educational merits of the programs under focus. Ralph Garry argues that TV does have verifiable effects in children. But what exactly such effects are and which children are prone to what kinds of effects is uncertain (p. 44). Despite a decade and a half of research, one irrefutable fact remained: Most researchers seemed to agree that effects remained elusive. Garry calls for a better-orchestrated set of broadcasting policies to govern children's TV, one in which "philosophy, policy, and action" coincide (p. 45).

This article introduced policy-related issues regarding children's TV—which had circulated predominantly in the more communications/broadcasting-oriented journals (e.g., *Journal of Broadcasting, Journal of Communication*)—to the educational discourse, and introduced the most detailed and comprehensive transcriptions to date of the audio and visual tracks of numerous children's programs. Child viewers since the advent of TV had been demographically and statistically dissected and exposed on grids of intersecting variables; the TV program, by contrast, had heretofore escaped such scrutiny.

S. H. Lovibond (1967) examined "The Effect of Media Stressing Crime and Violence Upon Children's Attitudes," published in *Social Problems*. This text classifies media effects on children as a social problem. Lovibond administered Likert scales to 374 eleven- to 15-year-old boys; one scale sought to measure exposure to violent media (comics, movies, TV), the other to measure exposure to "constructive moral influences" (p. 91). Seven pages of the 10-page paper are devoted to "method," "analysis," and an appendix of the "Children's CF [ideology of fascism] Scale" (pp. 92, 99–100). Instead of conclusions, Lovibond ends with a section entitled "Ideology and Action" (p. 98). In a rather unusual mix of critical theory and empiricism, Lovibond finds "effects" on one hand and invokes Adorno on ideology on the other. His Likert scale data revealed that increased media violence exposure is related to an increased "CF Scale score": children who prefer TV crime and violence are also heavy viewers and tend to hold attitudes that reflect an "ideology of crime and violence" (p. 96). However, such an ideology need not "manifest . . . in delinquent acts" (p. 98), for "if as Adorno and his associates argue, 'ideology in words and ideology in action are essentially the same stuff,' one would expect that, under appropriate circumstances, acceptance of an ideology will result in active behavior congruent with such a system of ideas. Under other circumstances . . . acceptance of an ideology may manifest itself in a *failure to take action*" (p. 98).

Lovibond speculates that children who are exposed to substantial media violence will tend to commit delinquent acts if countervening moral influences and legal sanctions are weak, and if opportunities for such acts present themselves. Yet, for the "majority of children," exposure to media violence is more likely to manifest itself in decreased opposition to delinquency and a "decreased readiness to take humanitarian principled action when the situation demands that such action be taken" (p. 98). Lovibond proposes here that exposure to media violence does have empirically verifiable attitudinal effects, but that behavioral manifestations of such attitudes are not necessarily predictable or consistent. Whereas Bandura et al. (1961, 1963) proposed that exposure to media violence causes aggressive action, Lovibond links media violence not with action, but with inaction. Finally, although Lovibond presents evidence for effects, he dismisses a "one-way causal relationship": "It is probably that there is a circular feedback component in the causal chain, such that a taste for violence is reinforced by exposure to portrayals of violence in the various media, leading to increased exposure" (p. 98).

Walters and Donna C. Willows (1968) and Donald P. Hartman (1969) sought to support Bandura's social learning theory by experimenting with male adolescent delinquents and "disturbed" and "non-disturbed" children, respectively. Both studies argued against catharsis theory and, instead, claimed to have shown that "observation of filmed or televised violence is likely to generate violence in the observers" (Walter & Willows, 1968:80).

"Imitative Behavior of Disturbed and Nondisturbed Children Following Exposure to Aggressive and Nonaggressive Models" (Walters

& Willows, 1968) was published in *Child Development* and follows the rule system of the methodological model of 1960s experimental psychology: a detailed description of methodological design and procedure and analysis of statistical treatment takes precedence over theoretical considerations. Hartman's (1969) study noted below is similarly preoccupied with methodological minutiae. Implying that Himmelweit et al.'s (1958) and Schramm et al.'s (1961) large-scale field studies have not shown any influence of violent TV on children's behaviors because their data was not derived from direct observation in a laboratory setting, the authors set out to show that under controlled conditions both disturbed and nondisturbed children will display varying levels of aggressive behaviors following exposure to modelled (filmed) aggression. In contrast to Bandura et al. (1961, 1963), Walters and Willows's data suggested a rather low incidence of imitative responses. But this discrepancy is attributed to a difference in testing period, a "procedural difference" (p. 87). Although admitting to a low "incidence of aggressive behavior following exposure to an aggressive model" (p. 87), the authors conclude that their findings nevertheless support the hypothesis that children exposed to an aggressive model will display more aggressive behavior than non-exposed children, "at least within a short time-span after exposure to the model" (p. 87).

In support of Bandura's research, Hartman (1969) also set out "to assess the effects of exposure to instrumental aggressive responses and pain reactions upon subsequent aggressive behavior" (p. 281). Hartman produced these findings: under all conditions, subjects—72 "male adolescents who were under court commitment to the California Youth Authority" (p. 282)—exposed to modelled aggression behaved more punitively (measured through shock intensity administered to the provocateur). Subjects who witnessed "pain cues" from the victim behaved more punitively than subjects exposed only to instrumental aggression. Subjects with "longer records of antisocial behavior delivered more aversive stimulation than subjects with less extensive records" (p. 280). Noting that his findings contradict the traditional catharsis hypothesis, Hartman makes his case for conceptualizing a positive relationship between modelled (filmed) aggression and aggressive behaviors. Of the experimental subjects, "22 percent were institutionalized for highly aggressive offenses, for example, strong-armed robbery, assault, and fighting, while the remaining 78 percent had committed a wide variety of lesser crimes" (p. 282). Generalizing to the general male adolescent populace from an incarcerated sample is conceptually highly suspect. Yet, Hartman provides no indication that he even recognizes the need for qualifications of his data or conclusions.

In what by the late 1960s was seen by academic psychologists as an established domain of inquiry—experimental research guided by social learning, instigation, and, to a lesser degree, catharsis theory—children and TV came to be a focus of intense scrutiny and research activity. Children emerged on the disciplinary field of experimental psychology in the context of Bandura's initial work on social learning theory: a construct that focused on a crucial formative stage of development. And, as Bandura maintained, children learn from their social context, of which the modelling of behaviors by family, school, and peers is but one component.

By the late 1960s, TV was an integral part of family life, seen to be one such modelling agent. At this juncture in the discourse, the intersection of a particular theoretical elaboration with a prevailing dominant (methodological) rule system reflected an epistemological stance that viewed social action in terms of quantifiable, observable microbehaviors, made possible by a particular discursive formation—a particular set of knowledges about the subject. Within this discursive network, children and TV emerged as a theoretical and methodological construct that tried to circumvent the problem of the highly contingent TV-child relationship. In the estimation of researchers committed to experimental psychology as the most objective human science, the laboratory experiment was seen to ensure the kind of rigorous and unadulterated analysis required by the TV-child problem: it was seen as free from interference from uncontrollable social context, experimenter bias, and the inaccuracies of subjects' self-reports.

Hence, the discourse of experimental psychology quickly established itself as a very influential research approach yielding scientific, incontravertible evidence of TV's effects on children. Already in 1968, a selective bibliography of children's TV use and effects (Abel, 1968–1969) categorized effects research separately from research on TV use. The entries under "Psychological Effects" research far outnumber the studies listed under "Children's Use of Television" and nearly half of the psychological studies are experimental. Most of these were published in the *Journal of Abnormal and Social Psychology*.

The years 1968 and 1969 saw a minor surge of studies on a widely neglected variable in the TV-child relationship: parents. Parents previously had figured in the discourse only as background classifications of their televiewing children. The most common symbolic representation of parents had been constituted in categories of SES, income, and educational level. Although the apparent widespread lack of parental involvement in children's viewing had not gone unnoticed (e.g., Witty, 1950, 1967; Himmelweit et al., 1958; Schramm et al., 1961), parental attitudes towards, perceptions of, and role in their children's televiewing had been largely neglected. Studies by L. Erwin Atwood (1968), Barbara Wand (1968), Ruth Young, (1969–70), and F. Earle Barcus (1969) situate parents in a prominent position within the discourse. The general suggestion of these studies, with the exception of Atwood, is that the traditional TV-child relationship has been miscast because it has excluded parents who are, in the first instance, the most important influence on that relationship. Instead, the authors argue that effects or uses can only accurately be accounted for if the TV-child relation is reconceptualized into a triadic model of TV, children, and parents.

How well parents and teenagers predict each others' viewing preferences is the topic of Atwood's (1968) *Journal of Broadcasting* study, "Perception of Television Program Preferences among Teenagers and Their Parents." Q-sorts and factor analysis were used to study 11 high school students and their parents. What hypotheses Atwood sought to test, or what he hoped to uncover by an analysis of perception of program preferences, is not clearly set out. One obvious intent of this kind of study would be a comparison between perceived preferences and actual viewing patterns, but as Atwood puts it, "the extent to which any of the stated or perceived preference patterns reflects actual viewing behavior is unknown" (p. 378). In short, Atwood found that "teenagers are only slightly better at predicting the strong likes and dislikes of their mothers and fathers than are the parents at predicting the strong likes and dislikes of their teenagers" (p. 381). Fathers, typically, are cast as absentee parents. Fathers are said to make more errors in predicting their children's program preferences than mothers, predicting falsely, for instance, that their teenagers like "Lawrence Welk" and dislike "Shindig."

Although Atwood admits that "the small number of people in each of the preference type groups tends to make these data unreliable, and no conclusions can safely be drawn" (p. 385), he does venture beyond the obvious and suggests that "parents may be predicting the teenager's viewing behavior rather than program preferences (p. 386). This, he speculates, could be the result of parents basing their predictions on observed viewing behaviors: "teenagers watching programs their parents have selected while the parents . . . refuse to watch the programs the teenagers would have otherwise chosen" (p. 386). In light of the absence of conclusions, the unstated implications of such a study, as Witty had noted for over a decade, are that parents do not participate in their children's viewing and, hence, in regard to teenagers, the adolescent is a solitary viewer of the programs s/he likes.

Differences of choice in family viewing was investigated by Wand (1968) in "Television Viewing and Family Choice Differences" published in *Public Opinion Quarterly*. Based in part upon a 1964 study of 198 Ottawa (Canada) households and 180 Sydney (Australia) households, Wand used interviews and viewing diaries to determine to what extent individual choice and conflicting choices among household members influence family viewing patterns. Wand rejects the notion that viewers watch indiscriminately, and that viewers are passive participants being led by "lead-ins" from one program to the next: "The concept of inertia, and the broadcasting term, 'lead-in,' assumes that watching one program increases the probability that the following program will be watched. Both concepts tend to further the idea that viewing is not a matter of choosing in an active sense but is, rather, the resultant of forces operating outside the control of the person" (pp. 84–85). Instead, she claims that her data provides "some basis for arguing that television viewing is a much more sensible, orderly, and even purposeful kind of behavior" (p. 85).

The data from her sample suggested that in the case of conflict over program choice between children and parents, final selection decision falls equally between parents and children. Selection tends to be dominated by parents in families where children are "younger," presumably preadolescent. In older families, mothers and fathers reported less choice differences between young and old, and children in these families "were involved in a larger proportion of the family choice differences" (p. 92). In choice differences between parents of older children, fathers were reported as making the final decision in the first set of interviews, whereas mothers were reported as final selectors in the last set of interviews. This discrepancy, Wand speculates, may have to do with a "discrepancy between role expectations for the father and his actual behavior . . . [and] an attempt to present the father in his idealized role" (p. 89). Overall, Wand finds that most viewing is "related to expressed choice" (p. 86). What Wand means is that "viewing appeared to be less passive than it has often been supposed. Individuals did not tend to view programs in which they had not previously expressed an interest. Second, families were not as likely to subordinate personal choice to family viewing 'togetherness' . . . [and] did not tend to view as a group unless the program reflected some interest common to parents and children" (p. 93). Finally, for Wand it seems that TV does not bring the family unit together: "Perhaps the concept of television as a family medium has been misleading in some ways" (p. 93). Here Wand suggests that adult and young viewers watch TV more in isolation than in the family group. In Atwood's (1968) study, too, the teenage viewer was a solitary viewer. For Wand, however, this reflects viewers' purposive and active selection of TV programs.

Suggesting that "'children and television' has become a popular though false issue in many circles," Young (1969–1970) also implies that the familial context within which children's viewing occurs generally has been overlooked by researchers. Young provides no original research: "Television in the Lives of Our Parents," published in the *Journal of Broadcasting* (1969), is written in essay form and relies predominantly on Schramm et al.'s (1961) and Himmelweit et al.'s (1958) studies, from which she draws research evidence in support of her argument. The *Journal of Broadcasting*, strongly committed to quantitative research, here makes an exception with the publication of a polemical essay.

Young argues that the search for effects in response to two decades of public complaints about alleged TV effects on children has falsely centered on the wrong issues. The key to understanding children's use of TV—and, hence, potential effects—here is seen to lie with parental use of and attitudes toward TV. Parental decision, or indecision, about the use of TV in the home is a critical factor in children's exposure to TV. According to Young, parents inherently are the most closely involved with children's viewing, yet "it is generally the parent who is least informed of the real issues at stake, and even if informed, is often least capable of coping with the situation" (p. 37).

For Young, parents, rather than effects inferred from test scores, school grades, or observed behaviors, are the real issue in the TV-children debate. And because of the intrinsic diversity of family values, behaviors, and attitudes even within the same demographic grouping, the "effects of television can never be generalized to all individuals" (p. 37). Whereas Smith (1961–1962), Atwood (1968), and Wand (1968) had hinted at the importance of parental influence in children's viewing, Young considers parental use of and attitudes toward TV as fundamental to a more realistic and comprehensive understanding of the "larger problem" of TV and children. Young's selective use and combination of the Schramm et al. and Himmelweit et al. data associates her concept of the child viewer more closely with the uses and gratifications model of televiewing. Moreover, the child's use of the medium is seen as strongly influenced by parental use of TV. The alleged indifference most parents show for their children's viewing, however, suggests that children's use of the medium is mediated by parental influence only insofar as such mediation is absent. Paul W. Musgrave (1969) draws the same conclusions from his study of parental control over TV use by Scottish children, and is left wondering "what effect this comparative freedom from control has on children" (p. 278).

Published in *Television Quarterly*, "Parental Influence on Children's Television Viewing" (Barcus, 1969) proposes an analytic model for examining parental influences on children's viewing. This is the first appearance in the discourse of a conceptual frame with which to analyze parental influence. A decade later, this conceptual template would become a fundamental component for the promotion of media literacy: constructive parental intervention. The "time influence" dimension, for instance, is categorized according to differential levels of parental involvement prior, during, and after viewing. This involvement is identified in terms of "discussion," "selection," and "explanation." "Formal and informal controls" are examined in terms of set rules and regulations and "de facto controls—discussions, viewing with children" (p. 65). Here a whole new dimension of parental influence on children's viewing was proposed, one that transcended the static indicators of SES or educational level conventionally used to signify parental influence.

Barcus, like Young and Atwood, also comments on the lack of parental supervision of children's viewing, noting that if and when parents do exercise controls, these are commonly regulations for time and amount viewed, not specific TV content (p. 64). Forty-four mothers were interviewed and given questionnaires; Barcus provides no statistical analyses, no tables, and no lengthy description of methodological design and procedure. Instead, he provides a detailed account of the mothers' responses, weaving their voice throughout his argument. This "phenomenistic" approach, as Klapper (1957) had called it, never did take hold in the discourse on TV and children—children, parents, and viewing habits all had remained fixed on the grids of statistical quantification. Himmelweit et al.'s and Schramm et al.'s studies, which appeared in monograph form, are exceptions: they did give subjects a voice, perhaps because the monograph—unlike the more restricted, rule-bound journal article—enabled the material space on which to elaborate subjects' responses beyond their numerical quantification. On the other hand, the discursive rules governing the production of discourse in *Television Quarterly* were less scientifically oriented than, say, *Child Development*, in which the essayist's prose or qualitative data had no place whatsoever.

In all, Barcus found that almost half of his sample claimed to regulate and participate in their children's viewing. For the most part, mothers reported that they exercised control after viewing, rather than prior or during viewing, and the two most commonly cited reasons for imposing viewing controls were "fear that the child may be adversely affected by premature exposure to the adult world, and . . . a general belief that TV viewing is less important for a child than other activities" (p. 71). However, Barcus found that "parents generally have positive attitudes toward TV and its influence on their children" (p. 72). Apparently all mothers in his sample, those who exercise controls and those who do not, "believe that their children derive more good than bad from TV, especially in social interaction and ethics" (p. 72). Finally, Barcus shies away from prescriptions for channeling children's viewing toward exclusively quality programs and, instead, suggests that, "with proper interpretation, even *Peyton Place* might offer the parent an opportunity to discuss 'real life' topics that could help bridge the generation gap" (p. 73).

Two studies published in 1969 (Thelen & Soltz, 1969; Greenberg & Dominick, 1969) focused on racial differences among young viewers and their use of and learning from TV. Both approached the same topic, albeit from radically divergent disciplinary perspectives. Both, however, helped shape and give prominence to an emergent construct of the black viewer.

"The Effect of Vicarious Reinforcement on Imitation in Two Social-Racial Groups" (Thelen & Soltz, 1969), published in *Child Development*, reports on a replication study of Bandura's Bobo doll experiments. Two experiments are reported, the second of which was conducted "because of unexpected results in the first experiment" (p. 879). A control group, a human (reinforcement) model, an inflated clown, an aggressive film strip, an adjacent room for postexposure observation through a screen, an impartial observer unfamiliar with the experiment—all replicated precisely the Bandura procedure.

The principal finding from the first experiment "demonstrated that children of lower socioeconomic class imitated aggressive behavior of an adult model" (p. 882). Importantly, however, the sample consisted of 86 percent black children (4-to-6-year-old males) who "observed a white model in an experiment conducted by a white experimenter" (p. 883); this prompted the "unexpected results." Imitation of aggressive behaviors was found to be much lower among black than white children in both the continuous ("CR") and interrupted ("IR") reinforcement conditions. Mark H. Thelen and William Soltz explain this "unexpected result"—the "limited imitation in the IR and CR groups"—in terms of the racial composition of the sample: "Perhaps these Negro subjects had learned that imitating certain behavior, such as aggression performed by a white adult, may have consequences quite different or even opposite from the positive reinforcement obtained by the white model" (p. 883). Low SES white boys more readily imitate aggressive behaviors, whereas low SES black boys have already been socialized—that is, "negatively reinforced"—to take "positive reinforcement to a white model . . . [as] a cue to a young Negro that he would be punished if he would perform the same behavior" (p. 885).

In the second experiment, conducted with 30 white 4-to-6-year-old boys enrolled at the University Laboratory School, and whose parents "are of middle or upper socioeconomic class" (p. 884), quite different results were derived. Middle-class white boys apparently scored "significantly higher . . . on TI [total imitation]" (p. 885) than the sample in the first experiment. Other than noting that sanctions are already in place among young black males which militate against copying "white" behaviors in the presence of a white adult male, Thelen and Soltz draw no further implications. Given the license experimental psychologists took with transferring laboratory-based findings to everyday social contexts, the implication of this study is that if modelling of filmed or actual behaviors by white models inhibits imitation of those behaviors among black children, they should be less prone to effects of televised violence—portrayed in the late 1960s still predominantly by white males—than their white counterparts. In sum, though, the central statement of the Thelen and Soltz study is that lower class black boys react very differently to filmed aggression than middle- and upper-class white boys, regardless of differential levels of reinforcement.

Published in a 1969 special issue of the *Journal of Broadcasting* "devoted to questions of the mass communications behavior of the poor" (Greenberg & Dominick, 1969:331), "Racial and Social Class Differences in Teen-Agers' Use of Television" also examines the influence of economic status and race on adolescents' uses of and attitudes toward TV (p. 332). Data was accumulated through viewing logs and questionnaires administered to 200 high school students "from the outskirts of a ghetto from which the school enrolls all its black students" (p. 334), and from 100 middle-class students in another school in the same city. The sample was comprised of an equal number of males and females. The aim of the study was to test two hypotheses: that low SES teenagers would spend more time with TV than middle SES youths, and that the former would hold more favorable attitudes towards TV. Additionally, "further segmentation of the low-income teen-agers into black and white sub-groups was expected to accentuate the hypothesized differences" (p. 333).

Black low SES teenagers, according to the data, watch more TV daily (6.3 hours) than their white counterparts (4.6 hours), and also more than middle-class white adolescents. Parents in these respective households were reported to watch proportionately less than their children, but along those same class-based differences (p. 337). Use of other media was reportedly class based: middle-class youths read more newspapers and magazines, and blacks spend more time listening to the radio and using record players than whites (pp. 337–338). Low-income black teenagers scored higher on items testing for perceived reality of TV programs, followed by low-income white and middle-income white adolescents. Gender differences were significant only for middle-class females, who attributed a greater reality factor to TV than middle-class boys.

In order to determine reasons for viewing, the authors derived statements for the questionnaire from a "content analysis of 75 essays written by separate groups of middle and low-income high school students on the topic 'Why I Watch Television?'" (p. 340). This procedure comes a little closer to a "phenomenistic" approach: the use of children's definitions of their TV experience as a basis for questioning them about that experience. And, in line with a phenomenological approach, the authors provide data not encoded in tables and numbers, but report the students' verbal responses. And, in terms of reasons for viewing, black teenagers apparently "were the most dependent on TV . . . as a learning device" (p. 341), followed by low-income white youths.

Gerson (1966) claimed to have found a similar trend, noting that black teenagers used TV to learn about certain social behaviors (e.g., dating). He speculated that the need to learn about "white" social behaviors was a consequence of increased integration. Greenberg and Joseph R. Dominick, however, construe low-income black or white adolescents as living "in a world where contacts with the [white] middle-class are infrequent and limited in diversity" (p. 333). Therefore, "the amount of information about the middle-class world possessed by a young person from a lower-income environment would be minimal" (p. 333). Accordingly, they argue that TV affords the low SES black or white adolescent a window to the white, middle-class world, an environment s/he otherwise is said to have no contact with. Greenberg and Dominick construct an unassimilated black viewer, whereas Gerson a decade earlier conceptualized the black viewer in the process of assimilation; historically, integration here seems to be turned on its head. Yet relative levels of integration and isolation are seen in both studies as influential in black children's uses of TV.

Following Carey's (1966) study of TV preference differences among white and black (adult) viewers, Alan D. Fletcher (1969) examines differential preferences among white and black children. His aim was not "for the sole purpose of making comparisons with Carey's study . . . [but to] . . . show some interesting results that one can compare" (p. 359). Like Carey, Fletcher claimed substantial viewing preference differences between black and white viewers, but Fletcher noted even greater diversity within each racial group, reflecting intragroup age, gender, and parental SES differences. Peer group affiliations are seen as exerting influence on program preferences which, as Fletcher's sample revealed, are highly differentiated according to race. This lack of preference overlap between white and black children of, for instance, similar SES, age, or household composition, is due to "peer group influence [which] exists primarily, possibly only, in the individual member's own race. Because the students in this sample are not integrated to any great extent in their classes, influence of one race upon the other probably cannot develop in the school system" (p. 364). In Fletcher's view, "cultural factors are even more important in a young audience than in an adult audience" since children's social experience, through the family, community, and segregated schooling, is more confined to same-race contact, unlike black adults who have "a chance to become members of the total society rather than of just a segment of it" (p. 364).

Black children, then, are introduced here into the discourse as a distinct viewing audience with program preferences quite different from the previously conceptualized homogeneous black audience. For instance, whereas Carey's data suggested that black adult viewers show a strong preference for crime programs, the children in Fletcher's sample "preferred situation comedy over crime and violence" (p. 365). And although one might expect that young children, regardless of race, would prefer comedies over crime drama, few programs matched in preference order between black and white children. One significant sociocultural influence on program preferences among black children was revealed, in Fletcher's view, by "the Negro ranking . . . for programs in which the central character, or one of the central characters, is without a mate" (p. 360). Cultural differences and the circumstances of home background in terms of race are seen here as significant influences on differential TV use and program preferences between black and white children. By implication, effects are a function of programs selected in conjunction with the (home) viewing context, about which generalizations from data derived primarily from white children cannot be made. The laboratory studies conducted by experimental psychologists during these same years, by contrast, continued to make claims about a generic viewer devoid of any attributes other than age, sex, educational level, and varying levels of antisocial behaviors, arousal, or frustration.

Race also was included as a viewer categorization in another study published in 1969, "Mass Media and Political Socialization of Children and Pre-Adults" (Byrne, 1969). The political socialization of mass media users had a long-standing history dating back to the seminal work of, inter alia, Berelson (1949), Lazarsfeld and coauthors Berelson, Hazel Gaudet, and Stanton. Since the underage media audience was not of voting age, "studies interested in understanding the relationship between mass media and political behavior . . . [have] for the most part ignored one segment of the population—the media audience under 21" (p. 140). Here a child viewer is constituted as a viewer with political orientations: "characteristics [such] as attitudes toward authority, political party identification and perceptions of governmental effectiveness are well developed at early ages" (p. 140).

Political orientation among the young, according to Gary C. Byrne, differs between white and black children as a consequence of different media use. "Negro children have less exposure to newspapers" (p. 141) than white children, and low-SES white children watch less TV news and have significantly lower exposure to newspapers than upper-SES children (pp. 141–142). Consequently, black and low-SES white children are said to be less politically informed. Relatively high exposure among black children to TV rather than the print media accounts for their more "positive attitudes towards the government" than those of white children. In Byrne's view, "watching television does not call for the skill involvement that reading does and therefore does not contribute as fully to the development of these critical faculties which appear to influence generalized attitudes of the child and pre-adult toward govenment" (p. 142).

The reasoning here is that the visual treatment of political information is more topical on TV than in print, and that black children, generally heavier viewers than white children, do not develop the critical faculties associated with print comprehension. This, in turn, renders them acritical viewers of already simplified and shallow televisual political information. In sum, the child and adolescent viewer is constituted here as one with political sensibilities shaped, in part, by different race- and class-based uses of media in general and of TV in particular.

Also in 1969, *Developmental Psychology* published "Saturday Morning Television Cartoons: A Simple Apparatus for the Reinforcement of Behavior in Children" (Stumphauzer & Bishop, 1969) as part of the journal's research "Notes." Jerome S. Stumphauzer and Barbara Bishop's report consists of a one-page report and a half-page photo of a TV monitor with an on-off switch attached to an extension cord—the "reinforcement apparatus." Attention is drawn to a study by D.M. Baer (1962), who "was able to control thumb-sucking in three children by turning off movie cartoons when the children began sucking their thumbs and turning the cartoons back on when thumb-sucking ceased" (pp. 763–764). The point the authors make has little to do with cartoons, with children, or with Baer's study, other than to praise the relative inexpense of the "reinforcement apparatus" which "parents, teachers, and technicians . . . might be trained . . . [to] use in the home, school, or clinical setting" (p. 764). The implication here is the equation of TV as reinforcement apparatus with which to control children's behaviors.

At the close of the second decade of TV, Alton Harrison and Eldon G. Scriven reviewed "20 years . . . of the literature and research findings . . . of television's effect on youth" (1969:82). The authors note that "despite some rather strong feelings to the contrary, a review of the research findings to date indicates that television's impact on youth has been very slight" (p. 88). For Harrison and Scriven, the child's background and dispositions interact with TV content, but are not determined by TV: "Effect is the result of interaction between television and a given individual" (p. 88). Violent TV content in itself, then, is not seen to lead to aggressive or delinquent behaviors in children: "Television by itself cannot make a normal well-adjusted child become a delinquent" (p. 87). TV, according to the authors, "has no adverse effects on the physical health of children," and "school performance is neither raised nor lowered by televiewing" (p. 88). Both reject the notion of TV as generating passivity among children: "None of the research evidence indicates that television makes children passive or dependent" (p. 87).

Harrison and Scriven recognize the limitations of experimental research that assesses only short-term effects, and note that the survey method best exemplified by Schramm et al.'s (1961) and Himmelweit et al.'s (1958) studies "have carried survey methods about as far as possible in developing an understanding of the effects of television on children" (p. 88). The authors see the need to "greatly expand experimental and clinical research . . . [which] need to be longitudinal studies in order to reveal the cumulative effects of television" (p. 88). This proposal, in fact, would constitute a substantial segment of the research agenda the following decade.

THE 1960s: AN OVERVIEW

The early years of the 1960s saw a continuation of the research agenda established during the 1950s. Research on program preference and viewing pattern continued (Baxter, 1960–1961; Witty, 1961; Merrill, 1961), but ceased to be a research topic by the end of the decade. Differential program preferences among children came to be seen as a function primarily of age and sex.

Parental noninvolvement in children's viewing developed into an important object of inquiry. Parents increasingly came to be seen less as an adjunct variable to the child, and more as an active mediator of the child's experience with TV (e.g., Baxter, 1960–1961; Smith, 1961–1962; Niven, 1960; Appell, 1960; Hess & Goldman, 1962; Atwood, 1968; Wand, 1968; Young, 1969–1970; Barcus, 1969). Parental mediation was variously constructed as active control or absence of control over children's viewing. Yet for the most part, parents were judged guilty of indifference. Although parents apparently held strong opinions about TV and children, most reported only minimal, if any, supervision of and participation in their children's viewing (e.g., Schramm et al., 1961; Witty, 1961; Steiner, 1963; Hess & Goldman, 1962). After initial acknowledgements in the early 1950s that TV was reportedly reuniting families, the notion of the family as a primary social context which circumscribes children's TV experiences received inconsistent attention. This trend was reversed in the 1960s. In the context of the exponential increase of published studies on TV and children, the inclusion of parents as an influential source of possible effects forms one series of statements in the broader discourse on TV and children.

Other identifiable series which emerged during the 1960s can be grouped according to shared conceptual grounds (uses and gratifications, escapism), discipline-based methodological orientation (experimental psychology), and research topics (academic achievement, black viewers, violence). Also, a diverse range of statements wove through and across the discourse, questioning and assessing aspects of the TV-child relationship previously not considered: TV and library circulation (Parker, 1963), TV portrayal of father images (Foster, 1964), occupational role portrayal (DeFleur, 1964), value systems and communication among children's program producers (Greenberg, 1964), and televiewing and the physiology of eye movements (Guba et al., 1964).

The debate over mass media's escapist function subsided during the 1950s but re-emerged in re(de)fined form that self-declared itself as the uses and gratifications approach. Viewing choices were considered a function of viewers' psychological need to escape from the stresses and strains of alienating social circumstances or unsatisfactory social relations (Katz & Foulkes, 1962). So seen, the positive function of escapist viewing was located in the benefits of "feedback." This feedback transmitted to viewers social values that would assist in the performance of social roles, some of which the escapist viewer perceived as problematic. Escape viewing also was conceptualized as serving positive functions in children's development (e.g., Schramm et al., 1961; Parker, 1961). Children were thought to seek out TV fantasy content to escape the realities and contradictions of growing up and into a social world for which the egocentric understandings of childhood were ultimately inadequate. Needs gratification and the notion of escape were derived, somewhat obliquely, from the reality/pleasure principles of Freudian socialization theory. "Uses" connotes a utilitarian assumption and implies, moreover, a distinctly social source of and context for "uses." Hence, sociodemographic delineations of uses as SES-, age-, and sex-specific were a conceptual means of signposting, if not conceptualizing, context. The uses and gratifications model thus can be read as a somewhat curious pseudo-theoretical construct couching a social (not necessarily sociological) conceptualization of human activity in psychological concepts, and these cast within a mechanistic dynamic of functional utility.

The conflation of "the social" with "the psychological"—that is, the psychologizing of the social—discursively precludes sociopolitical and historical questions of structure by focusing on the individual, the primary group, and the psychologically motivated behaviors within and among groups and individuals. In this view, the social is con-stituted by subjects who engage in rational and purposive social activity on the basis of dynamics located principally in mind. Certain causal regularities between objects (TV) and individuals, and among individuals, however, can be established by reference to the social (e.g., SES, educational level). The primacy of the psychological dimen-sion attributed to the social, then, renders even social-situational context (e.g., the "stresses" and "strains" of life) intelligible only in terms of how individuals translate these structural features into psychological experience (i.e., stress, frustration, alienation) and so-cial action (i.e., watching TV to escape "problems"). The social dimen-sion, characterized, for instance, as SES, similarly is articulated in terms of how individuals within such groupings act and behave.

Moreover, the formalization of this epistemology in the mathemati-cal formulae of descriptive science generates conditions of theoretical possibility that limit investigation and theorizing to the measurable and the individual. Both behaviorism (social learning theory) and functionalism (uses and gratifications "theory") shared this scientific ideology. And despite the superficial distinctions and theoretical dis-tance the "uses and gratifications" advocates attempted to establish between their social orientation and the behavioral effects orientation, the 1960s "sociology of media" remained theoretically and epis-temologically unable to question, let alone investigate, the historical, sociopolitical, cultural, and institutional structural dynamics within which the media-subject relationship was located.

Arguing against the "effects camp" in behavioral psychology, Katz and Foulkes (1962) and Klapper (1963) formally inaugurated the uses and gratifications model. The discursive establishment of this model harnessed residual and emergent statements that rested on assump-tions about viewers' purposive and active engagement with media. The relationship between viewer and medium, however, remained in a functional framework. Active and intentional selection of media and media content was conceptualized as a function of individual social circumstances and psychological predispositions. Effects were con-sidered not as a function of content (as in social learning theory) but as a function of the needs for which individuals seek gratification from the media.

As Katz and Foulkes and, certainly, Klapper saw it, a uses and gratifications approach already had, by the 1960s, an established history. It only needed the articulation of a label in order for earlier studies to fall in line. The heralding of the formalization of the model—in Klapper's words, "Viva los uses and gratifications"—also established a formalized conceptual niche to which future statements could claim allegiance. In this way a research tradition and continuity was built. Through self-certification, then, the uses and gratifications model distinguished itself from a range of other empirical sociological, social psychological, and psychological orientations. As such, the approach, or model as it was alternately described, drew demarcations—and, thus, a discontinuity—with other approaches within the discourse. Although Klapper and others since (e.g., Blumler & Katz, 1974; Katz, Blumler & Gurevitch, 1974a, 1974b; Blumler, 1979) acknowledged the origins of uses and gratifications in the 1940s communications research of, inter alia, Lazarsfeld, Stanton, Herzog, Wolfe and Fiske, and Berelson (see Chapter 3)—the advent of the uses and gratifications model is still today dated during the late 1950s and early 1960s, when it gained the formal textual recognition and prominence described here. Hence, the Klapper (1963) and Katz and Foulkes (1962) texts constitute a marker of discontinuity, of difference, from all preceding works, including those that were labeled after the fact as studies "within the uses and gratifications tradition."

Alongside the uses and gratifications school, and diametrically opposed to it on theoretical and methodological grounds, experimental, behavioral and developmental psychologists had developed during the 1960s a research focus which quickly gained a substantial following and relatively widespread recognition. Unlike the more impressionistic data produced by researchers in the uses and gratifications tradition, the laboratory experiment produced hard scientific data that claimed to prove TV's irrefutable effects on children. After a decade of scattered research, inconclusive and contradictory findings, here was a methodology and a theory of learning and development that finally could claim scientific proof of effects on children. The assumption that learning could best be facilitated and assessed by providing children with the appropriate conditions, learning stimuli, and reinforcements which would generate observable learning behaviors in the form of written or verbal responses was already well entrenched in contemporary educational theory and practice.

The equation of learning as behavior thus was neither a particularly novel nor radical departure from existing scientific pedagogy. Schooling, however, was and is an institutionally controlled and rule-bound "condition," whereas watching TV is not. Yet by bringing the lived experiences of TV (or film) and the viewer under the control of the laboratory experiment, the effects of learning from visual, kinetic, electronically displayed information—not unlike the "controlled" school-based learning of text information—could be more closely observed, counted, and classified. Stripped of social context, personal social history, cognitive processes and background knowledges, the viewing subject was reconstituted as a passive behavioral response mechanism, one whose learning from a given stimulus could be accurately predicted by reference to that stimulus. A learning theory that claimed that children learn from and develop within a variety of social environments—hence, *social* learning theory—ironically was tested (and verified) in the most socially sterile environment conceivable. Individual behavior was experimentally miscontextualized and interpretively decontextualized.

Children and TV thus came under scrutiny by psychologists at a historical moment, when the laboratory experiment was considered the most sophisticated and scientifically rigorous analytical tool. Yet academic authorities of delimitation, by virtue of their particular labor at the production of disciplinary discourses, are as much historical products of discourse as the discourses they produce. Like the data produced by nonexperimental researchers, the findings derived from experimental psychological research are historical discursive constructs which may have very little, if any, correspondence to "the Real."

TV and children came under the dissecting gaze of a particular historical variant of North America's flagship discourse in the human sciences, a discourse preoccupied with method. Methodological design, procedures and apparatuses—from Bobo dolls and mallets, to electroshock levers and helmets—forced the object of inquiry (the human subject) to serve method, not vice versa. The "fact" that children in a laboratory setting behaved aggressively after watching a filmed portrayal of aggressive actions is only a fact or "truth" insofar as it is a behavioral consequence of a particular method applied to a manipulated "condition" according to procedural rules, rules that delimit and enable the extraction and constitution of knowledge. Similarly, facts derived from field studies of, say, viewing preferences, are truths only insofar as they are constructions by the survey or interview respondent reframed, in turn, by the researcher's reconstruction of such information into a methodological (e.g., delineating statistical significance) and conceptual framework.

Research is by definition hermeneutic, if only in the sense that what is observed and analyzed becomes known as formalized knowledge via the linguistic and conceptual structures of discourse. Simply put, "respondents" in one discourse are transformed into "Ss" in another; "socialization" in one discourse becomes "response inhibition" in another. While the recognition that all research is interpretive is not a radical revelation, the point here is that discourses form and constitute rules according to which authorized speakers within the discourse, themselves embodiments of discourses, construct objects and truths about those objects. And it is such critical self-reflection, or metacommentary, that modernist scientific discourses by and large fail to acknowledge as intrinsic to the dynamics of their labor of truth production. Importantly, such discursively constituted truths are often transposed from one authoritative domain to another: from scholarly documentation to, for example, a federal policy or curriculum document. In the process of intra- and interinstitutional circulation, discursive statements invariably filter into the public domain (via the press, and most notably TV) within which they rapidly assume the cloak of conventional wisdom and commonsense knowledge.

This chapter has shown that several concepts of the child viewer and explanations for the TV-child relationship were formally established during the 1960s. Taken as a whole, the discourse on TV and children cannot be taken as illustrative of what is today commonly referred to as the behavioral "effects paradigm" of the 1960s. While the social learning theorists, following Bandura, certainly carved out a very influential space in the field of TV/violence/children research, it coexisted with a range of, in Himmelweit's words, "widely scattered studies." Some of these explicitly identified with the uses and gratifications approach, others implicitly appeared to share its assumptions, while yet others bore no identifiable relation to any particular disciplinary orientation or common theoretical ground.

If one statement can be said to have remained constant across the first 20 years of TV research and commentary, it is the critique of then contemporary research models which, by and large, were judged as inadequate, inconclusive, narrow, and scattered. Indeed, according to Kuhn (1962), critique, refutation, and theory (re)construction are the hallmarks of "good science." Interestingly, however, within the mass media discourse, the TV discourse in general and its subbranch on TV and children in particular, critique traveled essentially one way: directed from those quarters concerned more with the social dimension and context of communications media to those concerned primarily with documenting observable media effects. In short, from what loosely can be labeled a sociological, albeit no less empirical, orientation came most of the critiques of what was amorphously referred to as "existing research."

Researchers within the psychological strand of mass communications research, by contrast, engaged silently in theory-building without much commentary on contending work. The only criticisms emanating from this field were focused on work within the paradigm, that is, on methodological or procedural inadequacies of earlier versions of a given experimental model. In brief, "effects" research based on experimental psychology seemed to have no argument with other approaches to the study of TV and children, whereas researchers arguing for the social as opposed to the psychological dimension of the mass media–audience relationship engaged in ritualized condemnation of the opposition. The uses and gratifications model—the only other model which can be labeled dominant—perhaps was seen by psychologists as posing no legitimate theoretical threat to the experimental effects model. Psychologists were able to isolate and verify effects, while survey research on social effects could not claim such unequivocal accuracy. In the historical-political context of the 1960s, when the public and ostensibly government were demanding evidence of effects to use as ammunition to force industry regulation, experimental research could deliver the evidence; nonexperimental research could not. Perhaps the defensive posturing of sociological and social-psychological orientations to mass media research reflects a more fundamental theoretical and methodological insecurity in the face of what may have seemed like a towering and well-entrenched opposition, one that had long claimed children as its privileged object of study via the discourse of educational psychology.

Generally invisible in the discourse prior to the 1960s, the black viewer surfaced in the discourse during this decade variously conceptualized as integrated within or segregated from mainstream society. In either site, s/he was construed as possessing different, socioculturally determined viewing patterns and preferences. Racial and ethnic minorities were TV viewers long before discourse constituted them as a viewing subgroup *in relation* to the construct of an average white, middle-class American viewing public. Race and ethnicity were in the 1960s still very much the privileged intellectual property of sociology and social psychology. Hence, it is not surprising that the black viewer initially appeared in communications and social issues journals, not in journals of psychology.

Notable by its omission in the 1960s, as in the 1950s, is the participation by what could be considered a distinctly educational discourse on commercial TV and children. TV became an object of educational study and classroom practice only insofar as its educational-instructional applications became a discursive focus (e.g., Green, 1962; Schramm, 1960b). Since the advent of mass public schooling, children have been by definition educational objects of study. As noted, the educational enterprise during these decades was well entrenched in a behaviorist orientation. Yet academic educators, with few exceptions (Sorelle & Walker, 1962; Ridder, 1963; Blumenfeld & Remmers, 1966), remained silent on the issue of commercial TV and children, and silent on the (print) surface of scholarly exchange. A separate study of teachers' professional journals might reveal their presence in that discourse (e.g., Witty, 1967).

Certain topics of study appeared and disappeared, leaving no identifiable patterned trace: TV advertising and consumer socialization, for instance, appeared only briefly in the 1950s (e.g., Brumbaugh, 1954; Munn, 1958) and did not resurface as a focus of inquiry until the early 1970s. Large-scale field studies remained the exception, not the rule (e.g., Schramm et al., 1961). Although calls for longitudinal studies to gauge long-term effects constituted a continuously repeated statement over two decades of research, none were undertaken after Witty's ten-year study until the following decade, when Monroe M. Lefkowitz, Eron, Leopold O. Walder and L. Rowell Huesman (1972) conducted a follow-up study of Eron's (1963) original sample for the 1972 Surgeon General's Report on *Television and Social Behavior*. Studies of comparative media use (TV, radio), a visible topic during the early years of TV, had disappeared by the late 1960s. Content analyses moved beyond broad general categorizations and began to focus on specific role portrayals (e.g., Foster, 1964; DeFleur, 1964).

In all, the research on TV and children during the 1960s cannot be said to have had any kind of unified internal logic, either theoretically or methodologically. Although, in retrospect, the evidence suggests that two approaches to the study of TV and children quite clearly emerged, these were embedded within what Himmelweit had termed a "widely scattered" research field. The search for effects, however, did comprise a unifying thread that reached back to the early studies on movies and children.

Effects of any phenomenon on human subjects can be varied even within one spectrum (e.g., the social, the psychological; positive or negative effects). Yet conceptualizations of effects of mass media on children were delimited since the 1920s in terms of negative effects: we have seen thus far that research on the relationship between media-portrayed crime and violence in drama, and juvenile delinquency has a longstanding history. Studies of the effects of what today is labeled "prosocial" TV have been historically sparse: e.g., teenagers' use of movies to learn about social behaviors, as noted in the 1933 Payne Fund studies; or, similarly, black viewers' use of TV as suggested by Gerson in 1966, and by Greenberg and Dominick in 1969. The 1960s research sharpened the focus on negative effects. This was a consequence of both the prolific research ouput on modelled aggression and, probably more importantly, the impending Surgeon General's Report on TV violence, which was published in 1972 but had already commissioned initial studies in the late 1960s.

POSTSCRIPT ON A DECADE: THE SURGEON GENERAL'S REPORT

The Surgeon General's Report titled *Television and growing up: The impact of televised violence* (1972) signified a summary underline to the 1960s research on TV and children and, as well, would serve as the definitive document upon which the research agenda for the 1970s was based. Initial work by advisory committees to commission research studies for the report began in 1969, yet the report was not made public until 1972. Hence, the text falls in between the discursive divisions that I have constructed here. As a summary textual marker of 1960s research, and as an agenda setting marker for 1970s research, I include here a brief commentary on the report's discursive and political function in the construction of an authoritative, (federally) formalized version of the discourse on TV and children. The history of communications policy lies, by virtue of this book's focus, beyond the possibility of in-depth analysis here. Nonetheless, in a poststructuralist reading, the lateral expansion of discourse across institutions and disciplines, and its historical extension together form the parameters of discourse. As such, the 1972 Surgeon General's Report figures prominently in the discourse on TV and children and hence warrants critical commentary.

What is of interest in the 1972 Surgeon General's Report is the network of authorities that helped shape the antecedant, selective organization of knowledge which, in turn, served as the authoritative research basis on which the report was founded. The production and formalization of a discourse, as the following explication will illustrate, is as much a product of ideologically embedded academic labor, as it is a product of concealed and powerful political and economic interests in shaping knowledge.

The reconstitution of the academic discourse on TV and children in a federal document legitimates and, certainly, formalizes a highly specialized set of statements as state sanctioned, public knowledge. The practical agenda that derives from the transformation of a scholarly discourse into a governmental political discourse, obviously enough, has significant implications. Among such practical consequences of the 1972 Surgeon General's Report were several subsequent attempts to legislate family viewing hours, with a mandate to exclude objectionable content (sex and violence). The conflict between a possible Federal Communications Commission (FCC) ruling and broadcasters' First Amendment rights was irresolvable constitutionally and, ultimately, control over objectionable programming remained at broadcasters' discretion (cf. Liebert & Sprafkin, 1988).

Liebert and Sprafkin (1988) recount the history of research and theory on TV and children in *The Early Window: Effects of Television on Children and Youth*, originally published in 1972. Published as part of Pergamon's General Psychology Series, it reconstructs the history of psychological research on TV and children. A substantial part of the monograph focuses on the 1972 Surgeon's General Report: the circumstances, groups, and individuals involved in the selection and appointment of advisors and researchers, the findings, and the "aftermath of the report." More than a decade after the publication of *The Early Window*, Rowland (1983) published *The Politics of TV Violence*, which is a revisionist history of the politics underlying the dynamics of social science in the service of government and industry. A significant part of this volume focuses on the 1972 Surgeon General's Report. Together, Rowland's political critique and Liebert and Sprafkin's positivist reconstruction provide sufficient conflicting and supporting evidence to suggest that the production of knowledge is delimited at least as much by epistemological and methodological rules of formation per se, as by power/knowledge relations that deploy tactics of discursive exclusion and inclusion.

Briefly, then, early in 1969 various academic and professional associations (e.g., American Sociological Association; American Anthropological Association; American Psychiatric Association; and American Psychological Association) were asked to submit names of social scientists to form a scientific advisory committee to advise the Surgeon General. According to Liebert and Sprafkin (1988:81), expertise was canvased from "distinguished social scientists, the NAB and the three major networks." From 200 names submitted, 40 were shortlisted and submitted to the National Association of Broadcasters (NAB) and the three national commercial networks (NBC, ABC, CBS). Incredibly, the broadcast industry was asked to indicate which of the 40 candidates "would *not* be appropriate for an impartial scientific investigation of this nature" (p. 82).

Political interests, according to Matilda B. Paisley (1972) and Rowland (1983), underlay the selection criteria of advisory members. Such political interests, in Foucault's (1980b) terms "the politics of truth," constitute implicit rules of discursive formation: who could be counted on to produce the kind of evidence sought by the Surgeon General. Rowland (1983:150), drawing on Paisley, suggests: "Much like the by then regular process in selecting other high level advisory groups, it appears that the final list was further influenced by questions of 'race, sex, political acceptability, and heterogeneity of background' (Paisley, 1972:21)." Rowland (1983:150–151) is worth citing at length here on the issue of selection and bias underlying the epistemology of an "impartial" government report, putatively based on objective findings of disinterested social science:

> Undiscussed by virtually all commentators was the more fundamental question of the particular scientific biases built into the advisory committee and its staff support from the outset. In keeping with the general scientific mandate established by Senator Pastore and the behavioral science context represented in the government agencies attached to the project, the SAC was weighted heavily toward the disciplines of experimental and clinical psychology and quantitative sociology and political science. Only one or two committee members had any roots in the qualitative social sciences or in the historical, critical, or cultural studies aspects of communications, and none came from the humanities. Under the circumstances of the advisory committee's origins, its subsequent character is hardly surprising.

Seven candidates, all of whose research except one has been reviewed in this chapter, were, in Liebert and Sprafkin's (1988:82) words, "secretly blackballed . . . in deference to the wishes of the industry whose product was under scrutiny." Moreover, the final appointment of 12 members to the advisory panel consisted of five additional members—industry executives and consultants (four from CBS, one from NBC, and none from ABC)—whose names had not previously been made available for review to either public interest groups or professional societies. The seven academic members of the 12-member advisory committee included only one academic researcher (Siegel) with a publication and research record directly related to TV and children. Siegel's research had been established since the mid-1950s as foundational to the catharsis theory of televiewing, a theory that claimed that TV violence serves as a release, not a trigger, for viewer aggression. Her anticipated role on the committee, in light of her research and theoretical orientation, cannot be seen independently of the discourse she represented, one which would invariably suggests a no-effects equation. The remaining academic recruits were professors in child development, psychiatry, anthropology, political science, and psychology.

The committee's mandate was to write the final report for the Surgeon General of all commissioned and submitted research. Under pressure to produce a single report instead of several, which more adequately would express conflicting research and viewpoints, the committee reconstructed the research under what one observer noted as tense conditions: "There was a big move by Government officials to get a consensus report. There was a lot of anger . . . meetings were extremely tense with the warring factions sitting at either end of the table, glaring at each other, particularly towards the end" (Rowland, 1983:99).

What was finally released to the public via the press was an 11-page summary of the 169-page report to the Surgeon General of a 2,000-page volume titled *Television and Growing Up: The Impact of Televised Violence* (1972). The report's overall message was that TV violence was one of several influences on children's aggressive behaviors and attitudes. TV was essentially absolved of blame as cause for aggression in youth. Despite (experimental) evidence to the contrary, the official state-sanctioned version of the research claimed that TV violence did not cause aggression in viewers. At best, it was claimed as one of many contributing factors within individual circumstances. The industry had acceded early during the study to a reasonable measure of blame, thereby hoping to preclude accusations of whitewashing the report. All subsequent attempts to legislate for a reduction of violent program content failed.

The publication of the report led to several Senate follow-up hearings, widespread public and academic debate, and a flurry of research activity the following decade on the effects of TV violence on children. The continuing research interest in TV violence stemmed from the mounting experimental evidence of positive effects in conjunction with the absence of federal industry regulations, which sanctioned the continuation of violent programming deemed unsuitable for children.

Government funding of university-based research projects, the selection of members for advisory committees to congressional or Senate subcommittees, and appointments of principal research investigators for a federal report together here constituted the politics of discursive practice. It is at this level of the political reorganization of knowledge production that "regimes of truth" establish and formalize discourses. Truth, in Foucault's view, "is centred on the form of scientific discourse and the institutions which produce it" (1980b:131). He explains: "Each society has its regime of truth, its 'general politics' of truth; that is, the types of discourse which it accepts and makes function as true; the mechanism and instances which enable one to distinguish true and false statements, the means by which each is sanctioned; . . . the status of those who are charged with saying what counts as true" (p. 131).

As I have shown in this chapter, the form of scientific discourse (i.e., the rules and relations of discursive formations) delimits which objects qualify for discursive inclusion and how those objects of study can be articulated. Institutional ensembles of rules and relations further delimit and enable what will count as scientific truth. As Foucault has noted, the power of the state does not operate downward from a monolithic center but is diffused laterally and surfaces in localized, "infinitesimal mechanisms, which each have their own history, their own trajectory, their own techniques and tactics" (p. 99). The procedures that produced the Surgeon General's Report constitute such mechanisms that have a (constitutional) history in the liberal democratic state, and that operate according to political and economic rules and tactics. The "politics of truth," Foucault (p. 132) observes, are historical "battles" of and for power and of and for knowledge:

> There is a battle 'for truth,' or at least 'around truth'—it being understood . . . that by truth I do not mean 'the ensemble of truths which are to be discovered and accepted,' but rather 'the ensemble of rules according to which the true and the false are separated and specific effects of power attached to the true,' it being understood also that it's not a matter of a battle 'on behalf' of the truth, but of a battle about the *status of truth* and the *economic* and *political* role it plays. (emphasis added)

The selective transposition of academic social science into a state authorized and highly publicized document that claimed, at the time, to represent an impartial scientific investigation exemplifies how ensembles of explicit and implicit rules underlay the dynamics of the "politics of truth."

5

1970–1979:
Constructing the Cognitive Subject

Following the release of the Surgeon's General's Report in 1972 amidst charges by the report's researchers of inaccurate and distorted representation of their work (Paisley, 1972; cf. Rowland, 1983), "the ten-year period from 1970 to 1979 was the golden age of television for social science, if not for the medium itself" (Liebert & Sprafkin, 1988:115). All the historically reconstructive connotations of a "golden age" not withstanding, the 1970s were marked by increasing and diverse research interests in TV and children. Research output increased at an unprecedented and accelerated rate, and the range of divergent topics of inquiry effectively dismantled any presupposed unities of research themes or methodological strangleholds.

Mass communications studies during the late 1970s began a subtle shift toward theoretical positions that conceptualized TV (and other mass media) as cultural product and audiences as embedded within and socialized by a cultural apparatus, of which TV was only one, albeit influential, socializing agency. Audiences and mass media were recast in the broader context of social systems: within, for example, national and global economic structures (Schiller, 1969, 1973), and cultural structures (Carey, 1977; Carey & Kreiling, 1974; Gerbner et al.'s cultural indicators project, 1976, 1977, 1978; Real, 1977). The impetus for the emergence of this orientation can be partially linked to McLuhan's (1962, 1964) interpretation of media influence in cultural-historical terms. McLuhan's media bias argument generated, inter alia, a flurry of academic commentary, and thus a reconsideration of the role of mass media in contemporary society. This emergent "cultural studies" approach to mass media did not displace empiricist models but developed, during the 1970s, as a distinct interdisciplinary line of inquiry that posed questions previously unarticulated by empirical mass communications research.

For the most part, the pursuit of "effects" continued throughout the 1970s. The range of effects, however, diversified, as did the identification of possible sources. The TV text was reexamined with a view toward uncovering more than violent content, and content was discovered to be embedded within medium-specific forms or symbolic codes. The audience was reexamined and was found to represent subgroups previously unaccounted for, and effects were reconceputalized from short-term behavioral outcomes to long-term socializing influences on morals, values, attitudes, and perceptions of social reality. Toward the end of the decade, the child viewer underwent a subtle reconceptualization, from a behavioral response mechanism to one who interacted with TV's form and content on the basis of, inter alia, developing cognitive abilities.

Preoccupation with TV violence effects on children did not cease abruptly. After the 1972 release of the Surgeon General's Report, debate over the validity of the report's findings and the report's implications for the direction of future research continued. But after two decades of "scattered" research, several Senate inquiries and, finally, the publication of the apparently long-awaited Surgeon General's Report, research on TV and children underwent a virtual explosion, both in terms of published output and diversity of topics. Many 1970s studies followed the implicit research agenda set by the Surgeon General's Report: evidence supporting and refuting TV violence effects proliferated. Yet the 1970s research also launched a search for effects beyond the violence-aggression equation established by the report, and new effects were identified as new content sources were articulated. Within the 1970s citation network, the Surgeon General's Report—the definitive text on TV effects—was systematically rearticulated throughout the decade.

Given the exponential growth of studies on TV and children during the third decade of TV, the kind of detailed textual analysis undertaken in the previous two chapters is more restricted in this chapter. The ordering of the data follows the format established in Chapters 3 and 4: research will be examined in chronological order and, because of the large number of studies published, these further will be ordered alphabetically for each year. The special journal issues on TV and children will be examined in the groupings in which they appeared in order to re-present the discursive textual unity established by special sections or special issues.

1970–1971

In "Mass Communication and Political Socialization," published in *Journalism Quarterly*, Steven H. Chaffee, L. Scott Ward, and Leonard P.

Tipton (1970) rejected the "two-step flow" and "reinforcement" explanations of media influence (p. 648), on the grounds that children do not have fully developed political views which are open to "conversion" by media or opinion leaders. Instead, the authors proposed that the role of media as influential in children's political development should be empirically delineated in order to identify how media, together with other sources of political socialization like the family, teachers, and peers, contribute to the formation of children's political knowledge and attitudes.

Toward this end, the authors conducted a field survey of 1,291 junior and senior high school students. Questionnaires, self-administered at "Time 1" and "Time 2," were given to students during the beginning and toward the end of the 1968 election primaries. Adolescents rated mass media as more influential in their political opinion formation than family, teachers, or peers. Newspapers, rather than TV, were found to be most influential in political knowledge acquisition. Class or gender differences were not noted. In the authors' view, "media use should be considered as an independent (or intervening) variable in the political socialization process, not merely as one of many dependent variables" (p. 658). The viewing child is here conceptualized as one whose behaviors, opinions and attitudes are only partially shaped by the media and who undergoes "a series of changes in . . . orientation to 'the outside world'" (p. 659) which are not seen as causally linked to media exposure. The use of children's "introspective self-description," rather than experimental evidence, precluded what the authors considered a significant shortcoming of most research on children's political socialization: namely, that researchers tend to define a priori and thus expect to find "media influences in *one* attitudinal direction" (p. 659). The object of inquiry in this study is a demographic group whose political attitudes and behaviors are only partially formed or perhaps not at all. Appropriately, the methodological rule system employed here to identify presence, absence, or direction of attitudes and attitude formation is an attempt to constitute the child as a political subject different from the adult.

Noting the absence in previous research of studies taking a developmental cognitive perspective, W. Andrew Collins (1970) steered social learning theory away from an emphasis on the learning of behaviors toward the learning of information content. No relevant recent research was available on which to base his research. Hence, Collins recirculates previous studies, dating back to the Payne Fund studies (1933) and Maccoby's research in the 1950s, that indirectly related to learning of media content. From his experimental data Collins found that children's abilities "to attend selectively to information inputs" increases with age (p. 1140). While this confirms common sense notions of children's cognitive development, Collins introduces the idea of learning "noncontent cues." By the end of the decade, these would be reconceptualized as "formal [technical] features" (Welch, Huston-Stein, Wright & Plehal, 1979). Young children, according to Collins, learn more noncontent information than adolescents, which "suggests that older children are better able than younger ones to ignore nonessential information" (p. 1140). And adolescent boys apparently "learn less central content than their girl age mates ... [which] suggest[s] that the ninth-grade boys were generally less skilled in selective attention than the girls"(p. 1141).

Collins does not develop any implications of his findings, nor does he elaborate what specific kinds of content his "Ss" centered on or rejected as peripheral, given differential ages. He does note, however, a gender difference: "Adolescent girls showed more incidental learning from a film depicting a domestic situation than adolescent boys, although the difference disappeared by adulthood" (p. 1141). In all, Collins introduced into the discourse experimental evidence that TV's effects on children have a cognitive dimension and that children's incidental and nonincidental learning of TV content is a function of age as well as gender.

In an overview of the historical directions and current state of mass media and audience research in "developed" countries (i.e., Britain and America), James Halloran (1970) articulated some concerns previously omitted in the discourse. Commenting on the historical nature of theory and theorizing, he suggests that historic-specific "models of society, concepts of human nature and images of man" (p. 20) underlie all conceptions of research problems and the data derived from methodologies applied to particular problems. In mass communications research, a coherent epistemology—or theory, for that matter—has been impossible to define or locate because "multi-faceted and inter-disciplinary approaches do not easily lend themselves to comprehensive theoretical developments" (p. 21). Echoing Himmelweit's characterization of mass media research as "ad hoc" and "widely scattered," Halloran cautions that "we should be aware of the shortcomings and inadequacies of piecemeal studies and the dangers of over concentration on isolated elements of what should be considered as a social process" (p. 20).

Research suffering such inadequacies is most evident in media crime and violence research, which has relied on a single concept in order to prove a direct causal relationship between filmed violence and viewer aggression. Dismissing experimental research for its simplistic conceptualization and methodological treatment of the problem, Halloran observes: "Experimental research in this field [violence/aggression] has been severely criticized amongst other things for its artificiality and lack of applicability to real life situations. Moreover, the results are conflicting. . . . What the apparently conflicting and confusing results show more than anything else is the mistake of trying to cover an extremely varied and complex set of relationships by the use of a single concept" (p. 23).

Important for Halloran is the recognition that what counts as a research problem, the methodological structuring of that problem, and the data derived from such research in one (developed) country may be quite different in another country. The problem, as he sees it, is that the research community tends to generalize data from one English-speaking country to another, often not recognizing the differences in the definition of the problem, and hence different research results. He notes, for instance, the virtual absence in "English universities" of research on "media-crime," whereas "in the U.S.A. . . . the same questions [media-crime] have been asked, and the same concern expressed time and time again" (p. 27). Lastly, he asks researchers to "take into account the research questions which have *not* been asked and the research which has *not* been carried out" (p. 22). He identifies the school as an arena for future inquiry—not for its traditional data on individual academic achievement scores and media habits—but in terms of the "role of the school-teacher in relation to the mass media tastes of pupils as well as the relationships between popular culture and school culture" (p. 32).

As noted in Chapter 4, research on TV and children in the 1960s was for the most part narrowly focused on isolated elements of the TV-child relation. Few acknowledged the epistemological specificity of their assumptions or the historical and ideological nature of the discursive practices in which media researchers engaged. Halloran, working in the distinctly British tradition of social science, clearly saw the importance of scientific research as ideological practice: "A set of rules has been developed for dealing with situations and sometimes the interpretations of these situations may be little more than the outcome of the rules and procedures that we have designed and imposed. Procedures . . . are not necessarily free from ideological considerations" (p. 33). Entrenched in an ideology of value-free scientific inquiry, American researchers, by contrast, were unable to make such claims.

Media Sociology: A Reader was published in 1970. Editor Jeremy Tunstall noted that "much research now talks of uses, gratifications, functions and interaction—rather than 'effects.' . . . Surveys of randomly selected national samples of the general population have also isolated respondents and cut them off artificially from the family groups where most . . . media consumption occurs. We need more broad-ranging research which studies the media within the family/socialization/domestic context and within the work/leisure/relaxation/life-style context. . . . Laboratory experiments and randomly selected samples . . . should be recognized as only two of the possible methodological approaches" (p. 23). The message from sociology was clear: experimental and survey research has been unsuccessful at providing data of an interactive TV-viewer relationship in its naturalistic context. Accordingly, U.S. and British researchers contributed to this volume what were seen to count as sociological studies of the mass media.

One paper by D. Harper, Joan Munro, and Himmelweit (1970) specifically focused on children and examined their program "tastes." The authors sought to draw a distinction between taste and the more traditional preference indices based on favorite program classsifications. According to the authors, "The most interesting contribution of this study lies in the establishment of the distinction between liking for programmes that reflected contemporary fashions and those which are liked because they satisfy psychological needs. . . . Preferences reflect the Zeitgeist rather than psychological needs" (p. 371). The point the authors make is that viewing choices are not simple behaviors that function to satisfy psychological needs but, rather, are embedded within a "complex interaction between the viewer and the medium" (p. 371). This interaction is further circumscribed by historic- and culture-specific "trends" over and above interacting psychological and intellectual variables within each child. "Interaction" is the key word not only in Harper et al.'s study but throughout most papers included in this monograph.

As noted in earlier chapters, what could be labeled a sociological perspective on media and children was not absent from, but marginal to the discourse (cf. Ball-Rokeach & Cantor, 1986), as was participation by sociological journals. The publication of Tunstall's sociological reader on mass media signaled an apparently extant sociological approach to the study of mass media—an approach ostensibly so wide-ranging that diverse studies were harnessed in what was to be considered a "reader." Although both Tunstall and Halloran were associated with British universities—Tunstall's anthology was published in England and Halloran's article appeared in a British journal—Harper et al.'s and Halloran's papers were recirculated in the citation network of the U.S.-based mass media discourse for at least the next decade.

John P. Murray, Oguz B. Nayman, and Charles K. Atkin (1971–1972) published a bibliography—part of which was originally commissioned by the Surgeon General's Advisory Committee—entitled "Television and the Child" in the *Journal of Broadcasting*. The 250 entries were divided into three sections: TV content and programing, general effects and viewing patterns, and effects of televised violence. Nearly half of all the items concerned children and TV directly, whereas the section on televised violence listed almost exclusively studies on children. Published in the same year that the Surgeon General's report was released, the main focus of inquiry into TV and children was linked to concerns over media violence. The preceding year, however, reflected none of the concerns so well publicized and associated with the pending government report. Only one study (Murray, Cole & Fedler, 1970) was published in 1970 that dealt with TV violence and children.

"Teenagers and TV Violence: How They Rate and View It" (Murray, Cole & Fedler, 1970), published in *Journalism Quarterly*, reports on a study that utilized "questionnaires, telephone interviews, content analysis and regression analysis" (p. 255) to identify possible relationships between adolescents' viewing of TV violence and "anomie or alienation" (p. 248). The findings suggested: "Of the variables considered, sex was the best predictor of violent viewing. . . . Alienation and viewing of violent content bear little relationship to each other . . . [and] few of the teenagers in the sample spent large amounts of time viewing television" (p. 255). Despite the seemingly sociological topic of this study, most of the text is not devoted to discussion of "the social" (either in terms of TV, viewing, adolescents, or anomie) but, rather, is devoted to lengthy discussion of the methodological fine points of procedure and statistical delineations of alienation and violence scores.

The use of electroencephalography to elucidate inhibiting or conducive conditions for learning from TV was proposed by Herbert E. Krugman and Eugene L. Hartley (1970) as an alternative to mainstream research which, in the authors' estimation, had "lost sight of man's animal, mechanical, and physical properties" (p. 185). Authors' institutional affiliations following the abstract identified Krugman as director for "corporate public relations and advertising research at the General Electric Company," and Hartley as "Dean of the College of Community Sciences at the University of Wisconsin." Following a lengthy discussion of the electroencephalography (EEG) literature, alpha brain waves and rhythms, EEG responses to LSD-dosed experimental subjects, and so forth, the authors suggest that learning about "serious matters" from TV is best facilitated under "calm" conditions in which the viewer is in a physiological state of nonexcitement, low arousal, and low resistance. This formulation of "passive" learning has implications for early childhood education, where the authors suggest that highly agitated children might benefit from "mild drugging" to induce a pseudoalpha state which would be "dramatically helpful to their educational achievement" (p. 189). Television research also might benefit from EEG research: "by comparing immediate physiological response with later measures of what has been learned, we may begin to answer questions about just how much attention (arousal, interest) is required to learn what" (p. 190). Like Guba et al.'s (1964) study of televiewing and eye movements, Krugman and Hartley conceptualize televiewing and learning as a physiological ("mechanical," "physical") "response activity" (p. 187) to "changing stimuli" (p. 186).

Drawing heavily on Carey's (1966) and Fletcher's (1969) studies of black viewing preferences, Stuart H. Surlin and Dominick (1970–1971) set out to reinterpret Carey's and Fletcher's findings—that black viewers prefer individual-centered, not family-oriented programs— in order to examine the influence of race and income on black children's viewing preferences. The (sub)discourse on TV and black children, by the early 1970s, had only a short history: short enough that Surlin and Dominick represented their, and Carey's and Fletcher's, findings in a table of "Similarities and Dissimilarities between Studies" (p. 61). Acknowledging the interval between studies and sample differences, Surlin and Dominick claim that the black adolescents in their study did not indicate significant preferences for programs focused on individual experiences. Carey and Fletcher both had suggested that such preferences among blacks reflect the social and cultural milieu among black families. In agreement with Gerson (1966), Surlin and Dominick suggest that both low-income white and black teenagers "are using TV as a learning device" from which "they acquire the behavior perceived as appropriate for family members in the predominantly white-middle-class world" (p. 62). For the low-income black adolescent, TV is thus seen to function "as a means of furthering understanding of the larger society from which he seems to have been excluded" (p. 62).

It seems plausible that during the 1960s and early 1970s the emergent discourse on TV and black viewers was linked to heightened political and public awareness and recognition of the black sector of the American populace. That the "sociological variables, such as race and social class" should become the seminal analytic grid on which black viewers initially would be mapped is not surprising. However, one aspect of social class which was left virtually unarticulated by researchers was educational attainment. The discursive exclusion of considerations of black viewers' educational levels in favor of an emphasis on the fragmented composition of the black family unit helped formulate a particular concept of the black viewer which, by omission, posited blacks as "under-educated" or "uneducated." At the least, this suggests that black viewers' educational backgrounds were considered irrelevant to studies of their social behaviors, whereas their culturally "aberrant," deprived familial circumstances were seen as central in explaining their viewing habits.

From Australia, Patricia M. Edgar and Donald E. Edgar (1971) reported in *Public Opinion Quarterly* on a study in progress in a rural community where TV had only recently been introduced. The authors discuss their research model and outline the pretest baseline data gathered to date; post-testing was to occur two years later. No research findings are reported. It seems that increasingly, during the early years of 1970, mass media studies conducted in places other than the United States were being published in American journals: Edgar and Edgar from Australia, Klaus R. Scherer (1971) from Germany, Smith (1971–1972) from Scotland, and Murray and Susan Kippax (1978) from Australia. Although none of these studies claimed any cross-cultural implications, the editorial establishment of, for example, the *Journal of Broadcasting* and *Public Opinion Quarterly* obviously considered the inclusion of non-American research in their journals to be a valuable addition to the U.S. academic discourse.

The appearance of overseas research in the U.S. mass media discourse at this particular historical juncture suggests a possible shift in discursive rules operant within discourse production. Mass media research and theory had as long and checkered a history in countries abroad (cf. Halloran, 1970) as in the U.S. Britain and the United States, according to Phillip G. Altbach (1987), "are the dominant forces in the distribution of scholarly and research knowledge"; academic journal and book publishers and distributors, as well as book and journal editors ("academic evaluators") "are located in these countries" (p. 171). Yet nonquantitative, distinctly European work was not being published in the United States. Much of the ideological left-leaning research and theorizing emanating from Britain, at least, ran counter to the kind of liberal assumptions and theories upon which the U.S. mass media discourse was based: European research tended to be theory-based, and operated from a distinct and different set of methodological canons. Non-American research that was finally incorporated in and circulated within the North American mass media discourse followed American theoretical and methodological models (Edgar & Edgar, 1971; Smith, 1971–1972; Murray & Kippax, 1978). Reflective of and contributing to the U.S. social and political sensibility of the day—of which "cultural awareness," "cultural difference," "multiculturalism," etc. are but variations of a then contemporary "theme of interest"—the sudden move to include research from other countries signals a perhaps conscious decision by journal editors to culturally diversify the discourse.

Surlin and Dominick (1970–1971) referred to TV as a "third parent." Neil Hollander (1971) in "Adolescents and the War: The Sources of Socialization," published in *Journalism Quarterly*, also suggested that "the new 'parent' is the mass media" (p. 479). For Hollander, however, the historical shift from family, church, and school as primary sources of political information, to the mass media, particularly TV, was of concern. His findings suggested that adolescents are most reliant on TV for political information, followed by the school, family, church, and radio. Hollander laments that the family, particularly the father, as a source of political socialization has "vanished." Repeatedly, he is disturbed over the church's loss of influence: for "a culture that is supposedly built upon a Christian morality this is extremely surprising" (p. 478).

With few exceptions (e.g., Byrne, 1969) previous studies on the political socialization of youth had focused on the print media, the family, or school. Furthermore, the study of TV as an important source of political socialization did not have much of a history, judging from the limited sources available to Byrne (1969) or to Hollander (1971). Research on political socialization, starting with Lazarsfeld's early 1940s research, had been concerned primarily with the political process itself. Just as the 1960s civil rights movement may have circuitously ensured a place for the black viewer in the mass media discourse, so the Vietnam war found its way into the mass media discourse by drawing attention to TV's political socialization of children and youth.

D.K. Osborn and R.C. Endsley (1971) in "Emotional Reactions of Young Children to TV Violence" set out to "demonstrate a causal link between a measure of emotional sweating in children and film episodes containing violence" (p. 322). Since the Dysinger and Ruckmick (1933) study, according to the authors, not much had been done on the effects of filmed violence and children's emotions. The "Ss"—12 boys and 13 girls from 4.5 to 5.5 years of age (p. 323)—were fitted with electrodes on their fingers to gauge "ES" (emotional sweating). In a testing room of the Preschool Laboratory, a room with "a couch, end tables, lamps, chairs, and a TV set" (p. 324), children were exposed to "four treatment films": HV (human violence), CV (cartoon violence), HNV (human nonviolence), and CNV (cartoon nonviolence). Some data was lost due to "apparatus failure" and other data discarded because of "carry-over effects" from one treatment to the other. From the data that remained and was judged as useful, the authors concluded that "Ss" responded more emotionally to and were able to recall more details from the violent segments than from the nonviolent segments. Although the authors do not explore the "statistically significant relationship" between "emotionality and recall" they do note that it "raises interesting questions" (p. 330). What is considered more important is methodological utility, which is the authors' concluding point: "By using film stimuli and electrodes which permit some hand and finger movement, the problems of measuring GSR (galvanic skin reflex) with young, active children appear surmountable" (p. 330). At the risk of stating the self-evident, the authors here have shown that children under experimental laboratory conditions will perspire on their fingers while watching filmed aggressive actions. The viewing child is constructed as one who reacts to TV violence affectively and affect is constructed as a measurable physiological process.

Krugman (1971) reported on a case study with one female subject to show that exposure to TV elicits more passive responses "composed primarily of slow brain waves" in comparison to print exposure, which generates active responses "composed of fast brain waves" (p. 8). His experimental design and procedure is reminiscent of Guba et al.'s (1964) apparatus set-up: a sound and light controlled cubicle with a monitor, the subject fixed with an electrode to the occipital region, and wires leading to an adjacent room equipped with polygraph, tape system, and computer. To simulate a natural environment, the cubicle included "drapes, a comfortable couch, magazines on a cocktail table" (p. 5). From his conclusion that "television is more passive [than print] simply because it is an easier form of communication," Krugman suggests that the next research question should be to "determine just how easy or hard different communication or even educational materials should be made for optimal learning by various audiences" (p. 9). Clearly, as in his earlier paper with Hartley (1970), and his 1966 paper "The Measurement of Advertising Involvement," the viewer is construed as passive: in "involvement," "thinking," and "attention." But, as Krugman sees it, passive does not mean that learning does not occur, or that active engagement (i.e., with print) is "better" than passive engagement with information "stimuli." Future research, he suggests, must seek to provide a better understanding of the qualitative differences between and the implications for learning of slow and fast brain waves (pp. 8–9).

The effects of antismoking commercials on students' and adults' attitudes about smoking and their smoking behaviors were examined by Timothy O'Keefe (1971), published in *Public Opinion Quarterly*. In agreement with Klapper (1960), O'Keefe noted that media campaigns do not affect attitudinal changes independent of other mediating influences. Adults and high school students reported behavioral changes as a result of televised antismoking campaigns only insofar as they were apparently already predisposed to give up smoking (p. 248). O'Keefe found that the majority of smokers were convinced of the harmful effects of smoking, but this attitudinal change had not transferred to behavioral changes. Nonsmokers and adolescent smokers reportedly were more likely than adult smokers to believe that anti-smoking commercials would persuade smokers to quit. The adolescent viewer here is seen as more susceptible to the televised message than the adult viewer. However, according to O'Keefe, because the adolescent smoker has a shorter behavioral pattern in place than the adult smoker, this may account for the greater frequency among adolescents to cease smoking.

Following Bandura and Walters' (1963) study, Walter G. Hapkiewicz and Aubrey H. Roden (1971) conducted an experimental study of 60 second-graders to test the effects of aggressive cartoons on children's play. Children's postexposure behavior was scored on aggressive and "prosocial" measures ("sharing responses"). This study is the first to replicate Bandura's research with provision for effects conceptualized as prosocial. Total aggressive scores indicated "no significant differences among the three treament groups": aggressive cartoon, nonaggressive cartoon, and no cartoon conditions (p. 1584). Girls exhibited less overall aggressive play than boys, sharing responses were noted as more frequent among all children than aggressive responses, and boys in the aggressive cartoon condition displayed the least amount of sharing behaviors (pp. 1584–1585).

The authors conclude: "Since . . . [this] investigation was conducted in a school, where such behaviors as standing in lines, waiting, and taking turns are encouraged and reinforced, it would be valuable to study the effects of aggressive films on prosocial behavior in a variety of other social contexts" (p. 1585). Here, then, was a break with the conceptual monopoly over negative effects and an admission that children are in command of behavioral modes other than aggression, which persist despite aggressive modelling. The experiment had moved out of the laboratory and into the school. The next breakthrough would be "other social contexts."

Scherer (1971) in "Stereotype Change Following Exposure to Counter-Stereotypical Media Heroes," published in the *Journal of Broadcasting,* also considered the notion of prosocial TV content. Basing his argument on earlier research by DeFleur (1964) and Smythe (1954) on program content analyses, and on Maccoby's (1964) and Larsen's (1964) research on the social effects of mass communication, Scherer hypothesized that televised stereotype reversals might influence viewers to change their opinions about and attitudes toward traditional human stereotypes. In agreement with Maccoby (1964), Scherer suggests that since character stereotyping of heroes and villains is endemic to TV and comics—children's favorite mass media fare—the mass media are a significant influence "for building up stereotyped thinking in children" (p. 92). Scherer's data—derived from subjects in Germany—indicated that adults and adolescents hold negative stereotyped attitudes toward dark-haired, dark-skinned, and dark-eyed characters (villains) and positive attitudes toward light-haired, blue-eyed, and fair-skinned characters (heroes). Stereotype reversals, he found, do change viewers' evaluation, but these findings were evident only in the short-term, posttest evaluation scores.

What can be considered, in retrospect, a classic uses and gratifications study—in terms of methodology and the research tradition to which it paid homage—was reported in "Some Uses of Mass Media by 14 Year Olds" (Smith, 1971–1972), published in the *Journal of Broadcasting*. This study was conducted among nearly 600 Scottish adolescents. Smith's study begins with the citation of founders (e.g., Berelson, 1949; Herzog, 1944), and then outlines proposals for a revised research model first suggested by Katz and Foulkes (1962). Media use, Smith suggests, should be delineated not only according to individual perceptions of why particular media or media content are used. But the perceived outcomes, or consequences for the viewer of that use, must be examined with a view to better understand how use patterns function for individuals: hence, "functional analysis." Smith's typology of uses is predominantly negative, fitting squarely with escapist notions of viewers seeking refuge from unsatisfactory situations: withdrawal from interaction, problem avoidance, lack of meaningful activity (p. 39). Yet Smith found that children reportedly chose TV viewing only rarely to escape boredom. Only a small number of children reported that they used TV to withdraw from social interaction and to avoid problems. The one positive use classified by Smith reportedly was widely shared: the majority of respondents claimed to use TV as a source of discussion, or "coin of exchange" with peers (p. 43).

Smith found that "in situations of choice between media and non-media sources of gratification nearly all children prefer non-media sources" (p. 48) such as "physical activity, sports, peer-group interaction, youth clubs, other organized group activities, and hobbies" (p. 40). This suggests that "media play a useful, though limited, part in the lives of our children" (p. 49). A clearer understanding of viewers' perceived functions of media use can only be developed when research questions include nonmedia alternatives. As Smith observes, "previous research, by depending upon media-specific questions regarding use, may exaggerate the importance of the mass media over other sources of gratifications" (p. 49). The viewer in Smith's refined uses and gratifications model is an active viewer who selects media for specific purposes, and who often chooses media by default to ameliorate unsatisfactory situations; for example, when playmates or organized activities are unavailable.

Noting that experimental research on the effects of televised aggression on children had focused only on aggression toward inanimate objects, Faye B. Steuer, James M. Applefield and Rodney Smith (1971) conducted a laboratory experiment to "determine the effect of filmed aggression on children's aggressive behavior toward other human beings" (p. 442). Published in the *Journal of Experimental Child Psychology*, the article's textual attention to methodological design and procedure predictably took precedence over discussion of theory, findings, or implications, which warrant only brief paragraphs. Ten preschoolers of mixed racial and socioeconomic background, equally divided for sex, and with a median age of 51 months, participated in this study; all were enrolled in the same university daycare facility. To "simulate natural play conditions" the experimental room was equipped with toys assumed as appropriate for this age group and these were laid out in what was taken to be a natural arrangement: "an inflated plastic punch-me doll, two wooden puzzles, six large cardboard blocks, two toy trucks, two plates, two cups and saucers, two spoons, a rubber knife, a plastic gun, a cowboy hat, a large cardboard carton, two plastic animals, a pail and shovel, and two bed pillows. At the start of each session, the toys were placed in predetermined standard positions about the room" (p. 444).

Here definitions of "play" and "toys" are circumscribed and delimited by the selection, arrangement, and location of toys which are to enable play. Disregarding the implications of such constructs, conclusions are drawn from the observational data: children in the "treatment conditions" substantially increased aggressive behaviors following exposure to the "television stimuli" compared to their "baseline conditions" at which time "subjects showed a marked tendency to keep peace with one another" (p. 446). In reference to Bandura et al.'s (1963) study of aggression against inanimate objects within a solitary play situation, Steuer et al. view their study as more naturalistic and, hence, more suitable to generalization: "The conditions of this study may be said to simulate the natural television-viewing and play situations of preschool children more closely than the conditions of other studies cited" (1971:446). What is striking here is the skewed logic underlying the conceptualization of what constitutes children's authentic interpersonal relations in the context of unmediated play. Complementing this conflation of naturalistic and laboratory-based "context" is the meticulous attention to methodological detail—from tracing the movements of the undergraduate "Os" (observers) to noting the model number of the Sony video tape recorders.

1972–1973

In the tradition of Bandura's research on filmed aggression and behavior, Glen Thomas Ellis and Francis Sekyra (1972) examined the effects of aggressive cartoons on 51 first graders. The authors observe that "most research in the area of film-mediated aggression has been conducted in laboratory setting . . . [which] may have altered their [children's] behavior" (p. 38). In order to rectify this methodological limitation, the authors conducted their study in a school: "a setting to which children are accustomed" (p. 38). Children underwent a three-day "pretreatment observation in the classroom" (p. 39). "Treatment" then proceeded on the fourth day, at which time "Ss . . . were escorted to separate viewing rooms isolated from normal school activity and other extraneous stimuli. The stimulus films were projected in their entirety, and the Ss were conducted back to their classrooms" (p. 40). Similarly, the control group was moved from the classroom "to an empty room" where assistants conducted a 5-minute "casual conversation" with the children, after which they were escorted back to their classroom (p. 40). The data derived from this experiment suggested "that the effect of viewing an aggressive cartoon sequence was an increased rate of emitted hostile behaviors by the Ss when observed in [their] natural environment" (p. 42).

Like Hapkiewicz and Roden (1971), Ellis and Sekyra moved the experiment out of the laboratory and into the school. But the substitution of an empty (class)room for the laboratory hardly counts as a "natural" setting. The possibility of increased "hostile" behaviors following viewing of aggressive cartoons notwithstanding, the authors fail to acknowledge the highly unusual circumstance—from the point of view of the children, at least—of removing children from the classroom and showing them a cartoon in an empty room. The point is that statements which qualify the specificity of and limitations for the generalizability of data derived from unique research situations are consistently absent from the (experimental) psychological discourse on media and children. Discursive emphasis on methodological design and procedure remained central to the research on TV and children. Whether the rules of discourse formation compelled researchers to report only that which is observable, or whether consideration of the circumscribing conditions of televiewing remained beyond the scientific imagination of researchers, is debatable.

In "Television and Political Socialization," published in *Educational Broadcasting Review*, Dominick (1972) "explores the role of television as a teacher of political facts and attitudes to children in sixth and seventh grades" (p. 48). Questionnaire data suggested that mass media, particularly TV, are primary sources of political information for children (p. 51). Dominick suggests that while TV may provide youngsters with political information, the actual "effects"—attitude or opinion formation, political behaviors—may be dependent upon other socialization agencies, namely family, friends, or school, which help children interpret and evaluate that information. Effects, then, are not seen as a direct function of TV exposure but are considered as a consequence of how the information derived by the child from TV is mediated by other socialization agents such as parents, friends, and teachers. The child is constructed here as one whose socialization by and learning from the media is conditioned by the social context within which the viewing experience occurs. Dominick would continue to argue for the importance of children's social context in attempts to locate effects (e.g., Dominick, 1974).

The first longitudinal study on long-term effects of TV violence and viewer aggression was Eron, Huesman, Lefkowitz and Walder's (1972) "Does Television Violence Cause Aggression?" published in *American Psychologist*. An initial sample of 875 third graders was recontacted 10 years after the first study in 1963 (Eron, Walder & Lefkowitz, 1963). In the 1972 study 427 members of the original sample participated. The data of the first study was derived from interviews with peers, subjects, and parents, which provided peer-rated aggression scores and parental reports of viewing preferences and amount; data sources a decade later used only the subject and his/her peers. In the 1963 study, a significantly strong relationship was found between exposure to violent programs and aggressive behaviors. A decade later, that relationship apparently was still found to hold (p. 263). Interestingly, the authors view dispositions and viewing preferences at age eight or nine as "strongly" related to preferences for violent programming and aggressive behaviors some ten years later in those same children: "By the use of cross-lagged correlations, partial correlations, and multiple regression, it was demonstrated that there is a probable causative influence of watching violent television programs in early formative years on later aggression" (p. 263). Admitting that perhaps other factors over a ten-year period may have influenced the sample's propensity for aggression, the authors, nonetheless, insist that "the effect of television violence on aggression is relatively independent of these other factors and explains a larger portion of the variance than does any other single factor . . . including IQ, social status, mobility aspirations, religious practice, ethnicity, and parental disharmony" (p. 262).

Accepting, for the moment, that exposure to violent TV content is strongly related to aggression in children, it does not then logically follow that watching violent programs as a child is necessarily related to aggressive behavior in adulthood. By analogy, watching a lot of prosocial programs during the formative years such as "Sesame Street" or "Mr. Rogers' Neighborhood" is not a good predictor of cooperative, helpful, nonprejudiced behavior in adulthood. The methodological rule system used by Eron et al. to isolate effects casts the subject, social context, and TV into this discursive grid: "the path coefficient from third-grade television violence to thirteenth-grade aggression is the coefficient of third-grade television in a regression equation predicting thirteenth-grade aggression with third-grade aggression controlled. The obtained pattern of path coefficients adds further credence to the argument that watching violent television contributes to the development of aggressive habits" (p. 260). In one sentence, empirical "proof" is established that the influence of TV violence on viewer aggression, already verified for short-term effects, was also applicable to explanations of long-term effects. This "truth" would provide theoretical ammunition for later pro-effects proponents (e.g., Andison, 1977; Liebert et al., 1982) and later longitudinal studies (e.g., Eron & Huesman, 1980; Singer & Singer, 1980).

Greenberg (1972) continued his research on black viewers and in "Children's Reactions to TV Blacks" extended his research to include the influence on black and white children of black TV character portrayals. In this study, Greenberg aimed to show to what extent TV portrayal of blacks in dramatic presentations helps structure black and white children's racial beliefs (p. 6). Four hundred 4th and 5th graders (approximately 300 white and 100 black) were interviewed during school hours. The white group was further divided into rural, urban, and suburban children; black children into urban only. Identification with black TV characters among white children was found to be strongly influenced by the groups' residential areas. The opposite pattern emerged from the data for white urban children. Black children reported watching more TV programs featuring blacks than white children but white children, also, apparently "find black TV characters with whom they identify" (p. 13). Greenberg claims that among white and black children, "identification [with black characters] has been tentatively established" (p. 13). But identification must further be examined in the context of "the possible mediational role of parents and/or peers including black peers" (p. 14). Interracial attitudes are not developed solely by exposure to TV black character portrayals or, for that matter, via dramatized programs alone. Greenberg maintains that it is important to consider "how a child cognitively fits together or processes the race riot with the comedy series, or the black dope addict with the black nurse" (p. 14). For Greenberg, TV is but one source, albeit for some viewers a primary one, of information about blacks for both white and black children. For Greenberg, interracial attitude formation is partially shaped by what children learn from TV, but how that learning occurs—in conjunction with learning from other media and nonmedia sources—is not explicable in simple behavioral terms.

The black child as potential consumer is considered in "How Race Affects Children's TV Commercials" (Barry & Hansen, 1973), published in the *Journal of Advertising*. An experimental study of 30 black and 30 white second grade children yielded data which suggested that: black and white children produced similar recall responses to two 60-second commercials ("Kellogg's Frosted Flakes" and "Kellogg's Smacks"); black children's product preferences are positively influenced by inclusion of a black character, and white children's product preferences are not adversely affected by the presence of a black character. In the authors' view, the positive relationship between black children's product recall and product preferences, and "the degree of 'blackness'" in advertisements targeted at children, has important marketing implications in view of "the opportunities posed by the existence of a black children's market which eagerly awaits marketing efforts specifically designed for it . . . [since] today's children are tomorrow's consumers" (p. 67).

The construction of the child as indirect consumer of televised products via product purchase demands of parents had been underway in market research quarters (Ward, 1972a, 1972b; Ward & Wackman, 1972) since the publication of "Children's Attention to Television Advertising" (Ward, Levinson & Wackman, 1972) in the Surgeon General's Report (1972). These studies, however, made only passing reference to the role of race in advertising. In Thomas E. Barry and Richard W. Hansen's study, the black child as consumer makes its first appearance in the discourse, albeit the market research discourse.

Extensive content analyses of TV portrayal of violence had been undertaken by George Gerbner (1972) for the Surgeon General's Report. In an attempt to get beyond mere violence "ratings," Gerbner and his associates had developed the concept of a violence "profile" or a set of "message configurations" (Eleey, Gerbner & Tedesco, 1972–1973) as a more reliable measure of TV's symbolic message system. Violence "ratings" provided indices to the number of violent acts coded in specific programs, across serials and program genres. The question of what counts as violent behavior was acknowledged as problematic then as it is today. Gerbner's violence "profile" attempted to refine "ratings" by including measures of symbolic violence: "contextual, structural and dynamic variables that measure various aspects of TV violence" (Eleey et al., 1972–1973:24).

Dominick (1973) applied Gerbner's analytic "profile" framework to a study of one week's prime-time programming in 1972. Like Gerbner,

Dominick found the portrayal of violence to be significantly dissimilar from the demographic patterns of crime evident in contemporary society. That is to say, "[TV] criminals bear little resemblance to their real life counterparts. Blacks, young people, and lower-class individuals are underrepresented in the TV criminal world" (p. 249). Nonwhites were found substantially underrepresented as victims of violence, violent crimes within families were underrepresented, and most TV criminal activity was directed at individuals, not at property, as is the case in "real-world crime" (p. 249). The TV criminal almost always was apprehended and brought to justice, although neither the legal proceedings nor long-term consequences (for the criminal) of incarceration are dealt with on TV. Moreover, the on-screen capture and bringing to justice of criminals, according to Dominick, far overstates a contrived effectiveness of a "legal system [which] is not nearly so efficient" (p. 249).

This profile of the symbolic messages of TV violence is quite different from what Smythe (1954), for example, had proposed nearly two decades earlier. The characterization and containment of screen violence now was seen as a highly unrealistic representation of real-life violence which, as Dominick speculates, provides society with the illusory message that "all is in order": "TV crime and TV violence are presented in ways that seem to minimize their potential threat to society. . . . Violence is typically set in the past or future, in relatively unfamiliar surroundings, and involves people who are not closely acquainted. . . . It has been pushed indoors and is portrayed as private, hidden, and unsuccessful. It is performed by one-dimensional caricatures who are motivated by personal failings, not by inadequacies existing in society" (1973:250).

This construct suggests that TV violence is harmless for viewers because it portrays an unrealistic picture of the social world. Dominick turns the argument on its head by implying that TV violence effects cannot be seen in terms of increased individual and societal violence but, rather, in terms of promoting an increased false sense of security and complacency that "all is in order." If this is the case, Dominick questions: What might be the implications for children of such distorted portrayals of crime and violence, and the underlying symbolic message of deviance allegedly regulated under the just control of law enforcement? To what extent grade-school children internalize "the norms of the TV world" (p. 242) is posited as the research Dominick proposes to undertake subsequent to the "baseline" data gathered in this study.

A departure from the paradigmatic conceptualizations of TV violence effects—increased aggression through observational learning (social learning theory), increased aggression in response to specific content (instigation theory), and decreased aggression in response to specific content (catharsis model)—was under way. Specific messages from specific TV texts would soon no longer be seen as accurate indicators of either TV content per se or of what the audience was learning. As Dominick, following Gerbner, proposed, the entire symbolic image of TV violence and crime required closer examination before any coherent model of effects could be postulated. Quantitative violence "ratings" can provide no more than a numerical count of coded "acts." A violence "profile," by contrast, promised to delineate how cultural norms and values are embedded within and transmitted via TV's symbolic code (p. 241). From such analysis, "the symbolic functions of this content" could then proceed.

This approach informed Dominick and Gail E. Rauch's (1972) study, "The Image of Women in Network TV Commercials," published that same year in the *Journal of Broadcasting*. The study reports on a content analysis of prime-time commercials, followed by a review of "the criticisms made by feminist writers" (p. 260). This is one of the first studies that examined the symbolic role of women on TV. For the most part, women in professional positions were found "conspicuously absent from commercials" (p. 264), women primarily are shown as preoccupied with household cleaning products and their appearance, and "in the world of the television commercials, women are housewives or low-level employees" (p. 265). The implications for children's socialization are summed up this way: "Our main quarrel with television is that it does not provide human models for a bright 13-year-old girl who would like to grow up to be something more than an ecstatic floor waxer" (p. 260).

In "Mass Communication and Socialization" Herbert H. Hyman (1973–1974) assessed the current position of socialization theory as applied to the study of mass media. He also noted the importance of extending empirical measurement units both in terms of media content and effects. Research on TV and children, he noted, must consider more than short-term effects, and needs to consider "prosocial" effects of TV as interacting with and possibly offsetting negative influences (pp. 532–533). Even the Surgeon General's Report, he observed, "implied by the title, to study both pro- and anti-social behavior," provided "no evidence" of TV's potentially prosocial effects (p. 532). The study of media socialization, in Hyman's opinion, must move away from the assumptions of social alienation and deprivation which underlie the escapist model of televiewing. Hyman argues instead: "In studying the socializing influences of the media, I stress the socialization of sentiments, about which we know so little" (p. 529). Although the kind of research he proposes, admittedly, may be a return to "old-fashioned audience research" (p. 527), he insists that viewers are not socialized by media only into a specific set of values, norms, attitudes, or knowledge, but into affective states and values neglected by contemporary research. "Research on sentiments would shed light not only on a new sphere of socialization that is important of itself, but also . . . on many *old* topics for which our research findings remain shallow or enigmatic" (p. 529).

Noting that "extensive research"—namely, Bandura et al.'s (1963) and Lövaas's (1961) filmed aggression experiments—has shown that exposure to filmed violence, with and without verbal reinforcements, leads to increased aggressive behaviors, C. Edward Wotring and Greenberg (1973) set out to examine the relationship between exposure to televised violence and verbal and physical aggression in adolescent boys. The data derived from two successive experiments suggested that social class did not influence aggression scores. Both lower- and middle-class boys demonstrated equal amounts of physical and verbal aggression, although middle-class boys apparently "show[ed] more intense verbal aggression" (p. 457). Aggression scores were reported higher for the experimental than the control groups. Of concern also was the effect of showing the consequences for victims of violent actions. It was hypothesized that exposure to the effects of violence on victims might inhibit aggression in viewers. Since no significant relationship was found between exposure to portrayed consequences of violent acts and decreased aggression, the authors suggest that adolescent boys' "consequence thresholds" might be far greater than anticipated. Seemingly dismayed at their findings, the researchers comment: "We wonder whether viewing scenes of torture, concentration camp victims, or similar holocaust events may be necessary to raise inhibitions to a sufficient level" (p. 459). The widely accepted postulate that viewing TV violence caused viewer aggression still held for Wotring and Greenberg, although, as they admitted, "there may be an interaction between preangering, social class, and television exposure treatments" (p. 458).

1974–1975

"British Children and Televised Violence" (Greenberg, 1974–1975), published in *Public Opinion Quarterly*, reported on a cross-cultural replication study of TV violence effects on children. With a sample of British children, Greenberg found "findings very similar to American data, in terms of both direction and magnitude of the relationship" (p. 531). His British sample consisted of 726 nine-, 12- and 15-year-olds, of whom 475 were from working-class backgrounds, 250 from middle-class backgrounds, 418 were white, and the rest comprised of "Asians,

Africans, and others" (p. 533); the sample was equally divided by sex. The data were derived from questionnaires self-administered during school hours. Two measures of aggression were used: perceived effectiveness of the use of violence to resolve conflicts, and a reported willingness to use aggressive means. The kinds of conflicts or problems the children were asked to respond to were not noted. It would seem that a stated willingness to use aggression for purposes of self-defense in a life-threatening situation, or for purposes of retrieving a candy bar from another child, involves significantly different moral and ethical justifications. Such inattention to considerations of what constitutes justified and unjustified aggression was typical of most violence effects studies. Observer-coded descriptions and enumerations of aggressive behaviors rarely took into account whether behaviors such as shoving, hitting, or shouting were justified in the context of play strategies or peer relations. Nonetheless, Greenberg claims to have established a positive, albeit moderate, relationship between exposure to televised violence and viewer aggression in a cross-cultural context but cautions that TV may not be the only source of children's aggressive attitudes (p. 545).

Greenberg concludes that the child viewer is not a "passive receiver" of TV information who "faces the medium with a blank mind, ready to accept whatever is forthcoming: quite the opposite, the child is actively seeking certain gratifications" (p. 547). Greenberg argues for an affective model over a behavioral or cognitive one, suggesting that if the viewer's motivations for viewing and the gratifications sought can be isolated, then a clearer understanding of what the viewer takes away from the medium can be determined: "The aggression theory view is being expanded here to encompass a broader spectrum of effects. It is a position that in essence argues for a more content-free, less cognitive approach to examining certain effects (p. 547).

"Uses and Gratifications Research" (Katz, Blumler & Gurevitch, 1974a)—often cited since its publication as the definitive text illustrative of this "approach"—made a plea for discarding the "label 'uses and gratifications approach' in favor of its recognition as theory" (p. 510). They discuss briefly the benefits of a uses and gratifications model for studying children's use of media and assert, citing Schramm et al. (1961), that "conventional effects designs may be unable to capture that child uses of the mass media for fantasizing might either drain off discontent caused by the hard blows of socialization or lead a child into withdrawal from the real world" (Katz et al., 1974a:519). Schramm et al.'s model posited a pseudocatharsis hypothesis ("drain off discontent") based on assumptions of a fundamental need among the young to escape, via fantasy, from "the real world" and the "hard blows of socialization" (p. 519). The child viewer is seen here as an active selector of media, but one whose motivations are grounded in negative social experiences. The origins of media uses thus are seen to lie in viewers' combined social and psychological conditions where the social (i.e., socialization), however, is seen to subsume the psychological (fantasy).

In 1974 the discourse of the *Journal of Communication* underwent a significant shift: from a relatively marginal position within the field of mass communications study to a highly visible forum of debate focused on contemporary issues. A change in discursive focus, in textual format, in editorship, and an institutional relocation all converged to reconstruct a forum for discourse on what would be seen to count as communications studies and research. A symposium on women in the media appeared in one issue of the 1974 volume, and a section on aging and the media appeared in a subsequent issue that same year, along with a special section on "Children's TV Commercials." Silent on questions of TV and children since TV's introduction in 1950, the journal abruptly transformed itself (along with a format transformation in 1973) to become, by middecade, the flagship journal for communications studies.

A 1973 change in the *Journal of Communication*'s editorship is significant insofar as it reflected a reconstitution of mass communications studies per se, and played a role in refocusing specific mass media topics of which children and TV headed the list. A change in journal editorship has the potential to change the discursive rules of the game: editorial changes can signal institutional relocation and, possibly, disciplinary reorientation. In the case of the *Journal of Communication*'s institutional and disciplinary shift from the Department of Speech Communication at the University of New Mexico to the Annenberg School of Communications at the University of Pennsylvania, this move can be read as a discursive event signaling difference and discontinuity.

"Archaeology," as Alan Sheridan (1980:109) explains, "takes as the object of its description what is usually regarded as an obstacle: its aim is not to overcome differences, but to analyse them." As noted in Chapter 1, an archeological enterprise seeks to identify and locate the dispersion, disappearance, emergence, or transformation of statements within discursive rule systems. As a material surface for the articulation of statements, the scholarly journal constitutes one such field upon which statements are inscribed under highly rule-bound constraints. When the rules change, an object of study potentially is relocated and resystematized within a new arrangement of rules: These may be disciplinary, theoretical, methodological, or material at the level of the physical text. And, indeed, the typographic layout for the 1974 issue signaled a new format conceptualization of what was to count as communications studies. This shift reflected the new editorship's institutional base in a school of communications not primarily devoted to speech studies. The visual impact of the journal's new format (e.g., typeset, graphics, color) clearly was to signify a concept of communication that was more than speech and rhetoric studies.

In its first year at the Annenberg School under the new editorship of George Gerbner, the journal textually organized a symposium on the study of women in the media. The text was augmented in addition to the obligatory statistical charts and graphs with graphics and photo illustrations. The cover assumed a magazine format replete with issue topics superimposed on collages, drawings, photo, or bold print backdrops, thus signifying a more contemporary look—a marketing strategy to promote communications studies. Furthermore, the material format changed as did the objects of communications study. Children and TV, absent along with other mass media topics from this particular channel of discourse for 24 years, were to emerge by the end of the decade as principal objects of study in the discourse of this journal. Few other journals consistently produced discursive units (special issues, special sections) centered on TV and children. By the end of the decade and well into the 1980s, the discourse on TV and children can be traced almost exclusively through the successive volume series of the *Journal of Communication*.

While Foucault suggests that an archeology of discourse should not be concerned with attributing statements to authorial authority or synthesizing disciplinary totalities, the archeological task must consider marginal events such as the one just outlined as significant in order to identify difference, discontinuity, or transformation. Although attempts to note such discontinuities run the risk of falling into the discourse of social history by virtue of identifying the minutiae of authors, editors, and institutional affiliations, these are, however, the very authorities of delimitation who, according to Foucault, wield invisible power over the (re)construction of knowledges.

Discourse is not a faceless text or set of practices. The archeologist is not interested in exactly who said what for which reasons—hence, author or editor "X" could just as well be labeled author "Y." But the notation (in fact, annotation) of scholarly statements requires author reference: the citation of author/editor function and institutional affiliation is an important part of scholarly text production. Such data preface every article, book, and every journal issue, and constitute the central rule by which the authority of statements is sustained. As such, the validity of truth statements *within* the discourse cannot be divorced from their authorial signifier. It is, ironically, what the scholarly enterprise of knowledge and truth production is founded upon. In short, under the editorship of Gerbner, the *Journal of Communication* redefined what was to count as state-of-the-art communications research.

Research on TV gender portrayal, particularly the portrayal of female images, had not achieved notable visibility in the discourse on TV and children. The civil rights movement appeared to generate interest in black viewers and the TV portrayal of blacks. The "American women's movement" was seen to focus interest on media sex-role portrayal: "especially with the growth of a newly organized American women's movement that has challenged traditional sex roles" (Busby, 1974:690). The TV portrayal of gender images and gender-based values and behaviors, sex-role socialization via the media, media stereotyping and personality development, attitude and value formation, had not been a visible focus of study prior to 1974, when the first group of studies on women and the mass media appeared in a special section of the Journal of Communication. Nine papers were included in this 1974 symposium on mass media and women. These are reviewed here in alphabetical order; they have not been inserted alphabetically throughout this chapter in order to retain the discursive unity within which they were textually sited in this journal volume.

Linda J. Busby (1974) in "Defining the Sex-Role Standard in Network Children's Programs" reports on a content analysis of 20 popular cartoon programs broadcast during the 1972 to 1973 season that represented the range of Saturday morning cartoon offerings. Busby had virtually no research on TV sex-role portrayal to draw from. Similarly, Dominick and Rauch's (1972) study of "The Image of Women in Network TV Commercials" had no research literature to draw from and, instead, relied solely on newspaper and TV Guide references. Busby found that the 20 cartoons analyzed presented an image of men and women in traditional gender-based characterizations: "Males assume complete responsibility for family financial support, and the females assume responsibility for child care and home maintenance. . . . No married females in the sample worked, [and] the few females who worked out-of-home jobs were in low level employment . . . [and] females tended to have low levels of personal aspirations" (p. 698).

Overall, a general negativism toward women outside the home was seen to pervade the scripts: women were shown consistently to impede everyday affairs, from creating traffic jams to crowding bus aisles. The message to (child) viewers, according to Busby, is clear: women belong in the home, not in the public life of work (p. 693). Since TV plays a significant role in children's socialization, then cartoons, young children's favorite fare, are a powerful source of children's learning. Busby sees cartoons as one source of children's socialization that does not promote contemporary norms of equitable gender roles but, instead, legitimates existing relations: "If television indeed plays a major part in the child's socialization, findings from this study indicate that the sex roles presented in the cartoon programs further the entrenchment of traditional sex roles" (p. 698).

Concurring with Busby, Michele L. Long and Rita J. Simon (1974) also found that "the general image of women continues to be one of tradition and sexism" (p. 110). In their study of 22 family- and child-oriented programs broadcast during Saturday morning, early after-noon, and prime-time hours, the image of women is one of dependency, low prestige, and powerlessness, cast into subordinate social and occupational roles, preoccupied with appearance and "trying to attract a man" (p. 110). Woman's subordinate status is reinforced by her on-screen label as a "girl" regardless of her age: "Women are referred to as girls, while men are men unless they are in fact boys" (p. 110). Long and Simon see TV as a negative socializing force for children of both sexes who are being socialized "toward a future that is based on the status quo," not "toward a future that is adjusting to and anticipating the changes that are already occurring in the business world, at the universities, in politics, and in other spheres" (p. 107).

Beuf (1974) reported in this symposium on interviews with 63 middle-class 3- to 6-year-olds (37 boys, 26 girls). Demystifying the popular belief that "the women's movement is changing American children's ideas about sex roles," she reports that her findings indicate that "sex role perception of children born since the women's move-ment shows little change" (p. 142). Children's career aspirations fell along traditional gendered lines: boys chose the more adventurous occupations of policeman, sports superstar and cowboy, whereas girls chose "quieter pastimes" such as nursing (p. 143). Girls specified opposite-sex career ambitions whereas boys did not. However, girls with opposite-sex career aspirations were quick to dismiss such am-bitions: "I'll never do it . . . because I'm not a boy" (p. 143). The male response to opposite-sex career ambitions, on the other hand, in the words of one boy: " . . . If I were a girl I'd have to grow up to be nothing," (p. 144), reflected both a socialized male perspective on female occupational options and, although Beuf does not imply this, can be read as an incisive encapsulation of the transparency of women's social, economic, and political status in society. In terms of media influence, Beuf found that moderate and light TV viewers indicated a "wider range of choice in career selection than heavy viewers" (p. 144), which suggested to her that sex-stereotyped role portrayals on TV do not expand but limit children's perceptions of same- and opposite-sex occupational choices.

Studies published in the *Journal of Communication*'s special section, "Women: A Symposium," all presented similar findings: in magazines (Franzwa, 1974), TV commercials (Courtney & Whipple, 1974), cartoons (Streicher, 1974), daytime soap operas (Downing, 1974; Turow, 1974), and prime-time drama (Turow, 1974; Tedesco, 1974), the message to the audience is that woman's place is in the home; that women do not make important "decisions or do important things; that women are dependent upon men and are regarded primarily as sexual objects" (Courtney & Whipple, 1974:110). Traditional sex-role stereotypes indeed were seen as entrenched in both the media and in viewers.

Five of the nine papers included in this symposium were content analyses based on statistical analyses of portrayal frequency counts, demographic (e.g., race, age, SES) and personality (e.g., assertive, emotional, "feminine," etc.) variables, speech modalities (e.g., advising, ordering, complying, agreeing) from which a (cultural) profile of what counts as being female on TV was derived. Compared with earlier quantitative accounts (Smythe, 1954; Head, 1954), which had not gone beyond noting that men outnumbered women on the screen by three to one, this set of studies reflected what could be considered a new sensitivity to sociocultural questions of symbolic gender portrayal in the mass media. A similar orientation would emerge the following year in another special section on gender studies in the same journal.

Sex traditionally had been defined within the social sciences as an essential characterizing variable along with age, SES, educational level, and so forth. Yet in the early 1970s, most social science discourses began a turn away from simplistic notions of sex as a biologically based variable to a recognition that sexual difference is embedded in culturally ascribed and produced gender attributes. Although gender remained conceptually framed in functionalist "sex-role" terminology, and the ideological production of gender was not an issue for publication until the mid-1980s, the recognition in the early 1970s that "cultural forces" shape or "cultivate" (Tedesco, 1974) "sex-role images" (Busby, 1975:127) marks the advent of a new series of conceptual statements superseding earlier categorizations of sex-differentiated portrayals and viewers.

Dominick (1974) examined the relationship between the portrayal of crime and law enforcement and children's formation of attitudes toward crime and police in "Crime and Law Enforcement on Prime-Time TV," published in *Public Opinion Quarterly*. An interactive relationship between TV exposure and the viewer is proposed for explaining "TV's role in the socialization process . . . [and] what the child brings to the viewing situation" (p. 6). A questionnaire survey of 371 fifth-graders from two New York schools in "blue-collar" and "white-collar" communities (p. 7) revealed that high amounts of TV exposure correlated positively with children's belief that criminals usually get caught, with increased knowledge of civil rights, and with greater identification with TV law enforcement characters (p. 11). However, for "both boys and girls, the strongest predictors of general evaluation of police were the perceived attitudes of friends and family" (p. 11). As such, children's attitudes toward crime and law enforcement cannot be said to be causally linked to TV, independent of other social mediating factors such as family and peers. The most disturbing finding for Dominick is the "low but persistent relationship between the amount of importance attributed to TV as an information source and the child's reluctance to indicate he would report witnessed crimes to police" (p. 12). Hence, as Dominick interprets his findings, this "exaggerated idea about police efficacy" convinces heavy viewers that "most criminals will be apprehended . . . [and thus] it matters little whether or not the person who witnessed a crime reports it since the criminal will be caught regardless" (p. 12). Gerbner and his associates would later postulate that heavy TV viewers develop a sense of fear and insecurity about a "mean world" (e.g., Gerbner & Gross, 1976)—an antithetical view to Dominick's conceptualization that heavy TV viewing engenders a sense of security and complacency derived from TV's myth of social order under the efficient control of law enforcement agencies.

The extent to which children's tolerance for aggressive behavior among peers is influenced by exposure to televised aggression was investigated by Ronald S. Drabman and Margaret Hanratty Thomas (1974) and reported in "Does Media Violence Increase Children's Real-Life Aggression?" published in *Developmental Psychology*. The experimental study of 22 male and 22 female third and fourth graders from a middle-class neighborhood was conducted in a trailer located in the schoolyard. The experimental group was shown a "cowboy film that depicted many violent events" (p. 418). In this group, younger children were placed who "at first played, quietly, then became progressively destructive . . . culminat[ing] in a physical fight ending with the apparent destruction of the television camera" (p. 418). The authors found that the experimental group appeared more tolerant of physical aggression among the younger children because this group took longer to seek adult help in mediating the fight than the control group. For Drabman and Thomas, "the frightening possibility [is] that while some children are incorporating such violent responses into their everyday behavior, even more may be learning to tolerate them"

(p. 421). Other than sex of subjects and "treatment conditions" no other mediating variables were considered. Unlike Bandura et al.'s premise a decade earlier that viewing televised violence leads to viewer aggression, exposure to TV violence, according to Drabman and Thomas, leads to the inverse of aggressive behaviors: a passivity marked by an increased tolerance of aggression, and a reluctance to intervene in physical altercations when encountered in real life situations (p. 419).

Following Collins' (1970) research on children's learning from TV, Bernard Z. Friedlander, Harriet S. Wetstone, and Christopher C. Scott (1974) examined preschoolers' learning of a "3-minute age-appropriate informational television program" (p. 561). The authors render effects problematic, noting that young children's comprehension of TV information cannot be taken for granted. Imitation of televised behaviors, as the authors see it, is only a partial account of effects. Comprehension of visual and verbal information, a function of cognitive development, has an equally significant if not greater influence on possible effects.

The notion that cognitive processes are at work in televiewing was beginning to gain ground. Despite the use of an age-appropriate televised segment (an animated segment on the sense of smell presented by an imaginary character and a talking bird companion), the authors found that "more than half of the 31 children demonstrated comprehension of less than half of the tested information" (p. 561). Although the preschoolers "did comprehend the general flow of ongoing activity . . . [they] failed to make contact with the central informational theme of the program" (p. 564). Moreover, the rapid action and animated format, generally assumed to sustain children's attention, "appeared to have low comprehension payoff" (p. 564). If such poor comprehension of program content specifically designed for this age group was evident, it implies that comprehension of regular TV fare, including children's programs, advertisements, and noninstructional cartoons, may very well be beyond the cognitive range of most preschoolers and early elementary school-age children. What children learn from programs which they only marginally comprehend, and what effects are indicative of such learning, then, remains questionable for the authors.

A field comparison study (Gadberry, 1974) of 22 white male preschoolers from a suburban neighborhood yielded yet another TV effect: TV viewing leads to decreased motor and verbal activity among preschool boys. Heavy viewers were observed to require less maternal interference than light viewers during play and televiewing conditions and were observed to engage in less verbal and physical activity and more attention shifts during play than light viewers. From "an operant learning point of view," a child's "reduced activity level" during televiewing seems to require less adult intervention, thereby reducing possibilities for parental selective reinforcements (p. 1135). In short, televiewing "may affect parental socialization practices, since less parental interference occurred during viewing, along with less behavior which was potentially reinforceable" (p. 1135). Here, following Bandura, early childhood socialization is conceptualized as a process of selective reinforcements. Sharon Gadberry finds no evidence that TV directly causes viewer aggression in preschool boys. However, she does find a negative effect: heavy viewing sets the conditions for less than optimal rates of parental reinforcements (p. 1135).

Another study on TV and socialization, "Children's Television: More than Mere Entertainment," was published in *Harvard Educational Review* (Leifer, Gordon & Graves, 1974). This journal had remained silent for the last two decades on the topic of TV and children. Following a review of the literature on TV effects, and an outline of the structure of the TV industry, Leifer et al. focus on the need for parental involvement in children's viewing. In order to make children more discerning viewers, they argue, parents and children need to be taught how to view TV critically. Instead of arguing for or against effects, the authors propose that: "Perhaps we can teach children about the roles of television, the types of information it presents, and the cues that indicate which type of information is presented. If young children can acquire this knowledge, they might understand when and how particular content relates to their lives" (p. 239). In other words, whatever alleged effects accrue from TV exposure can be mediated by critical viewing skills acquired by both the child and, preferably, by parents as well. The notion of "television literacy" (p. 239) surfaces here with the caveat that little is known about whether and how parents teach children to critically evaluate TV content or, for that matter, how children's understanding of TV content develops (pp. 240–241). A better understanding of the development of cognitive processes involved in the comprehension of TV information and of family interaction patterns "would provide parents the opportunity to teach children how to evaluate the applicability of television to their lives" (p. 241). The authors thus argue for a cognitive model of televiewing, one that assumes that viewers' learning from and socialization by TV is mediated by knowledge the viewer brings to the screen. That knowledge, moreover, has a social source in the family and parents are seen as a potential teaching resource to help elaborate children's critical comprehension skills. This construct positions the viewer as active, and televiewing as a cognitive, not behavioral, process.

Part of an apparent commitment to present its discourse via thematic groupings such as special sections, issues or symposia, the 1974 final issue of the *Journal of Communication* focused on TV advertising and children. The three papers included in this section examined policy issues related to advertisements targeted at children (Melody & Ehrlich, 1974), reported on a field study of "children's cognitive and attitudinal defenses to commercials" (Rossiter & Robertson, 1974), and reviewed existing research on children and TV advertising (Sheikh, Prasad & Rao, 1974). Anees A. Sheikh, V. Kanti Prasad, and Tanniru R. Rao found that the research "on TV ads and their effects on children lags behind more 'prestigious' areas of investigation" (p. 126). According to the authors, market research dominates investigation into TV advertisements for children, and only a handful of studies have analyzed children's attention and attitudes to commercials. As evidenced in the citations, most of the existing research was documented in unpublished conference papers and doctoral dissertations, and in research center working papers. A few such studies were reported in the Surgeon General's Report. In agreement with Ward's comment in the Surgeon General's Report on the low academic status of research on TV advertising, Sheikh et al. note that "this field is not considered sufficiently respectable in academic circles" (p. 133). This suggests that unlike, for instance, the rapid rise to prominence and respectability of studies on gender and media, research on TV commercials and children was still only at the level of a hesitant articulation.

The only empirical study in this grouping was "Children's TV Commercials: Testing the Defenses" (Rossiter & Robertson, 1974). Interviews were conducted with 289 primary school boys in first, third, and fifth grades from mixed social class backgrounds. The aim of the study was to examine "persuasibility in terms of children's cognitive and attitudinal defenses to commercials" (p. 137). Young children were found to utilize predominantly attitudinal defenses, whereas with increasing age, cognitive defenses were said to override attitudinal ones. By fifth grade, commercials' persuasive impact is mediated by cognitive defenses: discriminatory skills that distinguish between fact and fiction, program and advertisement, recognition of commercial intent and of target audience, and an understanding of symbolic constructs of product information. Cognition, then, "appears to be a higher order construct than attitude," and they propose that "future research on mediators of commercial persuasion should take cognitive processes into account as well as the more commonly utilized attitudinal measures" (p. 147). The viewer here is conceptualized along cognitive and developmental lines: televiewing is a cognitive process which, at some developmental stages, overlap (e.g., third graders who are said to utilize both attitudinal and cognitive defenses). Comprehension is seen to be further mediated by amount of TV exposure and home socialization.

Eli A. Rubinstein (1974), research director of the Surgeon General's Report, reviewed research published since the report's publication and outlined an agenda for future research on TV and children. For Rubinstein, the effects of TV violence on viewers were unambiguous: "We know there is a causal relation between televised violence and antisocial behavior which is sufficient to warrant immediate remedial action" (p. 81). Remedial action, for Rubinstein, means the remediation of both viewer and industry: Children must be taught by parents how to view more critically, and industry needs to be guided to provide better ("more positive") programming. The provision for better program choice, however, first requires research which investigates TV's social stereotypes: of women, ethnic groups, and social class (p. 86). Moreover, emphasis on negative effects must be refocused to "accentuate the positive. . . . The potential of television as a positive socializing influence has not been realized" (p. 87).

The Surgeon General's Report had constructed consensus about the "true facts" of the "causal relation" in experimental conditions between TV and antisocial behaviors in children. Parents, as the research had repeatedly shown, "do not now control their children's viewing activities" (p. 85). And, since TV undeniably had become a permanent fixture in family life, and the industry was "understandably opposed to any effort which adds new controls or restrictions to its operation" (p. 85), the only "antidote"—as Witty had put it over a decade ago—is to learn to live with the medium in a constructive relationship. This would mean reconceptualizing the TV-child relationship from an exclusive focus on negative to positive effects: the search for prosocial effects was next on the agenda. The discourse was in the process of reinventing itself, if not theoretically and methodologically, at least in terms of its objects of study.

From a symbolic interactionist perspective, Robert P. Snow (1974) critiques research on TV and children for its "failure to take the child's definition of the situation" into account and for its "failure to determine whether the situation is one of play or non-play" (p. 13). Most children, Snow argues, watch TV at home in the context of play. Since most play dynamics contain elements of make-believe or fantasy, children's reactions to TV may well be influenced by the fantasy context within which viewing and play occurs. "However, in most previous research fantasy has been defined in an adult perspective and interpreted as escapist, or the avoidance of reality" (p. 14). In light of this limitation, Snow sets out to let children define what play and TV means to them.

Twenty-three female and 27 male preadolescents were interviewed during a summer vacation program at a middle-class school. Preadolescent children, Snow found, apparently "are for the most part play oriented in their response to television" and, with respect to TV violence, "play and non-play appear to be especially important in that violent behaviors as defined by adults do not affect the child viewer adversely when interpreted within a play context. Instead, violence in a play setting is something funny as in a cartoon or seen as enjoyable in a gun battle" (p. 21). Children, Snow claims, are not as socially or cognitively naive as research has indicated, and they do not take the lesson of TV at a literal, object level. Rather, their interpretation and definition of TV is framed by the social context within which viewing occurs and, moreover, by the ways in which the child makes sense of the social world. The preadolescent child, following Mead, is at the "game stage" in which role playing is "normal" and not an escapist strategy to avoid reality. Children's adeptness at playing out roles or trying out different characters makes them as adept in identifying the make-believe fantasy of TV. For Snow, then, children are not as easily duped by TV as commonly assumed. Children do not turn to TV for escapist reasons but, rather, incorporate TV into their world of play and use TV to extend that world of play. Children are seen as active viewers who select certain kinds of TV content to suit their age-specific definitions of reality, a significant part of which is the reality of play and fantasy.

Published in one of the 1974 *Journal of Communication* issues was "Children Talk About Television" (Streicher & Bonney, 1974). Through open-ended interviews children were allowed to define what TV meant to them. Six- to 12-year-old boys and girls from "professional and managerial" families were interviewed at summer day camps; the children had an average of three TV sets in the home. Contrary to expectations of less familial conflict over viewing in multiple-set households, the children reported that despite the number of available sets, conflict arose over the use of color sets. Parents intervened primarily to settle disputes over set use and to forbid viewing in order to enforce mealtimes, bedtimes, or household chores. The children claimed to like watching TV because it is "fun"; they disliked news, talk shows, and commercials. The authors found that the children seemed to have a host of critical discriminating attitudes in place, with which they accept programs as realistic or reject others as lacking credibility. Commonly, dramatic plots and characterizations were judged valid or invalid on the basis of matches or mismatches with personal experience. Programs which were not believed as credible tended to be fantasy programs. Sports, news, and dramas allegedly based on "true facts" (e.g., "FBI," "Dragnet," "Adam-12") were judged as credible.

Since parental guidance was reported as minimal, and children in this sample watched only what they liked, this suggests to the authors that indirect learning of self-selected, preferred content probably confirms and strengthens already existing values and plausibility structures. The authors' typology of "discriminating attitudes" and concept of "indirect learning" is not theoretically supported. Nonetheless, what is proposed here is that children invoke certain criteria, reality principles, according to which they make sense of TV through rejection and selection of specific content.

In 1975 the *Journal of Communication* published another symposium: "TV's Effects on Children and Adolescents," which comprised the bulk of research reported in this issue. Eleven studies ranging from sex-role research (Werner, 1975; Dohrmann, 1975; Busby, 1975) and TV violence (McCarthy, Langner, Gersten, Eisenberg & Orzeck, 1975; Drabman & Thomas, 1975) to children's cognitive development (Collins, 1975), prosocial learning (Poulos, Rubinstein & Liebert, 1975), TV and hyperactivity (Halpern, 1975), and reviews of (Siegel, 1975; Comstock, 1975) and agendas for (Fowles & Horner, 1975) research were included.

This unit of discourse very clearly intends to represent the dawn of a new era: the first two papers reassess outmoded models and assumptions (Siegel) and outline some basic agreements established by research to date (Comstock). Much as Rubinstein (1974) attempted to draw closure to a preceding research era preoccupied with negative effects, so Siegel attempts to purge the discourse of what she deems outdated models and misguided assumptions. Most of the studies in this issue do not, in fact, represent a new research orientation—although, for instance, the link drawn by Werner I. Halpern between high TV exposure and hyperactivity is certainly a new line of thought. Yet the strategic surface location of Siegel's metacommentary frames this group of studies as indicative of what McLuhan (1975), in this same issue of the journal, referred to as a new paradigm in communications studies.

Siegel (1975) admits that the stimulus-response model was an inadequate explanation and conceptual tool. She comments: "We thought learning occurred when reinforcement was contingent on the learner's behavior. There is nothing which happens on radio, the movies, or TV which is contingent on the behavior of the listener, except turning on or off. . . . Since it was not clear how TV could enter into a chain of reinforcing or punishing sequences, psychologists found difficulty in conceptualizing how TV could be significant in modifying behavior" (p. 18). Catharsis theory, of which Siegel was an early proponent (1956, 1958), also had provided no insights. In Siegel's estimation, "There is little or no evidence of catharsis of aggression through media experience; much of the evidence is inconclusive, and where positive findings do exist they are in the opposite direction" (1975:18). Social learning theory, too, framed as it was in "the context of behavior theory" and experimental methodology, gave prominence to negative and immediate effects at the expense of considerations of nonmeasurable, long-term, nonbehavioral effects. Bandura, the undisputed torchbearer of the laboratory-constituted violence-aggression equation, had redeemed himself, "partly as he has written about his own explanation of his findings [a decade after the fact] and partly as he has extended his research to other classes of responses including prosocial behaviors" (p. 19).

Finally, Siegel indicts "our commitment to the experiment": "This commitment is at once our glory and our constraint. We know that experiments are more informative than correlational studies in identifying the sources of effects, in clarifying the direction of relations between events. . . . But experiments are inefficient for the study of cultivation, erosion and corrosion" (p. 19). Isolating one variable "from the others with which it is interwoven in ordinary life" cannot account for those "insidious effects" (p. 19) that may accrue during 15,000 hours of televiewing by age 16 (p. 22).

In his review of research, Comstock (1975) notes that apart from "some exceptions, most of the reviews agree on the interpretation of the findings [of violence/aggression studies]" (p. 30). The problem is not in the interpretation of data but, as Comstock sees it, in the questions asked and the methodologies employed with which to answer those questions. In his words: "The context in which the evidence is placed, the concepts employed, and the way findings are organized around those concepts, and the degree to which formal theory is used strongly affect the emphasis of the conclusion" (p. 30). And past research, according to Comstock, has been divided principally into two camps, each reflecting different epistemological assumptions: nonalarmists who see no evidence of harmful effects, and alarmists who provide evidence of effects worthy of alarm (p. 30). What all this suggests for Comstock is that before recommendations for change (via programming policy) can be proposed, the "hidden nature of the true debate"—"the true areas of difference"—need to be revealed. That is, "alternative conceptual schemas" for evaluating the evidence need to be considered in order to bridge the division established over 20 years of research, before any "corrective action" can be proposed.

For Siegel, research on TV and children has recognized its past limitations and is mending its conceptual fences. For Comstock, the field is irreconcilably divisive unless the research community can agree on common "conceptual schemas" with which to evaluate divergent effects evidence. Following this discursive self-reflection, the remaining studies are indicative of both Siegel's new conceptual ground prediction and Comstock's divergent evidence premise.

Collins (1975), in "The Developing Child as Viewer," insisted that age-related comprehension abilities mediate any behavioral effects of TV. Cognition, the selection, processing, and evaluation of incoming information, precedes behavior. Cognitive skills are age-dependent in terms of the ability to select central from peripheral information, to interpret, evaluate, and draw inferences from information cues. And since so much of TV information is symbolic, the question for Collins is how well young children, at a predominantly literal, object-level stage of cognitive development, make sense of TV's complex message system. In brief, the data suggested that "children as old as seven and eight do very poorly at perceiving, organizing, and understanding the information" (p. 37). This lack of comprehension, Collins notes, may account for "their tendency toward antisocial acts after viewing" (p. 37). Children's inability to link, say, motive to consequence in portrayals of violent acts, may lead children to draw incorrect inferences, because violence may have been evaluated independent of a motive or other extenuating social and moral circumstances. Preschoolers, for instance, typically recalled only the aggressive act of a videotaped TV segment. With increasing age, Collins claims, information processing skills become more complex in tandem with increased social maturity, which provides an experiential basis against which to evaluate the moral and social legitimacy of on-screen action. For Collins, "younger viewers fail to derive meaning from much of what they watch" and these "confusions over television plots gradually give way to a recognition of the orderly sequences that help them make sense of social events, on or off television" (p. 43). The child viewer is conceptualized as one who constructs different meanings from TV content on the basis of age-related cognitive, social, and moral maturity. Behaviors, in turn, are seen to be determined by varying levels of viewer comprehension.

Two studies conducted in Scandinavia, one in Norway (Werner, 1975) and one in Sweden (Feilitzen & Linne, 1975), were included in this symposium. Werner examined the effects of a TV book-buying campaign and Cecilia Feilitzen and Olga Linne took a developmental perspective to explain children's identification with TV characters. Children under 8 years old were found to identify predominantly with child characters of similar age, whereas older children tend to identify with characters slightly older than themselves. Although program content, sex, nationality, and social circumstance influence viewer identification, the authors found that "individual characteristics of the child are crucial in determining with whom he or she identifies" (p. 53). Besides contributing to what appears to be an increasing trend in the discourse toward developmental explanations of the televiewing process, Feilitzen and Linne provide one of the first indications of a conceptual and linguistic shift in attempts to specify gender. The authors go to great lengths to avoid referring to children via male pronouns: "his/her" and "himself/herself" couplets appear throughout the paper. These gender distinctions in print break the visual landscape of the taken-for-granted organization of words in sentences. In this or any other discourse the male conception of "the individual" was textually and conceptually dominant. The textual appearance of a dual-gendered pronoun set is as significant a conceptual, visual, and linguistic marker denoting "difference" than, say, the more subtle conceptual shift from behavioral to cognitive explanations. The reader virtually stumbles over this new linguistic construct, and the expression of its visual (print) form foregrounds "difference," signaling gendered difference previously subsumed.

Rita Dohrman (1975) analyzed children's educational programs for gender portrayal and noted the same patterns of stereotyped sex-role portrayal reported by Nancy S. Tedesco (1974), Joseph Turow (1974), and Long and Simon (1974) for prime-time programs; by Alice E. Courtney and Thomas W. Whipple (1974) for TV commercials; by Helen W. Streicher (1974) and Busby (1974) for cartoons; and by Mildred Downing (1974) for daytime soap operas. In Dohrman's estimation, because "the programs containing these powerful gender codes are also acclaimed as the best and the brightest of children's television fare" (p. 64), the portrayal of stereotyped sex-roles has serious implications for children's socialization: "Children are exposed from an early age to this symbolic message of comparative gender worth. By observing the powerful adult male ... the boy viewer is being socialized to accept and bask in his dominant societal rank ... the girl viewer is learning the fateful outcome of female existence" (p. 64).

Extending the meaning of content, Dohrman suggests that children do not learn isolated units of meaning (a program, an act, a role) but derive from TV a "symbolic" message system of gendered inequality, the foundation for which is laid in the preschool years via what are considered "quality" children's programs. The shift here is away from atomistic object-level conceptions of content (e.g., frequency counts of gender or occupational role portrayal) toward a reconceptualization of the total spectrum of TV messages as symbolically constitutive of definitions of gender. Dohrman considers enumerations of how often women and girls appear on screen and in what kinds of roles as insufficient and simplistic accounts of sex-role messages. "Codes" such as music, color, language patterns, spatial distribution, camera angles, and so on, symbolize, subsume, and enhance the more overt and literate messages of comparative gender worth revealed by mere frequency counts.

Halpern's (1975) "Turned-on Toddlers" was a critique of "Sesame Street," considered at the time the leading quality program for preschoolers (cf. Dohrman, 1975). In short, Halpern suggested that the fast-paced action of "Sesame Street" produced a "sensory overload" in very young children, which can lead to hyperactive behaviors. Halpern's evidence was derived from what he judged a dramatic increase in the number of children brought to a child guidance clinic, of which he was director, with complaints of children's irritability, restlessness, prolonged sleep resistance and uncontrolled overactivity. His patients reportedly were all avid "Sesame Street" fans. Some of the children were so "jived-up" by "Sesame Street" residue that they "compulsively recited serial numbers and letters . . . [and] delivered themselves of . . . speech fragments . . . [while] inspect[ing] their inanimate surroundings like restless, wound-up robots" (p. 68). Monkeys, he noted, had been observed to react similarly: when their sensory capacities are overtaxed, they exhibit destructiveness and aimless play. Taking a developmental perspective, following Bruner and Piaget, Halpern suggests that the average three-year-old does not have the "coping readiness" of older children with which to fend off the "stimulus barrage" of most TV content, including "Sesame Street." In a subsequent popularization of the TV and children debate (Moody, 1980), Halpern's findings were presented as factual evidence of TV's "physical effects." Referring to Halpern's 1975 study, Kate Moody embellished the findings by adding that a dramatic decrease in "overactive" behaviors was observed once parents reduced their children's "Sesame Street" viewing.

Elizabeth D. McCarthy, Thomas S. Langner, Joanne C. Gerston, Jeanne G. Eisenberg, and Lida Orzeck (1975) argued for imitative learning from modelling as a "mediating mechanism through which the connection is assumed to be made between viewing and behaving" (p. 71). The notion of mediation as a mechanism, particularly in the context of social processes, bears the residual mechanistic construction of the stimulus-response model of human behavior. This conceptualization the authors seemingly attempted to refine by inserting a "mediating mechanism" between "viewing and behaving." The authors found that children (6- to 18-year-olds) from economically depressed family backgrounds watch the greatest amount of TV and are more likely to be exposed to, and often are victims of, domestic violence. Differential perceptions of violence in one's immediate social environment "may explain some of the differences in amount of violent TV watched by different sectors of society" (p. 81). This, in turn, may explain the relationship between watching violent TV and aggressive behaviors. Family use of violence in conflict situations reflects family attitudes toward aggression which children tend to imitate. Parental use of violence to solve interpersonal problems is conceptualized as the "mediating mechanism" which, for some viewers, legitimates on-screen violence and aggressive behaviors. TV is considered by the authors to affect the child only in combination with other social environmental influences, which include parental viewing habits and parental use of and attitudes toward the use of violence.

Drabman and Thomas's 1974 study, originally published in *Developmental Psychology*, was republished as part of the *Journal of Communication* 1975 symposium on TV and youth. Two further studies had been undertaken since the 1974 publication and these were added to the report of the original study and published as "Does TV Violence Breed Indifference?" (1975). The following year the authors republished their studies in *Pediatrics* (Drabman & Thomas, 1976). In all three studies, children in the experimental groups were shown "Hopalong Cassidy." Subjects in the second study were 20 male and 20 female third graders; subjects in the third study were 20 male and 20 female fourth graders. The methodological design and procedure of the first study, outlined earlier in this chapter, was replicated in the subsequent studies. Age, the authors found, did not mediate the "toleration effect": children in all three experimental groups took significantly longer than the control groups to seek adult help in order to intervene in a physical conflict among other children.

The long-term implications appear grim: continued exposure to TV violence "may be having the dual effect of exacerbating some children's violent behavior while at the same time teaching the rest to tolerate their aggression" (p. 88). As noted earlier in the discussion of Drabman and Thomas' first study published in 1974, TV crime and violence does not necessarily lead to increased aggression but can lead to inaction and indifference. The notion that TV violence could desensitize viewers to both televised and real-life aggression was certainly a radical departure from conventional wisdom and scholarly proof of the "TV violence equals viewer aggression" equation.

Following these three sequentially placed studies on TV's negative effects (Halpern, 1975; McCarthy et al., 1975; Drabman & Thomas, 1975), the discourse switches to positive effects with "Positive Social Learning" (Poulos, Rubinstein & Liebert, 1975). This experimental laboratory study of 30 middle-class, white first graders (15 boys, 15 girls) used attention as a measure of learning prosocial behaviors. The experimental group was videotaped from an adjoining room while watching "Lassie." After viewing, the children were asked to play a board game for points and to "monitor the care of puppies in a distant dog kennel by listening to earphones" (p. 93). When the dogs were heard barking, the children could either press a help button to solicit adult help for the distraught puppies or continue playing the boardgame.

The data suggested that the group in the prosocial "Lassie" viewing condition showed significantly more "helping behaviors" than the control group. Learning is conceptualized as attention behaviors matched with subsequent interpersonal behaviors; positive "stimulus materials" have been substituted for negative stimuli. The viewing child, in the author's observational learning schema, is socialized by and learns from TV by exposure and attention to specific examples which s/he accepts "as a guide to his or her own actions" (pp. 90–91). Although the exposure-behavior relationship is modified here by attention levels, the fundamental stimulus-response model still holds: cognitive or social-situational factors that may influence (in)attention are not considered relevant. The stimulus-viewer-effects relationship methodologically constructed in this study reflects unmistakably behaviorist assumptions.

Attempts to resharpen a behaviorist emphasis in TV and children research are outlined in "A Suggested Research Strategy" (Fowles & Horner, 1975). The problem with most of the research, as the authors see it, is that it "has characteristically concerned itself with effects of continued exposure to violent and aggressive programming . . . [which] is generally guided by social learning theory," and which has tended to measure "*unintended side effects* of *programming*" (p. 99). More important would be to "relate actual messages to specific outcomes rather than to assumptions about possible consequences" (p. 98). More rigorous delineations of TV content and viewer "outcomes" would avoid a "fuzzy conception of appropriate outcome variables" (p. 100). "Larger questions" of long-term attitude and value cultivation or unintended "side effects" are "inappropriate . . . for the social scientist" for they "may cause researchers to overlook smaller but detrimental effects to all viewers" (p. 100). Mass media researchers would do well, the authors admonish, to take cues from educational research: "Researchers will do better to take the stance that identifying *specific* behavioral outcomes is as legitimate an approach here as it is in explicitly educational research" (p. 100). The call here is for research to focus more narrowly on specific and measurable behavioral outcomes rather than waste time with fuzzy conceptions of long-term consequences.

Busby's (1975) review of research on sex roles concludes the symposium. Her analysis of research on sex-role portrayal in newspapers, magazines, print advertising, school textbooks, literature, instruction-al and entertainment films, and comics compares with research by Dohrman (1975), Tedesco (1974), Courtney and Whipple (1974), Streicher (1974), Downing (1974), Turow (1974), and Long and Simon (1974): "Sex roles in the mass media are traditional and do not yet reflect the impact of the recent woman's movement" (Busby, 1975:122). Research on children's modelling of sex-typed behaviors is dated back to Maccoby et al.'s (1958) study and includes Beuf's (1974) study published the previous year. Although research on sex-role modelling in children is not as extensive as that on violence and aggression, Busby maintains that enough evidence exists to support the need for concern "about the images of males and females in the media, especially in media where children are heavy users" (p. 126). Previously not articulated in gender and media studies, the role of males as "media gatekeepers" is noted as one important area for future research: "Since the mass media have been dominated primarily by one group—white, American males—it is not surprising to find a similarity of imagery in all the media" (p. 127).

The *Journal of Communication* symposium on "TV's Effects on Children and Adolescents" suggests an ostensible break with the past in terms of research topics, and yet also signified a continuation of established research orientations toward TV and children. The Surgeon General's Report was used as a discursive marker of research completed and facts established about the effects of violence on children. Next on the research agenda was a reversal of the original question: prosocial effects would be substituted for antisocial effects. The established, blue-ribbon tradition in North American social science of locating institutional, cultural, social, and ideological processes at the level of individual behavior was not easily dislodged. Apart from speculations about children's cognitive processes (Collins, 1975) and sex-role content analyses, the information-input/behavior-output model prevailed.

The four identifiable emergent series which surfaced in the dis-course in the early 1970s, then, were research on children's com-prehension of TV, TV advertising and children, sex-role media portrayal linked to gender socialization research, and research on long-term media ("cultivation") effects. The first of the "Cultural Indicators" studies was published in the Surgeon General's Report and would not circulate in an academic journal until 1976 (Gerbner & Gross, 1976). A total of ten annual analyses of TV's symbolic message system and the cultivation of these messages in viewers would be published by the end of the decade. Some researchers (e.g., Tedesco, 1974), however, already claimed to be working within the "cultivation hypothesis" tradition. Yet the most highly profiled entry into the discourse, by virtue of sheer volume of publications, was the study of TV sex-role portrayal and gender socialization.

Lynette K. Friedrich and Aletha H. Stein (1975) examined the effects of prosocial TV on "learning and helping behavior" (p. 27) in "Prosocial Television and Young Children: The Effects of Verbal Labeling and Role Playing Learning and Behavior," published in *Child Development*. Thirty-eight boys and 35 girls, ages 3 to 6 years, from white middle- to lower-class families were assigned to four combined viewing/training conditions. The "training" components consisted of role-playing and verbal-labeling as single sessions or in combination, and these configured with the various prosocial and neutral viewing conditions. Three measures of learning were used: first, a 39-item content test was administered to all children on the final day of treatment. Experimenters read a brief (narrative) "stem" of specific "Mr. Rogers' Neighborhood" content to the children, and "then read a brief description of the two [pictorial] alternatives" (p. 31), which provided a choice of generalization to a Mr. Rogers-linked situation or a situation not explicitly linked to the program. Second, a "puppet measure" was used to assess children's "spontaneous production of verbal and non-verbal content" (p. 31). Third, a "behavioral helping measure" (helping to reassemble a torn and knocked-down collage) was used to measure the frequency, duration, and latency of helping behavior (p. 35).

According to the authors, statistical support was found "for the prediction that training enhances verbal learning and affects actual helping behavior" and "that children learn the prosocial content of television programs and generalize that learning to other situations" (p. 27). The substitution of a "prosocial" for an "antisocial" stimulus, and the relabeling of behavioral measures (from aggression to helping) and reinforcements (from Bobo doll to hand puppets), all within the "framework of observational learning" and "experimental treatment," is no more than a discursive recirculation of the by then traditional stimulus/response model of learning and televiewing.

By the mid-1970s, the search for behavioral effects of prosocial TV content was underway. Brian Coates and H. Allison Pusser (1975) examined positive and negative verbal and physical reinforcements on two of America's most popular children's programs in "Positive Reinforcement and Punishment in 'Sesame Street' and 'Mister Rogers.'" Frequency counts of "positive reinforcements (e.g., giving positive attentions such as praise and approval, giving physical affection, giving tokens) and punishments (e.g., verbal criticism, physical abuse or attack, withdrawal of tokens or privileges)" (p. 144) revealed that "more positive reinforcement [was] given on 'Mister Rogers' than on 'Sesame Street' whereas there was more punishment given on 'Sesame Street' than on 'Mister Rogers'" (p. 149). Given that "millions of children are being exposed every day to positive reinforcement, rather than punishment, for social behaviors on the two programs" (p. 148) and, given the tenets of "modeling theory," which hold that children will imitate behaviors positively reinforced, the authors read the outcomes of the social lessons taught on both programs as "very encouraging." As in earlier behaviorist research on the effects of televised violence, the assumption here is that children will virtually reenact TV content given the appropriate behavioral stimuli and reinforcements.

M. Margaret Conway, A. Jay Stevens and Robert G. Smith (1975) examined "The Relation Between Media Use and Children's Civic Awareness." The authors suggest that since children have few if any political attitudes that can be "reinforced"—and hence, empirically tested—research has tended to avoid this area of inquiry. Moreover, "the focus on reinforcement of attitudes, opinions and controversial issues ignores the development of cognitions as well as of interest and involvement in children of this age" (p. 531). A questionnaire survey was administered in classrooms to 284 fourth, fifth, and sixth graders from a suburban and a rural area. The hypothesis was "that children's orientations to the political system var[ies] with the type and amount of media consumption." Arguing from a Piagetian perspective, mass media were seen potentially to influence "both affective and cognitive orientations to the political system" (p. 532). The two measures of "mass media" were TV (total amount watched and frequency of watching news programs) and newspapers (frequency of reading public affairs content). Political awareness measures included "children's membership identification with a political party," children's voting choice, recognition of party differences, evaluation of party platforms judged to be most responsive to interest groups, understanding of roles of governmental sectors, and perceptions of "the nature of laws" (p. 532).

The data suggests to the authors that children derive most of their political information from the mass media, particularly TV, which play "a significant role in [children's] political socialization" (p. 538). Children at the "concrete stage of cognitive development" reportedly were more influenced by the media in terms of their localized, "personalized" political knowledge such as preferred political parties or political roles encountered in a community context. Abstract political ideas, however, such as the "perceived importance of political parties and the ease and extent of change over time in laws tend not to be fostered by media usage patterns among children at this stage of mental development" (p. 538). Media, then, are seen to contribute significantly to children's political socialization, and age-dependent cognitive abilities are considered as most influential in what kinds of political information children can comprehend. The Piagetian child is here constituted as a political subject, one whose political attitude and opinion formation are abstracted from the politics of school and family influence and family social class. In this conceptualization, cognitive developmental age determines media use independent of the child's sociopolitical, economic, and cultural context.

Thomas R. Donohue (1975) notes the paucity of research on the relationship between TV exposure and "the acquisition of . . . moral and cultural values" (p. 153), particularly in young black children. Since "a young child's mind is a relatively 'clean slate'" (p. 153), TV's influence on very young children's moral and cultural value development is considerable. A field comparison study of 247 black children, grades one through three, was conducted. "The interview technique used open-ended questions" (p. 156) to enable children to define their TV experience in their own terms. Comparisons were drawn with data of white middle-class children derived from an earlier study conducted by Timothy P. Meyer (1973). Donohue's interviewers described four problem "situations" to which children were asked to provide solutions that would entail a moral and behavioral choice. Children also were asked to indicate how they thought others (e.g., favorite TV character, parents, best friend) might resolve the same dilemmas. "The overall findings indicated that television provided mostly innocuous behavioral models for black children and in a few cases negative behavioral models" (p. 165). Comparing his data with Meyer's findings of white middle-class children, Donohue proposes that his research "strongly suggests that black children may be influenced by their parents more than is commonly believed" (p. 166). Donohue thus redeems the black family, which had been accused of fragmentation and of being unable to provide adequate role models for its children, who were increasingly being integrated into a white world (cf. Gerson, 1966). Contrary to what "is commonly believed," Donohue suggests that black parents play a role in their children's socialization that is at least as significant as TV.

The influence of "Sesame Street" on what was conceptualized as "reading readiness" among 500 kindergarten children was examined by Judith H. Minton (1975). Metropolitan Readiness Test (MRT) scores from children (siblings of the test sample) attending kindergarten prior to "Sesame Street's" first broadcast season were compared with those children's scores who were enrolled in kindergarten during the program's first broadcast season. This "simulated before-after design" was utilized because no "data for the group prior to the experimental treatment" was available (p. 143). A questionnaire was designed to gather data on viewing amounts and interviews took place in separate rooms within the schools. MRT scores were analyzed for a 3-year period of the total group. Minton found that children from what she classified as "advantaged" backgrounds watched more "Sesame Street" and scored higher on the alphabet subtest than children from disadvantaged homes. Boys and girls reported viewing similar amounts of "Sesame Street" but boys scored higher on the alphabet subtest. Although "Sesame Street" did not appear to improve total readiness nor particular skills involved in the separate subtests . . . "Sesame Street" did prove itself a capable teacher of letter recognition" (p. 150). One unanticipated finding was the apparent absence of "effects of 'Sesame Street' on the MRT . . . for Head Start children" (p. 150). In view of the program's aim to bridge the "educational gap separating advantaged and disadvantaged children before they enter first grade" (p. 151), the lack of verifiable print literacy skills improvement ("effects" in Minton's terms) among Head Start children suggests to her that future research must go beyond mere "effects" and look, instead, more closely at individual variables. She agrees with Klapper (1960) that exposure to mass media cannot be taken to imply uniform "mass effects." The volume of effects studies which looked for effects, provided evidence of effects, and then argued for the need to go beyond effects was a recurring theme throughout the 1970s.

Minton's study appeared in *Sociology of Education*. As noted in the previous chapter, the discourse of education, sociology, and educational sociology remained at the margins of the academic debate over TV and children. Charles Wright (1986) speculates that "the social demands [in the 1960s and 1970s] for immediate research on the suspected 'evil' effects of television temporarily swamped the field. Sociologists were easily outnumbered in the process, and, as a result, sociological paradigms did not prevail" (p. 31). A similar argument can be applied to explain the lack of participation by academic educationists. Yet since the child was and is indisputably the privileged object of study of the educational discourse, and since education was, and is no less today, an applied extension of psychology, the muted voice of the educational discourse on matters concerning TV and children is slightly more difficult to explain. That children were learning TV's messages had long been established. And since learning is both a fundamental practice of schooling and a central concern of educational scholarship on education, the disregard for children and TV among academic educationists may have to do with the low status "TV knowledge" and TV watching has traditionally been accorded by educators of and for print.

1976–1977

On the fringes of the academic debate on TV and children, the *Journal of Marriage and the Family* made a singular contribution to the discourse in 1976 with the publication of "The Family and Child Television Viewing" (Abel, 1976) and "Birth Order, Club Membership and Mass Media Exposure" (Tomeh, 1976). Aida K. Tomeh's study was conducted in Lebanon with female college students of Lebanese and Jordanian origins. John D. Abel (1976) conducted a field study of 1,180 fifth and sixth graders and their mothers from a lower middle-class rural and middle-class university community. The aim of the study was to investigate to what extent family interpersonal communication patterns influence children's TV viewing preferences. Family interaction was mapped on two conceptual axes: the "socio-oriented family" (emphasis on rules and familial authority hierarchies) and the "idea-oriented" family (emphasis on the expression of ideas, encouragement of alternative viewpoints). Children from socio-oriented families tended to have "viewing preferences similar to what they perceive their parents would prefer them to watch" (p. 333). Children from idea-oriented families indicated more autonomous program preferences. For Abel, "parents and the interpersonal patterns of communication in the home are useful antecedant variables in identifying the effects of TV on children" (p. 335). A major limitation of most research on TV and children, according to Abel, is that "it has concentrated on the direct effects of the medium and not on how the medium is used by the family" (p. 335). For Abel, the social context of the family within which viewing occurs is what influences children's viewing choices which, in turn, can then be linked to specific effects.

Following a similar line of inquiry, Abel and Maureen E. Beninson (1976) published "Perceptions of TV Program Violence by Children and Mothers" in the *Journal of Broadcasting*. In view of the much publicized controversy over TV violence and children, the authors assumed that parents might have inflated definitions of TV violence whereas "Perhaps children do not perceive or interpret violence in the same way adults do" (p. 356). The authors hypothesized that mothers would rate programs as more violent than children (fifth and sixth graders), that girls would rate programs as more violent than boys, that boys would select violent programs more frequently than girls, that children would watch more TV violence than their mothers, and that mothers provided with a definition of violence would rate violence higher than those not provided with definitions (pp. 356–357). Questionnaire data from 191 mother/child pairs suggested that children perceived programs as more violent than their mothers' perceptions. Gender did not influence perceptions of violent content.

Boys reported watching more violent programs than girls, while children overall reported watching more violent programs than mothers. Those mothers given a definition of violence tended to rate programs as more violent than mothers not provided with definitions (p. 362). For Abel and Beninson, the data suggest that "Children and adults differ substantially in their perception of violence in television" (p. 362), which implies that it "should not be assumed that the adult-generated definition has a similar meaning for children" (p. 363). The implication of the differential violence ratings assigned by parents and children is not discussed. The authors do argue, however, that future research "designs should be flexible enough to permit children to define violence in their own way" (p. 363). Taken-for-granted assumptions and definitions of the child or, in this instance, violence were commonly not questioned. Abel and Beninson here call for a reconsideration and refinement of both the definition of (TV) violence and ways of measuring perceived violence.

Samuel Ball (1976), an "authority" on educational TV program assessment at the Educational Testing Service (p. 8), also expressed concern over prevailing measurement categories and procedures. His focus is on educational program assessment, which he views as fraught with three principal problems different from entertainment program research: methodological design, sampling, and measurement. At the outset of this text, Ball states that "it is not possible to assess accurately the impact of television in general" (p. 8). However, "the effects of specific television programs" can be measured as evidenced by assessment studies of "Sesame Street" both in the U.S. and Mexico, "The Electric Company," "Mr. Rogers' Neighborhood," and "Fat Albert" (pp. 8–9). Ball notes that since televiewing and TV impact studies take place in the "real world," the measurement instruments and techniques "suitable for a captive classroom or a psychological laboratory may need to be adapted" (p. 16). For Ball, "this is a depressing situation" for which his solution is a "combination of measurement techniques [which] should be used to supplement each other" (p. 16). Admittedly, "the net result might be confusing. . . . But better a degree of confusion than a sense of security with invalid results" (p. 16). What Ball suggests here is that the prevailing concept of the viewer—and, no less, definitions of program and "impact"—is at least partially the product of methodological construction.

In 1976 the *Journal of Communication* published a special issue on "Sesame Street." Seven papers and one review article were included in this special section entitled "Sesame Street Around the World." Four studies will be discussed here: (1) Stephen R. Levin and Daniel R. Anderson and (2) Gavriel Salomon because they report on empirical research; (3) Rogelio Diaz-Guerrero, Isabel Reyes-Lagunes, Donald B.

Witzke and Wayne H. Holtzman because their paper best exemplifies the problem of cultural imperialism raised in this issue of the journal; and (4) a review by Thomas D. Cook and Ross F. Conner of seven "impact" studies on children's learning gains following viewing of "Sesame Street." The latter paper is chosen for discussion here because it provides a condensed overview of the research on "Sesame Street" and learning gains. The remaining papers report on and critique "Sesame Street's" introduction into non-American cultures, which is discussed below in reference to Diaz et al.'s report on "Plaza Sesamo" in Mexico. The four studies chosen from the "Sesame Street" special issue for analysis here are discussed in the order in which they were published.

Levin and Anderson (1976) in "The Development of Attention" conducted an experimental study of 70 white, middle-class one- to two-year-olds. The aim of the study was to determine which production features increase or decrease preschoolers' attention to "Sesame Street" in particular, and to children's programs in general. The children were videotaped by a concealed camera in a room filled with toys, reading materials and coffee for parents, and a TV showing "Sesame Street." Children were free to play, watch TV, or interact with parents. Observers coded children's videotaped activities and recorded each "onset and offset" of visual attention to the screen. The findings suggested that children, regardless of sex, tend to increase their attention when adult females, children, puppets, and animation are screened, and when singing, repetition, rapid scene changes, reverse motion, and active movement are featured. Adult males, animals, stationary activity and scenery, and body parts other than the face were found to decrease attention. One-year-olds paid attention an average of 12 percent of the program time, compared to four-year-olds' average of 58 percent of program time. Age 2.5 years was judged to be a turning point in young children's attention focus. Levin and Anderson suggest that by that age, preschoolers have developed a concept of "watching TV."

No theory of cognition or development is provided in which to situate children's attention to TV. The failure to include language as one feature of the TV text which might deter or elicit attention limits the auditory dimension of attention cues to music and "other sound characteristics" (e.g., applause and laugh tracks, rhyming, alliteration, repetition) (p. 133). The child constructed in this model of viewing is one who is seen to react to, not interact with, TV in response to visual and nonlinguistic auditory cues. Looking (at TV) is not equivalent to comprehension. In view of the study's aim to provide guidelines for children's program production, the authors' implicit suggestion is that looking behaviors are what constitute preschoolers' viewing of children's programs. The epistemological assumptions underlying the study's methodology—measuring looking behaviors—and the failure to take into account children's cognitive processes and development or verbal ability situate this study within a behaviorist discourse. That is, TV text stimuli are seen to trigger children's attention; children's knowledge repertoire is not considered as a corequisite to "attention."

Salomon (1976) in "Cognitive Skills Learning Across Cultures" reports on empirical research, the theoretical framework that he had been working on since the early 1970s. Theoretical formulations about the interaction between media attributes and children's cognitive skills and abilities can be traced to David R. Olson and Jerome S. Bruner's (1974) and Salomon's (1974b) publications in the "73rd Year-book of the National Society for the Study of Education" entitled *Media and Symbols: The Forms of Expression, Communication, and Educa-tion* (1974). Salomon's 1976 study of "Sesame Street" in different cultural contexts, and his subsequent work in the late 1970s and 1980s, draws upon the early 1970s educational debate about cognition and media symbolic forms. Olson and Bruner (1974) and Salomon (1974b) argued that different media of instruction (e.g., written/oral lan-guage, observation/imitation, mathematical code systems, graphic illustrations, film) not only draw upon different cognitive skill reper-toires and life experience, but also produce in learners sets of medium-specific skills which frame how children think about and deal with the world.

Salomon (1976) questioned whether "Sesame Street" can equalize not only content (letter, number) mastery but cognitive skills across cultures. He hypothesized that children familiar with particular media codes, for instance, a zoom close-up which relates part to whole, will better understand content framed in such codes than children with poor initial code mastery. Children unfamiliar with media-specific codes will either fail to comprehend messages or will "imitate and internalize the code and use it as a new mental tool" (p. 139). In cases where a code explicitly models or "supplants" cognitive operations, viewers with low initial code mastery may internalize and imitate such processes, thereby improving their cognitive operations.

The Israeli children in the sample had relatively little experience with the American TV format that structures "Sesame Street": fast pacing and action, rapid scene changes, and magazine format. Since the Israeli children had less overall exposure to TV than American children, this group was judged to have lower skill mastery of TV's symbolic codes than American "Sesame Street" viewers. The sample consisted of 317 five-, seven-, and eight-year-olds. "Sesame Street" (adapted with Hebrew translations) was broadcast twice weekly for six months between November 1971 and April 1972. Tests (unspecified) were administered prior to the onset of broadcasting and five months after the final "Sesame Street" broadcasts. Medium-specific codes that were identified as relevant to cognitive skill modelling included: fragmentation/discontinuity of shots (relating part to whole); embedded messages (disengaging and engaging in context); differential camera angles (assuming points of view); "kaleidoscopic" magazine formats (rapid shifts among content issues and topics).

The findings suggested that, over and above social class and age differences, "children of all age groups learned what the program's designers declared it was intended to teach them" (p. 141). Knowledge gains were judged as directly related to amount of exposure. Older children showed increased improvement of skill mastery: "Age, or perhaps cognitive development, appeared to be a crucial factor in these results" (p. 143). Heavy viewers, particularly older heavy viewers, "significantly outperformed light viewers when initial differences were partialled out" (p. 143). Children who initially tested as "more skillful benefitted most from formats that called upon those skills. They showed no improvement where skills were supplanted" (p. 143). Salomon found that the reverse applied to children with initial low skill mastery: they failed to benefit when existing skills were required to make sense of content but benefitted when such skills were "supplanted," or modelled for them.

The child viewer is conceptualized as one who interacts cognitively with TV content on the basis of what is comprehensible. Comprehensibility, in turn, is dependant upon both general background knowledge and previously acquired knowledge of specific TV codes. Learning is seen as a function of the interaction between a medium's symbol system and the learner's background knowledge, which includes previous experience or inexperience with particular media symbol systems. The TV-child relationship is thus conceptualized by Salomon as a cognitive and interactive process between a dynamic symbol system and changing cognitive repertoires of the viewer. In contrast to Levin and Anderson's (1976) concept of comprehension as identifiable in attention behaviors, Salomon proposes a concept of comprehension that is identifiable in viewers' age-related cognitive abilities, as these are elaborated through viewers' knowledge and experience.

"Plaza Sesamo" was the first audio and visual adaptation of "Sesame Street" to a culture-specific context. Early adaptations for export entailed language translation only. The findings reported in "Plaza Sesamo in Mexico: An Evaluation" (Diaz-Guerrero et al., 1976) were similar to the U.S. impact studies of "Sesame Street" noted below (Cook & Conner, 1976). Disadvantaged (Mexican) children were said to have achieved lower learning gains than advantaged children, and older children (5-year-olds) showed more significant gains than younger children (3-year-olds). The greatest increases were said to be linked with the program's stated objectives: number, letter, and word recognition, and general knowledge (pp. 146–147). Pre-, during, and post-tests of Mexican children were Spanish adaptations of the ETS (Educational Testing Service) battery used in the earlier American studies. This use of equivalent instrumentation across cultures is based on assumptions that the underlying measurement categories are equivalent in different cultural contexts and are capable of yielding cross-cultural "truths."

Perhaps more problematic was the direct extension of the discourse into foreign (cultural) territory via the alleged Spanish adaptation of the program's form and content. As Diaz-Guerrero et al. point out, a group of American "educators, psychologists, psychiatrists, and other specialists" worked together to provide the formative data "to assist the producers of Plaza Sesamo in developing the program" (p. 145). Despite the substitution of Spanish for English, and Latin American for distinctly North American characters, the program remained a white middle-class North American interpretation of Latin American childhood. An urban, relatively affluent child of visibly European-Spanish descent constituted the image of the Latin American (in fact, Mexican) child. Identifiably indigenous or Indian Hispanic children, by contrast, were excluded from this image and served most often as cultural curios which urban TV children encountered on "trips to the country." The exportation of the North American discourse on what counts as "childhood" or "good" educational children's TV thus excluded the majority of Hispanic children—the urban and rural poor, and non-Europeans—to whom the program was ostensibly addressed.

Consequently, the discursive-cultural imperialism of "Plaza Sesamo" may account for the generally negative results in learning gains "among the lower-class four-year-old children in Mexico City" (p. 150). Much to the authors' surprise, "the most striking outcome of this study is the ineffectiveness of Plaza Sesamo to improve significantly the cognitive development of rural preschool children" (pp. 149–150). As a remedy, the authors propose that it "may well be necessary, especially with disadvantaged children, to provide . . . forms of stimulation and reinforcement" (p. 149). The "problem" is not with the ideological structure and imagery of the program but with disadvantaged children who might benefit from what must surely be termed the "classic" behaviorist solution: ensure effects with better reinforcements.

The last of the four studies in the "Sesame Street" special section to be discussed here is Cook and Conner's review of seven impact studies in "The Educational Impact." All seven studies investigated the differences in viewing in children's learning gains as a consequence of "adult encouragement" and the absence of such encouragements. The data so far suggested that increases in differential learning among children are attributable to social class differences, and the absence or presence of adult encouragement while viewing. Most of the "nonsignificant tests" indicated "mean differences which suggested that *Sesame Street* may have caused learning gains," the most significant of which were for letter recognition skills (p. 164). Learning gains were most evident among children whose viewing had been mediated by adult encouragement. In all seven studies, "encouragement" was defined as adult encouragement through verbal reinforcements and modelling of "attentive" viewing behaviors. Cook and Conner qualify the concept of "encouragement," noting that one major "difficulty is that we do not know what 'encouragement' is behaviorally or abstractly" (p. 164). Encouragement, which was seen as a significant mediating measure of cognitive gains, is reduced in the first instance to behavior. Nonetheless, the move here is to acknowledge the influence of reinforcements, euphemistically termed "encouragements," on learning effects here labeled as "gains."

The seven studies reviewed by Cook and Conner, and those grouped in the journal's "Sesame Street Around the World" special issue, comprise a subdiscourse: all shared the same objects of study (the program, the child viewer), posed the same research questions (effects), and adhered to the obligatory citation of foundational literature. This founding research was traced to two studies commissioned by the Children's Television Workshop, producers of "Sesame Street," to the Educational Testing Service, America's corporate measurement bastion (Ball & Bogatz, 1970; Bogatz & Ball, 1971). As Ball (1976) had observed, educational program "impact," or learning "effects," was the key question researchers of "Sesame Street" addressed.

John Dimmick (1976) reported on "Family Communication and TV Program Choice," published in *Journalism Quarterly*. Like John D. Abel (1976), he constructs a family typology derived from Chaffee et al.'s (1971), and Jack M. McLeod and Garrett J. O'Keefe's (1972) application of the concept of socio- and idea-oriented families to media use. Dimmick renames socio- and idea-oriented families as "pluralistic" and "protective" respectively; "laissez-faire" families stress neither orientation and "consensuals" stress both (p. 720). It was hypothesized that pluralistic families would resolve family viewing conflict by voting, and that in protective families parents would make viewing decisions for children to avoid conflict.

Questionnaires were administered during English classes to 234 students in grades seven through 11. The data suggested that two thirds of the children from what were classified as pluralistic families resolved conflict by voting and compromise, and two thirds of the protective family respondents reported that parents decided what to view or not to view. Age was one variable among protective family children to which differences in conflict resolution were attributable: younger adolescents reported more parental decision-making than older adolescents. In pluralistic families, by contrast, young and older adolescents reported voting and compromise as most frequently used by the family to resolve conflict over TV. Dimmick concludes: "The communication environment in the home is related to the modes of conflict resolution for families in which either the socio-orientation or the concept-orientation is stressed" (p. 723).

Like Abel (1976), Dimmick conceptualizes children's viewing as constrained by varying levels of parental imposition of controls. The child is alternately encouraged to make autonomous viewing choices (as in pluralist families) or is inhibited from self-determined choice by parental decisions (as in protective families). Dimmick's discursive construction of the child and of televiewing in a familial context, then, is contingent on correlative constructs of the family.

"Children and Television" (Feinbloom, 1974), published in *Pediatrics*, comments on recent violence research and proposes that health workers help families deal with children's viewing. Drabman and Thomas (1976) had published "Does Watching Violence on Television Cause Apathy?" in the same issue of this volume (a near identical paper to their 1974 and 1975 publications), and Richard I. Feinbloom uses their findings and numerous citations of the Surgeon General's Report as a springboard for his attack on TV. As he put it, "Violence is now a leading cause of morbidity and mortality in children and is a major problem in society" (p. 301). Since a "preponderance of evidence" has verified that, in the short term, "television violence makes children more willing to harm others, more aggressive in their play, and more likely to select aggression as a preferred response in conflict situations" (p. 301), Feinbloom views with alarm the implications for long-term effects, about which even "less is known" (p. 303). Add to this the influence of TV on children's nutritional health—the commercial glorification of "snack foods, soft drinks, candy and sugared cereals"—and children's emotional and physical health is severely at risk as a consequence of this "highly seductive medium" (p. 303). In fact, for Feinbloom, the link between TV and nationwide obesity is not so tenuous: "I am tempted to link the faulty nutritional patterns encouraged by television and the inactivity associated with viewing to our national problem of obesity" (p. 303).

Despite his negative effects position, Feinbloom does not suggest that parents turn the set off, but advocates that families view together in order to discuss and interpret content. The message to the health profession, then, is that TV affects children's emotional, behavioral, and physical development adversely, but these effects can be countered by family participation in their children's viewing. Circulating in the medical discourse of children's health, TV is diagnosed as the cause for a variety of physical and social maladies, the cure for which is seen to be in parental and health worker intervention.

Originally started in 1967 as an investigation of TV violence for the National Commission on the Causes and Prevention of Violence, the seventh of the "Cultural Indicators" studies under the direction of Gerbner was published in 1976 in the *Journal of Communication* (Gerbner & Gross, 1976). Following the 1972 release of the Surgeon General's Report, as Gerbner and Larry Gross explain: "then Secretary of Health, Education, and Welfare Caspar W. Weinberger reported to Senator John O. Pastore in the fall of 1973 that our research was 'broadened to encompass a number of additional dimensions and linked with viewers' perceptions of violence and its effects, as recommended by NIMH consultants and as incorporated by Dr. Gerbner in his renewal research" (p. 174). The 1976 study, "Living with Television: The Violence Profile," reports on that "renewal research." Gerbner and Gross suggest that the study of TV effects on viewers needs to be reconceptualized, at both the level of TV content and viewers. To this end, they propose that TV should be seen as: "the central cultural arm of American society . . . as an agency of the established order . . . [which] serves primarily to extend and maintain rather than to alter, threaten, or weaken conventional conceptions, beliefs and behaviors. Its chief cultural function is to spread and stabilize social patterns, to cultivate not change but resistance to change. . . . Its function is, in a word, enculturation" (p. 175).

To reconceptualize effects on viewers, "a model based on the concept of broad enculturation rather than of narrow changes in opinion or behavior" (p. 180) is proposed. "Message system analysis" was undertaken for all cultural indicators projects (until 1980) which mapped TV's symbolic message system. Attitude and opinion surveys of adults and children were to provide insights into how the "symbolic world" of TV is "discharged into the mainstream of community consciousness" (pp. 181–182). For each question asked of respondents, "there is a 'television answer,' which is like the way things appear in the world of television, and another and different answer which is biased in the opposite direction, closer to the way things are in the observable world" (p. 182). Heavy viewers tended to give "TV answers" and to report a greater sense of fear and risk in a world which TV depicts for them as more violent and threatening than the "real world." Gerbner and his colleagues would develop in later studies the notion that a heightened sense of fear and risk among heavy viewers is linked with increased support for law enforcement among this group.

This and subsequent "Cultural Index" studies steered clear of a critical theoretical analysis of its empirical findings and failed, inter alia, to provide a theoretical base for its seemingly unproblematic first principles: "culture," "enculturation," "institutional order," "reality," and "symbolic message systems." Preoccupation with method and statistical minutiae dominate the text. Although Gerbner and Gross shift conceptual attention from immediate (TV) individual effects to long-term "cultivation" effects on viewer cohorts, the viewer remains a passive recipient and "carrier" of TV messages. Viewers' learning of TV's "lessons" are seen as unrelated to other social-environmental influences. For instance, as Anthony D. Doob and Glenn E. Macdonald (1979) would point out, viewers who live in high crime areas tended to express more fear and sense of risk. Gerbner and Gross propose a consensus model of media and audiences. TV's symbolic worldview is seen to enculturate a homogenous audience into a dominant set of nonproblematic, albeit "distorted" values. This process of mass enculturation, as well as the socio-structural, political apparatus within which media and audiences and the symbolic world of ideas coexist, is rendered conflict free, ahistorical, and apolitical.

Meyer's (1976) "Impact of 'All in the Family' on Children" reports on individual interviews conducted with 320 children after exposure to the popular program "All in the Family." Meyer claims that his data showed that no children are missing the program's central messages and that they "are affected in distinctly different ways" (p. 32). Each episode centered around the main character (Archie, a white working-class male), his prejudiced worldview and his family's attempts to reform his biased attitudes toward then controversial social issues. At the time, the program had the largest child audience for any regular TV program: "nearly nine million children under the age of twelve" were regular viewers. The implications, then, for a generation of children regularly exposed to this program were seen by Meyer as significant.

The experimental episode centered around Archie's attempts to avoid paying federal income taxes by trying to bribe a black tax officer. The children, ages 6 to 10 years, were interviewed individually in small groups of five to ten after viewing one entire episode including commercials. Controls were tabulated for SES, age and grade level, sex, race, and "learning ability" (defined by school records of children's reading test scores). Meyer found that Archie's unethical characteristics, or the more ethical values of the rest of the family and the black tax officer, "had little impact on most children's character preferences." The "overwhelming" character preference by all children was for Archie. "The show's emphasis on comedy may well have obscured any moral lessons that could be imparted to children. . . . Doing what is right may be almost totally diminished by being funny, having a nice appearance, being nice, being quiet, etc." (p. 28). Despite the favorable portrayal of the black tax officer, neither black nor white children identified with this character.

Age, according to Meyer, was the most significant variable "affecting understanding of the show's contents." Reading ability appeared to make no significant difference in children's comprehension of the program: "the ability to read print messages [does] not apply to the ability to 'read' audio-visual messages" (p. 30). Meyer found, however, that children judged as slow readers also were more inclined to view cheating and bribery as acceptable behaviors. This trend reappeared among very young children who, in Meyer's view, may not have developed the cognitive and social maturity and skills with which to understand and judge motivation-consequence relationships. In Meyer's view, "different types of children, bringing different beliefs, attitudes, and values to the viewing of the show as a result of different socialization processes, are affected in distinctly different ways" (p. 32). Meyer here articulates an interactive concept of televiewing: TV effects, or "impact," are seen as meaningful only insofar as they are considered in relation to the individual viewer's knowledge, cognitive skills, and affective profile.

Reminiscent of Foster's (1964) study of children's perceptions of real-life and "TV fathers," William C. Miller and Thomas Beck (1976) examined children's perceptions of "television parents, their own parents, and good and bad parents" (p. 324). Questionnaires were administered during English class to 34 rural ninth graders from low- to middle-income backgrounds. The authors cite Klapper's (1960) observations that children tend to find their own parents wanting in contrast to the idealized portrayal of TV parents. Such contrasts, Klapper noted, "may bewilder children and hamper their perception of what attitudes and values are in fact socially accepted and approved" (Miller & Beck, 1976:324). Miller and Beck, however, produced "statistically significant" evidence to show "that respondents perceived their own parents as most often doing what they felt the good parent would do" (p. 326). With few exceptions, "TV parents . . . [were] seen as behaving much as the respondents feel a good parent would" (pp. 327–328). In the authors' view, the implications of this reported match between children's perceptions of TV families and their own families are that "as parents most of these television characters are acceptable behavior models, and that these adolescents are *not* overwhelmed by the larger-than-life television parents at the expense of their perception of their own parents" (p. 328). TV content is here conceptualized as a behavioral model for children which, in the case of TV families, the authors judge to provide "acceptable" status quo role models.

Miller and Byron Reeves (1976) in "Dramatic TV Content and Children's Sex-Role Stereotypes," published in the *Journal of Broadcasting*, examined "the impact of television on sex-role perceptions" (p. 35). Content analysis of prime-time progams and survey data of children from kindergarten to sixth grade suggested that heavy viewers had more sex-typed perceptions than light or moderate viewers. "The findings support the assertion that television helps shape children's sex-role perceptions. Children do nominate television characters as people they want to be like when they grow up. There is ample evidence that children can learn through imitation and it is reasonable to assume that they will imitate particular people whom they say they want to be like" (p. 47).

Children who reported to have watched counter-stereotype programs appeared to hold less stereotypical views of occupational roles. This trend indicated to the authors that exposure to counter-stereotypes "causes modifications in real-life sex-role perceptions" (p. 48). Since children tend to "choose primarily high stereotyped characters of their own sex" (p. 47), the authors speculate that TV either teaches directly or reinforces stereotypes that children have learned elsewhere. And since research also had shown that children do change stereotyped role perceptions after exposure to counter-stereotype roles, all the evidence for Miller and Reeves points to TV as cause for sex-role perceptions. This model of televiewing constructs the child as passive agent whose social learning is caused by observation and emulation of TV content.

Chaffee et al. (1970), Dominick (1972), Byrne (1969), and Carter and Greenberg (1965) had already established that TV was children's principal source of political information. Alan M. Rubin (1976) in "Television in Children's Political Socialization" hypothesized, inter alia, that above average viewers of public affairs and news programs would exhibit more political information than below average viewers, and that above average viewers of all types of TV fare would display more negative attitudes toward political institutions and individuals than light TV viewers. Rubin rationalizes his "heavy TV–negative attitude" hypothesis by noting that mass media tend to present a less than idealized account of government officials, processes, and political machinations. Rubin's appraisal of a critical media responsible for generating negative political attitudes among viewers must be seen in light of post-Watergate sensibilities: political journalism had redefined itself, and public sentiment regarding government and, relatedly, sentiment regarding the presidency were widely considered to be at an all-time low. This characterization of public opinion reflected a deviation from a long entrenched and deeply embedded national adulation of both "the presidency" and the "American way," thought to be institutionally and procedurally enshrined in "government."

From his questionnaire data Rubin found a statistically weak association between TV viewing and political information. Political knowledge, however, was somewhat tainted by what Rubin considered a negative attitude toward the (federal) political system. Rubin reads this negativity as a historically isolated instance: "the children's comparatively negative attitudes toward the president may have been directed at the occupant of the office at a time when Watergate dominated media journalism" (p. 59). Yet the evidence indicated for Rubin that children do learn from TV and that the media, particularly TV, play a significant and powerful role in children's political socialization.

In contrast to Gerbner and Gross's (1976) conservative enculturation model of media socialization, Rubin's construct of TV can be read to suggest TV's potentially subversive function. If, as his findings suggest, children do learn political information from TV, and if that information is politically counterhegemonic, then TV—at least, in principle—has the power to disrupt political hegemony. The post-Watergate media events, including the media mobilized wholesale public attitudinal change toward government, the presidency, and political processes, is testimony to Rubin's suggestion that TV is potentially subversive rather than unequivocally enculturative.

Rubinstein (1976) reassesses the Surgeon General's Report in "Warning: The Surgeon General's Research Program May Be Dangerous to Preconceived Notions." He endorses the "consensus" among the report's researchers over TV's negative effects on children and suggests that the empirical "truth" underlying the causal link between TV violence and viewer aggression would have been revealed even if different researchers had been chosen: "My own firm conviction, unfortunately untestable, is that any other equally diverse group of scientists given the same set of data would have come to essentially the same general conclusions" (p. 26). As one of the architects of the report, Rubinstein was unable to look beyond the taken-for-granted validity of the report itself, the research findings, or the very questions asked and methodologies applied to answer those questions. Rubinstein, principal organizer of the report's production of knowledge long before the project got off the ground, here was authorizing the knowledge base established and formalized by the report. As Paisley (1972:24) observed: "The NIMH staff, under the direction of Eli Rubinstein, had already made a number of decisions about the research project prior to the first convening of the committee. . . . The twelve committee members had almost nothing to say about conceptualizing the research to be funded by 'their' million dollars, about soliciting research contracts, or about any detail either theoretical or methodological."

Rubinstein's behaviorist orientation is transposed to his assessment of the aftermath of the report, which he considers to have significant "effects" itself: "If one looks at the total effort to study the effects of TV violence on the viewer, the [SRG] program does seem to have had some significant effects" (p. 29). Among these effects are follow-up Senate hearings (p. 29), the industry's response to the findings as evidenced in an apparent decrease in violent programming (p. 30) and, importantly, the possibility opened by the report for considering TV's potential for positive socialization: "Efforts to search for the positive side were only an incidental part of the surgeon general's program but are increasingly apparent in a number of more recent and ongoing research projects concerned with the relationship of prosocial programming to prosocial behavior" (p. 21). Since research had established a negative effects link between TV and viewers, then the time has come to reconsider that relationship and begin "to search" for positive effects.

At the purely discursive level of "what was said," Rubinstein here endorses a new agenda based on the assumptive base of the negative effects model which Rubinstein himself had selected and authorized. Willard D. Rowland (1983) reads into this a more calculating, mercenary appeal for further federal funding to underwrite the "natural" extension of violence effects research into prosocial effects research. With the advent of the Surgeon General's Report, in Rowland's estimation, "communication effects research had been admitted into the federal social science research establishment" (p. 195). Rubinstein had helped this research take a particular theoretical and methodological direction, one destined to produce negative effects.

Rubinstein's paper was the second of nine included in a special issue on "Television and Social Behavior" in the *Journal of Social Issues* (1976). Of the nine articles, five, excluding Rubinstein's discussion of the Surgeon General's Report, reported on research with children. Like the *Journal of Communication* (1975, 1976, 1977) special issues and sections on TV, this grouping of research harnessed statements and constituted them as a single discursive unit, which is reviewed next in the order that the works appear in their textual formation.

Following Rubinstein, Robert M. Kaplan and Robert D. Singer (editors of this issue) reexamined the evidence on TV and children in "Television Violence and Viewer Aggression: A Reexamination of the Evidence" (1976). Research, mostly on TV and children, is reviewed and organized according to three dominant positions: "activation," "catharsis," and "null view." The authors are critical of both the (causal) activation and (inhibitory) catharsis models on methodological grounds, noting limitations of laboratory or field experiments, nongeneralizability to long-term effects, problematic sample representativeness and aggression measures, and so forth. Hence, Kaplan and Singer align with the "null effects" view. In their estimation, "laboratory studies have in some cases shown that TV can be a possible cause of human aggression. However, this research has failed to demonstrate that TV appreciably affects aggression in our daily lives. At present it is not entirely clear whether the effect of television becomes less detectable in natural settings or if the laboratory is not a good prototype in this research area. . . . We are not contending that the null hypothesis is true, but that the no-effect view is currently the most plausible" (pp. 62–63).

Locating the TV experience within the context of "economic, developmental, social and cultural factors" (p. 63), Kaplan and Singer recommend that research turn its attention away from "laboratory studies with marginal, if any, external validity" (p. 64) and focus instead on social phenomena and relations which potentially combine to generate violence and aggression: "unemployment, racial prejudice, poor housing and lack of medical care, the prevalence of guns and the ease of obtaining alcohol, the high mobility of the population, the prevalence of broken families, the role of age, the still partly subservient role of women, the lack of public school courses in childrearing, and a possibly declining faith in the just nature of our political and judicial system" (p. 64). Kaplan and Singer here reposition TV as one of many sociocultural and political sources of human aggression, and relocate the viewer within an interlocking social network of potentially frustrating, aggression-inducing situations.

Feshbach's (1976) experimental study also supports this view, albeit from a slightly different perspective. Feshbach had been working on the catharsis hypothesis since the mid-1950s, and yet some two decades later the evidence was still considered unconvincing. Children with a strong "reality set" were observed to act aggressively following exposure to TV violence in a controlled setting. "Reality sets" were cues given to children prior to viewing which labeled the (experimental) program nonfictional. Conversely, children with a strong "fantasy set" (experimental program labeled "fantasy") were observed to act less aggressively: "the label 'fantasy' . . . acted as a discriminative stimulus, eliciting a differential set of reactions than the label 'real'" (p. 76). Feshbach posits a viewer who incorporates metamessages in the form of verbal cues into an existing cognitive schema, restructures that schema and uses that mind set to evaluate, comprehend, and react to TV messages. For Feshbach, children's cognitive options are located on either side of the fantasy/reality dichotomy. Potential effects are considered a function, presumably age-related, of differential "fantasy activities," fantasy needs, and the motivational and cognitive processes involved in pursuing gratification for those needs. Feshbach's concept of the viewer is based on combined affective-cognitive-developmental models based predominantly on Freudian developmental stage theory. His methodology and the language he employs, however, reveal a firm rootedness in the stimulus-response model of experimental psychology.

Greenberg and Reeves (1976) examined the perceptual levels of reality operant in children's perception of TV content. Perception of reality is seen as an intervening variable between exposure and effects (p. 86). Acknowledging Feshbach's contribution to the research, Greenberg and Reeves include TV content, TV use, and children's interpersonal communications as predictors of children's reality perceptions. The data from a field survey of 201 third to sixth graders, equally divided by sex and representing a "wide variety of lower; middle; and upper-middle-class backgrounds" (p. 88), suggested that specificity of TV content and interpersonal communications (friends and family) are principal mediating influences in children's perceptions of the reality of TV. Pointing to Feshbach's "clean" and simplistic distinction between fantasy and reality, Greenberg and Reeves argue for the use of a "multidimensional continuum of content perception for the observer" (p. 95). Such an approach, which the authors attempted to apply in their study, may explain more adequately why some children perceived "so-called fantasy content" as realistic, and why others may perceive content labeled realistic as implausible, unrealistic, and fictional.

What parents and peers label as realistic or fantasy content is applied by the child to comprehend that content. Viewing amount and TV content, the child's needs and motives, and gratifications sought are seen to mediate TV's effects. Although needs, motives, and gratifications are not methodologically delineated here, children's content abstractions and reported peer/family interactions suggest to Greenberg and Reeves that children do apply background knowledge to TV information. Background knowledge is seen to interact with content and that interaction constrains possible effects. Greenberg and Reeves steer clear of the role of cognition and comprehension in children's understanding of the televised text and stay, instead, with an affective socialization model that takes needs and gratifications as first principles and posits cognitive "sets" and process as universally given and unproblematic.

Also focusing on the social context of viewing, Chaffee and Albert R. Tims (1976) examine four viewing contexts (with parents, siblings, friends, or alone) which differentially influence children's uses and interpretations of TV. Data were derived from questionnaires administered during school hours to 82 middle school students and 112 high school students. Distribution for sex and social class was not noted. Children's viewing was found to be closely associated with parental viewing patterns in all four family types (protective, pluralistic, consensual, and laissez-faire), particularly among "socio-oriented" and "concept-oriented" families. Perceptions of reality were found to be greatest when children view with parents (particularly in socio-oriented families), and lowest when watching alone (p. 104). From a social learning theory perspective, it appears that "learning is greatest when the child is viewing with parents" (p. 98). However, "the association of violent content and perceptions of reality in the parent-accompanied program is . . . a disquieting finding, given that this combination of conditions has been found to maximize interpersonal aggression in both experimental . . . and field survey . . . studies" (pp. 104–105).

The communication patterns for each group setting are examined using a "variable A-B-X model" in which A and B denote two agents in a communicative exchange in relation to topic X. Since this study claims to examine the social context of viewing as a mediating factor in children's "uses of and reactions to television," the lack of a locus denoting context in this A-B-X model is peculiar. As it stands, this model posits two communicators (A and B) exchanging information about a topic (X) in a social vacuum; the position or role of speakers and the topic which constitutes their exchange are necessarily circumscribed by the environmental circumstances within which exchange occurs (cf. Wilden, 1980). Nonetheless, Chaffee and Tims formulated a conceptual base from which to theorize social influence—that of "interpersonal communication"—on children's uses and interpretations of TV. Here, an interactive TV-child relationship is constituted, one which supports the general orientation of the studies included in this special issue.

A longitudinal study of children's media use and taste (Himmelweit & Swift, 1976) and Comstock's discussion of the role of social science research for media policy decisions conclude this issue. Himmelweit and Betty Swift (1976) take a broader view of the role of media in people's lives and how media may affect individuals. The aim of their study was not so much to chart changes in media use and taste, but to chart TV's place as a socializing influence alongside "the effects of different socializing experiences (home, school, and at the later stage, work and marriage) on educational and job achievement and on adolescent and adult self-image, outlook and social attitudes" (pp. 135–136).

The field work followed a group of males at three intervals over two decades: "in 1951 when they were 13–14 years old, in 1962 (aged 24–25), and in 1970 (aged 32–33)" (p. 135). The data suggested that "cultural norms" circumscribe individual TV use and program taste and, as with peer norms, these change historically in tandem with individual development. Cultural norms are seen as closely associated with parental social class and education. "Stepwise block regression analyses" (p. 143) revealed a progressive order among these influences: "background and ability level predated that of family relations which, in turn, had an earlier influence than outlook and personality" (p. 144). Heavy TV use appeared to be most commonly associated with lower ability and educational levels, and lower social class membership. Less "well-adjusted" adolescents became relatively heavy TV users as adults, whereas well-adjusted teenagers developed interests in more diverse and "demanding" media as adults (p. 154). These two patterns, in the authors' view, tend to become established during adolescence and appear to maintain continuity over time, regardless of subsequent educational attainments or occupational status (p. 155).

Media, specifically TV, are not seen as cause for lack of educational and subsequent occupational success, poor social adjustment, or a "negative outlook." Rather, class-related cultural norms operant in a given sociocultural milieu, combined with individual social circumstances and demographic and psychological characteristics, are seen to condition individual media "tastes" and uses. Himmelweit and Swift support a nonpsychological model of TV use. The viewer is conceptualized as one whose media selection and uses are irreducible to simple affective predispositions or cognitive abilities. This special issue on "Television and Social Behavior" concluded with a discussion by George Comstock (1976) of "The Role of Social and Behavioral Science in Policymaking for Television." Here, as in the previous year's publication of his review of research and the Surgeon General's Report in the *Journal of Communication* (1975), he outlines the need for policy-oriented research to ensure qualitatively better children's programs.

In 1977 the *Journal of Communication* published another special issue on TV and children. Before turning to this issue, studies published elsewhere (Andison, 1977; Himmelweit, 1977; Lometti, Reeves & Bybee, 1977; Rubin, 1977; Salomon & Cohen, 1977) will be examined.

In "Yesterday's and Tomorrow's Television Research on Children," published in *Communication Research—A Half-Century Appraisal*, Himmelweit reviews two decades of research on TV and children, outlines then current trends, and concludes with an agenda for future research. Throughout she insists on the importance for research to take into account the influence of social context in any measurements of effects. Skeptical of research that has "examin[ed] the effects of content—that is, the stimulation . . . ," she proposes that "we need to go back to displacement effects and examine . . . how and why children spend so much time in front of the screen" (p. 29). Himmelweit supports the work of Gerbner and his colleagues on cultivation effects and the "symbolic culture" of TV content, and supports research by cognitive developmental psychologists on children's comprehension of TV content (pp. 30–31). Although Himmelweit does not contribute any original research here, her paper is indicative of an increasing trend in the late 1970s to attempt to inscribe some kind of a temporal marker on a nearly 30-year research history on TV and children. That TV and children should be included as the lead paper in a monograph marking a "half-century appraisal" locates TV and children within what is being claimed by this volume as an established field of inquiry. The mass communications discourse is situated at a historical threshold from which proclamations emanate about scholarly maturity, rites of passage to disciplinary status, and so forth. The discourse on TV and children, likewise, is gaining momentum and seeking legitimacy (cf. Siegel, 1975; Comstock, 1975, 1977).

The uses and gratifications model resurfaces in Guy E. Lometti, Reeves and Carl R. Bybee's (1977) study of middle school, high school and college students' perceptions of different "communication channels." Statistical analysis of the data showed that "respondents did not differentiate channels based on the characteristics of electronic, interpersonal, and print" (p. 335); older adolescents and college-age students tend to seek media ("channel") attributes that provide "behavioural guidance." What the authors admit they did not consider, and what "future research" should pursue, is the methodological distinction between channel and message attributes, and viewers' distinctions between channel and message gratifications. In other words, medium and message should not be conflated as one conceptual unit of medium attributes or perceived viewer gratifications. The authors conclude with a list of "future considerations" which are indicative of many of the shortcomings of this model: the need to identify the "social and psychological determinants of the cognitive processes" involved in making media choices, the "social structural constraints or personality variables," the "relationship between gratifications sought and actual gratifications," and the "causal order- ing of gratifications in relation to media effects" (p. 337). Despite claims that the uses and gratifications approach differs substantially from most other media research models because of its conceptualiza- tion of the audience as "active [and] possessing particular needs" (p. 321), the TV-viewer equation in this study remains functional. The mechanistic and determinist assumptions underlying this study reduce an allegedly active subject to a passive subject responsive to behavior-determining needs.

F. Scott Andison (1977) reviewed the literature on TV violence and viewer aggression and found that "the collective findings of previous studies indicate that such a relationship does exist" (p. 314). Three dominant "schools of thought" are outlined under which most studies can be categorized: the first holds that "watching TV violence will have a cathartic effect," the second that "violent television neither stimulates nor retards . . . aggressive levels of its viewers," and the third that "television violence can stimulate aggression in its viewers" (p. 315). Discussing the representativeness of his data, he notes the absence of studies that provide evidence of negative results: "Positive results are generally reported to a greater extent than negative ones" (p. 316). Andison cautions about the over-representation of studies indicating positive results and explains that even "a null result of any given study is of important significance and . . . is as apt to be reported as a positive result" (pp. 316–317).

Methodology, in Andison's view, dictates what will count as reported effects which, in turn, may account for the overwhelming U.S. research evidence for a positive relationship between TV violence and viewer aggression. Comparing U.S. with foreign studies, Andison finds that the former "show a substantially more skewed distribution to the positive. . . . This discrepancy might be a function of methodol- ogy" (p. 321). On the question of aggression measures, Andison finds that shock measures yielded "consistent, more highly positive skewed results in contrast to the overt physical aggression or questionnaire measures" (p. 321). Cautiously critical, he questions: "Does the degree of shock operationalization overestimate the true relationship or does it more accurately measure the correlation between watching violence and subsequent aggression?" (p. 321). Nonetheless, he judges "shock technique" as "the most scientifically rigorous measurement tool" (p. 321) and maintains that studies which utilize shock measures are "more valid than others" (p. 322).

Analysis of the differential results that different methodologies yield suggested that the laboratory experiment consistently shows more positive results than the two field methods (p. 322). Yet methodological bias clearly underlies results, Andison points out, noting, for instance, that since Bandura and others have "tried to put the 'values' of real life into their laboratory experiments," a "shift of their findings toward the Neutral category" has been noted. Field methods, on the other hand, generally have been considered insufficiently rigorous, and therefore have been assumed to underestimate the relationship (p. 322). Andison, again cautiously, suggests that what all this indicates is that "a methodology of research can, and does, affect the findings of a study quite substantially" (pp. 322–323). Here, then, is a key point which indicates not only the methodological bias of the studies revealed in his own survey of research but also exposes the fundamental epistemological assumptions upon which most of the "violence effects" research was articulated. Andison buries his insight, however, with a firm commitment to empiricism, noting that despite problems with results, the evidence stands in favor of positive results: "Although there do exist several problems with the results [ac]cumulated, it seems quite clear that according to the findings of the studies collected there is at least a weak positive relationship between watching violence on television and the subsequent aggression displayed by viewers of that violence" (p. 323). Methodology may be held accountable for skewed results but, in the final instance, the validity of empirical results is not easily challenged.

Rubin (1977) in "Television Usage, Attitudes and Viewing Behaviors of Children and Adolescents," published in the *Journal of Broadcasting*, argued for a "purposeful" viewer whose "viewing behaviors are more complex than the sheer volume of television exposure" (p. 355). Drawing heavily on Himmelweit et al.'s (1958), Schramm et al.'s (1961), and Greenberg's (1973) data on viewing patterns and program preferences—sources generally neglected since the 1960s—Rubin's questionnaire data suggested similar viewing and preference patterns among children and adolescents, as documented a decade earlier. Children and adolescents least preferred educational programs, news, and public affairs programs. Young children reportedly watched twice as much TV as adolescents, which Rubin attributes to a developmental trend in both amount of viewing and motivations for viewing: the young child seeks "pseudo-friendships" and "parasocial interaction" which TV provides. Yet, with "changing social needs, increased social demands and activities of the older group," the need for TV is said to be reduced (p. 367).

Habituation and nonpurposive viewing characterized the motivations for viewing among all age groups. Yet younger children who viewed more and held more favorable attitudes toward TV expressed stronger motivations for viewing. Adolescents, by contrast, provided more discriminating reasons for purposeful viewing. However, "when amount of viewing was partialled out, viewing to pass time or as a habit no longer significantly correlated with age" (p. 367). In other words, while adolescents may be able to indicate more clearly their specific viewing motivations than younger children, a large part of all children's viewing nonetheless is "spent with television without any specific object of gratification-seeking behavior in mind" (p. 368). What this suggests, then, is that much of children's viewing may be habitual and nonpurposive. This has serious theoretical implications for the uses and gratifications model, as Rubin (p. 368) notes in his concluding remarks: "This predominant mode of habitual viewing may not fit neatly within a uses and gratifications paradigm whose theoretical foundation is built upon the assumption of purposeful viewing. Future investigations may want to consider this supposition."

The child and adolescent viewer here is implicitly conceptualized within a uses and gratifications model: the viewer uses TV for a variety of reasons, one of which is "for no reason at all." For Rubin, nonpurposive viewing is nongratification-seeking viewing, which from a uses and gratifications perspective suggests that no effects would accrue since no gratifications are sought and no needs are perceived. Because this model failed to conceptualize "null" motivations and the absence of need—viewing without intent—the entire model moves into theoretical jeopardy. Yet given the insistence by uses and gratifications proponents that TV uses are motivated by identifiable needs, Rubin's text rightly throws the model's first principles into question.

Drawing on Salomon's earlier work (1972, 1974a, 1974b, 1976) on cognition and media attributes, Salomon and Akiba Cohen's (1977) "Television Formats, Mastery of Mental Skills, and the Acquisition of Knowledge" reported on an experimental study which claimed to demonstrate that when TV formats are varied with content held constant, children's cognitive skills and knowledge acquisition were differentially affected. Salomon and Cohen, following Olson and Bruner (1974), suggest that the symbolic codes within which content messages are embedded "may serve educational and psychological functions beyond those served by the content alone" (p. 612). They argue that in order to identify how and what children learn from a given medium, research must account for the "codes, formats, and methods" used to convey content in any particular medium: "Learning cannot be viewed as independent of the details of the instructional means" (p. 612).

Four groups of 44 fifth graders equally divided by sex were assigned to one of four experimental conditions. These consisted of four versions of a specially produced eight-minute video segment adapted for four different formats: fragmentation of space (FS condition), logical gaps (LG), close-ups interspersed with long-shots (CU), and zooms (Z). Six pretests for "specific mental skills" and two post-tests for specific and general knowledge were administered. After "the test items were factor analyzed together using a varimax rotation procedure" (p. 615), "the results . . . showed that different formats typical of the television medium differentially affect the mental skills that are called into play" (p. 618). What this means, for Salomon and Cohen, is that media codes, or formats, elicit specific cognitive strategies that viewers use to decode formats and message content. The authors construct a triadic model for knowledge acquisition from an audiovisual medium: "the three-way interaction between the mental requirements of the formats, the subjects' mental repertoire, and the mental requirements of the knowledge acquisition task" (p. 618).

Despite the highly mechanistic methodological delineation of cognition in this study, the authors propose an interactive cognitive model of learning and of televiewing. Viewing is conceptualized as an active cognitive process by which viewers are seen to bring to the viewing situation background knowledges and age-dependent repertoires of cognitive skills. These are said to be differentially applied to TV content depending on the kind of cognitive requirements stipulated by medium-specific codes or formats.

In 1977 the *Journal of Communication* again took the lead in constituting a discursive site for the debate on TV and children. The first volume that year graphically depicted TV and children on its cover, announcing yet another special issue: "How TV sells children: A 'state of the art' research symposium." In Sheikh, Prasad, and Rao's (1974) estimation several years earlier, the paucity of research on TV advertising and children was due to the lack of prestige associated by academics with this field of inquiry. Only a few studies on the influence of TV advertisements on children had been published in the Surgeon General's Report (e.g., Ward, Levinson & Wackman, 1972; Ward & Wackman, 1972). Following the report's publication, few researchers developed a sustained interest in this topic, with the exception of Scott Ward, Daniel B. Wackman and Ellen Wartella, who published *How children learn to buy: The development of consumer information-processing skills* in 1977. Ward and his associates initially had shown that young children fail to understand commercials' selling intent and fail to distinguish between program and commercial. This lack of comprehension, it was hypothesized, could leave young children defenseless against the audio and visual strategies commonly used to persuade viewers to buy.

Credibility was bestowed on TV advertising research in 1977 when, according to Robert M. Liebert and Joyce Sprafkin (1988), a "panel to review the research on the effects of television advertising on children and to recommend areas for future research" was commissioned by the National Science Foundation (p. 178). Recommendations were published in 1977, coinciding with the *Journal of Communication*'s publication of a symposium on children and TV advertising. The following year, several professional and public nonprofit organizations appealed to the Federal Trade Commission (FTC) to investigate the effects of TV advertising on children, to consider drawing up recommendations for banning commercials aimed at child audiences, and to develop industry guidelines for snack-food and heavily sugared food commercials. Federal hearings ensued, and in 1980 the FTC commissioned a staff report that outlined the hearings' findings and the future direction of the commission's proceedings. The report was released in 1981 and proposed the termination of further proceedings. Essentially, the commission refused to set federal industry guidelines for children's TV advertising. In light of what Liebert and Sprafkin claim was the advertising and broadcasters' "$30 million 'war chest' to fight the FTC" (p. 180), the capitulation of the federal government to industry pressure is not surprising. Federal and public attention to issues regarding TV advertising and children coincided with a burgeoning research industry, a great deal of which was located in faculties and schools of business. TV advertising and children had developed, with the help of much publicized federal concern, into a legitimate contemporary issue and area of research: the 1977 *Journal of Communication* capitalized on this with its timely publication of its symposium on "How TV Sells Children."

The search for effects continued. Since children were not consumers with disposable incomes whose purchasing behaviors could be observed and measured, advertising effects on behavior were not readily quantifiable. Children's consumer behaviors were most apparent in the kinds of purchase demands made on parents. Yet preceding measurable purchase demands, children's differential abilities to comprehend commercial messages were seen as crucial to their subsequent quasi-consumer behaviors. Hence, cognitive conceptualizations of effects were forced onto the research agenda which, of course, did not restrain the urgency with which behaviorists continued to view their task.

Thomas S. Robertson and John R. Rossiter (1977), for instance, whose study was the first of seven papers included in the symposium, deplored the lack of evidence for behavioral effects: "Although previous research has studied the effects of television advertising on children's cognitive beliefs and verbally expressed attitudes . . . there is a disappointing lack of evidence as to the behavioral effects of advertising on children" (p. 101). A field survey was conducted to identify "receiver factors," seen to mediate behavioral effects. The interview data of (presumably white) 92 first graders, 101 third graders, and 96 fifth graders of mixed socioeconomic backgrounds revealed that, after statistical treatment, "low [TV] exposure-high [parental] education children are least persuaded" (p. 105) by commercial messages; the reverse was indicated for high exposure, low education children. Important dispositional "receiver factors" are seen to be age (cognitive defenses) followed by peer integration and parental education, both of which can provide "alternative reality checks" for the child. Children, commonly labeled "Ss" or "respondents" in the discourse of the 1960s and 1970s, here are conceptually cast within a "sender-receiver" model. This construct reconfigures subjectivity implied by "Ss," and constructs an image of technical receivership not unlike the TV monitor-receiver itself.

Atkin and Gary Heald (1977) reported on a content analysis of commercials shown during two 4-hour Saturday morning segments in November of 1972 and 1973, the period of concentrated pre-Christmas toy commercials. The authors drew this profile of children's commercials: price is never mentioned and the product user is almost always shown as satisfied; information about accessories is commonly encoded in verbal messages; repetition of jingles is common; toy ads tend to have a more serious tone than food ads; toy ads tend to exaggerate product performance. In terms of consumer portrayal, minority groups appeared in only one fifth of all commercials analyzed, and most snack-food ads and toy ads featured children. Premium appeals appeared in only one quarter of the ads surveyed, even fewer ads used testimonials or celebrity endorsements, and few ads promised increases in social status as a consequence of product purchase (pp. 113–145). Cautiously, Atkin and Heald conclude that "while implications of these content dimensions for children's knowledge acquisition, attitude development, or behavioral patterns cannot be inferred . . . the findings provide a guide to the kinds of effects that might be expected" (p. 114).

Pat Burr and Richard M. Burr (1977) reported on a field survey of parental attitudes toward the use of premium appeals in commercials targeted at children. The sample's educational level, SES, occupational status, and race are not specified. The data suggested that parents tended to comply with children's product requests. The majority of parents reported dissatisfaction with the over-emphasis on premium appeals "to the point where children request the product just to get the prize." The authors conclude: "Generally . . . children . . . are very much in touch with the commercial messages on television; they do pass on the commercial information to parents in the form of a request to buy; and positive parental response varies depending upon the nature of the appeal used by the child" (p. 117). Perhaps parental SES may have shed some light on parents' ability or inability to comply with children's appeals.

Diane E. Liebert, Sprafkin, Liebert, and Rubinstein (1977) in "The Effects of TV Commercial Disclaimers on the Product Expectations of Children" reported that a standard verbal disclaimer such as "partial assembly required" was "totally ineffective" (p. 118) in communicating the message to children in the age range for which it was intended. Two experimental pilot studies of 240 white, middle-class kindergarten and second grade students, equally divided by sex, showed that "disclaimer messages can be clearly understood by young children if the wording is clear enough" (p. 120). In other words, when "partial assembly required" was rephrased to "you have to put it together," 50 percent of the sample understood the message, compared to less than 25 percent who understood the original message (p. 123). When the disclaimer was further simplified to "you have to put the legs on the horses," 100 percent of the children understood the message. Preschoolers and second graders found the original disclaimer equally difficult to understand, whereas older children "outperformed" younger ones in comprehension of the first modified disclaimer. The authors conclude that verbal disclaimers are "ineffective" with young children, which renders the more salient appeals (action, color, size) of commercials all the more effective.

Another survey of parental attitudes toward children's commercials was conducted by Shel Feldman, Abraham Wolf and Doris Warmouth (1977), who found that concern over TV advertising effects on children differs among parents, and that differential levels of concern are not attributable solely to demographic factors (p. 131). Parents reportedly do not control their children's viewing and therefore exert no control over the commercials children are exposed to. The authors view the relationship between parental concerns over and possible effects of advertising on children as complex: "The data seem to underline the complexity of the problem and the difficulty of generating any simple solution to parental concerns. Both resentment against encroachment in the socialization process and concern about effects on the child are probably involved, albeit in different proportions in different respondents" (p. 136). The authors speculate that parents may have less control over children's consumer socialization since peer pressure appears to be more influential on children's program choices. And, since these are almost exclusively broadcast on commercial channels, parents have virtually no control over the advertisements that children are exposed to. In this study, parental mediation of TV effects on children is ruled out.

Wackman, Wartella and Ward (1977) in "Learning to Be Consumers: The Role of the Family" explain how cognitive development theory and socialization theory can be combined to "form a cognitive developmental approach to socialization research" (p. 138). The central aim in this investigation was to examine how "general consumer skill development" evolves in children as a function of both cognitive development and consumer socialization by TV and the family. Two central factors seen to influence consumer information processing skills in children are the mother's use of information in purchasing decisions, and the informational aspects of mother/child interactions about and during purchases. The authors suggest that family consumer socialization variables may have some impact on the development of children's general cognitive abilities which, in turn, would influence performance of specific consumer skills (p. 146).

Drawing from Kohlberg's "'interactional' view of cognitive development" and Piaget's cognitive structuralism (p. 140), a combined "socialization perspective with cognitive development theory" (p. 150) is proposed to explain developmental phenomena in both naturalistic and long-term contexts. According to the authors, traditional socialization research has been unable to demonstrate social learning beyond short-term effects and to generalize learned behaviors "across a host of social situations" (p. 149). Wackman et al. propose that their reconceptualized model, applied to naturalistic settings of family life, will be able more adequately to specify "long-term socialization influences."

Following Wackman et al.'s study, Sheikh and Moleski (1977a) also base their investigation on a Piagetian perspective by utilizing the "Story Completion Method" to identify the development of children's moral judgment. The story completion method was seen as "effective in measuring emotional conflict" (p. 153). Unlike Wackman et al.'s attempts to theoretically reframe the consumer socialization issue, Sheikh and Moleski remain within a strictly behaviorist framework. "Respondents" were 144 white, upper middle-class urban children (first, third, and fifth graders), randomly chosen and assigned to one of three experimental groups, each consisting of 24 boys and 24 girls. Children were told a "story stem" which involved a main character watching TV "with his or her parents." The passage included repeated commercial interruptions. Following the story presentation children were given guided questions, the answers to which would reveal the child's perception of parent/child conflict over a product purchase request. The data "were analyzed on TRI-CHI, a program for interpreting three-dimensional contingency tables by means of log-linear models. The results are discussed under the assumption that whatever the child is saying about the main character . . . reveals his/her own true feelings" (p. 155). The processed results indicated that age is linked with a decrease in acceptance of parental refusals of product requests, and an increase in aggression: "It appears that by the third grade level, the commercials are having a strong effect on the children: not only do they make more purchase requests, but they also seem less prone to accept parental refusal and more likely to act aggressively when faced with frustration" (p. 157).

Here the results depend on children's verbal responses to an oral story about TV and their description of commercials, and the TRI-CHI program's quantification of those responses. Children's reactions to televised commercials, or their "true feelings," appear to have little to do in this study with anything other than whatever truths have been methodologically produced and measured. The authors conducted a similar study to investigate children's perceptions of the value of an advertised product, published that same year in the *Journal of Broadcasting* (1977b). In this experimental study of 68 white, middle-class fifth graders, one group viewed a commercial of a gender neutral vibrating action game, the other group examined the product. Results suggested that girls were less misled by the commercial version than boys, and that girls' value judgments were apparently more realistic than boys' judgments. Taking a functionalist (and patently sexist) perspective of role socialization, the authors interpret their findings to suggest that perhaps fifth grade girls have not yet learned their "appropriate" sex-typed role of persuadability.

The *Journal of Communication*'s "state of the art" symposium on "How TV sells children" reported on the most recent research on a relatively new and novel topic. Yet Wackman et al.'s study was the only attempt to move away from traditional assumptions about and approaches to the study of TV and children. Methodologically, the field experiment (Liebert et al., 1977; Sheikh & Moleski; 1977a, 1977b), field survey (Robertson & Rossiter, 1977; Feldman et al., 1977; Wackman et al., 1977), and quantitative content analysis (Burr & Burr, 1977) prevailed. Notably absent is the laboratory experiment. Yet, behaviorist assumptions continued to underpin the epistemological orientation of all studies included in the symposium. Effects of TV (consumer) socialization were seen only in terms of individual behaviors ("purchase requests") or, alternately, as "non-behaviors" seen as a function of children's inability to understand complex verbal messages (disclaimers). Here was a new research topic: the cultural production (socialization) of the consumer as both active economic subject and passive (audience) product to be sold to sponsors. Yet researchers failed to seize this opportunity to transcend the narrow empiricism focused on the minutiae of measurable individual effects. The possibility was missed to recast "consumer socialization" within a sociopolitical framework from which to theorize about the ideological implications of the mass media production of consumption: the production and disciplining of consumer society. While an ostensibly new research topic is elevated here to "state-of-the-art" importance, the only change evident was a shift of focus from program to commercial: theoretical and methodological conventions remained firmly entrenched.

Two more special sections on TV and children appeared in the *Journal of Communication* in 1977: the second issue of the journal that year included six studies grouped under "Sex, Violence, and the Rules of the Game," and the third issue consisted of five studies in a section titled "Effects of Television." Clearly, concern with effects remained paramount.

Susan Franzblau, Sprafkin and Rubinstein (1977) commented on the recent shift of public attention to TV portrayal of sexuality. This emergence of interest the authors linked to the adoption in 1975 by the three networks and the National Association of Broadcasters of a "family viewing code." Violence, "an issue for public debate and scientific research for almost two decades" (p. 164), and sex-role portrayal had become established research topics. The negative effects of both had been verified. TV sex and sexuality, however, had not been taken to task, although concerns about immodest and immoral sexual conduct on the (movie) screen had been expressed as early as the Payne Fund Studies.

Franzblau et al.'s content analysis covered prime-time programs broadcast during the 1975–1976 seasons. Their principal finding "was that physical intimacy appeared most often in less sensuous forms than one would expect from the public criticism of the portrayal of sexuality on current television programming" (p. 164). The problem with TV sex and sexuality for children, in the estimation of Franzblau et al. and most of the authors in this special section, was the lack of clear programming guidelines which would prevent the broadcast of "inappropriate" programs during the family viewing hour (Wiley, 1977:189). Initially, the problem implied between TV sex and child viewers was articulated indirectly as a policy problem of inadequate broadcast regulation. The danger for children was seen to be both with content and with inadequacies in policy governing family viewing. Richard E. Wiley (1977), in fact, suggests that the problem may be at a more fundamental conceptual level of what family viewing should mean for the public, the industry, and the federal courts.

An effects logic was not as readily transposable to questions of TV sex, sexuality, and child viewers. What children might be learning from TV's construction of sexual relationships was not as easily measurable in pre- and post-treatment schemes as measurements of effects of violent and prosocial TV content. Hence, effects of TV sex on children initially were speculative. Public and academic concern over the kinds of moral harm the portrayal of sexual innuendo on TV might inflict on the young was sidetracked, from the beginning of the debate, to concerns over policy: to industry regulation of TV content and programming. As Liebert, Sprafkin and Emily S. Davidson noted in 1982: "Speculations on the effects of TV sex on young viewers abound ... [yet] how children react to TV sex remains to be systematically studied. To date, there have not been any studies of how children's attitudes and behaviors are affected. Due to moral and ethical issues, it is extremely difficult to do such studies" (p. 177). Based on widely shared public assumptions and on mounting scientific evidence about children's susceptibility to TV modelling of violent and prosocial behaviors, it appears that those same assumptions transferred to speculations about the behavioral and attitudinal effects of the portrayal of sexual conduct and relationships. In a social order that claims to have strong taboos against violence institutionalized in sites such as the school and family, children nonetheless were said to behave aggressively as a direct consequence of exposure to TV violence. It is reasonable to assume, then, that conventional wisdom and the scientific imagination would anticipate that youth might also imitate and learn from TV's messages of sex and sexuality, despite equally strong taboos.

The second of the "Cultural Indicators" studies published in the *Journal of Communication* was included in this section: "TV Violence Profile No. 8: The Highlights" (Gerbner, Gross, Eleey, Jackson-Beeck, Jeffries-Fox & Signorielli, 1977). The violence profile series claimed no allegiance to any preceding or contemporaneous research on TV violence. Two references are cited: one to the 1976 violence profile, the other to an earlier version—an in-house technical report—of the 1977 (No. 8) TV violence profile. This cumulative series of self-legitimating and self-referential statements established an autonomous subdiscourse: each of Gerbner et al.'s studies located itself serially in a numerical sequence, each precipitating a follow-up study, of which each would refer back only to its antecedents in the series.

As the authors stated in 1976, the "violence profile" or "index" was meant to be read as a "cultural indicator"—an indicator of the ways in which TV cultivates and distorts viewers' perceptions of "social reality." TV is seen to create a system of symbolic images into which mass audiences are enculturated. This view posits media influence as long-term and posits "effects" as ostensibly ideological, rather than as behavioral. The authors found that heavy-viewing adults also "overestimate the prevalence of violence" (p. 178), and heavy-viewing children (and adults) "consistently ... reflected a sense of mistrust and suspicion" of their environment (p. 179). The data also revealed that "the cultivation of these conceptions of a 'mean world' and other aspects of social reality are not significantly altered by sex, age, education, income, newspaper reading, and church attendance" (p. 171). Race, however, appeared to make a difference: "Blacks, as a whole, do not show this association, although those blacks in the sample who are college educated or whose income is over $8,000 do show the cultivation pattern found among white respondents" (p. 179). Presumably, the college educated, relatively affluent black viewer is economically sheltered from the "mean world," which for working class or inner-city blacks is a de facto social reality, one that undoubtedly influences perceptions of a mean world—televised or real.

This "violence index" in the journal's special section stands apart from the other five studies, all devoted to issues relating to TV sex. Discursive rules stipulate not only the conceptual organization of ideas within the textual format of a given discourse, but stipulate how textual "unities" (i.e., scholarly articles) will be sequentially organized, classified and labeled within a discursive forum such as an academic journal. As such, the inclusion of the violence profile amidst a series of texts grouped according to a shared "thematic orientation" (i.e., TV sex, not violence) may be explained by reference to the editorial basis of the journal. The senior author of the "Cultural Indicators Project" was also the editor of the *Journal of Communication*. The final authority over the invocation of rules delimiting inclusion and exclusion of texts thus rested in his position as author of and authority over this particular discourse. Unquestionably, a social history of this or other academic journals would reveal a network of institutional and personal relationships (cf. Rowland, 1983) which would reveal "the making of rules" below the threshold of discursive articulation.

The special section of the third issue of the journal in 1977, "Effects of Television," included five studies. In the first of these, "Sex and Violence: Can Research Have It Both Ways?" Richard A. Dienstbier (1977) argues that the behaviorist model which has guided research on TV violence and children is not applicable to the study of effects of TV sex on children because "preadolescent children seem to be less subject to strong influence by explicit sexuality since their ability to sustain sexual arousal is slight compared to their potential for feelings of anger" (p. 182). In place of the "insufficient" behaviorist model, Dienstbier offers an alternative model based on Freud's dual concepts of negative/positive fixation. According to Dienstbier's reading of Freud, for the sexually uninformed or misinformed, "some exposure to explicit sexuality during the adolescent or preadolescent years might be useful in reducing . . . naivete" (p. 184). Accordingly, TV sex might balance negative fixations ("underexposure ... to explicit sexual information") among some children, whereas for those with a positive fixation ("overexposure"), media exposure might mediate such imbalance. Once guidelines for appropriate sexual content on TV are agreed upon, Dienstbier foresees a valuable educational potential of TV for children, particularly in view of the paucity of sex education programs in the schools.

Dienstbier's "personality model approach" (p. 176) locates the source of potential effects at the nexus of interaction between the individual and the medium. And, because of the "timing factors of age" (p. 182), children's sexual responses, unlike aggressive responses to TV violence, are unlikely. As such, the effects of "exposure to explicit sexual material" are more likely to be "non-harmful cathartic effects" (p. 182). Locating TV effects in developmentally delayed behavior, then, Dienstbier cannot conceive of the ideological, cultural, and social implications of TV gender/sexual politics on the youth audiences.

The second paper in this section, "Types of Portrayal and Aggressive Behavior" by Comstock (1977), attacks the interpretations of "null effects" studies of the catharsis theory literature. Comstock admits that the findings of laboratory experiments are suspect: "The surroundings are artificial; the 'television' is brief, usually shown out of context, and often something quite unlike anything ever seen on a home screen; ... the target for the aggression is an object actually designed for playful violence, the Bobo doll ... [and] the operationalization of aggression typically is an act, such as the delivery of electric shocks ... that is in mode if not in motive unlike behavior in which persons normally engage" (p. 192). Despite his apparent sensitivity to such constraints, he insists that "nevertheless, the experiment is the best means for exploring contingent factors because it tests causal relationships in the most rigorous and sensitive way possible" (p. 192). By contrast, studies which fail to find effects, such as those based on the catharsis hypothesis, should be interpreted as showing no more than "that under some conditions there may be no effect" (p. 196). Hence, such findings "should not be interpreted as invalidating the many studies which do demonstrate some effect" (p. 196).

In defense of "the certainty of effects," Comstock invokes history— the allegedly indisputable track record and sheer volume of positive effects studies: "When a scientific literature is young, positive versus null results may be taken as canceling each other out. When a literature has matured to substantial size, which is the case with the literature on television and the performance of aggressive and deviant acts, the situation is quite different. Then, if positive findings have become replicated across numerous, varied studies, a null result . . . ceases to be invalidating and becomes instead a modification of the certainty of effects. That is where we now stand in regard to research on television portrayal and aggressive behavior" (p. 196). Here the maturity of the literature, gauged in terms of published output, is to be taken as legitimating the validity of its findings. Comstock, "senior social psychologist at the Rand Corporation" (p. 189) and part architect of the Surgeon General's Report, here rearticulates credentialed authorization and discursive formalization on the "mature" positive effects discourse. Following Comstock's proclamation of "the certainty of effects," Drabman and Thomas' (1977) study confirms that certainty. Their classic replication study of the Bobo doll experiments showed that "witnessing filmed action [in the trailer laboratory] . . . enhances assaultive behavior" in male preschoolers (p. 199), which "serves further to emphasize the potential undesirable effects of televised violence" (p. 205).

The final paper in this section, "Predispositions Revisited" (Liebert, Cohen, Joyce, Murrel, Nisonoff and Sonnenschein, 1977), reviewed "the report of eleven research projects supported over a period of five years and published by the American Broadcasting Company" (p. 217). All the studies in this industry-funded project dealt with children and adolescents. A central criticism of the project is its alleged methodological inaccuracy and confusion: "We found . . . a veritable casebook of basic methodological and careless reasoning, and some startling appeals to psychiatric authority" (p. 216). One criticism, among many others, was levelled at one of the studies which apparently allowed children to watch TV during a four day interval between experimental condition and post-exposure observation. Subjects were thus engaging in normal everyday viewing activities. Yet for Liebert et al., this methodological lapse invalidates the study since it renders unmeasurable the "impact of [a] single show introduced for experimental purposes" (p. 218). The logic here of judging invalid children's behavioral responses because they were seen as contaminated by a four-day interval of normal activities that included watching TV can only be justified by reference to the acute insights on the social context of viewing derived from the epistemological basis of behaviorist psychology. Yet for the authors, of greater significance is that the project "give[s] the impression that they have acquitted the medium of any serious responsibility" (p. 219). Given Liebert et al.'s charge that the industry framed its research endeavor in order to ensure null effects, their rejection of an industry-funded research project on methodological grounds is to be expected. In all, this paper draws an apt conclusion to the journal's special section on "Effects of Television": Comstock vouches for the maturity and dominance of a positive effects paradigm, which is followed by confirmation from laboratory and field evidence, to which Liebert et al. add a critique of methodologically fallible attempts to counter the irrefutable "truths" of the discourse on the "Effects of Television."

1978–1979

"TV News Is First Choice in Survey of High Schools" (Atkins & Elwood, 1978), published in *Journalism Quarterly*, reports on a questionnaire survey designed to identify adolescents' consumption of and preference for news media. The data suggested that TV "is the No. 1 news of a sample of more than 200 students in six high schools" (p. 596). The majority of the sample ranked "believability" as the primary reason for their preference of TV as a source of news. Students reportedly devoted more than 30 minutes daily to TV compared with one to five minutes spent with newspapers. Newspaper reading apparently had declined by 10 percent among 18- to 24-year-olds since 1964 "to the point that only 61 percent of young adults are reading papers" (p. 598). That trend prompted this study: "A major purpose of this survey was to see if high schoolers followed the pattern of the older youth. Broadly they do" (p. 598).

Bandura (1978) outlined his "refined" social learning theory in "Social Learning Theory of Aggression," published in the *Journal of Communication*. In acknowledgment of the ascendant model of cognitive psychology, Bandura agrees that "people are not simpy reactors to external influences; through self-generated inducements and self-produced consequences they exercise influence over their behavior" (p. 23). This is Bandura's conceptual modification that Siegel (1975) had alluded to. Nonetheless, his shift to prosocial effects and his acknowledgment that cognition might play a role in social behavior remain firmly grounded in the assumptions and language of behaviorism: social and cognitive processes are seen to entail "mechanisms," "disinhibitory factors," "impulse actions," and so forth. So while the surface terms of the debate shifted ground, as had been the case so often during the 1960s and 1970s, the epistemological deep structure remained intact and continued to define social behavior in terms of what was seen as methodologically expedient and measurable at the level of the sovereign individual.

A shift in direction toward a tentative acceptance of TV's place as only one among many sources of influence in children's socialization was indicated in Comstock's (1978) review of research, "The Impact of Television on American Institutions." He acknowledges that despite irrefutable experimental evidence of TV's short-term effects on children's behaviors, "what is less clear is the degree to which it contributes to truly harmful antisocial aggression or criminal acts or heightens the level of aggressive interaction among the adults young viewers eventually become" (p. 16). Comstock grants that "non-vicarious agents, such as teachers and parents" do intervene in children's viewing, and help shape the "socializing prowess of television" (p. 17). In Comstock's (1975, 1977) earlier view, the effects evidence pointed to a seemingly irrefutable violence/aggression equation. The following year (1978) he readily admitted to the possibility that nonvicarious socialization agents might mediate the alleged power of TV. A shift in direction was clearly underway, one authorized by Comstock who, since the Surgeon General's Report, had taken the discursive role of commentator on and reviewer of research. In short, Comstock was setting out "flags," discursive markers, that indicated new research agendas, new orientations, and a potential reformation of the object of study.

From a Piagetian perspective, Roger J. Desmond (1978) reports on a study of TV effects on children's play in "Cognitive Development and Television Comprehension," published in *Communication Research*. Observations over a one-year period of preschool and primary children indicated that "individual differences among children partially explain the amount and kind of social learning from the medium, while chronological age is the most accurate index of content-learning" (p. 202). Noting the "effects tradition's" preoccupation with measurement of aggressive behaviors, Desmond comments that "while aggressive and pro-social behavior are important aspects of the potential effects of television, there are numerous other possibilities. . . . [TV] presents examples of people at work, models of family communication patterns, examples of appropriate and inappropriate forms of addressing others, and a myriad of forms which fall outside of the classes of behavior studied by behavioral scientists" (p. 203). The study of other kinds of behaviors, then, might provide new insights into children's use of TV information and, hence, potential effects. For instance, Desmond suggests that "children who are skillful role takers will infer the methods and motives of program characters, and modify what they view, adapting knowledge about how a character usually behaves to a specific social [play] situation. This process of inference, identification, and adaptation, while more difficult to study than imitation, is potentially more pervasive" (p. 219).

The child here is constituted as an active cognate viewer. Even within homogenous cognitive age groupings, children are seen to differently process and adapt TV information for use in other social situations. Young children do understand how TV heroes solve problems, and children apply that understanding of motive and consequence to "playground vignettes" (p. 219). Countering the simplistic conceptualization of direct imitation in social learning theory, Desmond proposes that cognitive development theory can shed light on "why children do not directly imitate vast amounts of behavior from television." This, he argues, can be achieved by a study of the interpretive structures which enable children to transform TV content into conversations and play strategies "filled with concepts and ideas attributable to the medium" (pp. 219–220).

The ninth violence profile (Gerbner, Gross, Jackson-Beeck, Jeffries-Fox & Signorielli, 1978), published in the *Journal of Communication*, focused exclusively on "methodology, current findings of the distribution of power in television drama, and the behavioral correlates of viewing" (p. 176). TV's ideological form and content are construed as "stories": "stories about what things exist, stories about how things work and stories about what to do . . . television tells them all through news, drama, and advertising to almost everybody most of the time" (p. 178). One such story this violence index is concerned with is the "lessons" of power. Power is conceptualized thus: "Indices of power are expressed in terms of chances for involvement in violence and the balance of risks in some kind of hurting and/or killing" (p. 186). This construct individualizes power and locates it within relationships of violence and aggression. Content analysis (the "television view") is matched with "social reality" (the "real world"): TV violence, for instance, is matched with data about actual crime rates. Attitude and opinion survey data, analyzed "in terms of age, education, sex, and other social and personal characteristics" (p. 195), can reveal how and to what extent viewers have cultivated a view of the social world that resembles TV's definition of social reality.

While Gerbner et al. hint at the institutional, political origins and functions of TV's symbolic message system, the empirical analysis focuses on individual attitudinal effects of the decidedly apolitical construct of "TV stories." As indicated, this study is concerned primarily with methodology and, indeed, charts, graphs, and discussion of statistical delineations of indices (e.g., Rosenberg's "faith in the people" index, NORC General Social Survey) dominate the discourse. And although questions of theory or the politics of TV's "symbolic environment" were not focal in this study, the Gerbner et al. studies did suggest the conceptual possibilities that TV is "more than mere entertainment" and that effects are derivative of more than a single exposure. Yet, any discussion of, or reference to theories of culture, power, symbolic violence or, for instance, the "economic (i.e., marketing) goals as well as the goals of socialization into a power structure" (p. 205) is curiously absent.

In "Television Access and the Slowing of Cognitive Growth," published in *American Educational Research Journal*, Robert C. Hornik (1978) took his research to El Salvador to examine the effects of TV on school performance among children with different access to TV. Since all urban and almost all rural American communities had access to TV, comparative studies of TV effects on children from communities with and without TV were rare (cf. Murray & Kippax, 1978, in Australia; Schramm et al., 1961, in Canada; Himmelweit et al., 1958, in Britain). Hornik posits two questions: First, does TV watching displace more intellectually demanding activities such as reading and thus diminish the rate of intellectual growth? Second, given that most entertainment programs are based on life in America's middle-class, white urban culture, might such content not be meaningless to rural American children or to children in developing countries where a fair amount of imported U.S. content is broadcast? Hornik questions whether culturally alien content might lead either to intellectual acceleration, since children "strain" to incorporate "alien" content, or to null effects on intellectual growth, since content is seen as meaningless fantasy.

Hornik's study sampled seventh to eighth graders over a two-year period. Three groups were isolated for study: never owned TV, always owned TV, and recently acquired TV. The data suggested that for all three cohorts "there seems to be no evidence of a television exposure effect in specific subject achievement" (p. 10). However, a "striking negative association" between TV exposure and long-term reading growth was evident for all three groups. That is, taking into consideration a two-year (age/developmental) gain minus TV viewing effects, Hornik found a 10 percent loss in reading scores for all three groups over a two-year period. Students with lower general ability and reading scores who recently had acquired TV showed a drop on both measures; their gain in the subsequent two years lagged behind middle and high ability students. Hornik speculates that "for these students, the acquisition of a television set had a more noticeable impact than it had on relatively better-off students" (p. 13).

The (educational) construct of the child is based here on a numerical reading score measured against an equally abstract reading skill "ideal" or "average." TV effects are seen as mere access to the medium, not amount or specific content watched in particular social circumstances. The transposition of U.S.-constructed reading skill criteria and tests for both general ability and reading as measurements of educational achievement to a developing country is thus fraught with similar measurement and equivalence problems, as outlined earlier in discussion of "Plaza Sesamo" (Diaz-Guerrero et al., 1975).

In "Children's Social Behavior in Three Towns with Differing Television Experience," published in the *Journal of Communication*,

Murray and Kippax (1978) reported on the effects of TV on children in three Australian communities: high-TV town (five years of access); low-TV town (one year); and no-TV town (no TV). The demographic composition of the three towns was judged equivalent with slight variations in educational levels and family size. The sample consisted of 128 eight- to twelve-year-olds almost equally divided by sex. Interviews were conducted in the homes with mothers, fathers, and one child. Murray and Kippax, like Hornik, retrieved the displacement hypothesis to question the influence of variable TV access on children. While Hornik's concern was with TV and reading achievement, Murray and Kippax examined TV and children's social activities.

Children reportedly decreased social activities when TV was a relative novelty in the home, but tended "to return to their former levels of interest in other media and social participation opportunities" after several years of set ownership (p. 27). Children's perception of the function of TV reflected their "experiential differences": those with less TV experience valued TV more than those with more experience. From a uses and gratifications perspective, these trends were seen to parallel high-TV town children's perception of TV as more entertaining, which increased their use of TV for diversion and the relief of boredom. By contrast, low-TV town children with less TV experience perceived TV as more informative, and thus tended to be more selective and to use TV for informative purposes. For Murray and Kippax, the social context of viewing is important. The child is seen to use TV according to specific perceptions of the medium which are partially determined by differential experience with the medium. Whatever effects potentially accrue are seen as a consequence of the "interaction between media content and the social context" (p. 20).

Concern with displacement theory as an explanation for TV effects was prevalent in the early years of TV (e.g., Lewis, 1949; Riley & Riley, 1951; Baxter, 1960–1961). Since then, research had argued that viewers resume initially displaced activities after several years of TV ownership, and the concept of displacement came to be viewed as a useful explanatory tool only for groups which had recently acquired TV. Displacement theory could not account for effects in children who had grown up with TV since, even by the early 1960s, TV had passed the "novelty effect" threshold in most U.S. households. Displacement theory thus had ceased to circulate within the discourse. Semirural Australia and Central America, however, could still provide data for the application of a concept no longer applicable to most U.S. viewers.

Foucault (1972) has suggested that once concepts have been articulated as "truths," once established or "epistemologized" within a field of discourse, even if these "are no longer discussed" (p. 58), concepts and statements still exist at the margins of an enunciative field in a "field of memory." He explains: "The enunciative field involves what might be called a *field of memory* (statements that are no longer accepted or discussed, and which consequently no longer define either a body of truth or a domain of validity, but in relation to which relations of filiation, genesis, transformation, continuity, and historical discontinuity can be established" (p. 58). Hence, statements appear, disappear, or are transformed, marginalized, or reinstated. Hornik's and Murray and Kippax's studies exemplify such retrieval and reinscription of a concept. Recalled from the textual discursive memory, displacement theory was rearticulated and reinscribed with new empirical content (i.e., El Salvadorean and Australian data). The thematic unity of these two studies as they appear here in this book is itself a discursive structuring by virtue of the alphabetic and chronological sequencing imposed by the discursive rule under which this present text operates. In that sense, their colocation is purely coincidental yet, at the same time, illustrative of how discursive rule systems can recombine and (re)construct the discourse.

Salomon and Cohen (1978) asked "what *is* television and what is it that we measure?" (p. 266) in "On the Meaning and Validity of Television Viewing," published in *Human Communications Research*. Salomon and Cohen attempt to define a TV viewing construct that entails a socio-situational factor, transmission of content, the source of content messages, and message perceptions. In the authors' view, since both medium and viewer are engaged in a "multifaceted" interaction, simple measures of viewing amount or even program exposure are inadequate: "Viewing is a behavioral variable which hides many, and different, surplus meanings, and needs to be considered as representing a (some) theoretical construct(s). . . . It is unwarranted to consider 'amount of viewing' as one general measure which is equally valid for all purposes, and within all frames of reference. Rather, there are a number of loosely interrelated constructs which belong to different nomological networks" (p. 269). This conceptual expansion posits viewing as a social situation within which coded messages are transmitted via a medium to a viewer who has specific "perceptions of messages," has differential knowledge of a medium-specific "language," and is engaged in a "cognitive" and "emotional act" (pp. 266–268). The construction of meaning and, hence, effects on viewers are generated within this interaction.

Rossiter (1978) reviews "American Research on TV Advertising's General Impact on Children" to examine the findings on behavioral, attitudinal, and cognitive effects. He conceptualizes behavioral effects as children's purchase requests, attitudinal effects as likes and dislikes for commercials, and cognitive effects as the ability to comprehend commercial intent. He concurs with much of the research on cognitive effects of TV commercials: More exposure does not lead to greater susceptibility to advertising strategies but, rather, improves children's ability to comprehend intents underlying those strategies. In support of Ward, Wackman, and Wartella's (1975, 1977) use of Piagetian theory to explain TV advertising effects, Rossiter emphasizes the importance of considering age-related cognitive abilities and TV exposure as coconstitutive of effects. Similarly, behavioral effects must be interpreted with caution: "Before interpreting request frequencies as data on 'effects,' we must consider the problem referred to earlier—namely, that requesting behavior is under the control of factors other than advertising-induced intent" (p. 17).

Rossiter acknowledges that TV advertising does have effects: adults and children are persuaded to want and buy certain products. But, he argues, the developing child "selects those products which are interesting and attractive, and asks for them" on the basis of what s/he understands in an ad. Age-related cognitive abilities are seen to mediate "purchase requests" along with the kinds of social influences (parental buying habits and use of consumer information) outlined by Ward et al. (1975, 1977). Rossiter posits an interactive model of televiewing in which the child is seen to attend and respond to TV messages on the basis of cognitive abilities and sociosituational and family influences.

A field survey of 124 nine-year-olds, 146 thirteen-year-olds, and 131 seventeen-year-olds, representative of "various ability levels . . . [and] racial and socioeconomic composition" (Rubin, 1978:126), sought to identify the relationship between "patterns of television viewing and political-socialization measures" (pp. 125–126). TV-use measures were correlated with political socialization indices for each age level. Rubin found that younger children reportedly watched fewer current affairs programs and were less politically informed than older children. Yet younger children who watched above average amounts of news programs scored higher on political information indices than their light- or moderate-viewing counterparts. Rubin notes that "earlier political socialization studies generally concentrated on the impact of the family, school, or peer group," and that his study does not account for these nonmedia influences. Subsequent research, he proposes, should recombine data on both media and nonmedia sources of influence on children's political socialization. Yet he also insists that the isolation of media influences from children's everyday social context is warranted because of the importance of TV in children's lives. Further research, Rubin hopes, should enable a clearer specification of TV's "functional role" in children's political socialization. The epistemological problems associated with the methodological utility of separating socializing contexts into measurable bits notwithstanding, the viewer is constituted here as a passive recipient of TV information seen to affect viewers independent of other mediating or countervailing political influences.

"Children's Viewing of Television and Recognition Memory of Commercials" (Zuckerman, Ziegler and Stevenson, 1978), published in *Child Development*, reports on a study of the relationship between children's attention (to TV) and information retention (of breakfast cereal commercials). This experimental study of 112 white, middle-class second, third, and fourth graders was conducted in an on-campus experimental laboratory. Room size, monitor size, furniture arrangement, toys, experimental commercials, background and reliability of the undergraduate coders, and the hardware setup used to videotape the children were all meticulously described. Following exposure to a 15-minute video interspersed with commercials, children were asked to complete a pencil and paper test that required that they circle "yes" or "no" in response to the experimenter's queries about content. To help the children recall specific content, the experimenter then replayed seven video and seven audio segments of the experimental video they had just viewed. "This procedure was continued until all 58 segments were presented," and during this presentation, the "experimenter called out the number of the segment about to appear so that the children were on the correct number and ready for the segment" (p. 99).

After laborious discussion of statistical results, Zuckerman et al. concluded that children of this age group do not pay much attention to commercials. Children were observed to attend more to the visual than auditory component of a commercial. Their attention was recorded as "highest at the onset of a commercial and decreased rapidly after this," with a further decline for a second commercial in a series (p. 102). Children's behaviors during the commercials were considered "low or moderate": they rarely engaged in play or social interaction, focusing, instead, on a toy. When "they talked it was predominantly about something other than what was on television" (p. 102). These attention patterns suggested to the authors that "children are so familiar with the content and techniques used in commercials that they rapidly habituate to them" (p. 102). Since children paid so little attention to commercials, their recall ("recognition memory") was correlatively poor; attention thus was found as a moderately strong predictor of visual information retention.

A "construct of viewing" (Salomon & Cohen, 1978) is here reduced to attention levels. Moreover, whatever attention was measured had little to do with children's attention to TV or their recall of advertising content. Rather, the results provide evidence of children's different abilities to link information from a 15-minute video to 58 video segments, and of their numerical abilities to match an experimenter's number calls with equivalent numbers on a "pencil and paper" instrument. In other words, what this study measured indicates more about attention paid to an experimenter's task instructions, to 58 video segments, and to numeracy and literacy skills than to levels of attention paid to TV or commercial messages under "normal" viewing conditions.

Stanley J. Baran, Lawrence J. Chase and John A. Courtright (1979) conducted an experimental field study of 81 second- and third-grade children to determine the effects of prosocial programming on behaviors. Noting that only a few studies have used actual TV programs (e.g., Meyer, 1976; Sprafkin et al., 1975) in their experimental designs, the authors point to the importance of using programs that are actually broadcast, rather than using edited or specially produced video segments. Zuckerman et al.'s (1978) study is a case in point of the approach Baran et al. (1979) critique. Yet the prosocial stimulus chosen for this experiment was an edited, 12-minute condensed version of one episode of "The Waltons." A natural social encounter was added to the traditional experimental procedure of control and experimental group division, film treatment, and post-treatment interviews. In this natural encounter the subject "accidentally" met a confederate "by the doorway . . . [who] dropped an armful of books" (p. 279). The subject's behavioral response to this incident (to help or not help pick up the books) was recorded by the confederate. The data indicated that a prosocial program such as "The Waltons" can "transmit prosocial behaviors to children": "One viewing of an edited episode was sufficient stimulus to elicit cooperative behavior from those who viewed it" (p. 282). Although the authors recognize the limitations of their findings in terms of long-term effects, this dilemma is seen as resolvable by more of the same kind of research. Other possible sources of learning "cooperative" behaviors—peers, family, school—are not considered, not even bearing a mention in the obligatory concluding agenda for further research.

Apparently under siege, the uses and gratifications approach took a defensive stand in Jay G. Blumler's (1979) tract "The Role of Theory in Uses and Gratifications Studies." Blumler reviews the criticisms leveled at uses and gratifications "theory"—its atheoreticism heading the list—and insists throughout on the model's important contribution of the "active audience" to mass media research. In some ways, Blumler's text already had been presaged by the general decline throughout the 1970s of published studies based on the uses and gratifications model. As I have pointed out earlier, one of the major conceptual problems of this model is the a priori methodological ascription of particular needs to audiences. How individuals perceive their needs, moreover, is conditioned by the gratifications they perceive media to fill. Self-ascribed needs and gratifications indeed would be learned from school, family, peers, or even the media themselves. The tautology of uses and gratifications is further exacerbated by the methodological constraints of the field survey. Himmelweit and Swift (1976:135) explain that "the danger of circularity becomes acute in such gratification research where perception of needs and their satisfaction depends on questioning the same individual." Although nonexperimental research continued to consider media uses as a context for "effects," studies based on a formalized uses and gratifications model declined throughout the 1970s.

John B. Christiansen (1979) used a linear recursive path model to examine "Television Role Models and Adolescent Occupational Goals," published in *Human Communication Research*. In 1979 this journal was only in its fifth year of publication, yet at the vanguard of quantitative communications research. Christiansen's methodological choice aimed to show a "logical, causal model" of socialization in which "each independent variable is seen as causing change in the dependent variable, as well as in the two intervening variables . . . [and] each intervening variable is seen as causally prior to the dependent variable" (p. 336). Agreeing with DeFleur and DeFleur (1967) that viewing amount is related to children's increased knowledge about TV occupations, Christiansen found in his sample of 387 high school students (of undesignated sex or SES) that TV exposure does not "develop specific occupational goals" in adolescents (p. 337). TV may teach about TV occupations, but this knowledge is not used by adolescents to form occupational goals. In this study, the linear recursive path model constructs a viewer cast in a cause-effect model of socialization and learning.

In "Problem-Solving in TV Shows Popular with Children: Assertion vs. Aggression" (Dominick, Richman & Wurtzel, 1979), published in *Journalism Quarterly*, the authors reported that during prime-time viewing, helping and assertion are shown most frequently as problem solving means, whereas during the Saturday morning cartoon hours, aggression features prominently. Males primarily use aggressive behaviors to resolve conflict, whereas females use assertive behaviors. Plot structures on Saturday morning cartoons were found to be more simplistic than during prime time, consisting mostly of physical chase and avoidance sequences. Hence, solutions to simple problems were correlatively simple and focused on physical aggression rather than verbal negotiation. For Dominick et al., since children spend a lot of time watching Saturday cartoons, they are exposed to substantial amounts of antisocial modelling which, from an observational learning perspective, has serious implications.

Drawing on Bandura's (1975), and Bandura and Walters' (1963) premise that attention precedes learning, Dominick et al. suggest that children probably more readily attend to physically aggressive rather than verbally assertive behaviors, and thus are more likely to learn aggressive behaviors. Moreover, Bandura and Walters's "theory also posits that if behavior is successful, the probability of modeling increases" (Dominick et al. 1979:463). Since aggression is commonly portrayed on TV as a successful problem-solving strategy, this models for children predominantly antisocial, rather than prosocial interpersonal behaviors. Although the concept of the child articulated here is along classic behaviorist lines, the authors nonetheless suggest that children may be attending to other portrayed behaviors coded as violent. For example, "Bionic Woman," the authors note, "was the third most aggressive prime time program but also ranked third in helping behavior," and "'Bugs Bunny' ranked number one in aggression but was also number two in assertive attempts" (p. 463). Recognizing that more than one content element is intrinsic to any program and that children attend to more than a singular element coded by the researcher, Dominick et al. maintain that children "could be attending to the nonviolent behaviors as well as (or instead of) the violent ones" (p. 463).

Comstock, writing with Robin E. Cobbey (1979), in "Television and the Children of Ethnic Minorities" switches from his "pro-effects" stance by outlining reasons why research on TV and children must transcend the narrow conceptualization of minority children as blacks, as low SES blacks, and as heavy viewers. They review and summarize the research on TV and black children and conclude that explanations for black children's viewing habits have been narrow and simplistic: they propose either a "'political adaptation' explanation" (p. 106) or posit TV as "a symbol of assimilation" (p. 107) explanation. The former holds that "the civil rights movement inspired information-seeking" (p. 106) from TV by blacks, and the latter proposes an integrationist explanation that suggests that blacks use TV information to learn about and participate vicariously in mainstream white society. The authors, however, suggest that within any minority group there are viewing differences which should not be reduced to single factors of race, ethnicity, or social class. Moreover, research preoccupation with blacks as representative of "race/ethnicity" has failed to consider Hispanic, "Oriental, or American Indian children" (p. 112).

Comstock had already acknowledged the previous year that TV may not be as powerful as laboratory evidence had confirmed. In 1979 he was ready to admit that "it may be that television is actually more subordinate to other influences among minority children, or that its influence among all children comparatively is minor" (p. 111). But in the absence of research evidence "that would provide a ready answer," Comstock and Cobbey propose parental and school intervention: "In the case of parents, the questions become those of focus (when might the parent most effectively intervene), technique (how), and *constancy*—for childrearing is an everyday task, not a laboratory experiment. . . . In the case of schools, we return to a theme as old as the empirical investigation of television's impact on children" (p. 111). Comstock's revelations about childrearing, about the sociocultural diversity of ethnicity, and about the potential influence of other sources of socialization besides TV are significant if only in the sense that such statements authorize what many with lesser academic status had been claiming for some time.

Gerbner's "cultural indicators" research which, by 1979, had established a series of studies nearly a decade in progress, was itself generating research—replication studies—by others not working with Gerbner and colleagues at the Annenberg School. Doob and Macdonald (1979), for instance, reported on a replication study of Gerbner's violence profiles but included one previously omitted factor: "the actual incidence of crime in the neighborhood" (p. 170). The interview data from randomly selected households in four areas (low/high crime suburban, low/high crime urban) revealed that "when actual incidence of crime is controlled for, there is no overall relationship between television viewing and fear of being a victim of crime" (p. 170). Hence, Gerbner et al.'s claim that heavy viewers feel more at risk in a "mean world," are more suspicious of the outside world, and more inclined to support law enforcement agencies and tactics is a simplistic explanation of a complex social context within which attitudes toward crime, violence, and law enforcement develop. Moreover, in the absence of a theory and analysis of that elusive variable of social context, the cultivation hypothesis can lead to the attribution of unrealistic and overdetermined powers to TV. Doob and Macdonald thus point to the importance of considering viewers' environmental context as a significant influence on perceptions of victimization in a "mean world."

Phillip J. Mohr (1979) examined "Parental Guidance of Children's Viewing of Evening TV Programs" and found "little parental guidance on specific evening television programs" (p. 225). Responses were obtained from a probability-sample survey of 5,167 fourth to ninth graders, and 4,882 of their parents. Questionnaires were administered to children during school hours and self-administered by parents. Mohr noted that black parents reported more positive guidance ("should watch") than white parents, who reported more negative guidance ("should not watch"), and that "parents with no college education reported more positive guidance than those with one or more years of college" (p. 223). Mohr comments that both the PTA of his sample and the House subcommittee "concluded that parents share responsibility with the television industry for the amount of violence to which children are exposed" (p. 213). If, by extension, protecting children from potentially harmful effects of TV violence is a shared responsibility between industry and parents, and parents are remiss in their share of responsibility, then the industry, in principle, cannot be held entirely accountable for "harmful effects." Funded by the "American Broadcasting Companies, Inc.," Mohr's study articulates this logic and, by constituting parents as ineffective mediators between TV and children, it in effect absolves the industry from sole responsibility for any effects that TV violence may have on children.

Patricia Morison, Margaret McCarthy, and Howard Gardner (1979) in "Exploring the Realities of Television with Children," published in the *Journal of Broadcasting*, suggested that age, not viewing amount or program content, correlated with children's abilities to distinguish between TV reality and fantasy. Open-ended interviews followed "the procedure devised initially by Piaget" (p. 455). Eighteen boys and 18 girls from first, third, and sixth grades in a multiethnic, working-class community comprised the sample. The data suggested that "the ability to assess the reality status of various types of television is relatively independent of the child's familiarity with a variety of television programs, and, possibly, independent also of the amount of television watched" (p. 461). TV content and amount viewed are considered inadequate measures by which to gauge children's perceptions of TV reality and fanatasy. Other factors such as "knowledge of the television medium [seem] very important in the achievement of sophistication"; such medium-specific knowledge indeed may "exceed the sheer effects of watching a variety of programs" (p. 462). This, in turn, suggests that children could benefit from being taught TV concepts which would "facilitate their abilities to discriminate [TV] reality from fiction" (p. 462).

Cognitive stage and background knowledge—specifically, knowledge of TV's "conventions" or symbolic system—increasingly were seen as significant factors in explanations of children's abilities to distinguish between TV fact and fantasy. Efforts to theorize background knowledge began foregrounding considerations of what would soon be conceptualized by the discourse as media literacy, or literate viewing. Given a theory that posited viewers' experience, knowledge, and comprehension abilities in interaction with specific TV codes, the teaching of TV comprehension skills became conceptually possible. This reconceptualization became most apparent to those working within variations of Piagetian cognitive development theory. Salomon and Cohen (1978) were articulating similar views in their redefinition of "viewing constructs"; Morison et al. (1979), Wackman et al. (1977), and Andrew F. Newcomb and W. Andrew Collins (1979) were also, in Foucault's terms, at the same threshold of articulation.

Extending and recirculating nearly a decade of research on children's cognitive processing of TV information pioneered by Collins and colleagues (Collins, 1970, 1975; Collins, Berndt & Hess, 1974; Collins, Wellman, Keniston & Westby, 1978), Newcomb and Collins (1979) again argue for cognitive development theory to explain children's learning from TV. The shift here, however, is toward efforts to incorporate "children's prior social experiences" as part of their cognitive scaffolding. Age-related differences in universal cognitive stages are seen as an inadequate explanation of comprehension differences among children at similar developmental levels. Newcomb and Collins gave tentative acknowledgment to what in reading psychology had been formalized as "schema theory" of reading comprehension with the publication two years earlier of Schooling and the Acquisition of Knowledge (Anderson, Spiro & Montague, 1977).

Although the processing of print and audiovisual information may not draw on the same classes of cognitive skills, the authors speculate that knowledge "sets" or "schemes" might also be involved in comprehension of the TV text: "Older children and adolescents may remember the content of particular shows better than younger viewers because they have existing information sets or schemes that facilitate processing of program detail whereas the younger viewers have no such sets, or perhaps have less adequate ones" (p. 418). Similarly, children from certain class or ethnic subcultures might better comprehend TV content which features characters and social settings similar to their own backgrounds, than children with different sociocultural backgrounds.

The sample consisted of 578 middle- and lower-SES, white and black children in second, fifth, and eighth grade who participated in "two fully-crossed replications of the same design" (p. 417). Children viewed one of two edited "conflict resolution" TV dramas: one portraying a middle-class white family, the other a working-class black family. The data suggested that children's comprehension is related to familiarity with content, and not solely to age-dependent elaboration of cognitive structures: "Second graders whose own backgrounds were similar to the portrayal in the program comprehended program content better than second graders whose socioeconomic backgrounds were relatively different from the portrayal" (p. 421).

At issue here are not effects or what children learn from TV but, rather, how children learn. The TV-viewer relationship here is constituted as interactive: meaning for the viewer is seen as coconstituted by the TV text, and the knowledge and cognitive abilities which the viewer brings to bear on that text. And since "young viewers whose backgrounds diverge from the heavily middle-class bias in most television portrayals" are "most at risk for the negative effects" because of the "miscomprehension that often occurs in children of their age" (p. 423), this failure to comprehend the "TV curriculum" can be seen as analogous to the failure syndrome of working-class children to comprehend that same "middle-class bias" of the school curriculum. To extend Newcomb and Collins' hypothesis, children's miscomprehension or "mis-reading," then, of both the lessons of TV and of the school can be seen as a function of cultural capital (Bourdieu, 1973), not of cognitive deficit.

Robertson (1979) in "Parental Mediation of Television Advertising Effects," published in the *Journal of Communication*, reported on a "comprehensive review of research" which suggested that research is "scattered and incomplete" (p. 12). Some trends, however, did appear to emerge from the scattered research evidence: children's purchase requests were seen to vary with age and, to a lesser extent, with social class. Children's product requests provide opportunities for parental consumer socialization, but this line of inquiry "has not been pursued by the literature" (p. 21). One consistent research finding points to parent-child conflict and the child's disappointment and frustration following parental denial of a purchase request. This prevalent finding of negative affective effects of exposure to TV advertising, in Robertson's view, is more of a consequence of the research question posed than a generalizable effect of TV commercials (p. 22). Robertson suggests that since any effects of TV advertising are inherently "handled" by parents, "a more complex model might better explain these relationships than the simple linear flow model of advertising to requests and mediation. The impact of advertising is a function of a complex set of family, child, and situational factors" (p. 24). The construct of the child here is located within a network of social influences that conditions apprehension of and the learning of (consumer) values and behaviors from the commercial message. The child-TV relationship is constituted as interactive, not unilinear, and parental (non)involvement is considered as a central mediating force in TV advertising effects on children.

In "Media and Symbol Systems as Related to Cognition and Learning," published in the *Journal of Educational Psychology*, Salomon (1979a) outlines a cognitive information processing model. This model, he claims, is based on the triadic interactive dynamics of cognition, learning and TV. This paper was a condensed version of his monograph published that same year, *Interaction of Media, Cognition and Learning* (1979b). By 1979, Salomon had added a third dimension to his interactive cognitive model, first outlined in 1976. He proposed that in addition to viewers' background knowledge interacting with the cognitive skill demands of a medium's symbol and code system, task perception also influences information processing. How children perceive a decoding task is seen to influence the amount of mental effort invested in extracting information from print or audiovisual text. Children, given an information-seeking task, will tend to "deep process" text, whereas absence of a task-orientation will lead children to more "shallow processing" of text. According to this model, deeper processing, in turn, "require[s] more handling of the coded messages and enhance[s] the cultivation of the relevant skills" (p. 143). The interactive processes involved in the service of decoding text are reciprocal, or what Salomon would later call "spiral" processes (1987:16).

Drawing on a Piagetian framework via the works of Olson and Bruner (1974) and others, Salomon locates his model in the discourse of educational psychology—more to the point, in the locus where the discourse of developmental psychology intersected with reading psychology. Of course, Bandura and advocates of observational learning theory had long been concerned with learning. But that concern was a psychological, not educational, one, a concern with behavior and not cognition. Once TV content was reconstituted as "text" and the learning of that text as a cognitive, not behavioral, process, the child was remapped along what Foucault calls the "grid of specification." The attribution to TV of the status of text relocated TV from the social domain of domestic leisure to the educational domain of institutionalized learning. Correspondingly, the child's relationship with the TV text was relocated from body to mind: from inscriptions on bodily behaviors to inscriptions on cognitive structures and processes. The reconceptualization of TV as text enabled the conceptual and disciplinary move that the reading of that text should be a privileged educational object of study. Moreover, once the notion of "reading TV text" is invoked, questions of literacy and the teaching of literate competencies arise. Since institutionalized teaching of decoding and comprehension skills is required to enable children to read the symbol system of print text, then, in principle at least, the same requirements could be suggested for the acquisition of skills with which to decode and comprehend the TV text. The discursive possibility of "media literacy," then, was enabled by the respecification of the child as a cognate subject and of TV as text.

James G. Webster and William C. Coscarelli (1979) examined children's program preferences and discussed the implications of their findings for regulatory guidelines in "The Relative Appeal to

Children of Adult vs. Children's TV Programming," published in the *Journal of Broadcasting*. Fifty third graders and 46 fifth graders were randomly assigned by grade level to one of two treatment groups. Sex and SES distribution were not noted. One group received a questionnaire with forced choice preference items "to measure the relative appeal to children of adult versus children's programming" (p. 438). The second group was shown a video with 48-second program segments meant to replicate "the essence of the shows as if the child was switching channels 'to see what's on'" (p. 442). Children viewed this videotape individually with the investigator "to avoid peer group pressures when stating a program preference" (p. 442). The data indicated that, when given a choice, children prefer adult programs. Whether children prefer adult prime-time programs because children's programs are not available during that time, or whether they would prefer children's programs if these were substituted for adult programs, are issues that the authors acknowledge their study did not address, but which policy makers need to address.

The following and final group of studies to be discussed in this chapter was published in the *Journal of Communication*'s 1979 special section entitled "Growing Up With Television." As with previous special sections in journals, I discuss these in the order in which they were textually grouped.

Cohen and Salomon (1979) headed this section with "Children's Literate Television Viewing: Surprises and Possible Explanations." A comparative study between U.S. and Israeli children sought to identify differences in "literate viewing," given different viewing amounts. Israeli children watched less and produced higher "literate viewing" scores than U.S. children. The "deep processing" of TV information among Israeli children the authors see as related to medium-specific and situational factors: TV was positively evaluated by children and parents, and children reportedly viewed TV more frequently with parents. Thus, "a social norm that favored more 'serious' televiewing [led] them to invest more mental effort in their viewing" (p. 162). Less entertainment programs and the absence of color broadcasts (which typify U.S. TV), as well as the need to "concentrate more . . . since they often have to read subtitles," required more mental effort among Israeli children (p. 162). In the authors' view, the empirical data show that "depth of information processing depends on the amount of mental effort invested in the process . . . [which] in turn, depends on (a) the way the information is structured, (b) cognitive makeup of the individual, and (c) the perception of the task to be performed" (p. 161).

Drawing support from "recent studies in psycholinguistics" and the cognitive branch of reading psychology, the authors make a case for the conceptual transfer of mental elaboration invested in print text to the TV text: "Given that the likelihood of remembering an element of a story varies according to the perspective, or mental scheme, a reader brings to the material, it is reasonable to argue that story elements that do not match the 'slots' readied in the reader's perspective are processed more shallowly and are thus less well remembered" (p. 161). "Generalizing to television," Cohen and Salomon argue that the level of processing applied will depend, as with reading print, on "how a person wants to perceive (or is told to perceive) the information" (pp. 161–162). Intentionality, available skills and social situational factors influence what is taken to and from the text: "When children view television at home . . . [t]he extent to which they are likely to engage in deeper or shallower processing will depend on motivation, situational possibilities, and constraints, as well as on the prevailing social norms pertaining to the televiewing situation" (p. 162).

Following Cohen and Salomon's educational reframing of televiewing and the child, the next paper also considered the educational implications of TV. Sydney G. Burton, James M. Calonico and Dennis R. McSeveney (1979) linked preschool viewing habits with school achievement and social relationships at first grade level in "Effects of Preschool Television Watching on First-Grade Children." Multiple regression analysis of data from a field survey of 174 first graders and their parents from a multiracial, lower-SES community and from a predominantly white middle-SES community suggested that "first graders who watched a lot of television in their preschool years earned lower grades than those who watched less—and tended to choose each other as friends" (p. 164). Heavy viewing was seen to reduce the chances of "successful social integration" and to reduce time spent with other scholastic and social activities. Thus, in "addition to taking away from time a child might be spending in more clearly social activities, TV viewing may also hinder the growth of certain skills necessary for the development of adequate communicative abilities" (p. 165) which, in turn, may account for why heavy viewers choose each other as playmates. These friendships among heavy viewing, less "successful" socially integrated children is said to reinforce already existing low sociability among them. Although no claims for causal effects are made, preschool viewing amount is conceptualized here as a singular influence, "a good predictor . . . of academic success and choice of friends among first-graders" (p.169). The only mediating characteristics the child is seen to bring to the viewing situation is a personal history of amount viewed.

Also concerned with TV's influence on children's school achievement, Elliott A. Medrich (1979), in "Constant Television: A Background to Daily Life," examined the "constant TV household." He interviewed 764 eleven- and twelve-year-olds (269 families) from mixed racial and SES backgrounds. Achievement scores were obtained from the schools and children's mothers were given self-administered questionnaires. The sample comprised: "black—59.8%, white—24.2%, Asian—9.2%, Hispanic—4.6%, and other—2.2%" (p. 172). The data showed that one third of inner city families were constant TV households. Low income and low education households comprised the majority of constant TV households: "The poor and less well-educated . . . those with fewer material and cultural resources and those who also often live with less privacy in crowded homes . . . represent the majority of constant television households. . . . Children in these households have generally limited out-of-school opportunities or fewer time use alternatives in the home" (p. 174).

Test score data suggested that children from constant TV homes tended to perform poorly at school and were "more likely to be reading well below grade level than children from non-constant television households" (p. 174). Parents or guardians apparently exercised minimal control over children's viewing. Children claimed to watch when and whatever they wanted, and "whatever is on . . . because they feel they have nothing else to do" (p. 175). Medrich (p. 176) proposes that "research may have to shift from its emphasis on television content to emcompass a notion of television as a pervasive environment in many American homes. The effects of television content are often thought to be the principal problem, but television's role as constant background to daily life may ultimately prove to have greater significance." Medrich turns the TV-child effects equation on its head by suggesting a viewing construct not based on content exposure or viewing amount, but on reports that TV is on all day long in some households whether someone is watching or not. As such, he does not consider TV as a singular cause of low academic achievement, but as an integrated and constant element within a network of social influences which, in combination, appears to account for poor educational performance.

The tenth violence profile by Gerbner and a new combination of graduate students (Gerbner, Gross, Signorielli, Morgan & Jackson-Beeck, 1979) followed next. TV violence apparently had increased across all networks, but the most alarming increases were noted for programs broadcast during the children's hours. Yet findings suggested that "imitative aggression among children may be frequent but . . . relatively low-level" (p. 179). Like previous violence profiles, this study discusses the long-term cultivation of cultural myths symbolically recoded by TV and made to appear as social reality (p. 180). Especially among heavy viewers, TV cultivates a view of the world as hostile and violent which, in turn, is said to promote fear of violence and a correlative support of law enforcement (p. 193). The mass cultivation of a dominant image system, via the technological production of a violent symbolic environment, has serious implications: "The meaning of violence is in the kinds of social relationships it presents and the lessons of power . . . and fear of power . . . that may derive from them. . . . It is . . . important to look at the large majority of people who become more fearful, insecure . . . dependent on authority, and who may grow up demanding protection and even welcoming repression in the name of security" (p. 196).

While the TV text is seen here to transmit a uniform set of dominant and distorted messages about social reality, viewers likewise are seen to constitute a uniform mass audience—a manipulable mass, victimized by a prescriptive ideological/technological apparatus. Ideology per se is not in question here: in fact, the term is never used in this or any other of Gerbner's works. But the discursive shift across the violence studies from a focus on specific program content to notions of a symbolic order upheld and perpetuated by "representatives of established order" (p. 195) suggests a resurfacing of the arguments made by Horkheimer and Adorno (1972 [1944]) 30 years earlier, and by Williams (1976 [1962]) and Hall (1977) in England since the 1960s. While today (cf. McQuail, 1987) the violence profile studies and related work are being labeled as critical theory of sorts, only a decade ago it was empirical work overlaid on theory which, at best, was obliquely implied but not articulated. The effective camouflage of any discursive links, that is, citations to "schools of thought" ostensibly too left of center, veiled any political implications of the "cultivation hypothesis." Thus stripped of any overt neo-Marxist or Frankfurtian traces, the discourse of the cultural indicators project was rendered sufficiently palatable to fit into the dominant positivist U.S. discourse of mass communication. Claims of a "left" orientation, an affiliation with critical theory, would not eventuate until the mid-1980s when Gerbner himself announced, via another special issue, the field's discursive reformation from a positivist to a critical orientation.

Following the violence profile, the discourse shifts direction back to the viewer. Edward L. Palmer and Cynthia N. McDowell (1979) in "Program/Commercial Separators in Children's Television Programming" reported on a study that sought to identify "what cues children use to make program/commercial distinctions . . . and their awareness of the commercial's selling intent" (pp. 197–198). This experimental study assigned 60 kindergarten and first graders to one of four treatment groups equally divided for age, race, and sex (p. 198). At four different points in the program, children were interviewed individually and asked whether what they had just seen "was 'part of the show' or a 'commercial,' and how they could tell" (p. 198). The data suggested that awareness of selling intent was low for all groups. Children in the control and experimental groups were equally able to distinguish between program and commercial, although when an animated commercial followed an animated program, children identified both as a program more frequently. The most frequent cues used by children to identify ads were found to be format, not content features. Typical responses included "because it wasn't long" or "because commercials are short" (p. 199). The child is here seen to respond to, or rather be confused by, the format features of the medium. The only discriminatory skill the child viewer brings to the screen is the knowledge that commercials are short. The authors conclude by proposing that children should be taught awareness of commercials' intent and that research "questions must go beyond technique to educating *about* technique" (p. 200).

In this special section, concern with TV form preempted concern with TV content. "Subtle Sex-Role Cues in Children's Commercials" (Welch, Huston-Stein, Wright & Plehal, 1979) examined production techniques and argued that "formal features" carry gender stereotype messages that "may be more influential than the blatant stereotypes presented in content" (p. 208). Sixty toy commercials broadcast during the Saturday morning cartoon hours were analyzed for four categories: action, pace, visual, and auditory techniques. The data suggested that "commercials directed at boys contained highly active toys, varied scenes, high rates of camera cuts, and high levels of sound effects and loud music . . . characters were frequently aggressive to each other or to objects, and the narrators were male. Commercials directed at girls had frequent fades, dissolves, and background music; the narrators were usually female" (p. 207). Dissolves and accompanying soft music "convey images of softness, gentleness, predictability and slow gradual change" which the authors see as promoting "the stereotype of females as quiet, soft, gentle, and inactive" (p. 207). In the authors' view, cumulative effects of exposure to content encoded in stereotypic forms can lead children to link "*any* content with which these features are subsequently associated" (p. 208). Children's "media literacy," according to Renate L. Welch et al., has as much to do with knowledge of the structural, symbolic form within which messages are embedded, as with the messages themselves.

"Children's Understanding of the Nature of Television Characters" (Quarforth, 1979) concludes this special section. Beginning from a Piagetian concept of "animism," Joanne M. Quarforth hypothesized that 6- to 11-year-olds might erroneously attribute consciousness (being alive) to animated characters because children at this age are thought to "attribute consciousness only to those organisms that move of their own accord and that experience a finite life span" (p. 211). Older children, by contrast, are seen to have developed more dis- criminating categories for distinguishing between organic and inor- ganic objects. Quarforth set her sample of 34 predominantly white, middle-class kindergarten to fourth graders four tasks, ranging from "concrete picture sorting to abstract interview questions" (p. 212). Additionally, "each child verbally completed three questionnaires" (p. 213). Kindergarteners and first graders were found to have little understanding of the mechanics of TV "and this seemed to affect their perceptions about the reality of television." Of this age group, 20 percent believed that "people seen on programs are really standing *inside* the television set" (p. 216), and that cartoon characters are "alive." Typical explanations included: "'Those people are made smaller than us and when you turn the TV on, they're lowered down by a rope,' or 'God put them there'" (p. 216). Half the children in this group could not explain how characters appeared on the screen, but agreed that people are not actually "in the TV." Second to fourth graders were almost equally confused about the dynamics of cartoon characters. One fourth of the second and third graders suggested that "cartoon characters have 'people inside them making them move and talk,'" or that "Tony the Tiger," for instance, wears a costume making him "move and talk" (p. 217).

The child's understanding of TV content and any effects that ensue from exposure are here construed as a consequence of the interaction between TV form (animation) and age-related cognitive abilities. Yet children's abilities to distinguish between reality and fantasy are considered independent of social, situational, or experiential media- tion. The omission of mention of the potential for media literacy instruction in, say, animation techniques, reflects Quarforth's agree- ment with Piaget's genetic epistemology: cognitive abilities are in- herited, universal, and "set" in stages, which conceptually limits the possibility for sociocultural, environmental, or educational media- tion.

"Growing Up With TV" was both the title cover and a special section in this issue of the *Journal of Communication*. More than in previous special sections or issues, statements about "media literacy" recur throughout. Not all the studies fall under the aegis of a reconceptual- ized, interactive TV-child relationship. Yet simple unilinear causal explanations are absent from this particular unit of discourse. Over half of the studies base their argument either on an identifiable theoretical orientation (Burton et al., 1979; Quarforth, 1979) or attempt theory-building around their object of study (Cohen & Salomon, 1979; Gerbner et al., 1979; Welch et al., 1979). The atheoreticism so typical of experimental psychology—the fascination with methodology and quantification of behavioral minutiae—has no place in this emergent conception of TV and children. But this is not to say that empiricism had been marginalized. The methodological (and visual) importance of representing the child, TV, televiewing, or cognitive processes in quantitative terms—the discursive mapping of the object of study on graphs, charts, tables—remained. Stirring underfoot, however, not at the margins of discourse but beneath the established scholarly order of "how to speak," were attempts to theorize the acknowledged multiplicity of influences on the TV-viewer relationship. This shift, of course, was not exclusively articulated in this particular journal issue, but is evident in the decade-long reassessment of the TV-child "problem."

THE 1970s: AN OVERVIEW

To suggest that the 1970s research on TV and children can be characterized by one broad orientation in topic choice, theory, or method is to oversimplify and misrepresent the diversity and overlap evident in the research literature. Nonetheless, two notable differences between the 1960s and 1970s discourse can be identified: (1) the emergence of a divergent array of research topics, and (2) the emergence of a more cognitively based, interactive explanation of TV's effects on children. I will discuss the former first and then discuss the shift from a behaviorist to a cognitive construct of the TV-child relation.

The 1960s had witnessed the emergence of the black viewer. In the 1970s, research on the black child audience continued but remained marginal (Comstock & Cobbey, 1979; Greenberg, 1972; Surlin & Dominick, 1970–1971). Similarly, the role of parents in mediating children's viewing remained a marginal concern (Abel, 1976; Chaffee & Tims, 1976; Dimmick, 1976; Greenberg & Reeves, 1976; Mohr, 1979). From a focus in the 1960s on parental controls over children's viewing, interest shifted in the 1970s toward the role of specific family types (i.e., idea- or socio-oriented) in mediating TV effects.

The role of media in the political socialization of children became a relatively focal concern (Atkins & Elwood, 1978; Conway et al., 1975; Dominick, 1972; Rubin, 1976, 1978). This emphasis on TV's role in children's political socialization was seen by researchers as partially related to both heightened media coverage and public awareness of political issues during the Vietnam-Nixon era. Questions regarding TV and children's school achievement (Burton et al., 1979; Hornik, 1978; Medrich, 1979), their occupational goals (Christiansen, 1979), their perceptions of TV parents in relation to real-life parents (Miller

& Beck, 1976), TV's physical effects (Halpern, 1975; Krugman, 1971; Krugman & Hartley, 1970), and children's viewing habits and program preferences (Rubin, 1977; Webster & Coscarelli, 1979) all remained peripheral to more dominant concerns, such as effects of TV violence, advertising, sex-role portrayal, prosocial TV, and the role of cognition in mediating effects.

Following the 1972 release of the Surgeon General's Report, violence effects research continued to provide evidence to support the scientific facts produced for and in the report. TV violence research continued within the methodological and theoretical parameters established in the 1960s by imitative learning proponents in experimental psychology (e.g., Drabman & Thomas, 1974, 1975, 1977; Ellis & Sekyra, 1972; Greenberg, 1974–1975; Hapkiewicz & Roden, 1971; Steuer, Applefield & Smith, 1971; Wotring & Greenberg, 1973). However, Drabman and Thomas (1974, 1975, 1977), Dominick (1973, 1974) and Feinbloom (1976) reframed the TV violence-viewer aggression equation: they claimed that TV violence indeed did have effects, but that these were manifest in "non-responses," or nonbehaviors seen as indicative of apathy toward violence.

The violence desensitization argument closely approximated Feshbach's (e.g., 1976) ongoing research on catharsis theory. Both positions claimed that TV violence had effects but that these were in the opposite direction from those posited by social learning theory. Catharsis theory, based on Freudian developmental stage theory, held that TV violence "drains off" viewers' needs to act out repressed aggression. By contrast, the desensitization hypothesis, based on socialization theory, held that repeated and long-term exposure to TV stimuli and reinforcements causes viewers' eventual acceptance of violence, which leads to apathy and insensitivity toward televised and real-life aggression.

Such seemingly contradictory evidence Foucault (1972) terms discursive "points of diffraction." Apparent incompatibility among statements within a field of discursive diffraction also can constitute "points of equivalence" (p. 65). Never one to admit to a potentially dialectical dynamic underlying his counter-theory theorizing, Foucault explains the emergence of contradictory yet complementary, equivalent yet incompatible elements from within the same discourse: "Points of equivalence: the two incompatible elements are formed in the same way and on the basis of the same rules; the conditions of their appearance are identical; they are situated at the same level; and instead of constituting a mere defect of coherence, they form an alternative: even if, chronologically speaking, they do not appear at the same time, . . . have the same importance, and . . . were not equally represented in the population of effective statements, they appear in the form of 'either . . . or'" (pp. 65–66). Both possibilities, desensitization or catharsis, were products of one methodological rule system that already had confirmed to the point of canonization the "truth" that TV causes behaviors. Within a behaviorist framework, the absence of observable behaviors nonetheless would have to be reconceptualized as behaviors, even if this meant relocating them in subjects' behavioral repertoire.

Drabman and Thomas's, Dominick's, and Feinbloom's research found legitimate methodological means to argue that the absence of observable aggressive behaviors following exposure to TV violence did not mean that behavioral responses did not occur. Thus, for example, when children in an experimental treatment condition are asked to choose between continuing to play a game for points (egocentric behavior) or press a buzzer to solicit adult help for mediating conflict (altruistic behavior), either choice implies a behavior: not pressing the buzzer does not imply absence of behaviors. Such contrived forced choice suggests a methodological procedure which elicits behavioral choice merely different from those prompted by the Bobo doll studies. While on the surface level, the same stimulus (TV violence) appears to have generated contradictory and incompatible findings, nonbehaviors were indeed behaviors, albeit experimentally manipulated. The concept of positive effects (aggressive behaviors) was reconstituted to include null effects (nonaggressive behaviors) which, in turn, were *interpreted* as signs of apathy and insensitivity toward violence and aggression. These may be mutually exclusive elements, but these ostensible oppositional elements were based on and derived from an assumed first principle: the inevitability and validity of behavioral responses.

The emergence of prosocial TV and prosocial effects research followed the same discursive logic. Since antisocial TV had been shown conclusively to generate aggression in viewers (notwithstanding the equivalent possibility of nonaggression), substituting prosocial for antisocial TV was seen potentially to elicit prosocial behaviors in viewers. Research quickly confirmed this hypothesis (Baran et al., 1979; Friedrich & Stein, 1975; Hapkiewicz & Roden, 1971; Poulos et al., 1975; Scherer, 1971). The prosocial TV debate initially sprang from and centered on "Sesame Street."

The 1976 *Journal of Communication* special section on "Sesame Street" rallied the positive effects literature around a single program and positioned "Sesame Street" as synonymous with "prosocial TV." The pedagogical objectives claimed by the program's producers drew theories of learning previously lodged in educational discourses into subsequent "impact" research. The measurement of learning "gains" required the borrowing of standardized assessment instruments from adjacent discourses. TV had been discursively transformed into an electronic school. Designed initially as a compensatory program targeted at educationally disadvantaged inner city children, the "Sesame Street" curriculum, like the school curriculum, was found to benefit primarily middle-class urban children. Through the cross-cultural deployment of ETS assessment instruments, these findings reappeared in Mexican "Sesame Street" viewers. Billed as a prototype of quality educational prosocial TV, "Sesame Street"'s culturally adapted versions became a viable export commodity which, unlike other TV exports such as "Bonanza," "FBI," or "Ed Sullivan," brought with it a veritable industry of authoritative expertise: attendant corporate and academic formative and summative research on program and audience. This research and development discourse, in turn, was used to guide program production and broadcasting, and the making of the "Sesame Street" viewer—the making of a discursive subject. In terms of the circulation of the discourse on TV and children, the "Sesame Street" (sub)discourse was the first to break national and cultural boundaries.

Throughout the decade, several studies on TV and children conducted outside North America were admitted into the discourse (Edgar & Edgar, 1971; Feilitzen & Linne, 1975; Werner, 1975; Hornik, 1978; Murray & Kippax, 1978). The key to this admission, as well as to the cross-cultural deployment of the "Sesame Street" discourse, was the application of assumed universally applicable methodology, hypotheses, and concepts to fields of study previously excluded. The assumed universality of the "Sesame Street" program and research discourse enabled its transnational extension outward from its institutional and discursive center (e.g., ETS, CTW). This cross-cultural extension, in turn, enabled the harnessing of colonized data to be returned to the discursive-institutional fold where these data filled a discursive space previously uninscribed.

Research on TV's symbol system or "formal features" exemplifies a similar inscription. Foucault (1972) explains the articulation of the "yet not said": "We are not dealing with a silent content that has remained implicit, that has been said and yet not said, and which constitutes beneath manifest statements a sort of sub-discourse that is more fundamental. . . . What we are dealing with is a modification in the principle of exclusion and the principle of the possibility of choices; a modification that is due to an insertion in a new discursive constellation" (p. 67). The 1970s exemplifies such a discursive constellation: a remodification of themes, theories, concepts, and methodologies which invested TV and the child with new dimensions. After all, symbolic codes structured TV content before discourse articulated their presence, and viewers were cognate before discourse discovered and verified cognition.

Research on TV advertising and children had circulated at the margins of discourse during the 1960s but surfaced in the 1970s as a legitimate topic of inquiry. Linked to emergent concerns with TV form and the role of cognition in effects, commercials were seen as different from entertainment programs in technical format and code systems, which children were seen to comprehend or miscomprehend, depending on age and corresponding cognitive abilities. As was the case with TV violence effects research, research on TV advertising and children generated an administrative/policy discourse which circulated at the level of federal hearings, reports, and research commissions. The circulation of this discourse in the high profile domain of federal discussion eventually forced broadcasters to adopt self-regulatory practices for airing commercials aimed at the child audience (cf. Liebert & Sprafkin, 1988). Implicit in this change in practice, and in the discourse that enabled the possibility for such change, was a reconstitution of the child as product consumer, as consumer of TV text form and content, and as a cognitively vulnerable viewer in need of special protection.

Effects research had proven its point early in the decade: in carefully controlled experimental conditions, TV did change behaviors. Cognitive and developmental psychologists (e.g., Salomon, 1979b; Collins, 1970, 1975), however, saw comprehension as implicated in behavioral responses. Hence, intervening cognitive processes between the TV stimulus and behavior formed a discursive blank space—the "not said"—that became inscribed during the 1970s. In the educational discourse, the cognitive domain and development of the (Piagetian) child was already well entrenched, while in the mass media discourse the child was only belatedly attributed cognitive faculties.

The possibility of delineating the complexity of cognition, however, remained problematic. The problem with theorizing and verifying cognition lay in the inflexibility of a dominant methodological rule system that did not lend itself easily to measurements beyond observable viewer behaviors. Claims about children's comprehension of TV form and content were constructed on the basis of empirical verifications of children's "looking behaviors," or attention. Research on the effects of TV advertising on children relied much on children's assumed comprehension or miscomprehension, conceptualized on the basis of different levels of attention paid to program/advertisement separators and commercials' salient features. Questions of comprehension of a multicoded medium such as TV, with its simultaneous transmission of speech codes, visual imagery, music, print, and technical and cultural symbolism, brought to the fore newly constructed questions regarding learning, memory, attention, cognitive development, background knowledge, information storage and retrieval, and so forth.

As early as 1933, Holaday and Stoddard had attempted to delineate what and how much information viewers of different ages acquired and recalled from movies. Maccoby and colleagues in the 1950s also used attention measures as explanation for learning and recall of audiovisual information. During the 1970s, questions of comprehension of the audiovisual text continued, yet cognition remained framed in the discourse of behavioral psychology: the experimental treatment, standardized instruments, and correlational analyses. Comprehension could only be articulated insofar as pre-tests could document baseline knowledge and posttests could verify learning gains in terms of information recall of specific (experimental) program content. Historically entrenched preoccupations with short-term individual effects maintained the discourse on the child viewer at an apolitical microanalytic level.

Attempts to politicize the TV discourse, to go beyond descriptive content frequency counts and to conceptualize TV's "lessons" along more sociopolitical lines, also remained anchored in the discourses of positivism and liberalism (e.g., Gerbner et al., 1976, 1977, 1978, 1979). The cultural indicators project revealed the ideological "distortions of reality" to which a national community was ritualistically exposed. But even at its most political, ideology was masked to read, for example, "the common symbolic environment that cultivates the most widely shared conceptions of reality" (Gerbner & Gross, 1976:178). By the end of the decade the ideological underpinnings of TV's symbolic environment remained camouflaged metaphorically as TV's "storytelling" function. The correlative conception of the human subject was a construction of "respondents" as heavy or light viewers first who also, secondarily, happened to have various social class and educational backgrounds, anxieties, fears, and so forth.

Research topics, or "thematic choices," on the TV-viewer relationship diversified throughout the 1970s in attempts to identify and evaluate the processes constituting that relationship. That diversity, however, itself was irrevocably grounded in what must be seen as a deep mistrust among social scientists of theoretical formulations that could not deliver the empirical goods on immediate effects. As McQuail (1987:284), for instance, comments on the cultivation hypothesis: "However plausible the [cultivation] theory, it is almost impossible to deal convincingly with the complexity of posited relationships, between symbolic structures, audience behavior and audience views, given the many intervening and powerful social background factors." The problem here was that any new theorization could only deal convincingly with complexity on the basis of authoritative and established frameworks and categories. Despite the diversity of research topics, the shift toward cognition from behavior, and attempts to reconstruct the TV-viewer relationship as interactive, the body of work produced during the 1970s retained and propagated a firm allegiance to an apolitical individual effects rationality.

Foucault (1972) explains that discourse is constituted by multiple branchings of discursive formations which, like a "tree," contain in modified form the base principles of regularities at each node. Each node and subsequent branching makes possible more detailed specification of an object of study, and modification of the rule system which structures and enables the articulation of a discourse in the first place.

> One can thus describe a tree of enunciative *derivation*: at its base are the statements that put into operation rules of formation at their most extended form; at its summit, and after a number of branchings, are the statements that put into operation the same regularity, but one more delicately articulated, more clearly delimited and localized in its extension. Archaeology—and this is one of its principal themes—may thus constitute the tree of derivation of a discourse. (p. 147)

A newly established discourse—such as TV and children in the 1950s—can be seen to extend Foucault's metaphor, to have an unelaborated branching system. After three decades, discursive branching had increased exponentially, yet retained its reiterative links to the "base" where the initial "statements that put into operation rules of formation" were located. Topics or "themes" of inquiry diversified in the 1970s, as did conceptions of the child viewer. Yet despite divergent, even contradictory evidence of effects, the TV-child relationship remained rooted in the very construct of effects. Even when, toward the middle and end of the decade, the discourse veered toward attempts to transform the unilinear effects model into an interactive model, the focus remained on *immediate* effects on *individual* viewers. At the level of rules of formation, the procedural regularities which make possible discursive formations—methodological design, procedure, and instrumentation—were themselves a reflection of an individualist and utilitarian epistemology. Regardless, then, of what research questions were pursued, the "discursive regularity" of U.S. social science compelled the imposition of methodological procedures and concepts which contained within them the firm conviction that the subject and the social were reducible to numerical measurements. This severely limited the constitution of the subject, the medium, and the relation between them.

6

The Discourse on Television and Children

This chapter comments on post-1980 developments in the discourse on TV and children. In keeping with the structure imposed on history in this book, the last chapter ended in 1979 and a further chapter would have begun in 1980. However, given textual and editorial constraints, a detailed reading of 1980s research was not possible. But since the 1980s are widely acknowledged to constitute a "natural" break in the history of mass communication theory and research, I will discuss this work in light of what has been construed by the research community as a landmark event in the history of mass communication studies: the self-professed "ferment" and shift in 1983 to a new "critical paradigm," said to be indicative of "the emergence of a vital new discipline" (Gerbner, 1983:4). This move, like many such reappraisals in the social sciences, has entailed a selective reconstruction of the past, a rereading by contemporary authorities of the history of their discourse. Following a reappraisal of that reconstruction, this chapter concludes with a discussion of larger theoretical implications and methodological problems of "doing" an archeology of knowledge.

THE MAKING OF THE MEDIA-LITERATE CHILD

Foucault (1981:8) maintains that a given discourse is manifest in and deploys statements along two axes: the textual production of truths commonly undertaken in institutional sites of knowledge production, and the practices and procedures emanating from and justified by such discursive truths. The discourse on TV and children during the 1950s, 1960s, and most of the 1970s had constructed a set of scientifically validated truths about the child viewer as a behavioral response mechanism, as passive and devoid of cognitive abilities. The possibility that viewers bring anything other than demographic variables to the screen was conceptually excluded. Such a unilinear model of learning and one-dimensional concept of the child excluded the possibility of proposing that children could be taught specific comprehension skills, which they could apply to reading the TV text. This explains the absence during those decades of a domain of practice (i.e., school-based media literacy programs) which constitutes the procedural, practical axis of any discourse. However, by reconstructing the subject as an active, cognitive agent whose actions in the social environment are seen as contingent upon the interactions between self and other, the discourse cleared a space for institutionalized practices of intervention. The teaching of literate viewing skills was assumed to provide children with critical competencies to mediate between self and other.

Once cognitive processes and constructs were posited as critical in the learning process, and once the TV text was reconceptualized from a mere behavioral stimulus to an information text with a structural grammar similar to print text, then, in theory at least, the conceptual possibility that children could be taught "literate" TV comprehension skills emerged. If, as with learning to comprehend print, children's abilities to decode and understand print information are seen to depend on acquiring specific cognitive skills and "relevant" background knowledge with which to make sense of, say, a story, then similar principles might be operant in "reading" TV. And, indeed, by the early 1980s, "critical viewing skills," "media literacy," "literate viewing," "the active viewer," and "interactive viewing" had become catchwords in a new educational rhetoric founded on the reconceptualization of the televiewing subject. As Aimee Dorr (1986:137) has pointed out, this new approach assumed that children could moderate TV's influence in their lives. This assumption, in turn, was based on the presupposition that "television is a medium that requires literacy instruction just as the medium of print does." The surge during the 1980s of school-based, regional, and statewide media literacy curricula and the correlative establishment of media-studies curriculum and resource centers can be read as a direct "knowledge effect" traceable to the discursive (re)construction of the child viewer as a cognitively active subject.

Educational discourse had long been at the margins of scientific inquiry into and academic debate on children and TV. Yet during the 1980s schooling became the institutional and discursive site for the teaching of media literate practices. The discourse of pedagogy and schooling practices, traditionally protective of its status as defender of print in an increasingly worrisome electronic information environment, never actively sought out and appropriated popular TV and children as a domain of academic inquiry or pedagogical practice. Instead, and rather ironically, the very model of the Piagetian print-learning child that permeated educational thought and practices in the 1970s enabled the newly formulated TV-learning child to occupy a space in educational discourse which for so long had resisted the intrusion of noneducational TV into the classroom. And yet today, the opposition between educational (print) traditionalists and media literacy proponents wages on (cf. Dorr, 1986; Hodge & Tripp, 1986; Palmer, 1986; Manley-Casimir & Luke, 1987).

FERMENT IN THE FIELD OR SELECTIVE RECONSTRUCTION?

George Gerbner edited, indeed engineered, the textual signification of a discursive shift in communication studies from a liberal empiricist model to what was claimed as a more critical-theoretic orientation. A 1983 special edition of the *Journal of Communication*, "Ferment in the Field," was devoted entirely to a discussion of the "coming of age" of communication studies. For Gerbner, this symposium was to be seen as "a milestone along the course of growth and rapid development of communications as a discipline, its 'coming of age' as an active participant in and observer of communications technologies and institutions" (1983a:5).

Communications research during the 1970s "had begun to experience a series of paradigmatic tremors and readjustments that were to further enhance not only its general intellectual status, but also its specific value as a forum for television inquiry" (Rowland & Watkins, 1984:20–21). During the 1980s, the discourse was undergoing a wholesale reinvention of its history, disciplinary status, and theoretical orientation. A shift toward a more critical and self-reflective stance within the social sciences Rowland and Bruce Watkins (p. 21) attribute partially to the "ferment" generated by the "civil rights, antiwar, and consumer protests of the 1960s and 1970s" and, in part, to an emergent recognition within the social science academy of "the ways in which human agency, with all its variable individual and group factors of cognitive frames, knowledge, perceptive capacity, experience, and institutional constraints, significantly shapes the data, the instruments, the event, and therefore finally the observations and conclusions about social and behavioral phenomena."

Rowland's (1983) *The Politics of TV Violence*—an exposé of the 30-year "ritual dance" among scientists, politicians, and captains of industry who promoted and controlled the TV violence research in-dustry—is itself reflective of what the academy would call "critical" research. Rowland and Watkins (1984) and, that same year, 35 con-tributors to the *Journal of Communication*'s "Ferment" issue all to varying degrees admitted that "in the debates about culture, ideology, power, symbol, and meaning the particular scientism of American thought has often been an inhibiting factor" (p. 23), and all claimed that theoretical, methodological, and epistemological change was well underway. Yet what most failed to recognize is that there did not exist, in fact, a debate centered on culture, ideology, power, class, and so forth. Even Carey's cultural-studies approach remained embedded in the "cheery optimism of pragmatism" (1983:313) and did not venture beyond a progressivist critique of quantitative social science. American cultural studies, according to Carey, historically had taken a benign view of the role of mass media: "The decisive position in the debate was the liberal American response: the effect of mass com-munications [was] modest and on the whole beneficial, the quality of American culture was democratic and improving, American politics was non-ideological and consensual and . . . American power was benign and progressive" (p. 312). The future task for cultural studies, in Carey's view, is to consider those issues such as "power, dominance, subordination, and ideology" (p. 313) which British cul-tural studies (then signified by the Birmingham Centre for Contem-porary Cultural Studies) had long held as central. Carey suggests here that American communications research historically had been any-thing but critical, and had much to gain by considering those ques-tions deemed essential by European scholars.

Rowland and Watkins (1984) also acknowledge American resistance to and suppression of a European critical tradition which, in their estimation, "cost American intellectual thought dearly" (p. 23). How-ever, the discursive/textual flagging of a new era of critical research based on European influence combined with sudden U.S. enlighten-ment over the limitations of the positivist tradition contradicts what to this day stands as continued and ongoing resistance to any kind of critique associated with or derivative of, for instance, Frankfurtian critical social theory, French poststructuralism or structuralism, or the various strands of feminist or British cultural studies. There are, of course, noteworthy exceptions, varied attempts to retheorize mass media technologies, media texts, and subjects (e.g., Gitlin, 1986; Kaplan, 1987; Miller, 1988; Modleski, 1986; Real, 1989; Rowland & Watkins, 1984). But much of the more theoretically provocative work derives from disciplinary sites outside of communications studies per se. Theorists in, for instance, English and/or Literature departments have taken on the study of print and electronic popular culture as text, and the study of readers/viewers as positioned by and positioning themselves in multiple and fragmented relations to that text. Others, from feminist film and literary theorists to philosophers, attempt to reframe both modernist theory and modernist culture in what are considered by many still controversial "postmodernist" terms of debate/discourse. So, while TV and viewers, and the research models applied to explain them, are under critical theoretical scrutiny elsewhere, mass communications studies, including its cultural studies variant, continues to collect, triangulate, and quantify data on subjects, the social, and the cultural.

By the early 1980s, the American discourse of TV research, and particularly research on TV and children, had not veered toward attempts at critical structural or poststructural analyses of text, society, or culture, nor made attempts to theorize TV, audience, the subject, and the relation between them from a perspective even vaguely approximating what could pass as a critical orientation. Studies of TV and children, with few exceptions (e.g., Lull, 1980, 1982), have continued to be conducted primarily on paper (i.e., the measurement instrument) and in locations anywhere but the home context wherein children's leisure viewing occurs. And, questions of ideology, power, or culture continue to be absent from the research agenda and text. As Gitlin (1978:213) had noted, whether in American political, social, or communications science, questions of power historically have been "behavioralized" and individualized, reflecting "the tacit denial of patterns of structurally maintained power." Shrouded in apolitical euphemisms such as "TV as cultural storyteller" (cf. Gerbner, 1981), concerns central to European critical research remain buried. At best, they are only hesitantly articulated in the discursive modes of liberal social science.

The communications discourse relabeled its present and its past by claiming that the 1980s nonpositivist, critical orientation was based on a critical tradition dating back to Lasswell, Lazarsfeld and Stanton, Berelson, and others (e.g., Schramm, 1983). That the critical tradition Adorno sought to establish in the 1940s at Lazarsfeld's Bureau of Applied Statistics did not match the research interests or theoretical stance of utilitarian administrative research conducted at Columbia University is, in the 1980s "reworking" of history, quickly forgotten. The "initial abortive efforts of the Frankfurt School refugees" (Rowland & Watkins, 1984:17) at establishing a neo-Marxist critique of culture and communications did not constitute even a marginal discourse. Critical social theory, transposed to U.S. liberal discourse, was exscribed before it even reached the level of forming a discursive "node," from which even a marginalized "branching" could develop. Yet, even critics of the discourse like Rowland and Watkins invent in historical retrospect a tradition of a "cross-Atlantic" dialogue, which they claim influenced an already established critical vein in American social and cultural thought: "There is and has been considerable diversity of thought on the western side of the Atlantic that, while certainly open to and in dialogue with British and continental influences, is not simply the derivative creature of them" (p. 25). In other words, not only are claims made here of a long-established tradition of academic exchange and cross-fertilization of ideas, but in the spirit of remaking itself as part of a critical tradition, the discourse insists upon its own heritage as radically autonomous from and not derivative of European influence.

As I have noted in earlier chapters, the citation network rearticulated the same authorities, and thus reproduced itself without reference either to adjacent discourses, or to works authored outside of the United States. Raymond Williams (1974), for instance, made one guest appearance in the *Journal of Communication* in the 1970s. References to works by Barthes, Althusser, or Lévi-Strauss—well-cited during the 1970s by scholars of communications and culture who were not institutionally based in the United States—or the work produced since 1968 by the Birmingham Centre for Contemporary Cultural Studies are curiously absent from the historical record. Even Gerbner, the acknowledged dean of American critical research on culture and mass communications, did not cite those (e.g., Horkheimer and Adorno, 1972/1944) with whom he today claims intellectual allegiance.

Since its 1983 publication, the "Ferment" text has been discursively transformed into a benchmark text, a canonized historical marker according to which pre- and post-"Ferment" work is judged, historicized and located (cf. Hardt, 1986; Rowland & Watkins, 1984; Wartella, 1984; Whitney, 1985). This present text, too, writes the "Ferment" text as a discursive marker. The 35 solicited contributions for this issue, for the most part, were authored by senior, mostly American scholars (e.g., Schramm, Chaffee, Comstock, Tunstall, Smythe, Blumler, Halloran). Given the rather visible focus on children and TV in this journal during the 1970s and early 1980s, the omission of TV and children from this particular unit of discourse is a curious exclusion, particularly since many of the U.S. "social aspects" papers were authored by researchers who made what are generally considered substantial contributions to the TV and children discourse (e.g., Chaffee, Schramm, Comstock). All agreed, to varying degrees, that the behavioral paradigm was a thing of the past, in the process of replacement by a critical approach to communications. Yet how "critical" was defined by U.S. researchers differed substantially from definitions asserted by the European researchers in this volume. Chaffee, for instance, acknowledges that "historical, legal, critical, and other methods of inquiry are challenging the behavioral approach and some of us who used to think of ourselves as mainly concerned with individual behavior are now attempting to study structural factors and historical contexts of communication systems.... Two of the most prominent behaviorists, ... Wartella and Reeves, are undertaking a serious revisionist history of their specialty, the study of media and youth" (Rogers & Chaffee, 1983:22–23).

For Comstock (1983:47), the goal of any critical research must be to inform policy decisions. For Schramm (1983:14), linear explanations "now seem rather old-fashioned." Gerbner (1983b), too, speaks of a "newly emergent line of materialist analysis" (p. 357). Surprisingly, he breaks the very convention, the prohibition which he as long-time editor of the journal had established: the decade-long silent exclusion of any scholarly discussion bearing the mark of historical or cultural materialist theory. Here, however, Gerbner emerges as an advocate of such studies, claiming that the "study of the production, nature and role of messages in social life becomes an integral part of the study of the material 'base.'... If Marx were alive today, his principal work would be entitled *Communications* rather than *Capital*" (p. 358).

Within a material unit of discourse, or within the broader epistemological "oeuvre" of the social science or mass communication discourse, there are spaces for oppositional subdiscourses, or "*spaces of dissension*" (Foucault, 1972:152). The "Ferment" issue included such dissenting viewpoints. Stuart Ewen (1983) and Ithiel de Sola Pool (1983), two U.S. cultural studies scholars discursively linked with the Chicago pragmatist tradition commonly associated with Carey (cf. Whitney, 1985:143), claimed that self-professions of intellectual ferment and a shift in theoretical and methodological focus toward a critical approach is nothing more than the dressing up with new "in-words" of an old and very active paradigm. De Sola Pool's (1983:260) comments are worth citing at length:

> Some of the same people who write tirades about "the old paradigms" or about "positivism" do nothing different in their own work.... But the scores of methodological and ideological essays about the new approaches to the study of communications can hardly be honored by the term "ferment." There is a simple recipe for these essays: avoid measurement, add moral commitment, and throw in some of the following words: social system, capitalism, dependency, positivism, idealism, ideology, ... hegemony, contradition, problematic.... Nothing is particularly new in these critiques of empirical research, though the dictionary of in-words changes with each generation.

Ewen (1983:221), similarly, points to the continuing dominance of the logical-positivist paradigm in the instrumental service of government and industry: "Theoretical issues are unchanged and unchallenged within the U.S. academic mainstream. Out-of-context correlations between media forms and messages . . . and audience response . . . continue to dominate. Behind this faith lies the profession's instrumental roots—the service of business, government, and other institutions interested in 'reaching a public.'" Methodologically, the continued stress on empirically quantifiable units of analysis rules out the very possibility for speculative critical analysis: "When social experience is translated into data that do not perform efficiently, those data must be 'massaged' so that they will work. The approach, the years of training, after all, must not be questioned" (p. 221). Yet, more practical considerations that delimit research reside with institutional funding sources: "Policy-making institutions and foundations interested in influencing policy making are most likely to fund the more 'feasible' research questions" (Haight, 1983:232). Sender, message, receiver, and effects are simple to isolate methodologically and to recombine into statistically constructed relationships. Such data provide ready-to-use ammunition for defensible policy-related arguments. By contrast, research that theorizes the influence of media's symbolic systems as inseparable from, for example, larger political, economic, and cultural processes does not provide the kinds of data or answers that policy administrators can readily translate into government documents, industry guidelines, or better ads.

While at the textual level contributors to "Ferment" seem to have recognized the need for and, indeed, assumed an apparent reorientation toward critical research, the practical reality of alignments of the research process with economic and political interests remained, then and now. As William H. Melody and Robin E. Mansell (1983:103) put it, "There is no safe harbor in which researchers can avoid the power structure." And so despite the collective turn to a relabeled enterprise, "the tightly controlled laboratory study that so dominated early research efforts is still much in evidence" (Miller, 1983:39).

The authors in "Ferment" who heralded the dawn of a new critical paradigm outnumbered the skeptics. Yet several papers were included by scholars with a stated commitment to a historical materialist perspective (e.g., Smythe, Ewen, Rosengren, Szescko, Schiller). These voices of dissent are not signifiers of an actual paradigmatic philosophical shift, but must be seen as statements which, according to Foucault (1972:155), potentially may "induce a *reorganization* of the discursive field." Such apparent incompatible, oppositional, or dissenting statements (i.e., oppositional to an alleged pre-"Ferment" positivism) serve, in the case of the "Ferment" text, to legitimate and formalize a new discursive identity. Foucault explains that "other oppositions play a *critical* role: they put into operation the existence of the 'acceptability' of the discursive practice; they define the point of its effective impossibility and of its historical reflexion [sic]" (p. 155). Among these "multiple dissensions," some oppositions serve the critical role of self-legitimation and historical reflection—the kind of metacommentary the "Ferment" text precisely embodies.

There is ferment in the academy, but for now only at the level of a rehistoricization and a discursive reframing of aims and terms of reference. Contemporary communications discourse is reinventing itself as a formalized and self-contained discourse: no longer a field, but a discipline. It acknowledges the influence of European critical scholarship despite the verifiable lack of such influence. This reinvention persists despite the continuing proliferation of empirical, administrative research wherein the subject remains individuated, psychologized, and locked within a traditional effects equation. What counts as critical communications research is, as de Sola Pool (1983:260) noted, but a discursive self-transformation: what "used to be called a conservative critique of empiricism [but] is now often called a radical critique of empiricism."

Claims of a radical departure from the old empirical model have spread across the discourse. More recently, sociology is restaking its claim in the revival of interest in mass communications research, acknowledging the need for more contextual, socially and culturally sensitive research (e.g., Ball-Rokeach & Cantor, 1986). Where mainstream communications studies attest to a continual recycling of research problems and methods, sociology is announcing the end of a "famine in American mass communications research" (p. 10). Unable to "meet the social demands for immediate research on the suspected 'evil' effects of television" (Wright, 1986:31) in contrast to experimental psychology's plethora of answers during the 1960s and 1970s, a "new generation" of sociology scholars and students is now ready to take on the "social contexts and social nature of communication, including mass communication" (pp. 30–31). In the opening paper of *Media, Audience and Social Structure*, Wright (1986) proposes that this revival of interest should be directed toward the "instructive" application of "concepts such as reference groups, lines of authority and responsibility, occupational statuses and roles, status sets and role sets . . . to the study of mass media organizations" (p. 32). In other words: Wright advocates the recycling of functionalist models. Only one author in Sandra J. Ball-Rokeach and Muriel G. Cantor's volume makes an understated appeal to critical research by proposing a non-theoretically grounded feminist reading of film (Press, 1986). The rest of the volume is a reaffirmation of the enduring strength of empirical functionalist sociology, albeit in its allegedly "new wave" critical variant.

Hanno Hardt (1986) has pointed out U.S. isolation from the current critical discourse, which continues despite the Americanization by post-"Ferment" scholarship of the terminology of feminist or critical theory, structuralism, or poststructuralism: "There is no evidence that an Americanization of these ideas, . . . an adaptation of their practical consequences (research strategies), will also include an appropriation of their ideological (cultural, economic, political) foundations. It remains to be seen whether this field will move beyond its acquired designation as a methodological specialization" (p. 145).

The atheoreticism and ahistoricism of American logical positivism does not at present include the kind of critical analysis undertaken here: a deconstructive analysis of intellectual history as a history of discourse. This partially accounts for the paucity of historical research on children and media undertaken to date (e.g., Hearold, 1986; Wartella & Reeves, 1985). S. Hearold's metaanalysis is no more than a statistical reconfirmation of 230 effects studies. Wartella and Reeves' history, not yet published in its entirety, is a revisionist history which also seems unable to read beyond the historical text as a series of empirical benchmarks and developments. Hearold, Wartella and Reeves, and others (cf. Liebert & Sprafkin, 1988) who carry the contemporary TV-child debate fail to recognize the discursive character of the historical production of knowledge about TV and children.

Rowland and Watkins' (1984:26) comments on communications research aptly apply to current research on TV and children: "Many studies currently published in mainsteam communication journals seem filled with sophisticated treatments of trivial data, which, while showing effects significant at $p < .05$, make slight contributions to what we really know about human mass-mediated communication." Nonetheless, researchers are still grappling with attempts to make the uses and gratifications more effective and to make the linear effects model more socially contextual (cf. Kubey, 1986). Some have resorted to replication studies such as of the cognitive effects of TV versus radio (Greenfield & Beagles-Roos, 1988)—a sign of an exhausted framework. Others merely have added variables to either side of the effects equation. Creativity, imagination, cognitive developmental levels, and TV knowledge scores have been added to the child (e.g., Buerkel-Rothfuss, Greenberg, Atkin, & Neuendorf, 1982; Cantor & Sparks, 1984; Salomon, 1984; Singer, Singer & Rapaczynski, 1984; Zuckerman, Singer & Singer, 1980). And definitions of TV content have been expanded to include the medium's formal features (e.g., Huston et al., 1981, 1984) and symbolic reality structure (Gerbner & Gross, 1980).

The noticeable decrease since the mid-1980s of published studies on TV and children partially attests to the possibility that the effects model, despite its reinvention as an interactive model, has run its course. After nearly four decades of research on TV and children, researchers still call upon each other "to make a concerted effort to understand behavior as it occurs in the ordinary environment and in the context of natural purposeful activity" (Neisser [1976] in Kubey, 1986:109). Classification and description of individual purposive behavior remain the means and ends of the research enterprise. Researchers (e.g., Lemish, 1982; Lull, 1980, 1982; Rubin, 1983, 1984) still lament the impossibility of observing viewers and viewing in a naturalistic environment. While U.S. researchers continue their woeful, obligatory lament over the limitations of empirical research, and yet simultaneously press on with producing statistically significant effects at "$p < .05$" or better, research elsewhere is delineating the social and cultural, political-ideological, and cognitive/linguistic/semiotic relationships between children and TV from a range of nonbehavioral, critical theoretic vantage points (e.g., Hodge & Tripp, 1986; Palmer, 1986; Morley, 1980, 1986). But, as Hardt (1986) observed, even if U.S. research were to attempt qualitative research and to incorporate the terminology of what historically has been and continues to be associated with "social and ideological 'bad company'" (Gerbner, 1983b:359), that in itself is no guarantee that fundamental epistemological assumptions would be reconfigured below a resurfaced veneer of discourse.

POSTSTRUCTURALIST DISCOURSE ANALYSIS: REIFICATION OR CRITIQUE?

From an archeological perspective, knowledge is not natural, nor does it disclose truths about a natural order of things in the world. Instead, knowledge is seen as a product of discursive practices. Such practices reside in and are legitimated by discourses which have been nominated and valorized by a culture as authoritative true knowledges. Sites of truth production are institutionally organized around procedural rules of formation, which authorize authorities of delimitation—"fellowships of discourse" (Foucault, 1972:225)—and which invest them with de jure powers to produce authoritative knowledge. An archeology of discourse "shows how rules of formation of discourses are linked to the operation of a particular kind of social power" (Gordon, 1980:245). Discourse invests those qualified to speak with the power to "construct programmes for the formation of a social reality," and thus with the power to prescribe and enforce social practices that establish specific relations among elements and human subjects (Gordon, p. 245). Authorized speakers within formalized discourses are thus themselves implicated in and subject(ed) to particular versions or formations of social reality and social practices which they are instrumental in producing.

Although a fully formed theorization of power implicated in knowledge was absent in Foucault's *Archaeology of Knowledge* (1972), the institutional sociopolitical strategies underlying and sanctioning the production of knowledge are vested in what Foucault insists must be central questions in archeological analyses: "First question: who is speaking? . . . Who is qualified to do so? Who derives from it his [sic] own special quality, his prestige, and from whom, in return, does he receive if not the assurance, at least the presumption that what he says is true?" (p. 50). Second, the archeologist must "describe the institutional *sites*" from which authorities of delimitation are empowered to speak, to which "should be added the positions that the subject can occupy in the information networks . . . ; in the system of oral communication or of written document . . . [and] the circulation of information" (pp. 52–53). Underlying this productive network are epistemological and procedural regularities which both make and are remade by discursive practices. And, once discursive practices are exposed as having vested interests, institutional locations, and a politics of authorship (not to be confused here with an essentialism of authorial identity or intent), then the question of power implicated in the politics of truth production becomes apparent. For Foucault, statements are "assets" because statements in discourse "have value . . . which one tries to appropriate," which are "transmitted and preserved . . . repeated, reproduced, and transformed; to which pre-established networks are adapted, and to which a status is given in the institution" (p. 120). Access to the "economy of discourse" within which truths (valuable assets) are produced necessarily "poses the question of power; an asset that is, by nature, the object of a struggle, a political struggle" (p. 120). "Discourse," Collin Gordon (1980:245) comments, "is a political commodity."

This archeological history of the discourse on TV and children has tried to outline the politics of knowledge production as it is invested in and "preserved by virtue of a number of supports and material techniques (of which the book is, of course, only one example), in accordance with certain types of institutions . . . and with certain statutory modalities, . . . techniques that put them into operation, in practices that derive from them, in the social relations that they form, or, through those relations, modify" (Foucault, 1972:123–124). Accordingly, I have here illustrated how certain methodological rules were established as dominant and as "science" which, in turn, delimited specific procedures for the production of statements about children. We have seen how statements are deployed according to institutional procedural rules (of publication) that formalize statements and launch them into circulation on the material surface of authoritative texts (journals and books), themselves authorized by discourse as authoritative.

Foucault maintained that the "science of the individual" is a discursively produced epistemology: as an epistemological construct, the science of the individual is reified and operationalized in discourse. And discursive constructs of the human subject both confirm and (re)produce the epistemological field which, in turn, sets the conditions of possibility within which knowledges can be produced and articulated. Yet within an epistemological field, discourses and sub-discourses are dynamic configurations with several levels of "events" that, nonetheless, remain "always in the element of a single positivity" (Foucault, 1972:171).

Thus, at "the level of the appearance of objects, types of enunciation, concepts, strategic choices (or transformations that affect those that already exist)" (p. 171), the following "events" were noted. The appearance of the televiewing child was articulated through various combined definitions of the child (educational, sociological, psychological) in tandem with definitions of the TV-child relationship (active, passive, unilinear, interactive). At "the level of the derivation of new rules of formation on the basis of rules that are already in operation" (p. 171), the relatively short period of 30 years under scrutiny here evidenced a reformation of rules for the production of knowledge about children and TV. From simple percentage enumeration or verbal accounts of program preferences and amount watched matched with IQ scores, SES, sex, age, and school grades, such numerical groupings and classifications became more minutely quantified and categorized, both at the level of the practice of knowledge extraction (statistical analyses of data produced in laboratory experiments) and at the level of reproducing that knowledge into the technicist conceptual and textual framework of the scientific article. And, despite the later emergence of a cognitive concept of the child, and despite more recent claims of a shift from positivist to critical research, such discursively constructed "events" remain embedded within "the element of a single positivity." Cousins and Hussain (1984:256) aptly comment: "As it were, behaviourism only expels the subject through the front door in order to let it slip back in through the back door."

Three decades in the history of a social science discourse is but a brief historical instance. And the observations possible in this study, like those Foucault mapped for the emergence and transformations of the human subject in the human sciences over a three-century period, admittedly were limited. What I have been able to show, however, is that an archeology of discourse can uncover those strategies taken as politically neutral and scientifically objective that systematically produce knowledges and actively construct the human subject. Discourses, moreover, not only construct the products of their labor but (re)construct themselves through the strategic deployment of justificatory truths about the scientificity and legitimacy of their respective regimes of truth production. Accordingly, I have argued that claims of "ferment" heralding a new critical "paradigm," or the presentation of objective data specifying a cognitive, active viewer, are discursive strategies—officially recognized statements made by qualified speakers—that enable and justify the continuation of self-accredited discursive practices of truth production.

Yet, within the logic of discourse that an archeology claims to expose and subvert, how does a discourse on discourse distinguish itself as anything other than a criticism of positivism? How can archeology as critique claim to be any more representative of the "Real" than the "Imaginary" discourse of positivism that it exposes and opposes? How does any critique of discourse escape the discursive nature of its own enterprise? In other words, critiques of positivism, of scientific humanism, abound within the empirical social sciences as part of what seems to be a current discursive strategy of self-criticism, redefinition and rejustification. This text, too, deployed from within and according to the ritualized rules of institutional discourse production, circulates within the very domain that it critiques, and one that institutionalizes its self-critique. As such, what this text has accomplished is, at one level, another rewriting, another textual unification and formalization of the very discourse it has sought to deconstruct. The rules of discourse forced this text into the same delimiting procedural rules that it sought to undermine: chapter headings and textual units forced periodization; referencing forced recirculation of authorial authority; theory (Foucauldian poststructuralism) forced a position from which to critique the other which, in turn, forced the debate into an unfortunate binarist confrontation.

Finally, and most disconcerting, method (i.e., archeology) forced a genealogical search for the marginal, the previously excluded and "not said," the hidden ruptures, agendas, and voices. Yet working with the formalized texts of history, all that was "not said" is by definition unavailable to the archeologist. Hence, the politics historically operant in the university laboratory, the academic department, the publisher's office, or among professors and graduate research students, industry executives, and government agents are irretrievable. The inaccessibility of the social relations and political agendas among Foucault's authorities of delimitation—those who make and remake and are contained by discourse—rendered my work here as only a partial account of the rules of formation that structure and produce knowledges. Given that this text too was produced within the politics and formal rule structure of an institutional and disciplinary site of knowledge production, what I thought started out as a text and history with a difference ended up in many ways a colonized text, and I a colonized author-authority. Karlis Racevskis (1983:140) poses this dilemma, citing Foucault: "Under the conditions that prevail in a university, in a technocratic society, a Foucauldian critical enterprise appears doomed from the start because, as Foucault himself realizes, 'after all, is it not perhaps the case that these fragments of genealogies are no sooner brought to light, that the particular elements of the knowledge that one seeks to disinter are no sooner accredited and put into circulation, than they run the risk of re-codification, re-colonization'?"

The recodification and colonization of Foucault's power/knowledge doublet is already accomplished. That subjects are constructed in and by discourse is, among many feminist, postmodernist and poststructuralist social theorists, no longer a novel revelation. Institutionalized left and liberal-left theorists are already sketching the theoretical terms of reference for future emancipatory social action and social theory on the basis of an understanding that, once freed from the "terror of reason," of scientific rationality, critical discursive practice will liberate the human subject from the historical encumberments of a discursively imposed technocratic rationality. Located, as this study is, in the historical presence of a form of critique only now reaching a marginal level of epistemologization, it remains speculative as to what extent archeological critiques can generate transformative powers—whether in social (public) practice or discursive (academic) practice—or to what extent exposing the allegedly Real practices underlying Imaginary knowledge constructs becomes co-opted and colonized as part of a discursive strategy of self-criticism, reformation, and self-legitimation. It may be, as Foucault (1972:235) had noted, that in our attempts "to flee Hegel," "whether through Marx or through Nietzsche," we should recognize that "our anti-Hegelianism is possibly one of his tricks directed against us, at the end of which he stands, motionless, waiting for us."

References

Abel, J. D. (1968–1969). Television and children: A selective bibliography of use and effects. *Journal of Broadcasting, 13,* 101–105.

———.(1976). The family and child television viewing. *Journal of Marriage and the Family, 38*(2), 331–335.

Abel, J. D., & Beninson, M. E. (1976). Perceptions of TV program violence by children and mothers. *Journal of Broadcasting, 20*(3), 355–363.

Adorno, T. W. (1954). How to look at television. *Quarterly of Film, Radio and Television, 8,* 213–235.

Agee, W., Ault, P., & Emery, E. (1985). *Introduction to mass communication.* New York: Harper and Row.

Albert, R. S. (1957). The role of mass media and the effect of aggressive film content upon children's aggressive responses and identification choices. *Genetic Psychology Monographs, 55,* 221–285.

Albert, R. S., & Meline, G. (1958). The influence of social status on the uses of television. *Public Opinion Quarterly, 22,* 145–151.

Altbach, P. G. (1987). *The knowledge context: Comparative perspectives on the distribution of knowledge.* Albany, NY: State University of New York Press.

Anderson, R. C., Spiro, R. J., & Montague, W. E. (Eds.). (1977). *Schooling and the acquisition of knowledge.* Hillsdale, NJ: Lawrence Erlbaum.

Andison, F. S. (1977). TV violence and viewer aggression: A cumulation of study results 1956–1976. *Public Opinion Quarterly, 41,* 314–331.

Appell, C. T. (1960). Television's impact upon middle class family life. *Teachers College Record, 61,* 265–274.

Aries, P. (1962). *Centuries of Childhood: A Social History of the Family* (R. Baldick, Trans.). New York: Alfred Knopf.

Atkin, C., & Heald, G. (1977). The content of children's toy and food commercials. *Journal of Communication, 27*(1), 107–114.

Atkins, P. A., & Elwood, H. (1978). TV news is first choice in survey of high schools. *Journalism Quarterly, 55*(4), 596–599.

Atwood, L. E. (1968). Perception of television program preferences among teenagers and their parents. *Journal of Broadcasting, 12,* 377–388.

Baer, D. M. (1962). Laboratory control of thumbsucking by withdrawal and representation of reinforcement. *Journal of the Experimental Analysis of Behavior, 5,* 525–528.

Ball, S. (1976). Methodological problems in assessing the impact of television programs. *Journal of Social Issues, 32*(4), 8–17.

Ball, S., & Bogatz, G. A. (1970). *The first year of Sesame Street: An evaluation.* Princeton, NJ: Educational Testing Service.

Ball-Rokeach, S. J., & Cantor, M. G. (Eds.). (1986). *Media, audience, and social structure.* Beverly Hills, CA: Sage.

Balogh, J. (1959). Television viewing habits of high school boys. *Educational Research Bulletin, 38,* 66–71.

Bandura, A. (1975). *Psychological modeling: Conflicts and issues.* Chicago: Aldine Press.

———. (1978). Social learning theory of aggression. *Journal of Communication, 28*(3), 12–29.

Bandura, A., Ross, D., & Ross, S. (1961). Transmission of aggression through imitation of aggressive models. *Journal of Abnormal and Social Psychology, 63*(3), 575–582.

———. (1963). Imitation of film-mediated aggressive models. *Journal of Abnormal and Social Psychology, 66*(1), 3–11.

Bandura, A., & Walters, R. H. (1963). *Social learning and personality development.* New York: Holt, Rinehart & Winston.

Banning, E. (1955). Social influences on children and youth. *Review of Educational Research, 25*(1), 36–47.

Baran, S. J., Chase, L. J., & Courtright, J. A. (1979). Television drama as a facilitator of prosocial behavior: "The Waltons." *Journal of Broadcasting, 23*(3), 277–284.

Barcus, F. E. (1969). Parental influence on children's television viewing. *Television Quarterly, 8,* 63–73.

Barrett, D. (1986). *Media sociology.* London: Tavistock.

Barry, T. E., & Hansen, R. W. (1973). How race affects children's TV commercials. *Journal of Advertising Research, 13,* 63–67.

Baxter, W. (1960–1961). The mass media and young people. *Journal of Broadcasting, 5,* 49–58.

Baylin, L. (1959). Mass media and children: A study of exposure habits and cognitive effects. *Psychological Monographs: General and Applied, 73*(1), 1–48.

———. (1962). Approaches to the study of TV. *Journal of Social Issues, 18*(2), 1–5.

Berelson, B. (1949). What 'missing the newspaper' means. In P. F. Lazarsfeld & F. N. Stanton (Eds.), *Communications Research, 1948–1949* (pp. 111–129). New York: Harper & Brothers.

———. (1960). Communications and public opinion. In W. Schramm (Ed.). *Mass Communications* (pp. 527–543). Urbana: University of Illinois Press.

Berkowitz, L. (1964). Aggressive cues in aggressive behavior and hostility catharsis. *Psychological Review, 71,* 104–122.

———. (1965). Some aspects of observed aggression. *Journal of Personality and Social Psychology, 2*, 359–369.

Berkowitz, L., & Geen, R. (1966). Film violence and the cue properties of available targets. *Journal of Personality and Social Psychology, 3*(5), 525–530.

———. (1967). Stimulus qualities of the target of aggression: A further study. *Journal of Personality and Social Psychology, 5*(3), 364–368.

Beuf, A. (1974). Doctor, lawyer, household drudge. *Journal of Communication, 24*(2), 142–145.

Beuick, M. D. (1927). The limited social effect of radio broadcasting. *American Journal of Sociology, 32*, 615–622.

Blumenfeld, W. S., & Remmers, H. H. (1966). Television program preferences and their relationship to self-reported high school grades. *The Journal of Educational Research, 59*(8), 358–359.

Blumer, H. (1933). *Movies and conduct.* New York: Macmillan.

Blumer, H., & Hauser, P. M. (1933). *Movies, delinquency, and crime.* New York: Macmillan.

Blumler, J. G. (1979). The role of theory in uses and gratification studies. *Communication Research, 6*(1), 9–36.

Blumler, J. G., & Katz, E. (Eds.). (1974). *The uses of mass communication.* London: Faber.

Bogart, L. (1962). American television: A brief survey of findings. *Journal of Social Issues, 18*(2), 36–42.

———. (1972 [1958]). *The age of television* (3rd ed.). New York: Frederick Ungar Publishing.

Bogatz, G. A. & Ball, S. (1971). *The second year of Sesame Street: A continuing evaluation* (Vols. 1 & 2). Princeton, NJ: Educational Testing Service.

Bourdieu, P. (1973). Cultural reproduction and social reproduction. In R. Brown (Ed.). *Knowledge, education, and cultural change* (pp. 71–99). London: Tavistock.

Bowers, C. A. (1980). Ideological continuities in technicism, liberalism, and education. *Teachers College Record, 80*, 293–321.

Brumbraugh, F. (1954). What effect does TV advertising have on children? *Education Digest, 19*, 32–33.

Buerkel-Rothfuss, N. L., Greenberg, B. S., Atkin, C. K., & Neuendorf, K. (1982). Learning about the family from television. *Journal of Communication, 32*(3), 191–201.

Burr, P., & Burr, R. M. (1977). Product recognition and premium appeal. *Journal of Communication, 27*(1), 115–117.

Burton, S. G., Calonico, J. M., & McSeveney, D. R. (1979). Effects of preschool television watching on first-grade children. *Journal of Communication, 29*(3), 164–170.

Busby, L. (1974). Defining the sex-role standard in network children's programs. *Journalism Quarterly, 51*(4), 690–696.

———. (1975). Sex-role research on the mass media. *Journal of Communication, 25*(4), 107–131.

Byrne, G. C. (1969). Mass media and political socialization of children and pre-adults. *Journalism Quarterly, 46*(1), 140–142.

Cantor, J., & Sparks, G. G. (1984). Children's fear responses to mass media: Testing some Piagetian predictions. *Journal of Communication, 34*(2), 90–103.

Carey, J. W. (1966). Variation in Negro-White television preferences. *Journal of Broadcasting, 10,* 199–211.

———. (1977). Mass communication research and cultural studies. In J. Curran, M. Gurevitch & J. Woolacott (Eds.), *Mass communication and society* (pp. 315–348). London: Edward Arnold.

———. (1983). The origins of the radical discourse on cultural studies in the United States. *Journal of Communication, 33*(3), 311–313.

Carey, J. W., & Kreiling, A. L. (1974). Popular culture and uses and gratifications: Notes toward an accommodation. In J. Blumler and E. Katz (Eds.), *The uses of mass communications: Current perspectives on gratifications research* (pp. 225–248). Sage Annual Reviews of Communication Research (Vol. 3). Beverly Hills, CA: Sage.

Carpenter, C. (1955). Psychological research using television. *American Psychologist, 10,* 606–610.

Carter, R., & Greenberg, B. S. (1965). Newspapers or television? Which do you believe? *Journalism Quarterly, 42,* 29–34.

Chaffee, S. H., McLeod, J. M., & Atkin, C. K. (1971). Parental influences on adolescent media use. *American Behavioral Scientist, 14,* 323–340.

Chaffee, S. H., & Tims, A. R. (1976). Interpersonal factors in adolescent television use. *Journal of Social Issues, 32*(4), 98–113.

Chaffee, S. H., Ward, L. S., & Tipton, L. P. (1970). Mass communication and political socialization. *Journalism Quarterly, 47,* 647–666.

Charters, W. W. (1933). *Motion pictures and youth: A summary.* New York: Macmillan.

Christiansen, J. B. (1979). Television role models and adolescent occupational goals. *Human Communication Research, 5*(4), 335–337.

Clark, W. R. (1939). Radio listening activities of children. *Journal of Experimental Education, 8,* 44–48.

Clifford, K. (1948). Common sense about comics. *Parents Magazine.* n.p.

Coates, B., & Pusser, H. E. (1975). Positive reinforcement and punishment in "Sesame Street" and "Mister Rogers." *Journal of Broadcasting, 19,* 143–151.

Coffin, T. E. (1948). Television's effects on leisuretime activities. *Journal of Applied Psychology, 32*(4), 550–558.

———. (1955). Television's impact on society. *American Psychologist, 10,* 630–641.

Cohen, A., & Salomon, G. (1979). Children's literate television viewing: Surprises and possible explanations. *Journal of Communication, 29*(3), 156–163.

Collins, W. A. (1970). Learning of media content: A developmental study. *Child Development, 40,* 1133–1142.

———. (1975) The developing child as viewer. *Journal of Communication, 25*(4), 35–44.

Collins, W. A., Berndt, T., & Hess, V. (1974). Observational learning of motives and consequences for television aggression: A developmental study. *Child Development, 45,* 799–802.

Collins, W. A., Wellman, H., Keniston, A. H., & Westby, S. (1978). Age-related aspects of comprehension and inference from a televised dramatic narrative. *Child Development, 49,* 389–399.

Comstock, G. (1975). The evidence so far. *Journal of Communication, 25*(4), 25–34.

———. (1976). The role of social and behavioral science in policymaking for television. *Journal of Social Issues, 32*(4), 157–178.

———. (1977). Types of portrayal and aggressive behavior. *Journal of Communication, 24*(3), 189–198.

———. (1978). The impact of television on American institutions. *Journal of Communication, 28*(2), 12–28.

———. (1980). *Television in America.* Beverly Hills, CA: Sage.

———. (1983). The legacy of the past. *Journal of Communication, 33*(3), 42–50.

Comstock, G., & Cobbey, R. E. (1979). Television and the children of ethnic minorities. *Journal of Communication, 29*(1), 104–115.

Conway, M. M., Stevens, A. J., & Smith, R. G. (1975). The relation between media use and children's civic awareness. *Journalism Quarterly, 52*(3), 531–538.

Cook, T. D., & Conner, R. F. (1976). The educational impact. *Journal of Communication, 26*(2), 155–164.

Courtney, A. E., & Whipple, T. E. (1974). Women in TV commercials. *Journal of Communication, 24*(2), 110–118.

Cousins, M., & Hussain, A. (1984). *Michel Foucault.* London: Macmillan.

Cressey, P. (1934). The motion picture as informal education. *The Journal of Educational Sociology, 7,* 504–515.

———. (1938). The motion picture experience as modified by social background and personality. *American Sociological Review, 3*(4), 516–525.

Cressey, P., & Thrasher, F. M. (1933). *Boys, movies, and city streets.* New York: Macmillan.

Dale, E. (1933a). *The content of motion pictures.* New York: Macmillan.

———. (1933b). *How to appreciate motion pictures.* New York: Macmillan.

———. (1933c). *Children's attendance at motion pictures.* New York: Macmillan.

D'Amico, R. (1982). What is discourse? *Humanities in Society, 5*(3 & 4), 201–212.

Darby, C. L., & Riopelle, A. J. (1959). Observational learning in the rhesus monkey. *Journal of Comparative Physiology and Psychology, 52,* 94–98.

DeBoer, J. J. (1937). The determination of children's interests in radio drama. *Journal of Applied Psychology, 21,* 456–463.

———. (1939a). Radio and children's emotions. *School and Society, 50*(1290), 369–373.

———. (1939b). Radio: The pied piper of education. *Childhood Education, 16,* 74–79.

DeFleur, M. L. (1964). Occupational roles as portrayed on television. *Public Opinion Quarterly, 28,* 57–74.

DeFleur, M. L., & Ball-Rokeach, S. (1982). *Theories of mass communication* (2nd ed.). New York: David McKay.

DeFleur, M. L., & DeFleur, L. (1967). The relative contribution of television as a learning source of children's occupational knowledge. *American Sociological Review, 32,* 777–789.

Desmond, R. J. (1978). Cognitive development and television comprehension. *Communication Research, 5*(2), 202–220.

de Sola Pool, I. (1983). What ferment? A challenge for empirical research. *Journal of Communication, 33*(3), 258–261.

DeVito, J. A. (1985). *Human communication* (3rd ed.). New York: Harper & Row.

Diaz-Guerrero, R., Reyes-Lagunes, I., Witzke, D. B., & Holtzman, W. H. (1976). Plaza Sesamo in Mexico: An evaluation. *Journal of Communication, 26*(2), 145–149.

Dienstbier, R. A. (1977). Sex and violence: Can research have it both ways? *Journal of Communication, 27*(3), 176–188.

Dimmick, J. (1976). Family communication and TV program choice. *Journalism Quarterly, 53*(4), 720–723.

Dohrman, R. (1975). A gender profile of children's educational TV. *Journal of Communication, 25*(4), 56–65.

Dominick, J. R. (1972). Television and political socialization. *Educational Broadcasting Review, 6,* 48–56.

———. (1973). Crime and law enforcement on prime-time television. *Public Opinion Quarterly, 37,* 241–250.

———. (1974). Children's viewing of crime shows and attitudes towards law enforcement. *Journalism Quarterly, 51,* 5–12.

Dominick, J. R., & Rauch, G. E. (1972). The image of women in network TV commercials. *Journal of Broadcasting, 16*(3), 259–265.

Dominick, J. R., Richman, S., & Wurtzel, A. (1979). Problem-solving on TV shows popular with children: Assertion vs. aggression. *Journalism Quarterly, 56,* 455–463.

Donald, J. (1985). Beacons of the future: Schooling, subjection and subjectification. In V. Beechey & J. Donald (Eds.), *Subjectivity and social relations* (pp. 214–249). London: Open University Press.

Donohue, T. R. (1975). Black children's perceptions of favorite TV characters as models of antisocial behaviors. *Journal of Broadcasting, 19*(2), 153–167.

Doob, A. N., & Macdonald, G. E. (1979). Television viewing and fear of victimization: Is the relationship causal? *Journal of Personality and Social Psychology, 37*(2), 170–179.

Dorr, A. (1986). *Television and children: A special medium for a special audience.* Beverly Hills, CA: Sage.

Downing, M. (1974). Heroine of the daytime serial. *Journal of Communication, 24*(2), 130–137.

Drabman, R., & Thomas, M. H. (1974). Does media violence increase children's toleration of real-life aggression? *Developmental Psychology, 10*(3), 418–421.

———. (1975). Does TV violence breed indifference? *Journal of Communication, 25*(4), 86–89.

———. (1976). Does watching violence on TV cause apathy? *Pediatrics, 57,* 329–333.

———. (1977). Children's imitation of aggressive and prosocial behavior when viewing alone and in pairs. *Journal of Communication, 14*(3), 199–205.

Dreyfus, H., & Rabinow, P. (1982). *Michel Foucault: Beyond structuralism and hermeneutics* (2nd ed.). Chicago: University of Chicago Press.

Dunham, F. (1952). Effect of television on school achievement of children. *School Life, 34,* 88–89, 91.

Dysinger, W. S., & Ruckmick, C. A. (1933). *The emotional responses of children to the motion picture situation.* New York: Macmillan.

Eco, U. (1987). *Travels in hyper-reality.* London: Picador.

Edgar, P., & Edgar, D. (1971). TV violence and socialization theory. *Public Opinion Quarterly, 35,* 607–612.

Eisenberg, A. (1936). *Children and radio programs.* New York: Columbia University Press.

Eleey, M. F., Gerbner, G., & Tedesco, N. (1972–1973). Apples, oranges, and the kitchen sink: An analysis and guide to the comparison of "Violence Ratings". *Journal of Broadcasting, 17*(1), 21–31.

Ellis, G. T., & Sekyra, F. (1972). The effect of aggressive cartoons on the behavior of first grade children. *Journal of Psychology, 81,* 37–43.

Emery, J. N. (1944). Those vicious comics. *Journal of Education, 127,* 90.

Engelhardt, T. (1986). Children's television: The shortcake strategy. In T. Gitlin (Ed.), *Watching television.* New York: Pantheon.

Eron, L. D. (1963). Relationship of TV viewing habits and aggressive behavior in children. *Journal of Abnormal and Social Psychology, 67*(2), 193–196.

Eron, L. D., & Huesman, L. R. (1980). Adolescent aggression and television. *Annals of the New York Academy of Sciences, 347,* 319–331.

Eron, L. D., Huesman, L. R., Lefkowitz, M. M., & Walder, L. O. (1972). Does television violence cause aggression? *American Psychologist, 27,* 253–263.

Eron, L. D., Walder, L. O., & Lefkowitz, M. M. (1963). Relationship of television viewing habits and aggressive behaviors in children. *Journal of Abnormal and Social Psychology, 67,* 193–196.

Ewen, S. (1983). The implications of empiricism. *Journal of Communication, 33*(3), 219–225.

Feilitzen, C., & Linne, O. (1975). Identifying with television characters. *Journal of Communication, 25*(4), 51–55.

Feinbloom, R. I. (1976). Children and television. *Pediatrics, 57*(3), 301–303.

Feldman, S., Wolf, A., & Warmouth, D. (1977). Parental concern about child-directed commercials. *Journal of Communication, 27*(1), 125–137.

Feshbach, S. (1955). The drive-reducing function of fantasy behavior. *Journal of Abnormal and Social Psychology, 50,* 311.

———. (1956). The catharsis hypothesis and some consequences of interaction with aggressive and neutral play objects. *Journal of Personality, 24,* 409–462.

———. (1976). The role of fantasy in the response to television. *Journal of Social Issues, 32*(4), 71–85.

Fletcher, A. (1969). Negro and white children's television program preferences. *Journal of Broadcasting, 13*(4), 359–366.

Foster, J. (1964). Father images: Television and ideal. *Journal of Marriage and the Family*, August 1964, 353–355.

Foucault, M. (1972). *The archaeology of knowledge and the discourse on language* (A. Sheridan Smith, Trans.). New York: Vintage Books.

——. (1973). *Madness and civilization: A history of insanity in the age of reason* (R. Howard, Trans.). New York: Vintage Books.

——. (1977). *Language, counter-memory, practice*. Ithaca, New York: Cornell University Press.

——. (1979). *Discipline and punish: The birth of the prison* (A. Sheridan, Trans.). New York: Vintage Books.

——. (1980a). *The history of sexuality, volume I: An introduction* (R. Hurley, Trans.). New York: Vintage Books.

——. (1980b). *Power/knowledge: Selected interviews and other writings* (C. Gordon, Ed.; C. Gordon, L. Marshall, J. Mepham & K. Soper, Trans.). New York: Pantheon.

——. (1981). Questions of method: An interview with Michel Foucault. *Ideology and Consciousness, 8*, 4–14.

——. (1982). The subject and power. In H. L. Dreyfus & P. Rabinow, *Michel Foucault: Beyond structuralism and hermeneutics* (pp. 208–226). Chicago: University of Chicago Press.

Fowles, B. R., & Horner, V. M. (1975). A suggested research strategy. *Journal of Communication, 25*(4), 98–101.

Frakes, M. (1942). Comics are no longer comic. *Christian Century*, November 4, 1348–1352.

Frank, J. (1944). What's in the comics? *Journal of Educational Sociology, 18*, 220.

Franzblau, S., Sprafkin, J. N., & Rubinstein, E. A. (1977). Sex on TV: A content analysis. *Journal of Communication, 27*(2), 164–170.

Franzwa, H. H. (1974). Working women in fact and fiction. *Journal of Communication, 24*(2), 104–109.

Friedlander, B. Z., Wetstone, H., & Scott, C. S. (1974). Suburban preschool children's comprehension of an age-appropriate informational television program. *Child Development, 45*, 561–565.

Friedrich, L. K., & Stein, A. H. (1975). Prosocial television and young children: The effects of verbal labeling and role playing on learning and behavior. *Child Development, 46*, 27–38.

Gadberry, S. (1974). Television as baby-sitter: A field comparison of preschoolers' behavior during playtime and during television viewing. *Child Development, 45*, 1132–1136.

Garry, R. (1967). Television for children. *Journal of Education, 150*(1), 1–46.

Geen, R., & Berkowitz, L. (1966). Name-mediated aggressive cue properties. *Journal of Personality, 34*, 456–465.

——. (1967). Some conditions facilitating the occurrence of aggression after the observation of violence. *Journal of Personality, 35*, 666–676.

Geiger, J. R. (1923). The effects of the motion picture on the mind and morals of the young. *International Journal of Ethics, 34*, 69–83.

Gerbner, G. (1972). Violence in television drama: Trends in symbolic functions. In G. Comstock & E. Rubinstein (Eds.), *Television and social behavior*.

Vol. 1: Media content and control (pp. 28–187). Washington, DC: United States Government Printing Office.

———. (1981). Education for the age of television. In M. E. Ploghoft & J. A. Anderson (Eds.), *Education for the television age* (pp. 173–178). Athens, OH: College of Education, Ohio University.

———. (Ed.). (1983a). Ferment in the field. *Journal of Communication, 33*(3).

———. (1983b). The importance of being critical—in one's own fashion. *Journal of Communication, 33*(3), 355–362.

Gerbner, G., & Gross, L. (1976). Living with TV: The violence profile no. 7. *Journal of Communication, 26*(2), 172–194.

———. (1980). The violent face of television and its lessons. In E. L. Palmer & A. Dorr (Eds.), *Children and the faces of television: Teaching, violence, selling* (pp. 149–162). New York: Academic Press.

Gerbner, G., Gross, L., Eleey, M. F., Jackson-Beeck, M., Jeffries-Fox, S., & Signorielli, N. (1977). TV violence profile no. 8: The highlights. *Journal of Communication, 27*(2), 171–180.

Gerbner, G., Gross, L., Jackson-Beeck, M., Jeffries-Fox, S., & Signorielli, N. (1978). Cultural indicators: Violence profile no. 9. *Journal of Communication, 28*(3), 176–207.

Gerbner, G., Gross, L., Signorielli, N. Morgan, M., & Jackson-Beeck, M. (1979). The demonstration of power: Violence profile no. 10. *Journal of Communication, 29*(3), 177–196.

Gerson, W. M. (1966). Mass media socialization behavior: Negro-White differences. *Social Forces, 45,* 40–50.

Gesselman, D. (1951). Television and reading. *Elementary English, 28*(7), 385–391.

Gilligan, C. (1982). *In a different voice: Psychological theory and women's development.* Cambridge, MA: Harvard University Press.

Gitlin, T. (1978). Media sociology: The dominant paradigm. *Theory & Society, 6,* 205–253.

———. (Ed.). (1986). *Watching television.* New York: Pantheon.

Gordon, C. (1980). Afterword. In C. Gordon (Ed.), *Power/knowledge: Selected interviews & other writings 1972–1977* (pp. 227–259). New York: Pantheon.

Gray, B. (1950). The social effects of film. *Sociological Review, 42,* 135–144.

Green, E. J. (1962). *The learning process and programmed instruction.* New York: Holt, Rinehart & Winston.

Greenberg, B. S. (1964). The effects of communicator incompatibility on children's judgments of television programs. *Journal of Broadcasting, 8,* 157–171.

———. (1972). Children's reactions to TV blacks. *Journalism Quarterly, 49*(1), 5–14.

———. (1973). Viewing and listening parameters among British youngsters. *Journal of Broadcasting, 17*(2), 173–188.

———. (1974–1975). British children and televised violence. *Public Opinion Quarterly, 38,* 531–547.

Greenberg, B. S., & Dominick, J. (1969). Social differences in teenagers' use of television. *Journal of Broadcasting, 13,* 331–344.

Greenberg, B. S., & Reeves, B. (1976). Children and the perceived reality of television. *Journal of Social Issues, 32*(4), 86–97.

Greenfield, P., & Beagles-Roos, J. (1988). Radio vs. television: Their cognitive impact on children of different socioeconomic and ethnic groups. *Journal of Communication, 38*(2), 71–92.

Greenstein, J. (1954). Effect of television upon elementary school grades. *Journal of Educational Research, 48*(3), 161–176.

Grumbine, E. E. (1938). *Reaching juvenile markets.* New York: McGraw-Hill.

Guba, E., Wolf, W., DeGroot, S., Knemeyer, M., Van Atta R., & Light, L. (1964). Eye movements and television viewing in children. *Audio-Visual Communications Review, 12*, 386–401.

Hacking, I. (1981). How should we do the history of statistics? *Ideology and Consciousness, 8*, 15–26.

———. (1982). Biopower and the avalanche of printed numbers. *Humanities in Society, 5*(3 & 4), 279–295.

———. (1986). The archaeology of Foucault. In D.C. Hoy (Ed.), *Foucault: A critical reader* (pp.27–40). Oxford: Blackwell.

Haight, T. R. (1983). The critical researchers' dilemma. *Journal of Communication, 33*(3), 226–236.

Haines, W. H. (1955). Juvenile delinquency and television. *Corrective Psychiatry and the Journal of Social Therapy, 1*, 193–198.

Hall, S. (1977). Culture, the media and the 'ideological effect.' In J. Curran, M. Gurevitch & J. Woollacott (Eds.), *Mass Communication and Society* (pp. 315–348). London: Edward Arnold.

Halloran, J. (1970). Mass communication in society: The need for research. *Educational Broadcasting Review, 4*, 17–33.

Halpern, W. (1975). Turned-on toddlers. *Journal of Communication, 25*(4), 66–72.

Hapkiewicz, W. G., & Roden, A. H. (1971). The effect of aggressive cartoons on children's interpersonal play. *Child Development, 42*, 1583–1585.

Hardt, H. (1986). Critical theory in historical perspective. *Journal of Communication, 36*(3), 144–154.

Harper, D., Munro, J., & Himmelweit, H. (1970). Social and personality factors associated with children's tastes in television viewing. In J. Tunstall (Ed.), *Media sociology: A reader* (pp. 363–371). London: Constable.

Harrison, A., & Scriven E. (1969). TV and youth: Literature and research reviewed. *Clearing House, 44*(22), 82–90.

Hartman, D. (1969). Influence of symbolically modeled instrumental aggression and pain cues on aggressive behavior. *Journal of Personality and Social Psychology, 11*(3), 280–288.

Harvey, D. (1989). *The condition of postmodernity.* Oxford: Blackwell.

Head, S. W. (1954). Content analysis of television drama programs. *Quarterly of Film, Radio and Television, 9*, 175–194.

Hearold, S. (1986). A synthesis of 1043 effects of television on social behavior. In G. Comstock (Ed.), *Public communications and behavior: Volume I* (pp. 65–133). New York: Academic Press.

Heisler, F. (1947). A comparison of comic book and non–comic book readers of the elementary school. *Journal of Educational Research, 40,* 458–464.

———. (1948a). A comparison between those elementary school children who attend moving pictures, read comic books and listen to serial radio programs to an excess, with those who indulge in these activities seldom or not at all. *Journal of Educational Research, 42*(3), 182–190.

———. (1948b). A comparison of the movie and non-movie goers of the elementary school. *Journal of Educational Research, 41*(7), 541–546.

Herzog, H. (1941). *Children's radio listening.* New York: Office of Radio Research, Columbia University.

———. (1944). What do we really know about daytime serial listeners? In P. F. Lazarsfeld and F. N. Stanton (Eds.), *Radio Research 1942–1943.* New York: Duell, Sloan and Pearce.

Hess, R. D., & Goldman, H. (1962). Parents' views of the effect of television on their children. *Child Development, 33,* 411–426.

Hicks, D. (1965). Imitation and retention of film-mediated aggressive peer and adult models. *Journal of Personality and Social Psychology, 2*(1), 97–100.

Himmelweit, H. (1962). A theoretical framework for the consideration of the effects of television: A British report. *Journal of Social Issues, 18*(2), 16–25.

———. (1977). Yesterday's and tomorrow's television research on children. In D. Lerner & C. Nelson (Eds.), *Communication research—A half-century appraisal* (pp. 9–36). Honolulu: University of Hawaii Press.

Himmelweit, H., Oppenheim, A. N., & Vince, P. (1958). *Television and the child.* London: Oxford University Press.

Himmelweit, H., & Swift, B. (1976). Continuities and discontinuities in media usage and taste: A longitudinal study. *Journal of Social Issues, 32*(4), 133–156.

Hodge, B., & Tripp, D. (1986). *Children and television.* London: Polity.

Holaday, P. W., & Stoddard, G. D. (1933). *Getting ideas from the movies.* New York: Macmillan.

Hollander, N. (1971). Adolescents and the war: The sources of socialization. *Journalism Quarterly, 48*(3), 472–479.

Horkheimer, M., & Adorno, T. W. (1972 [1944]). *Dialectic of enlightenment* (J. Cumming, Trans.). New York: Herder and Herder.

Hornik, R. C. (1978). Television access and the slowing of cognitive growth. *American Educational Research Journal, 15*(1), 1–15.

Hoult, T. F. (1949). Comic books and juvenile delinquency. *Sociology and Social Research, 33,* 279–284.

Huey, E. G. (1906). *The psychology of reading.* New York: Macmillan.

Huston, A. C., Greer, D., Wright, J. C., Welch, R., & Ross, R. (1984). Children's comprehension of televised formal features with masculine and feminine connotations. *Developmental Psychology, 20*(4), 707–716.

Huston, A. C., Wright, J. C., Wartella, E., Rice, M. L., Watkins, B., Campbell, T., & Potts, R. (1981). Communicating more than content: Formal features of children's television programs. *Journal of Communication, 31*(3), 32–48.

Hyman, H. H. (1973–1974). Mass communication and socialization. *Public Opinion Quarterly, 37*(4), 524–540.

Johnson, J. S. (1917). Children and their movies. *Social Service Review, 6,* 11–12.

Kaplan, E. A. (1987). *Rocking around the clock: Music television, postmodernism and consumer culture.* London: Methuen.

Kaplan, R. M., & Singer, R. D. (1976). Television violence and viewer aggression. *Journal of Social Issues, 32*(4), 35–69.

Katz, E., Blumler, J. G., & Gurevitch, M. (1974a). Uses and gratifications research. *Public Opinion Quarterly, 37,* 509–523.

———. (1974b). Utilization of mass communication by the individual. In J. G. Blumler & E. Katz (Eds.), *The uses of mass communication* (pp. 19–32). London: Faber.

Katz, E., & Foulkes, D. (1962). Use of mass media as 'escape': Clarification of a concept. *Public Opinion Quarterly, 26,* 377–388.

Klapper, J. T. (1957). What we know about the effects of mass communication: The brink of hope. *Public Opinion Quarterly, 21,* 453–474.

———. (1960). *The effects of mass communication.* New York: Free Press.

———. (1963). Mass communication research: An old road resurveyed. *Public Opinion Quarterly, 27,* 515–527.

Krugman, H. E. (1966). The measurement of advertising involvement. *Public Opinion Quarterly, 30*(4), 583–596.

———. (1971). Brain wave measures of media involvement. *Journal of Advertising Research, 11*(1), 3–9.

Krugman, H. E., & Hartley, E. L. (1970). Passive learning from television. *Public Opinion Quarterly, 34,* 184–190.

Kubey, R. W. (1986). Television use in everyday life: Coping with unstructured time. *Journal of Communication, 36*(3), 108–123.

Kuhn, T. (1962). *The structure of scientific revolutions* (2nd ed.). Chicago: University of Chicago Press.

Laclau, E., & Mouffe, C. (1982). Recasting Marxism: Hegemony and new political movements. *Socialist Review, 12*(6), 91–113.

Larsen, O. N. (1962). Innovators and early adopters of television. *Sociological Inquiry, 2,* 16–34.

———. (1964). Social effects of mass communication. In E. L. Faris (Ed.), *Handbook of modern sociology* (pp. 348–381). New York: Rand McNally.

Lasswell, H.D. (1948). The structure and function of communication in society. In L. Bryson (Ed.), *The communication of ideas* (pp. 37–51). New York: Harper & Row.

———. (1972). Communications research and public policy. *Public Opinion Quarterly, 36*(3), 301–310.

Lazarsfeld, P. (1940). *Radio and the printed page.* New York: Duell, Sloan, and Pearce.

———. (1955). Why so little is known about the effects of TV on children and what can be done? *Public Opinion Quarterly, 19,* 243–251.

Lazarsfeld, P., Berelson, B., & Gaudet, H. (1944). *The people's choice.* New York: Columbia University Press.

Lazarsfeld, P., & Stanton, F. (1941). *Radio research, 1941.* New York: Duell, Sloan and Pearce.

———. (1944). *Radio research, 1942–1943.* New York: Duell, Sloan, and Pearce.

———. (1949). *Communications research, 1948–1949.* New York: Harper.

Lefkowitz, M. M., Eron, L. D., Walter, L. O., & Huesmann, L. R. (1972). Television violence and child aggression: A follow-up study. In G. A. Comstock & E. A. Rubinstein (Eds.), *Television and social behavior. Vol. 3: Television and adolescent aggressiveness* (pp. 35–135). Washington, DC: United States Government Printing Office.

Leifer, A. D., Gordon, N. J., & Graves, S. B. (1974). Children's television: More than mere entertainment. *Harvard Educational Review, 44*(2), 213–245.

Lemish, D. (1982). The rules of viewing television in public places. *Journal of Broadcasting, 26,* 757–781.

Lever, J. (1976). Sex differences in the games children play. *Social Problems, 23,* 478–487.

Levin, S. R., & Anderson, D. R. (1976). The development of attention. *Journal of Communication, 26*(2), 126–135.

Lewis, P. (1949). TV and teenagers. *Educational Screen, 28,* 159–161.

———. (1951). TV's impact on teenagers. *Phi Delta Kappan, 33,* 118–121.

Liebert, D. E., Sprafkin, J. N., Liebert, R. M., & Rubinstein, E. A. (1977). Effects of television commercial disclaimers on the product expectations of children. *Journal of Communication, 27*(1), 118–124.

Liebert, R. M., Cohen, L. A., Joyce, C., Murrel, S., Nisonoff, L., & Sonnenschein, S. (1977). Predispositions revisited. *Journal of Communication, 24*(3), 217–221.

Liebert, R. M., & Sprafkin, J. N. (1988). *The early window: Effects of television on children and youth* (3rd ed.). New York: Pergamon.

Liebert, R. M., Sprafkin, J. N., & Davidson, E. S. (1982). *The early window: Effects of television on children and youth* (2nd ed.). New York: Pergamon.

Lometti, G. E., Reeves, B., & Bybee, C. R. (1977). Investigating the assumptions of uses and gratifications research. *Communication Research, 4*(3), 321–338.

Long, M. L., & Simon, R. J. (1974). The roles and statuses of women on children and family TV programs. *Journalism Quarterly, 51*(1), 107–110.

Longstaff, H. P. (1936). Effectiveness of children's radio programs. *Journal of Applied Psychology, 20,* 208–220.

Lövaas, O. I. (1961). Effect of exposure to symbolic aggression on aggressive behavior. *Child Development, 32,* 37–44.

Lovibond, S. H. (1967). The effect of media stressing crime violence upon children's attitudes. *Social Problems, 15,* 91–100.

Luke, C. (1987). A discourse analysis of knowledge production: A poststructuralist agenda for doing the history of research on mass media and children. Paper presented at the Annual Sociological Association of Australia and New Zealand.

———. (1989). *Pedagogy, printing, and Protestantism: The discourse on childhood.* Albany, New York: State University of New York Press.

Lull, J. (1980). Family communication patterns and the social uses of television. *Communication Research, 7,* 319–334.

———. (1982). How families select television programs: A mass-observational study. *Journal of Broadcasting, 26,* 801–811.

Lyness, P. (1951). Patterns in the mass communications tastes of the young audience. *The Journal of Educational Psychology, 42*(8), 449–467.

———. (1952). The place of the media in the lives of boys and girls. *Journalism Quarterly, 29*, 43–54.

Maccoby, E. (1951). Television: Its impact on school children. *Public Opinion Quarterly, 15*, 421–444.

———. (1954). Why do children watch television? *Public Opinion Quarterly, 18*, 239–244.

———. (1963). The effects of television on children. In W. Schramm (Ed.), *The science of human communication* (pp. 116–127). New York: Basic Books.

———. (1964). Effects of the mass media. In M. Hoofman & L. Hoffman (Eds.), *Review of Child Development Research* (pp. 323–348). New York: Russell Sage.

Maccoby, E., & Wilson, W. C. (1957). Identification and observational learning from films. *Journal of Abnormal and Social Psychology, 55*, 76–87.

Maccoby, E., Wilson, W. C., & Burton, R. V. (1958). Differential movie-viewing behavior of male and female viewers. *Journal of Personality, 6*, 259–267.

Mahoney, K. (1953). Elementary school pupils' TV habits and choice. *Catholic Educational Review, 51*, 234–245.

Manley-Casimir, M., & Luke, C. (Eds.). (1987). *Children and television: A challenge to education.* New York: Praeger.

Maruyama, M. (1980). Information and communication in poly-epistemological systems. In K. Woodward (Ed.), *The myths of information: Technology and postindustrial culture.* Madison, WI: Coda Press.

McCarthy, E. D., Langner, T. S., Gersten, J. C., Eisenberg, J. G., & Orzeck, L. (1975). Violence and behavior disorders. *Journal of Communication, 5*(4), 71–85.

McDonagh, E. C. (1950). Television and the family. *Sociology and Social Research, 35*, 113–122.

McLeod, J. M., & O'Keefe, G. J. (1972). The socialization perspective and communication behavior. In F. G. Kline & P. J. Tichnor (Eds.), *Current perspectives in mass communication research* (pp. 133–150). Beverly Hills, CA: Sage.

McLuhan, M. (1962). *The Gutenberg galaxy.* Toronto: Toronto University Press.

———. (1964). *Understanding media: The extensions of man.* New York: McGraw-Hill.

———. (1975). At the flip point of time—The point of more return? *Journal of Communication, 25*(4), 102–106.

McQuail, D. (1987). *Mass communication theory: An introduction* (2nd ed.). Beverly Hills, CA: Sage.

Medrich, E. A. (1979). Constant television: A background to daily life. *Journal of Communication, 29*(3), 171–176.

Meerloo, J. (1954). Television addiction and reactive empathy. *Journal of Nervous and Mental Disease, 120*, 290–291.

Mehling, R. (1960). Television's value to the American family member. *Journal of Broadcasting, 4*, 303–313.

Melody, W. H., & Ehrlich, W. (1974). Children's TV commercials: The vanishing policy options. *Journal of Communication, 24*(4), 113–125.

Melody, W. H., & Mansell, R. E. (1983). The debate over critical vs. administrative research: circularity or challenge. *Journal of Communication, 33*(3), 103–116.

Merrill, I. R. (1961). Broadcasting viewing and listening by children. *Public Opinion Quarterly, 25,* 263–276.

Meyer, T. P. (1973). Television's behavioral models and children's perceptions. *Educational Broadcasting Review, 7*(1), 25–33.

———. (1976). Impact of "All in the Family" on children. *Journal of Broadcasting, 20*(1), 23–33.

Meyerson, R. B. (1957). What we know about audiences. *Journal of Broadcasting, 1,* 220–231.

Miller, G. R. (1983). Taking stock of a discipline. *Journal of Communication, 33*(3), 31–41.

Miller, M. C. (1988). *Boxed in: The culture of TV.* Evanston, IL: Northwestern University Press.

Miller, M. M., & Reeves, B. (1976). Dramatic TV content and children's sex-role stereotypes. *Journal of Broadcasting, 20*(1), 35–50.

Miller, W. C., & Beck, T. (1976). How do TV parents compare to real parents? *Journalism Quarterly, 53*(2), 324–328.

Minton, J. H. (1975). The impact of Sesame Street on readiness. *Sociology of Education, 48,* 141–151.

Mitchell, A. H. (1949). The effect of radio programs on silent reading achievement of ninety-one sixth grade students. *Journal of Educational Research, 42,* 460–470.

Mitchell, A. M. (1929). *Children and movies.* Chicago: University of Chicago Press.

Modleski, T. (Ed.). (1986). *Studies in entertainment.* Bloomington, IN: Indiana University Press.

Mohr, P. S. (1979). Parental guidance of children's viewing of evening television programs. *Journal of Broadcasting, 23*(2), 213–228.

Moody, K. (1980). *Growing up on television: A report to parents.* New York: McGraw-Hill.

Morison, P., McCarthy M., & Gardner, H. (1979). Exploring the realities of television with children. *Journal of Broadcasting, 23*(4), 453–463.

Morley, D. (1980). *The nationwide audience.* London: British Film Institute.

———. (1986). *Family television: Cultural power and domestic leisure.* London: Comedia.

Munn, M. (1958). The effect of parental buying habits on children exposed to children's television programs. *Journal of Broadcasting, 2,* 253–258.

Murray, J. P., & Kippax, S. (1978). Children's social behavior in three towns with differing television experience. *Journal of Communication, 28*(1), 19–29.

Murray, J. P., Nayman, O. B., & Atkin, C. K. (1971–1972). Television and the child: A comprehensive research bibliography. *Journal of Broadcasting, 16*(1), 3–20.

Murray, R. L., Cole, R. R., & Fedler, F. (1970). Teenagers and TV violence: How they rate and view it. *Journalism Quarterly, 47,* 247–255.

Musgrave, P. W. (1969). How children use television. *New Society, 13,* 277–278.

Mussen, P., & Rutherford, E. (1961). Effects of aggressive cartoons on children's aggressive play. *Journal of Abnormal and Social Psychology, 62*(2), 461–464.

Neisser, U. (1976). *Cognition and reality.* San Francisco: W. H. Freeman.

Newcomb, A. F., & Collins, W. A. (1979). Children's comprehension of family role portrayals in televised dramas: Effects of socioeconomic status, ethnicity, and age. *Developmental Psychology, 15*(4), 417–423.

Niven, H. (1960). Who in the family selects the TV program? *Journalism Quarterly, 37*(1), 110–111.

O'Keefe, M. T. (1971). The anti-smoking commercials: A study of television's impact on behavior. *Public Opinion Quarterly, 35,* 242–248.

Olson, D. R., & Bruner, J. S. (1974). Learning through experience and learning through media. In D. R. Olson (Ed.), *Media and symbols: The form of expression, communication, and education* (pp. 125–150). Chicago: University of Chicago Press.

Osborn, D. K., & Endsley, R. C. (1971). Emotional reactions of young children to TV violence. *Child Development, 42,* 321–331.

Paisley, M. B. (1972). *Social policy research and the realities of the system: Violence done to TV research.* Institute of Communication Research, Stanford University, CA: Stanford University Press.

Palmer, E. L., & McDowell, C. N. (1979). Program/commercial separators in children's television programming. *Journal of Communication, 29*(3), 197–201.

Palmer, P. (1986). *The lively audience.* Sydney: Allen & Unwin.

Parker, E. B. (1961a). Changes in the function of radio with the adoption of television. *Journal of Broadcasting, 5,* 39–48.

———. (1961b). Television and the process of cultural change. *Journalism Quarterly, 38,* 537–540.

———. (1963). The effects of television on public library circulation. *Public Opinion Quarterly, 27,* 578–589.

Pearlin, L. (1959). Social and personal stress and escape television viewing. *Public Opinion Quarterly, 23,* 255–259.

Peatman, J. G., & Hallonquist, T. (1945). The patterning of listener attitudes toward radio broadcasts. *Applied Psychology Monographs, 4,* n.p.

Peterson, R. C., & Thurstone, L. L. (1933). *Motion pictures and the social attitudes of children.* New York: Macmillan.

Poster, M. (1984). *Foucault, Marxism and history: Mode of production versus mode of information.* Cambridge: Polity.

———. (1989). *Critical theory and poststructuralism: In search of a context.* Ithaca, NY: Cornell University Press.

Postman, N. (1982). *The Disappearance of Childhood.* New York: Delacorte Press.

Poulos, R. W., Rubinstein, E. A., & Liebert, R. M. (1975). Positive social learning. *Journal of Communication, 25*(4), 90–97.

Press, A. L. (1986). Ideologies of femininity: Film and popular consciousness in the postwar era. In S. J. Ball-Rokeach & M. G. Cantor (Eds.), *Media, audience, and social structure* (pp. 313–323). Beverly Hills, CA: Sage.

Preston, M. I. (1941). Children's reactions to movie horrors and radio crime. *Journal of Pediatrics, 19*(2), 147–168.

Quarforth, J. M. (1979). Children's understanding of the nature of television characters. *Journal of Communication, 29*(3), 210–218.

Racevskis, K. (1983). *Michel Foucault and the subversion of the intellect.* Ithaca, NY: Cornell University Press.

Real, M. (1977). *Mass-mediated culture.* Englewood Cliffs, NJ: Prentice-Hall.

——. (1989). *Supermedia.* Beverly Hills, CA: Sage.

Renshaw, S., Miller, V. L., & Marquis, D. (1933). *Children's sleep.* New York: Macmillan.

Ricciuti, E. A. (1951). Children and radio: A study of listeners and non-listeners to various types of radio programs in terms of selected ability, attitude, and behavior measures. *Genetic Psychology Monographs, 44,* 69–143.

Ridder, J. M. (1963). Public opinion and the relationship of TV viewing to academic achievement. *Journal of Educational Research, 57*(4), 204–206.

Riley, J. W., Cantwell, F. V., & Ruttiger, K. (1949). Some observations on the social effects of television. *Public Opinion Quarterly, 13,* 223–234.

Riley, M. W., & Riley, J. W. (1951). A sociological approach to communications research. *Public Opinion Quarterly, 15,* 445–460.

Robertson, T. S. (1979). Parental mediation of television advertising effects. *Journal of Communication, 2*(1), 12–25.

Robertson, T. S., & Rossiter, R. J. (1977). Children's responsiveness to commercials. *Journal of Communication, 27*(1), 101–106.

Rogers, E. M., & Chaffee, S. H. (1983). Communication as an academic discipline: A dialogue. *Journal of Communication, 33*(3), 18–30.

Roody, S. (1952). Effects of radio, television, and motion pictures on the development of maturity. *English Journal, 41,* 245–250.

Rossiter, R. J. (1978). American research on TV advertising's general impact on children. *Australian Journal of Early Childhood, 3*(1), 15–19.

Rossiter, R. J., & Robertson, T. S. (1974). Children's TV commercials: Testing the defenses. *Journal of Communication, 24*(4), 137–144.

Rowland, W. D. (1983). *The politics of TV violence.* Beverly Hills, CA: Sage.

Rowland, W. D., & Watkins, B. (Eds.). (1984). *Interpreting television: Current research perspectives.* Beverly Hills, CA: Sage.

Rubin, A. M. (1976). Television in children's political socialization. *Journal of Broadcasting, 20*(1), 51–59.

——. (1977). Television usage, attitudes and viewing behaviors of children and adolescents. *Journal of Broadcasting, 21*(3), 355–369.

——. (1978). Child and adolescent television use and political socialization. *Journalism Quarterly, 55,* 125–129.

——. (1983). Television uses and gratifications: The interactions of viewing patterns and motivations. *Journal of Broadcasting, 27,* 37–51.

——. (1984). Ritualized and instrumental television viewing. *Journal of Communication, 34*(3), 67–77.

Rubinstein, E. A. (1974). The TV violence report: What's next? *Journal of Communication, 24*(1), 80–88.

———. (1976). Warning: The surgeon general's research program may be dangerous to preconceived notions. *Journal of Social Issues, 32*(4), 18–34.

Rush, W. (1965). Some factors influencing children's use of the mass media of communication. *Journal of Experimental Research, 33*(3), 301–304.

Salomon, G. (1972). Can we affect cognitive skills through visual media? An hypothesis and initial findings. *Audio-Visual Communication Review, 20*, 401–422.

———. (1974a). Internalization of filmic schematic operations in interaction with learners' aptitudes. *Journal of Educational Psychology, 66*, 499–511.

———. (1974b). What is learned and how it is taught: The interaction between media, message, task, and learner. In D. R. Olson (Ed.), *Media and symbols: The forms of expression, communication, and education* (pp. 383–406). Chicago: University of Chicago Press.

———. (1976). Cognitive skill learning across cultures. *Journal of Communication, 26*(2), 138–144.

———. (1979a). Media and symbols systems as related to cognition and learning. *Journal of Educational Psychology, 71*(2), 131–148.

———. (1979b). *Interaction of media, cognition, and learning.* San Francisco: Jossey Bass.

———. (1984). Television is 'easy' and print is 'tough': The differential investment of mental effort in learning as a function of perceptions and attributions. *Journal of Educational Psychology, 76*(4), 647–658.

———. (1987). Television and reading: The roles of orientations and reciprocal relations. In M. Manley-Casimir & C. Luke (Eds.), *Children and television: A challenge for education* (pp. 15–33). New York: Praeger.

Salomon, G., & Cohen, A. (1977). Television formats, mastery of mental skills, and the acquisition of knowledge. *Journal of Educational Psychology, 95*, 612–619.

———. (1978). On the meaning and validity of television viewing. *Human Communications Research, 4*(3), 265–270.

Scherer, K. R. (1971). Stereotype change following exposure to counter-stereotypical media heroes. *Journal of Broadcasting, 15*, 91–100.

Schiller, H. (1969). *Mass communications and American empire.* New York: Kelley.

———. (1973). *The mind managers.* Boston: Beacon.

Schramm, W. (1948). *Communications in modern society.* Urbana, IL: University of Illinois Press.

———. (1960a). *Mass communications* (2nd ed.). Urbana, IL: University of Illinois Press.

———. (1960b). *The impact of educational television.* Urbana, IL: University of Illinois Press.

———. (Ed.). (1963). *The science of communication.* New York: Basic Books.

———. (1983). The unique perspective of communication: A retrospective view. *Journal of Communication, 33*(3), 6–17.

Schramm, W., Lyle, J., & Parker, E. B. (1961). *Television in the lives of our children.* Stanford: Stanford University Press.

Scott, L. (1954). Social attitudes of children revealed by responses to television programs. *California Journal of Elementary Education, 22,* 176–179.

——. (1956). Television and school achievement. *Phi Delta Kappan, 38,* 25–28.

——. (1958). Relationships between elementary school children and television. *Journal of Educational Research, 52*(4), 134–137.

Seagoe, M. (1951). Children's television habits and preferences. *Quarterly of Film, Radio and Television, 6,* 143–152.

Shayon, R. L. (1951). *Television and our children.* New York: Longmans.

Sheikh, A. A., & Moleski, M. L. (1977a). Conflict in the family over commercials. *Journal of Communication, 27*(1), 152–157.

——. (1977b). Children's perception of the value of an advertised product. *Journal of Broadcasting, 21*(3), 347–354.

Sheikh, A. A., Prasad, V. K., & Rao, T. R. (1974). Children's TV commercials: A review of research. *Journal of Communication, 24*(4), 126–135.

Shelby, M. E. (1964). Children's programming trends on network television. *Journal of Broadcasting, 8,* 247–256.

Sheridan, A. (1980). *Michel Foucault: The will to truth.* London: Tavistock.

Shuttleworth, F. K., & May, M. A. (1933). *The social conduct and attitudes of movie fans.* New York: Macmillan.

Siegel, A. (1956). Film-mediated fantasy aggression and strength of aggressive drive. *Child Development, 27*(3), 365–378.

——. (1958). The influence of violence in the mass media upon children's role expectations. *Child Development, 29*(1), 35–56.

——. (1975). Communicating with the next generation. *Journal of Communication, 25*(4), 14–24.

Singer, D. G., & Singer, J. L. (1980). Television viewing and aggressive behavior in preschool children: A field study. *Forensic Psychology and Psychiatry, 347,* 289–303.

Singer, J. L., Singer, D. G., & Rapaczynski, W. S. (1984). Family patterns and television viewing as predictors of children's beliefs and aggression. *Journal of Communication, 33*(3), 73–89.

Skinner, B. F. (1938). *The behavior of organisms.* New York: Appleton-Century-Crofts.

Smith, B. L., Lasswell, H. D., & Casey, R. D. (1946). *Propaganda, communications, and public opinion.* Princeton: Princeton University Press.

Smith, D. C. (1961–1962). The selectors of television programs. *Journal of Broadcasting, 6,* 35–44.

Smith, D. M. (1971–1972). Some uses of mass media by fourteen year olds. *Journal of Broadcasting, 16,* 37–50.

Smythe, D. (1954). Reality as presented by television. *Public Opinion Quarterly, 18,* 143–156.

——. (1955). Dimensions of violence. *Audio-Visual Communication Review, 3,* 58–63.

Snow, R. P. (1974). How children interpret TV violence in play contexts. *Journalism Quarterly, 51*(1), 13–21.

Sorelle, Z., & Walker, J. (1962). What is television doing to our children? *The Journal of Educational Research, 56,* 236–237.

Sprafkin, J. N., Liebert, R. M., & Poulos, R. W. (1975). Effects of a prosocial and televised example of children's helping. *Journal of Experimental Child Psychology, 20*, 119–126.

Steiner, G. (1963). *The people look at television.* New York: Alfred Knopf.

Steuer, F. B., Applefield, J. M., & Smith, R. (1971). Televised aggression and the interpersonal aggression of preschool children. *Journal of Experimental Child Psychology, 11*, 442–447.

Streicher, H. W. (1974). The girls in the cartoons. *Journal of Communication, 24*(2), 125–129.

Streicher, L. H., & Bonney, N. L. (1974). Children talk about television. *Journal of Communication, 24*(3), 54–61.

Stumphauzer, J. H., & Bishop, B. R. (1969). Saturday morning television cartoons: A simple apparatus for the reinforcement of behavior in children. *Developmental Psychology, 1*(6), 763–764.

Surgeon General's Report (1972). *Television and growing up: The impact of televised violence.* Washington, DC: United States Government Printing Office.

Surlin, S. H., & Dominick, J. R. (1970–1971). Television's function as a "third parent" for black and white teenagers. *Journal of Broadcasting, 15*, 55–64.

Sweetser, F. L. Jr. (1955). Home television and behavior: some tentative conclusions. *Public Opinion Research, 19*, 79–84.

Tedesco, N. S. (1974). Patterns in prime time. *Journal of Communication, 24*(2), 118–124.

Thayer, J. (1963). The relationship of various audience composition factors to television program types. *Journal of Broadcasting, 7*, 215–217.

Thelen, M. H., & Soltz, W. (1969). The effect of vicarious reinforcement on imitation in two social-racial groups. *Child Development, 40*, 879–887.

Thrasher, F. M. (1949). The comics and delinquency: Cause or scapegoat? *Journal of Educational Sociology, 23*, 195–205.

Tomeh, A. K. (1976). Birth order, club membership and mass media exposure. *Journal of Marriage and the Family, 38*(1), 151–164.

Tunstall, J. (Ed.), (1970). *Media sociology: A reader.* London: Constable.

Turow, J. (1974). Advising and ordering: Daytime, prime time. *Journal of Communication, 24*(2), 138–141.

Wackman, D. B., Wartella, E., & Ward, S. (1977). Learning to be consumers: The role of the family. *Journal of Communication, 27*(1), 138–151.

Walters, R., & Willows, D. (1968). Imitative behavior of disturbed and non-disturbed children following exposure to aggressive and nonaggressive models. *Child Development, 39*, 78–89.

Wand, B. (1968). Television viewing and family choice differences. *Public Opinion Quarterly, 32*, 84–94.

Ward, S. (1972a). Children's reactions to commercials. *Journal of Advertising Research, 12*(2), 37–45.

Ward, S. (1972b). Kids' TV—Marketers on hot seat. *Harvard Business Review, 50*(4), 16–18.

———. (1974). Consumer socialization. *Journal of Consumer Research, 1*(2), 1–14.

Ward, S., Levinson, D., & Wackman, D. (1972). Children's attention to television advertising. In E. A. Rubinstein, G. A. Comstock & J. P. Murray (Eds.), *Television and social behavior. Vol. 4: Television in day-to-day life: Patterns of use* (pp. 491–515). Washington, DC: United States Government Printing Office.

Ward, S., & Wackman, D. (1972). Television advertising and intrafamily influence: Children's purchase influence attempts and parental yielding. In E. A. Rubinstein, G. A. Comstock & J. P. Murray (Eds.), *Television and social behavior, Vol. IV. Television in day-to-day life: Patterns of use* (pp. 516–525). Washington, DC: United States Government Printing Office.

Ward, S., Wackman, D., & Wartella, E. (1975). *Children learning to buy: The development of consumer information processing skills.* Cambridge, MA: Marketing Science Institute.

———. (1977). *How children learn to buy: The development of consumer information-processing skills.* Beverly Hills, CA: Sage.

Warden, C. J., Fjeld, H. A., & Koch, A. M. (1940). Imitative behavior in cebus and rhesus monkeys. *Journal of Genetic Psychology, 56,* 311–322.

Wartella, E. (1984). Review of "Ferment in the Field." *Journalism Quarterly, 61*(3), 720–721.

Wartella, E., & Reeves, B. (1985). Historical trends in research on children and the media: 1900–1960. *Journal of Communication, 35*(2), 118–133.

Webster, J. G., & Coscarelli, W. C. (1979). The relative appeal to children of adult vs. children's TV programming. *Journal of Broadcasting, 23*(4), 437–451.

Weeks, J. (1982). Foucault for historians. *History Workshop, 14,* 106–119.

Welch, R. L., Huston-Stein, A., Wright, J. C., & Plehal, R. (1979). Subtle sex-role cues in children's commercials. *Journal of Communication, 29*(3), 202–209.

Wells, C., & Lynch, T. (1954). The amount of free reading engaged in by intermediate pupils who have viewed television for one year or more. *Journal of Educational Research, 47,* 473–477.

Werner, A. (1975). A case of sex and class socialization. *Journal of Communication, 25*(4), 45–50.

Wertham, F. (1953). *The seduction of the innocent.* New York: Holt, Rinehart & Winston.

Wexler, P. (1987). *Social analysis of education: After the new sociology.* New York: Routledge & Kegan Paul.

Whitney, D.C. (1985). Review essay: Ferment and the field. *Communication Research, 12*(1), 133–143.

Wilden, A. (1980). *System and structure: Essays in communication and exchange* (2nd ed.). London: Tavistock.

Wiley, R. E. (1977). Family viewing: A balancing of interests. *Journal of Communication, 27*(2), 188–192.

Williams, R. (1962). Television in Britain. *Journal of Social Issues, 18*(2), 6–15.

———. (1974). Communications as cultural science. *Journal of Communication, 24*(2), 17–25.

———. (1976 [1962]). *Communications* (3rd ed.). Harmondsworth: Penguin.

——. (1980). *Problems in materialism and culture*. London: Verso.

Wimmer, R. D., & Dominick, J. R. (1983). *Mass media research: An introduction*. Belmont, CA: Wadsworth.

Witty, P. (1950). Children's, parents' and teachers' reactions to television. *Elementary English, 27*(6), 349–396.

——. (1951). Television and the high school student. *Education, 72,* 242–251.

——. (1952). Children's reactions to TV: A third report. *Elementary English, 29,* 469–473.

——. (1953). Children's reactions to TV: A fourth report. *Elementary English, 30,* 444–451.

——. (1961). Televiewing by children and youth. *Elementary English, 38,* 103–113.

——. (1966). Studies of mass media: 1949–1965. *Science Education, 50,* 119–126.

——. (1967). Children of the TV era. *Elementary English, 44,* 528–535.

Witty, P., & Coomer, A. (1943). Activities and preferences of a secondary school group. *Journal of Educational Psychology, 34*(3), 65–76.

Witty, P., Garfield, S., & Brink, W. (1941). Interests of high school students in motion pictures and radio. *Journal of Educational Psychology, 32*(3), 176–184.

Witty, P., & Gustafson, T. F. (1957). Studies of TV—An eighth yearly report. *Elementary English, 34,* 536–542.

Witty, P., & Kinesella, P. (1958). Children and TV—A ninth report. *Elementary English, 35,* 450–457.

Witty, P., Sizemore, R., Kinsella, P., & Coomer, A. (1959). A tenth yearly study and comments on a decade of television. *Elementary English, 36,* 581–586.

Wolf, K., & Fiske, M. (1949). The children talk about comics. In P. Lazarsfeld & F. Stanton (Eds.), *Communications research, 1948–1949*. New York: Harper Brothers.

Wotring, C. E., & Greenberg, B. S. (1973). Experiments in televised violence and verbal aggression: Two exploratory studies. *Journal of Communication, 23,* 446–460.

Wright, C. (1986). Mass communication rediscovered: Its past and future in American sociology. In S. J. Ball-Rokeach & M. G. Cantor (Eds.), *Media, audience, and social structure* (pp. 22–33). Beverly Hills, CA: Sage.

Young, R. (1969–1970). Television in the lives of our parents. *Journal of Broadcasting, 14*(1), 37–46.

Zuckerman, D., Singer, D., & Singer, J. L. (1980). TV viewing, children's reading, and related classroom behaviors. *Journal of Communication, 30*(1), 166–174.

Zuckerman, P., Ziegler, M., & Stevenson, H. (1978). Children's viewing of television and recognition memory of commercials. *Child Development, 49,* 96–104.

Author Index

Subject Index

academic texts, discourse and, 13–14

Advertising Age, 68

advertising effects: Atkin and Heald's 1977 study on, 242; Barry and Hansen's 1973 study on, 190; Bogart's 1958 study and, 103; Brumbaugh's 1954 study on, 78; Burr and Burr's 1977 study on, 242–43; Federal Trade Commission and, 241; Feldman et al.'s 1977 study on, 243; *Journal of Communication's* symposium on, 240, 241, 245; Liebert et al.'s 1977 study on, 243; Munn's 1958 study on, 98–99; Robertson and Rossiter's 1977 study on, 241–42; Rossiter's 1978 study on, 256–57; Sheikh and Moleski's 1977 study on, 244–45; Sheikh et al.'s 1974 study on, 203

Age of Television, The, 102, 104

aggression and effects of television, 70, 90, 92, 102, 111; Andison's 1977 study on, 237–38; Bandura et al.'s 1963 study on, 129–32; Berowitz and Geen's 1966–67 studies on, 145–46; Chaffee and Tims's 1976 study and, 234; Comstock's 1977 study on, 249–50; Dominick et al.'s 1979 study and, 260–61; Dominick's 1973 study on, 190–91; Drabman and Thomas's studies on, 200–201, 211, 225; Ellis and Sekyra's 1972 study on, 187; Eron et al.'s 1972 study on, 188; Eron's 1963 study on, 133–34; Feshbach's studies on, 89–90, 232–33; Gerbner et al.'s 1979 study on, 269–70; Gerbner's 1972 study on, 190; Greenberg's 1974–75 study on, 193–94; Halloran on study of, 176–77; Hapkiewicz and Roden's 1971 study on, 184; Hartman's 1969 study on, 148; Hicks's 1965 study on, 140–41; Himmelweit on 102; Kaplan and Singer's 1976 study on, 232; Lövaas's 1961 study on, 122; Lovibond's 1967 study on, 147; Maccoby on, 70; McCarthy et al.'s 1975 study and, 210–11; Murray et al.'s 1970 study on, 179; Osborn and Endsley's 1971 study on, 182–83; Rubinstein's 1974 study on, 204; Siegal's 1956 study on, 92–93; Siegal's position on, 169; Steuer et al.'s 1971 study on, 186; Surgeon General's Report on, 169–70; Thelen and Soltz's 1969 studies on, 154–55; Walters and Willows's 1968 study on, 147–48; Witty on, 144; Wotring and Greenberg's 1973 study on, 193. *See also* television and violence

"All in the Family," 227–28

American Broadcasting Company (ABC), 168, 169, 250

American Educational Research Journal, 254

American Journal of Sociology, 44

American Psychologist, 87, 188

Archaeology of Knowledge, 292

archeology: analysis of discourse via, 6–7, 19–20; Foucault quoted on, 36, 279; rules of discourse and, 291; Sheridan quoted on, 195

Audio-Visual Communcation Review, 86, 87, 138–39

authorities of delimitation, 16–17, 196

About the Author

CARMEN LUKE is Lecturer in sociology and communications in the Department of Social and Cultural Studies at James Cook University in Australia. She co-edited, with Mike Manley-Casimir, *Children and television: A challenge to education* (Praeger, 1987) and is the author of *Pedagogy, printing and Protestantism: The discourse on childhood* (1989).